TREE CARE

by John M. Haller

THEODORE AUDEL & CO.
a division of
HOWARD W. SAMS & CO., INC.
4300 West 62nd Street
Indianapolis, Indiana 46268

FIRST EDITION

FIRST PRINTING—1977

International Standard Book Number: 0-672-23280-4
Library of Congress Catalog Card Number: 76-50995

PREFACE

This book is about trees: how to plant them, feed them, prune them, shape them, repair their injuries, and defend them against their enemies.

Why should such a book be necessary? Because, simply, trees need all the care we can give them. Although apparently big enough and strong enough to look after themselves, they can, even the toughest of them, be benefited by intelligent care. Even the trees in the forest, while seemingly maintaining themselves against all comers, are frequently in need of help, while trees in the city are all too often cramped, stunted, starved, poisoned, plague-ridden, and mutilated. Growing under highly artificial conditions and subjected to every kind of environmental abuse, urban trees, in fact, need more or less continuous attention; that they survive at all is an on-going miracle.

Do we normally give them this care? Unfortunately we seldom do so; indeed, quite the reverse is true. Too often it happens that among the tree's many enemies we find at the top of the list — ourselves. We who owe to the tree so tremendous a debt — shade, shelter, food, fuel, timber, perhaps life itself — we are the exploiters who neglect and abuse our trees individually and on a larger scale log and burn them to the point of extinction. We have already put many a tree on the endangered species list, and we are potentially capable of destroying them all. We are more deadly than fungi, bacteria, viruses, leaf-miners, bark-riddlers, wood-borers, root-chewers, and all other of the tree's natural enemies combined; our capacity for destruction is unprecedented and unequaled.

As we continue to contaminate the atmosphere, poison the waters, and degrade the land while at the same time we work, through ignorance, carelessness, and malice, to reduce rather than to augment the numbers of our arboreal comrades, we march senselessly toward catastrophe. Is it not apparent that this mad course must be arrested — and reversed?

In our present environmental crisis, perhaps the most urgent lesson we have to learn is that trees are not objects to be taken for granted, much less to be wantonly destroyed. They are our brothers and allies, co-members of the complex ecological community so precariously sustained on this frail blue and green globe that constitutes, in the words of Jacques Cousteau, our "oasis in space." Their lives and our lives are inextricably intertwined; we must learn to care for them directly and individually in our yards and our patios and to care for them directly and individually in our yards and our patios and to care for them collectively in the wild by working socially and politically in the cause of fire prevention, good forest management, and continuous global reforestation. We must learn to be our brother's keeper.

JOHN M. HALLER

DEDICATION

To all the wonderful, unsung, anonymous trees that down through the years have felt the touch of my hand and supported the weight of my body I dedicate this book.

Contents

1

Planting

Few things are more satisfying spiritually than the setting out of a tree — and few things more important practically. In this simple act are exemplified both a spirit of altruism and a supreme instance of long-range planning. He who plants a tree, runs an old proverb, loves other people. While a past-oriented society may show a melancholy attachment for existing trees as a part of its general conservative set, it will take no steps to plant new ones. In marked contrast, any future-oriented society is certain to plant trees in abundance; to express the matter conversely, any society (or individual) that plants trees is by definition future-oriented. A present-oriented society, showing neither regard for the past nor concern for the future, will ruthlessly exploit its existing stock. One's attitude toward planting may, therfore, be both an indicator of scoietal norms and a significant personality key. With some people, planting becomes a passion: the activities of Johnny Appleseed, although legendary, have in fact been duplicated by certain dedicated individuals in every generation; Sir Walter Scott, for one, set out thousands — literally thousands — of trees with his own hands.

Planting may do more than reveal personality traits: it may modify them. By linking oneself to the future, one may make that future richer, perhaps even more likely to come true. There is the story of the young man who was advised by a friend to plant an apple tree. *"No"* he answered, *"it takes too long to grow."* His friend suggested the matter to the young man's father. *"I'm getting up in years,"* he said, *"and I'll be dead before any tree I plant grows up."* The friend then took the project to the young man's grandfather, who, agreeing that it was a good idea, planted the tree, watered it, tended it, and lived to enjoy its fruit.

Trees are front-line fighters in the war against pollution, our most dependable and least demanding allies in that grim struggle. Someone has worked out the ratio required for redressing the present pollution imbalance: we need to plant ten trees for every automobile and fifty for every large truck. Since we in this country are the worst offenders, in terms of vehicle numbers, let us consider our own case first. If we are 250 million strong and if we have 100 million or so cars on the road and perhaps a fifth that number of trucks, then each one of us, man, woman, and child, should plant — and the sooner the better — five or six trees. Surely this is very little to ask — an extraordinarily mild penance in relation to the sin.

But industrial and vehicular pollution, bad as it is, is by no means the only issue. Far worse is the active destruction of trees with none but the faintest attempt toward their replacement — a fatally short-sighted course now happily corrected in this country but rampant and raging throughout the underdeveloped nations as their exponentially increasing populations press on their fixed and limited resources.

With so many millions of men felling trees with no thought for tomorrow; with uncontrolled forest fires annually destroying hundreds of thousands of acres; with slash-and-burn primitive agricultural techniques opening up great gaping holes in the tropical forests (irreplaceable pools of genetic diversity); with the world-wide deserts advancing at the frightening pace of thirty miles a year, shall we stand idly by and watch our allies and brothers go down without raising a hand in their defense?

Tree Size

What size and what kind of tree to plant are the first questions that occur. Obviously, the smaller the tree, the more easily it is transplanted and the less it costs, but the longer it takes to grow. If you want immediate shade, you should get the largest tree available. If your budget is limited and your time unlimited, you may well start with a series of small trees.

Small trees survive the shock of moving better than large ones and usually manage to establish themselves, even though set out by unskilled hands. This—plus price and easy portability—is the main reason nurseries stock principally 1", 1-1/4", and 1-1/2" diameter trees in gallon or five gallon cans. Large trees, on the contrary, suffer a higher mortality rate after moving even though the job is entrusted to experts. If you want a large tree, try to select the most experienced, knowledgeable, and responsible arborist to move it for you, and insist on some kind of guarantee. (The usual guarantee is that if the tree dies within six months under reasonable care, it will be replaced at half the original cost.)

If there is an optimum size in selection of transplants, it is probably a tree 4 to 6 inches in trunk diameter and 18 to 20 feet in height. Such a tree is not too small to mean years of waiting for shade and not too large to make its moving costly and dangerous. Trees of this size, skillfully moved and properly watered and fertilized, will grow vigorously, producing appreciable shade in the second or third year.

Although theoretically no tree is too large to be moved, in practice, the cost and mortality risk on trees of 10 or 12

Courtesy of Mel's Tree Service, Lodi, California.

Moving 85-foot Deodar *(Cedrus deodara)*. The very heavy soil mass is enclosed in a wooden box bolted and chained together. Two large cranes are standing by to lift the tree off its 32-wheeled carrier and set it into the planting hole at upper center.

Courtesy of Mel's Tree Service, Lodi, California.

This California Pepper tree *(Schinus molle)* with a 50-inch trunk diameter, a 16-foot ball, and a total weight of 52 tons is perhaps the largest tree ever to be moved west of the Mississippi. Mounted on a special sled, it was pulled and pushed by bulldozers a distance of about 500 yards from one location on the University of the Pacific campus to another.

Moving a 45-foot, 35-ton Palm tree requires extra-heavy equipment. This giant crane swings the tree through the air as easily as if it were a match-stick and lowers it gently into the planting hole. The very numerous, much-branched, uniformly sized roots of the palm bind the soil mass securely; hence no wrappings are needed.

inches or more become disproportionately great. In parks and around commercial buildings, however, this risk is often taken. Trees 50 to 60 feet tall and 18 to 20 inches in trunk diameter are often successfully moved—in the East oaks and elms and in Calfornia palms and eucalypti. It is simply a matter of using heavy enough machinery. Habituated to instant coffee, instant car-wash, instant pants-pressing, Americans see no reason they should not have instant shade. And with enough money they get it.

In Stockton, California, a few years ago a large California Pepper Tree (*Schinus molle*) weighing 52 tons (including the ball of earth) was moved a distance of 400 feet, from one site on the college campus to another. The short distance, together with the extreme weight and bulk of the ball, favored sliding over and lifting as a means of transport. A 15-foot ball was dug, burlaped, laced, wired, and chained. A series of parallel, nearly contiguous six-inch diameter holes was drilled under the ball, a long heavy iron pipe was passed through each hole, the pipes were welded together at their ends, a pusher plate was welded on one side of the ball, and an upward curving plate on the opposite

side. An inclined plane running from the bottom of the ball upward to the soil line was scooped out, one bulldozer pushed while another one pulled, and the tree on its improvised sled was transported the whole distance in an upright position and then eased into the planting hole down a second inclined plane. This is the largest tree ever to be moved west of the Mississippi. Fortunately, the story has a happy ending: the tree took the moving in its stride and is today flourishing and happy.

Type of Tree

The question of size is intimately bound up with the question of kind. Some species are more easily moved than others, some grow faster, and some live longer.

Among the most desirable, all-purpose species are American elm and English elm (before the Dutch Elm disease and still, if control can be discovered), pin oak, red oak, and white oak, sycamore and London plane, hard maple, ginkgo, tulip tree, linden, sweet gum, and various species of ash.

Each section of the country has its favorites to add to the list. In the South there are live oaks, Spanish oaks, pecans, magnolias, mimosas; in the Northwest pines, firs, spruces, cedars, and redwoods; in the East and North birches, walnut, and hornbeam; in Florida and California palms, eucalypti, deodars, and many hundreds of exotics that make the landscape so interesting.

The ideal shade tree should be:

1. Naturally adapted to the climate and soil where it is to be placed, as proved by others of the same kind growing wild there or in some analogous region of the world.
2. Relatively immune to diseases and insect attack.
3. Of reasonably rapid growth.
4. Long-lived.
5. Straight and well formed (unless an exotic or nursery-produced variety chosen for its twisted and recurved pattern).
6. Adapted at mature size to the space it is intended to fill.
7. Strong-wooded enough to resist breakage by wind, snow, and ice.
8. Compatible with other plants—not preventing the growth of grass, shrubs, or annuals by too dense a shade or too greedy a root system.
9. Affording ample shade where shade is desired and conveniently shedding its leaves in cold weather where sunshine is wanted.
10. As nearly litter-free as possible.
11. Possessing roots that neither heave sidewalks nor invade sewer lines.
12. Beautiful in flower, foliage, bark, and general appearance.

Of these characteristics, rapidity of growth is probably the least important, while hardiness and soil- and climate-adaptation are probably the most important. Much depends on your objective. If you want immediate shade with no view to the future, plant some fast-growing tree, such as mulberry or chinaberry. If, however, you contemplate a permanent investment, then plant a nobler, sturdier, and longer-lived species, such as one of the oaks.

You may avoid the horns of this dilemma by planting two trees at the same time: one a slow-growing but highly desirable kind and the other a fast-growing species to be cut down at a later date when the first shall have developed to convenient size. Note, however, that while many "good" trees are slow-growing, it does not follow that all fast-growing varieties are necessarily "bad." The buttonwoods, the eucalypti, most of the elms, and some of the oaks grow rapidly and yet make excellent trees.

Although there are a number of species that will meet the above qualifications, there are more that will not. In choosing further among those that do qualify, your personal tastes must guide you. With trees, as with politics, there exist wide divergences of feeling even within an established frame of agreement. Some people catalogue the sycamore (buttonwood) among the most beautiful of trees; others curse it as a nuisance because of its large leaves and fluffy seed balls. Some believe the American elm the world's best shade tree; others hate it because of its ubiquitous roots. Some regard the tree of heaven as an object of beauty; others sneak out at night to pour kerosene around its roots. *De gustibus non est disputandum.* All the nurseryman or tree expert can do is to recommend a list of trees suited to a given locality; the final choice must be yours.

It should be noted that trees suitable for use around a residence are not necessarily suited for streets and avenues. Although lawn trees may (in some cases) be wide-spreading, short-lived, or even untidy; trees intended for parkways should have none of these characteristies — their qualifications are much more strictly delimited. Street trees should form a compact head affording much shade but should neither too tall nor too wide. If too tall, they conflict perpetually with overhead power lines and constitute a danger to pedestrians and automobiles beneath; if too wide, their branches hang out and down into the street. They should be exceptionally hardy and adaptable in order to resist the rigors of their environment: cement slab on one side, sidewalk on the other, thoughtless passersby who hack on their trunks, and errant automobiles that scrape and bump them. They should possess small, easily dispersible, easily decomposable leaves, small, inconspicuous flowers and seeds, and clean stems, for any, tree which makes conspicuous litter underfoot is sure to meet with public disapproval, however meritorious it may be in other respects. They should be strong-wooded, long-lived, insect-free, and disease-resistant, Finally, they should be well-shaped, attractive to

look at, and generous producers of shade, for this is their entire purpose.

To find a tree combining all these characteristics is indeed difficult, and the problem is complicated by the fact that each region must select those varieties suited for its particular climate, soil constitution, and biological and geographical peculiarities. Nurseries generally stock those species best adapted to local conditions; county agents and agricultural experiment stations are helpful consultants; and libraries usually have books and pamphlets in abundance. The National Shade Tree Conference publishes evaluations and recommendations for the different regions of the country from time to time.

Most cities manage to solve the problem sooner or later, some more successfully than others. Often the dominant impression a city makes upon us consists of its beautiful tree-lined avenues; these we remember long after the confused impressions of buildings, museums, and store windows have faded away. Berlin is (or was) famous for its avenue of lindens, Paris for its poplars and horse-chestnuts, Tokyo for its cherry trees, Mexico City for its ashes and Palms, Los Angeles for its Eucalyptus and Laurel Figs, Washington for its Ginkgoes, St. Louis for its Maples. An examination of the cities of the world will reveal that almost every kind of tree has been tried at some time or other as a street tree.

In this search for the ideal street tree a very important caution should be observed: not to plant one species exclusively, for in the event of an epidemic of some kind a one-tree city may be transformed almost overnight from an oasis to a barren desert. Such was the fate of Des Moines, Iowa, which lost 250,000 elms to the dreaded Dutch elm disease. Far better to plant a wide variety of species as biochemically different as possible; then when some varieties go, others will remain, for among plants as among animals epidemics rarely attack more than one kind of organism.

Tree Source

After deciding on the kind and the size, the third question is where to get the tree. Shall you dig it up in the woods, the neighbor's back yard, or buy it in the nursery? If the moving is to be done by a professional, that problem is of course his. But if you decide to do the work yourself, you'll find it helpful to learn something about soils and root systems first.

Trees growing in the woods and never having been moved or root-pruned tend to have a long, straggly root system that makes transplanting difficult; moreover,the soil is often rocky and hard to dig. Nursery-grown trees, on the contrary, are either kept in containers or are moved about from time to time in such a manner that they develop a dense, compact mass of roots confined within a reasonably small ball. In addition they are grown in the best possible kind of soil: rich, light, ideal for digging and balling. Wherever possible, the nursery-grown tree is to be preferred.

On occasions, however, where no large-sized or desirable nursery trees are available, or where you wish to move a particular tree from one location to another, then there is nothing to do but accept the adverse properties of the wilding tree and attempt to overcome them.

Whichever tree is settled on, nursery-grown or wilding, it should be thrifty, vigorous, full-limbed, free from cavities, bark disfigurations, twig or leaf diseases, or any other kind of abnormality. No tree in a declining condition should be moved. Nor should any tree be chosen for moving that is close to a sidewalk, street, building, or another tree, for half its root system will be unavailable for digging.

Remember also that the branches and crotches of a young tree will not increase their distance from the ground as the tree grows; a large limb or a low crotch three or four feet from the ground will always remain at that level unless cut off. (Many people are misled on this score, believing the tree to grow all over as an animal does.) Generally, it is preferable to select a tree with straight trunk, free of branches up to a height of 5 or 6 feet. However, low crotches or low branches are not always undesirable, much depending on the kind of tree, the location, and the purpose it is to serve.

Preparing the Hole

The hole should be prepared before the tree is moved. It should be dug larger than the root-system to be transplanted, preferably twice as large or in certain situations still larger. If the roots measure 4 feet across and 2-1/2 feet deep, the hole should measure 8 feet across and 4 to 5 feet deep. In poor soil, the enlargement of the hole is particularly necessary. Cart away all rocks and undesirable soil, and partly refill the hole with prepared soil of the mixture suited to the kind of tree you are planting. The reason for making the hole larger than apparently necessary is easily understandable, for when the root-system—which has been trimmed back to the edge of the ball—begins to grow, the thousands of new rootlets that push outward will more readily enter filled soil that has been loosened and enriched than they would the rocky inhospitable rim of the original excavation.

Ordinarily, the digging of an extra large hole and the refilling with imported soil is sufficient provision for giving the transplant a good start. In unusually rocky, clay, or tightly compressed soils, however, dynamiting is sometimes resorted to in order to loosen up the ground.

In some kinds of soils drainage provision must be made. A tree can be killed by too much water as well as by too little. Excess water damages plant roots not by any direct effect but by preventing proper aeration of the soil. Any tree whose root-system is completely and uninterruptedly sub-

merged in water for any length of time (which for some species may mean days, for others weeks, for still others possibly months) will die. Proof of this, in the form of dead trees, may be found in regions where floods have left water standing around trees or in regions where swamp levels or lake levels have suddenly risen and entrapped nearby trees. Even the species most intimately associated with water— willow, cypress, cottonwood, box elder—grow on the river bank, not in the river channel.

All tree roots must have air, and that air must come to them through the tiny pores of the soil. When the air supply is shut off by flooding (or by superimposing layers of heavy, impervious soil), the tree dies. Many times a heavy clay layer of soil exists, or is artificially made to exist by poor cultivating practices, under the surface soil. This hardpan prevents normal drainage, and in times of excessive rainfall or excessive watering, so much liquid accumulates in the surface soil that trees in the area die by asphyxiation. Such a hardpan layer sometimes exists many years, even around one's favorite trees, without coming to notice until certain changes in the environment develop its potential hazard. The most common example is that of a tree that suddenly dies after shrubbery has been planted around it. Why? Because the stepped-up watering program given the shrubs causes an unprecedented quantity of water to accumulate around the tree, and it dies of asphyxiation. In such cases the shrubs, with their shallower root system well above the hardpan layer, may live on, and the owner may never suspect the truth.

In locations where drainage is suspect, sandy loam and/or quantities of humus should be incorporated into the soil. The planting hole may be dug unusually deep and partly filled with gravel to make sure that water will drain away from the roots, at least in their immediate neighborhood. In extreme cases, it is advisable to install an underground drainage system consisting of tile pipes slanted in such a manner as to carry excess water away from the root area.

Some tree species, such as willows and redwoods, can sometimes overcome the threat of full or partial flooding by producing new roots near the new surface. When flood-swollen creeks subside, the willows and cottonwoods along the banks sometimes exhibit horizontal layers of adventitious roots along the trunk, indicating the various flood levels as surely as a man-made marker. Some species, such as the tropical almond (Terminalia catappa), can, when flooded, produce from their main roots thousands of tiny rootlets (pneumatophores) that grow straight upward until they rise above the water level, functioning, presumably, as air-intake tubes, and disappearing when the water level subsides.

Digging the Tree

With the tree selected and the hole dug, the next step is the actual moving. Digging out the tree, moving it to its new location, and planting it should be done as carefully as possible and without unnecessary waste of time. The less time lost in transit from old site to new site the better the chance of survival. Roots dry out rapidly in air and sun. A tree out of the ground is like a fish out of water; and although it may be made to survive in a state of suspended animation for weeks, months, or sometimes even years, its roots are nowhere so well off as in the ground.

Trees are moved in two ways: bare-rooted, and balled and burlaped. Bare-rooted trees are the easier to dig and move because of the lesser weight involved. Balled trees, except in the smallest sizes, must be moved with special equipment because of their weight.

Most deciduous trees may be moved bare-rooted if not over 3 or 4 inches in stem diameter. Some species, such as sycamore (buttonwood), American elms, willows and poplars, take transplanting in their stride. I moved (for a central Texas college) bare-rooted and in full leaf, 25 American elms of 4 and 5 inch stem diameter in the heat of August—under the worst possible conditions—with a 100% survival record. And in Mexico I once watched a friend, totally ignorant of gardening, dig up a 6 inch DBH lemon tree in full leaf and weighted down with fruit, move it across town without even bothering to cover the exposed roots, plant

it—and in spite of my scoffing went right on making his daily **cuba libre** with its aid for many years thereafter.

These exceptional cases are testimonials to the vitality of some species; they are not guide-lines to be followed. Most Temperate-Zone species need gentle treatment and should be moved, not in mid-summer but in early spring or late fall. The advantage of fall planting is that the roots have the opportunity to become active very early in the spring, benefiting from early rains and from melting snow. In regions where winters are severe and prolonged, tender trees are best planted in the spring.

A tree to be moved bare-rooted should be dug out with care, for not all movings will respond as gratifyingly as the Texas elms or the Mexican lemon. (Even with the best of care a certain percentage will fail to survive.) Dig a circular trench about 3 feet deep and 3 feet removed from the trunk. Cut off cleanly with axe or shears all roots encountered in this trench. Slowly and carefully work the dirt loose from the roots within the circle, cut off the tap root (if any) as low as possible, and lift the tree out of the hole. If the tree is small, one man can lift it without difficulty; if larger, two or three men may be needed; if still larger, a mechanical device of some kind may be necessary, such as a lifting arm mounted on a pick-up truck. If you use the lifting device, you may be able to transport the tree upright.

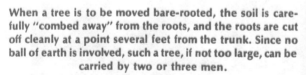

When a tree is to be moved bare-rooted, the soil is carefully "combed away" from the roots, and the roots are cut off cleanly at a point several feet from the trunk. Since no ball of earth is involved, such a tree, if not too large, can be carried by two or three men.

Digging an Elm tree for bare-rooted moving, the roots are cut off cleanly with axe or shears at two or three feet from the trunk, and the top is cut back correspondingly. It is important to get a good root pattern, including vertical roots as well as lateral ones.

A partly dug Elm tree that is to be moved bare-rooted. The roots must be "combed out" as carefully as possible and a good radial pattern must be sought.

If you do the job by hand, you will probably position the tree horizontally at one or more times; if so, rest the trunk across a saw-horse, bench, chair, or some similar object to prevent damage to the roots. With the tree out of the hole and the roots accessible, cut back all those that are broken or frayed, paint (with special tree paint) all cut and skinned surfaces, cut off any girdling roots that may be present, cover the roots with wet straw, wet newspapers, or better still, stick them into a mud bath, and take the tree as rapidly as possible to its destination. Cloudy, rainy days are the best for transplanting; if you do it on a sunny day, protect the roots from the light.

As many of the tiny fibrous roots as possible should be preserved: they are true feeders, and if they are destroyed, the muscular roots must grow new ones before the tree can function properly. Since the fibrous roots of balled trees are not disturbed, these suffer less shock, other things being equal, than bare-rooted trees.

Although some kinds of deciduous trees, such as elms, hackberries, poplars, and willows, can be moved bare-rooted in the wintertime in very large sizes, up to 50 or 60 feet tall and 18 to 20 inches in trunk diameter, most species that exceed a 4 or 5 inch stem diameter should be moved with a ball of earth surrounding the roots. All evergreens should be balled.

Balled trees are harder to move but easier to dig. As with a bare-rooted tree, the digging begins with a circular trench. As the trench is deepened, the roots are cut off cleanly with axe or shears and painted over. Care must be taken not to break the ball or to loosen the roots within. At the bottom, the trench is tapered in towards the center, thus rounding the ball. The final underneath cut is made by hand tools, if possible, or, if the ball is too big to be tipped over use a winch cable looped around and pulled through. The cable neatly separates the ball from the soil underneath it and severs all small down-pointing roots; any large roots encountered should, however, be cut by hand. (Burlaping, to be discussed in a moment, should precede this under-cutting.)

This size of the ball is, of course, proportioned to the size of the tree. The usual rule is 8 to 10 times the diameter of the trunk; thus a tree 6 inches in diameter is moved with a ball 48 to 60 inches across; one 4 inches in diameter should have a ball 32 to 40 inches across, etc.

In very large sizes (one foot or more through) the tree should be prepared for moving in stages covering a period of two, or sometimes three or more years. A circular trench is laid off as just described but is dug in sections. Suppose the trench to be divided into six segments. The first year three non-consecutive segments are dug, the roots severed and painted, and the dirt replaced. The next year the remaining three non-consecutive segments are dug, the roots in these areas cut, and the dirt replaced. The third year the trench is reopened all the way around, and the tree is

First step in moving a tree is digging the ball. The ratio of width to depth depends on the kind of soil and the kind of tree, root patterns varying widely. As the hole is deepened, all exposed roots are cut off cleanly with axe or a pair of pruning shears.

ready to be moved. If the tree is extra large, this procedure may be extended over a period of four or five years. Its purpose is to encourage the development of a compact root system within the ball and at the same time to prevent the perhaps fatal shock of severing all the large roots at the same time. (Spreading the procedure over too long a period, say 8 or 10 years, is not advisable, for by the time the last segments are dug, the roots in the first segments will have grown back to their original proportions, and the work will have been done in vain.)

The precise shape of the ball varies with the kind of tree. Species with a long taproot, such as the pecan, should have a long, conical ball. Those with shallow, wide-spreading roots should have a wide, flat ball. Those with deeper roots, such as most of the oaks, should have a ball more nearly equal in width and depth. Rarely is the "ball" actually a ball; more generally it is conical, truncated, ovaloid, or even square.

The objective, of course, is to shape the ball in such a manner that the greatest number of roots can be contained

This ball of earth has been carefully and skillfully dug, all roots cleanly severed with axe or shears. The proportion of depth to width depends on the kind of tree and the nature of the soil. For this type of tree (Spanish Oak, *Quercus falcata*) this shape is ideal. The next steps are burlaping and lacing to hold ball together.

within the smallest possible volume. The more roots that can be moved with the tree the better. On the other hand, dirt is unconscionably heavy, a cubic foot of average soil weighing about 110 pounds. A rapid way to estimate the weight of a ball is the following: Square its diameter (in inches); multiply this by its depth (also in inches); multiply this figure by .05. The result will be the weight in pounds. This formula, applied to a ball one foot across and one foot deep, gives 86.4 pounds. The difference between that figure and the figure of 110 pounds per cubic foot of soil is accounted for by the rounding of the ball toward the bottom.

Preparing the Ball

Once the ball is shaped, the problem is how to lift it out of the hole and hoist it onto the conveying vehicle without breaking it. This problem has several solutions.

In the North when the ground is deeply frozen, a ball of earth may sometimes be hacked out and moved as one frozen mass without wrapping of any kind. In some kinds of heavy, gumbo soil the same thing is true; the dirt can hardly be knocked loose with a hammer. Some kinds of palms, because of their numerous and tightly intertwined fibrous roots, can also be moved without wrapping, even in the loosest of soils.

In loose and sandy soil, however (palms excepted) it is as difficult to hold the ball together as it is to weave the traditional rope of sand. In such cases the box method is used. A trench is made as usual—but square not round, and tapering inward toward the bottom. A box of heavy oak boards bolted (not nailed) at the corners is built up around the square "ball". Other oak planks are worked under the bottom and bolted to the side boards. These bottom planks are cut longer than the width of the ball so that their ends protrude. Strong hooks are fastened to the protruding ends, ropes are tied to the hooks, and out of these a rope cradle is built up. A truck with winch and A-frame then hooks onto the rope cradle and hoists the box and tree straight upward. In this position the tree can be moved to any nearby planting site, or it can be transferred to a flat-bed truck, and positioned horizontally, if the haul is to be a long one.

The most common method, however, widely used in soils that are neither sandy nor sticky nor frozen, is to wrap the ball tightly with burlap. This material might not seem strong enough to hold together large balls of earth; but when wrapped tightly and properly it is adequate for all except the most unusual cases.

The burlap is used in the form of cut-open sacks. These are wrapped as tightly as possible around the ball and are pinned together with special nail-pins at every point where they overlap. For small balls one or two sacks may be enough; for large balls many sacks must be joined together.

After the ball is snugly burlaped, it is further secured by lacing. "Lacing" means the enwrapment of the ball by small ropes, about the size of a window sash cord. These ropes are wrapped in such a way as to form a tight net firmly holding the ball together. Interstices of the net may be 4, 5, or 6 inches wide, according to the manner of lacing. Small balls need not be laced; large ones must be.

If the ball is extra heavy and the burlaping and lacing are judged insufficient for holding it together, one to several heavy chains may be looped around it and tightened with load-binders. To prevent damage, two-by-fours may be inserted at intervals between chains and ball.

I once designed (and had manufactured by the local blacksmith) a series of iron plates 8 to 10 inches wide and of

Special tree-moving machine scoops palm tree out of ground, lowers it to horizontal position, and transports it to planting site. Under favorable conditions, the whole operation can be performed in less than an hour.

varying heights, (to be matched to the height of the ball), each plate curved in at the bottom like the fingers of a partially closed hand and each having an ear welded on its outer surface large enough to admit the passage of a chain. By fitting these all around the ball (with curved foot inward), passing a chain through the ears, and tightening with a load-binder, the ball can be secured very firmly without either burlaping or lacing.

Formerly, nearly all small nursery plants were balled and burlaped—hence the designation, widely used in the trade, "B and B"—and even today most of the medium-sized and larger nursery trees, especially those dug to order, continue to be balled and burlaped. But due to the great increase in the number of plants handled in recent years, the tendency among the nurserymen has been to grow plants in cans or to transfer them to cans at a very early stage. Heated discussions are often generated over the merits and demerits of this procedure.

Keeping the plants in cans makes watering easier and more effective (provided that the can have a drainage hole in its bottom), prevents disintegration of the soil ball (in this case a cylinder), and greatly facilitates handling. On the other hand, it has been shown repeatedly that roots kept within the inflexible confines of a metal can often twist and intertwine in such a manner that subsequent normal growth is impeded; that, in fact, the can is all too often a template for the production of girdling roots that eventually result in the plant's death by strangulation. A further disadvantage is that the metal cans, often carelessly left in full sunlight, heat up rapidly and damage the tender roots within.

Burlaping, although more time-consuming and less mechanically efficient, is horticulturally much the safer procedure. It represents for the plant what the modern cageless zoo represents for the animal: containment without restraint, detention without imprisonment. The soil mass is held firmly together, but at the same time the roots are free to grow in their natural direction—outward and downward—and they frequently do so when left long in one position, pushing through the flexible and loosely woven burlap in a way that the roots of canned plants can never do.

Recently a new kind of container, made not of metal but of compressed peat moss, has come into use in many nurseries. This need not be removed at time of planting—indeed, *should* not be removed, for by its quick disintegration, once in the hole, it fertilizes the roots as obligingly as it had previously contained them. Moreover, in common with burlap, which also may be left in the hole, it constitutes no disposal problem. At present this ingenious organic container is adequate for small plants only, not being strong enough to withstand the weight of larger balls; perhaps a similar, stronger product suited for the larger sizes will some day make its appearance.

Lifting and Loading

Once the ball is wrapped and laced, it still needs to be hoisted out of the hole and onto a conveyor. There are several methods by which this may be done.

The problem is not so much the weight of the ball—although this often runs into several tons—but rather the method of attachment, for the lifting must be done against the ball of earth, never against the trunk, which is easily damaged.

Preparing a Spanish Oak tree *(Quercus falcata)* for moving. The ball is first covered with burlap, pinned together as snugly as possible; next it is enclosed in a tight rope lacing. Additional chains are sometimes passed around it and drawn tight with load-binders.

Various kinds of rope or canvas slings are used for this purpose. The sling is placed around one side of the ball, and the ball is tilted over upon it. The ends of the sling are attached to a winch line suspended from an A-frame or to a chain hoist mounted on an overhead I-beam running the length of the truck. Improved types of slings, consisting of metal bands or rubberized belting, made to fit snugly about any size ball, may be purchased from tree-supply houses.

The advantage of the sling is that, like the box, it allows the tree to be carried in a horizontal position for a long haul. Also available are tongs, which work on the principle of those that carry blocks of ice. Instead of digging into the ball of earth, these embrace it with broad bands.

Another interesting method is to work a round iron plate under the ball, then to force a heavy iron rod through the ball in an upright position close to the trunk, taking care, of

Pulling the wrapped and laced ball of earth onto the iron bottom plate. The two upright bars in the foreground prevent the plate from slipping away until the ball is positioned. The iron rings welded around the plate's circumference are fastening points for chains which secure it firmly in place. The ball weighs several tons, and the weight of the man on top is negligible by comparison.

course, not to damage the roots. The rod fits into a special slot in the center of the plate, where it is secured by a heavy pin passed through a hole in its tip. The upper end of the rod, left sticking out of the ball a foot or so, terminates in an eye, to which a winch cable is fastened. The tree may then be lifted straight up and transported in this position to the new site. Disadvantages of this system are the difficulties of working the plate under the ball and of guiding the rod to find the slot. When it is possible to tilt the ball over slightly, these difficulties are obviated.

Amateurs sometimes attempt something similar by drilling through the trunk itself near its base, inserting a transverse rod, and applying a lifting device to the projecting ends of the rod. Although doubtless a certain number of trees have been moved in this manner, the technique is not to be recommended for the following reasons: (1) if the tree is soft-wooded and the ball of earth heavy, the trunk may split open when pressure is applied; (2) the drilling of a large hole unnecessarily opens up a potential avenue of infection into the very heart of the tree; (3) when lift is exerted on the trunk rather than on the ball, the ball tends to sag, to loosen, and to come apart.

A third method is to slide the ball onto a platform made of strong oak planks securely bolted together with stout cross pieces on the underside. One side of the trench is enlarged to form an inclined plane, and the platform—actually a kind

Balled, burlaped, laced, and chained, this tree is ready to be pulled up the inclined dirt ramp and onto a carrier. Chains passing over the top of the ball secure an iron plate firmly to its bottom.

Tree balled, burlaped, laced, and chained, ready for moving. The trunk diameter is 6 inches. The weight of the ball is approximately 4-1/2 tons. (Spanish Oak *Quercus falcata*).

of sled—is slid up the inclined plane to ground level. Instead of the oak platform, a heavy round iron plate with outward-pointing ears welded around its periphery, may be used.

For sliding the ball onto the platform or plate, a mat made of woven ropes, rubber strips, or close-meshed fence wire is useful. The mat is looped over the side of the ball and is pulled by ropes fastened to its ends, hammock fashion. The platform, like the plate, should have iron rings along its edges to which chains or cables may be attached for pulling it up the slope out of the hole. Motive power is furnished by

a winch truck, anchored in front to a distant tree or stump. When the tree reaches ground level, it may be slid onto a low-boy trailer and transported upright, if not too large.

Special tree-moving trucks and trailers are now manufactured that will load transplants easily and efficiently. For trees weighing up to 2000 pounds there are electric and manually operated cranes that fit in a corner of a pick-up and enables one man to load and unload the smaller-size balls with ease. For bigger balls there are bigger lifting units that require bigger trucks. Any large strong flatbed truck can be equipped to do the work for all except the very largest sizes.

Dug, balled, burlaped, and laced, this tree is being pulled by a winch truck up a dirt ramp preparatory to loading. An iron plate, not visible in the illustration, is under the bottom to prevent the dirt from crumbling away and to make sliding easier.

The essential elements are two overhead metal arches from which is suspended a horizontal I-beam with a traveling hoist.

Also available are special digging units designed to work off a front loader or a backhoe. These ingenious diggers, made in a wide range of sizes, up to 60 inches, penetrate the hardest soil, cut the roots as they go, scoop up the required ball, and transport it to any proximate planting site. Where space permits its use, such a machine saves many man-hours of work.

A large tree that is to be transported very far needs to be tied securely to the truck to prevent side-lash and damage to branches and/or trunk. Branches of spreading trees need to be drawn together with ropes. Right-of-way should be obtained ahead of time, the shortest route mapped out, bridges tested, etc. Four to seven men are needed to dig, transport, and plant a large tree.

Planting

When it reaches the planting site, the tree should be taken off of the truck with care and set into the prepared hole. If it is bare-rooted, it can be handled by a crew of 2 to 5

Large Spanish Oak weighing 5-6 tons being lifted off carrier truck by second truck with A-frame and winch for lowering into planting hole. With smaller trees a single truck is often equipped to handle the whole operation, but with larger trees two or more trucks are often necessary. The chains, ropes, and wrappings are removed after the transplant is positioned in the whole.

With an overhead rail mounted as shown, a tree can be picked up out of one hole and lowered into another with a minimum of effort. Note the iron plate under the ball to hold the soil in place. A winch mounted behind the cab provides the power.

A simple rig for moving medium-sized trees, consisting of nothing more than an overhead rail and a traveling hoist.

members, depending on its size. If it is balled and the ball is not too large, it can be rolled down an inclined plane made by leaning planks against the edge of the truck platform. If it has a large ball, it can be lifted by a chain hoist or a winch line passed through an A-frame, or some similar device.

The tree should be planted at the same level at which it was formerly growing. If set too deep, its roots may suffer from suffocation. If set too shallow, they may dry out in the air and sun. Elms, in particular, have roots very close to the surface, usually buttressing out from the trunk several inches above the soil-line.

There is an old wives' tale to the effect that a transplant should be oriented in its new location exactly as it was in its former location and that not to observe this rule spells disaster. While this is certainly not true of nursery trees and shrubs grown in cans and frequently moved about so that they have no fixed orientation, it may have a degree of applicability to a tree that has grown in one position all its life. Near the equator with an overhead sun, the applicability is perhaps less, but in high latitudes, where the difference between northern and southern exposure is considerable—where, indeed, trees grow moss on their north-facing side, as all Boy Scouts know—it is quite possible that a transplant turned on its axis 180° might suffer ill effects, at least temporarily. The north side—now suddenly become the south side—the trunk and branches might suffer sunburn (certainly the moss would shrivel off); the sun leaves and shade leaves might feel the shock when suddenly called upon to exchange places, and other, less measurable effects (perhaps altered relations to the earth's magnetic fields) might be experienced. Although this idea is often scoffed at, it bears investigation, and its violation might indeed account for the failure of some transplants to succeed in spite of all the care lavished on them.

Bare-rooted trees, although easier to lift and transport than balled trees, need more care in their planting. Broken and scarred roots should be cut back and painted over. Criss-crossing roots should be eliminated to a reasonable degree, girdling roots totally. The tree should be set in the center of the hole and lined up as straight as possible. If a small tree, one man can hold it upright while others shovel in the soil. If large, it can be conveniently kept supported by ropes. Planting boards, purchasable in many feed and seed stores, are sometimes used to help center the tree.

If there is a drainage problem, gravel or sand should be placed in the bottom of the hole to prevent water from standing around the roots. The hole is then filled with good, rich, porous, well broken-up soil. If there is no drainage problem, the gravel and sand may be dispensed with. The subsoil excavated during the digging, is of course, discarded.

Work the soil carefully around the roots, patting and tamping firmly with hands, fists, and, where no injury will result, with your feet. It is not enough just to shovel in the soil and assume that it will pack itself. Often it won't. Air pockets are sometimes left, with the result that some roots will remain out of contact with the soil, and later with the first rain or first heavy watering the soil will sink and puddle.

Fill all spaces under and in between roots. Try to bend and twist the roots as little as possible, and never double them upon themselves. Where one is too long for the hole, make the hole bigger or shorten the root; do not force it into a bent position. Extend, fill, pat, and tamp. Gradually build the fill up to the consistency and firmness of long-established soil. When the hole is filled and well packed, build up a ring of earth around its rim to make watering easier (by preventing it from running off).

Balled trees are easier to plant. The ball should be lowered carefully into the hole, which is previously measured so that when the ball comes to rest, its upper surface will be approximately even with the surrounding soil. When platform or iron plate is used, as a bottom support, it must be removed as gently as possible. This can be accomplished by tilting the ball—by manpower, if not too heavy, or by skillful use of winch cable and overhead pulley, if extra large. All such tilting and twisting, once the ball is in the hole, must be done before the lacing is removed, not afterward, for without this support the ball may be easily broken and the intimate contact between roots and soil disturbed. Once the tree has been positioned as straight as possible, the lacing and the burlap wrapping should be removed. Any burlap caught under the ball should be cut off and left rather than pulled out.

With the tree straight and all chains, ropes, cords, boards, and wrappings removed, all that remains is to shovel good, rich, loose dirt into the trench around the ball and to tamp it down firmly. A ring of earth may then be built up around the perimeter of the hole, just as with the bare-rooted tree.

Watering

Contrary to common practice, the hole should not be watered just before or during planting. Watering at this time makes working in the hole muddy and messy, prevents tamping, and causes the formation of clods, which when dry are broken up with difficulty. Watering is best done after the planting operation is finished.

Open the hose moderately, put a board or a rock within the ring of earth, and let the water fall on this and spray outward, thus preventing the concentrated stream from eroding a hole in the fresh earth. Let the water run three or four hours. Do not repeat until the soil shows signs of drying. This will mean watering—copiously but slowly—once or twice a week, according to the nature of the soil and the kind of weather.

Remember, too much water is as harmful as too little. Keep the soil moist but not saturated. Sprinkling and other forms of superficial watering are of little value; they may actually do harm by encouraging the roots to grow too close to the surface. Flooding is similarly of doubtful utility. Since water can be absorbed by the soil at only a certain rate, a great quantity of it poured out in a short time is largely wasted.

Feeding

Newly planted trees sometimes benefit from an application of plant food. Do not, however, use too much fertilizer or too concentrated a dose. Like watering, feeding can easily be overdone. Better to use no fertilizer at all than to use the wrong kind or to use the right kind in excess. Good rich soil placed in the planting hole is usually adequate.

Where some kind of plant food seems desirable, it may be added in the form of well-rooted manure or bone meal (the safest of fertilizers) in quantities not to exceed three pounds per inch of trunk diameter. The fertilizer should be thoroughly mixed with the dirt, not just dumped into one segment of the hole. In the case of balled trees, it may be mixed with the soil in the surrounding trench or applied directly within the ball through holes made very carefully with a small rod. Commercial fertilizers are not recommended for immediate use on transplants.

Bracing

The transplanted tree usually needs artificial support until it can establish itself. If allowed to sway in the wind, the new, developing rootlets will be broken.

Guy wires are most commonly used for this purpose. The size of the wire is, of course, proportionate to the size of the tree: slender wires for slender trees, and galvanized wire cable 1/8 or 3/16" diameter for tall, heavy trees. If the transplant is small, it may be secured by fastening the guy wires to three or four long stakes driven equidistantly around the tree; the stakes should be notched on the far side and inclined outwardly. The wires may be fastened to the tree by wrapping them around cushions of burlap or canvas or running them through short lengths of rubber hose. This method of attachment is strictly provisional, however; do not forget that all encircling wires must be removed in the second or third season, after the roots have taken hold. Too often, we forget (even trained city planting crews are guilty of this); and as the transplant begins to thicken, it crushes the protective boards, cushions, rubber strips, etc., and strangles itself against the unyielding wire.

An additional disadvantage of wires is that they are a tripping hazard and a temptation to little boys to pull and swing on them; moreover the stakes make a lawn unsightly and grass cutting difficult. Instead of using stakes, you may

One method of supporting a new, slender transplant. Notice than the stem is not encircled and that the wooden blocks are prevented from damaging the tender bark by the interposition of folds of burlap. If the two-by-fours are firmly fastened in the ground and if the pressure is even on all sides, the tree cannot sway.

prefer to drive a long wooden or iron rod into the ground close to the transplant's trunk and parallel with it, joining rod and trunk with loops of wire or cord with some kind of wooden block interposed to give rigidity. Although a good temporary measure, here, too, the danger lies in forgetting to remove the supporting arrangements after they have served their purpose.

Large transplants should be secured by large cables. These should be fastened at the ground end, not to wooden stakes, but to special holding devices consisting of a metal rod with an eye at one end and a flange, which is buried, at the other. The cables may be tightened by the use of turnbuckles or by the other ways explained in Chapter 3. Where necessary to avoid tripping, the cables may be rendered visible by attaching white strips of cloth along their lower portions.

Wrapping

The trunks of transplants, particularly small ones with thin, tender bark, should be wrapped with burlap or some other substance as a protection against sunburn, borer attack, clawing cats, chewing dogs, and gnawing rodents. A specially prepared tree-wrap material composed of two layers of crepe paper separated by a layer of asphaltum may be obtained from horticultural supply houses.

The wrapping should extend from the ground up to the first major branches, Put it on as you would tape a baseball bat, making it as snug as possible and giving sufficient overlap at every turn to insure full protection. Wrapping is also excellent for discouraging sapsuckers, which sometimes make a young tree look as if blasted with buck-shot. Leave the wrapping on for two or three seasons or until it begins to look unsightly. Since it is designed to yield and split under pressure, there is no danger of stem strangulation, as with wires, chains, and other inflexible materials.

Pruning

The transplanted tree should be top-pruned to compensate for the partial loss of its root system. This may be done at the time of digging or at the time of planting. If done at the time of digging, this excess weight and volume will not have to be transported. Also less evaporation will occur during transportation.

This reason for top-pruning is simple. Every transplant suffers some damage to its root system; hence the equilibrium between roots and top is upset. More water is evaporated from the leaves than can be supplied by the reduced number of roots. When outgo exceeds intake, the result is disastrous. The tree wilts, loses its foliage, and dies back part of the way, or, in unusually sensitive species, all of the way.

But if you reduce the top to conform to the unavoidable reduction of the root system, a balance between the two parts is restored. Leave the leader undisturbed, but cut back the side branches one-third or even one-half their length. Eliminate many small twigs altogether, particularly those pointing inward. If the tree is in full leaf, strip off 75% or so of the leaves. (Experiments have shown that some kinds of transplants, like some kinds of cuttings, do better when a few leaves are left on. While too many leaves permit too much evaporation, a bare minimum of leaves helps maintain life-processes and accelerates root initiation—probably through the production of hormones.) Such selective pruning, while effective in reducing the evaporative surface, does not destroy the tree's natural framework. The roots soon re-establish themselves, and in a short time the reduced top grows back to its original size.

Since the end result seems to be the same—a smaller tree, virtually devoid of leaves—the beginning gardener may

Special protective paper wrapped around trunk of newly transplanted American Elm. Composed of two layers separated by a coating of asphaltum, the paper helps discourage borer invasion, also prevents sunburning of the tender bark, which, as a part of normal transplanting procedure, is usually deprived of part of its normal leaf cover.

wonder, as I once did, why one should go to the trouble of producing that result artificially instead of letting the transplant die back naturally. But the two things are quite different. *Preventive* reduction of evaporative surface conserves moisture stored in the tree's roots and stems, permitting it to make a quick come-back, while the contrary practice of allowing the transplant to evaporate all its reserves, then wilt and die back, produces an exhausted specimen that will take much longer to recover or may never do so.

Since evergreens usually have a compact root system that is easily enclosed within a relatively small ball—and since they are always moved with a ball—they need less top pruning when transplanted.

Several wax preparations are on the market for use on transplants. Sprayed on foliage, branches, and trunk, they coat these surfaces with a thick layer of wax that serves very effectively to prevent evaporation. Many arborists use them routinely on evergreens and also on deciduous trees moved when in leaf.

Hormones

In the past thirty years or so a number of plant hormones have been discovered. A hormone is a chemical messenger, produced in minute quantities at one or more places within the plant body, often at a growing tip, and sent through the circulatory system to control a variety of life processes, including stem growth, the onset of flowering and fruiting, and the initiation of root activity. Now synthesized and produced in large quantities, some of these substances are sold as growth regulators. Of these, indolebutyric acid, often combined with naphthylacetamide and sold under various trade names, is perhaps the best known. It is widely used for rooting cuttings and is sometimes applied to the cut roots of a large transplant.

2

Grafting

Grafting means the nonsexual union of two (or more) individual plants. It is accomplished by bringing together, and holding together, the embryonic tissues (cambium layer) of each plant until they unite. Each member of a graft may be complete unto itself, being united with another plant at any point along its roots, stem, or branches. When two plants are so joined, each preserves its own identity, although partly influenced by the chemistry of the other.

On the other hand, each member of a graft may constitute only part of an organic whole, one plant commonly furnishing the roots, while another supplies the top, coming together in a mutually beneficial relationship, like the blind man who carried the lame man. Thus usually a top (called *scion,* with certain highly desirable characteristics, is grafted onto a root sytem (called *stock),* selected for its vigor and hardiness, so that both members grow to form a single individual superior to either one taken alone.

On most grafted trees the point of union is noticeable as a swelling or a sudden difference in diameter along the trunk. For most practical purposes such a tree is a perfect union. The roots supply the top with water and dissolved minerals; the top in turn supplies the roots with manufactured food. The tree lives and grows and bears leaves and fruit down through the years and is to all respects a normal tree.

Yet certain differences continue to obtain between stock and scion, despite all the years they remain united. Each stubbornly retains inborn characteristics. The stock strives continually to send up shoots from its stem below the line of graft, and the scion sometimes manages to become own-rooted, hence emancipating itself from the stock. affect the scion may leave the stock untouched, or vice versa. Furthermore, after many years of peaceable co-operation stock and scion may rather uddenly decide to march in step no longer, the affected tree exhibiting all the symptoms of pre-mature senescence, attributed, for want of a better explanation, to "delayed incompatibility."

The union of grafted parts is, therefore, not a perfect one, being something more than mere juxtaposition and something less than true blending. The wonder is, however, not that such unions occasionally fail but that they function as admirably as they do; only in sexual reproduction, involving as it does a restructuring of the contents of two parent cells, is a more intimate union to be found.

Grafting is not possible when stock and scion belong to different families. Although pecan may be grafted onto hickory, oak may not be grafted onto elm nor fig onto pear. However, even when stock and scion are closely related, grafts are not made with equal facility among all families. Some kinds of trees are quite easy to graft, such as the pecan; others extremely difficult, such as the oak.

Reasons for Grafting

Grafting is practiced for a variety of reasons, the chief of which is the desire to produce new individuals exactly like the parent one. Among valuable fruit or ornamental trees (or other plants), the valued characteristics—such as fruit of a certain size or flavor and flowers of a certain color—do not always appear in the offspring when these are reproduced sexually (that is, by pollination and fertilization). Plants, like animals, do not always "breed true"— in fact, almost never do. The offspring differ from their parents in unexpected and sometimes disconcerting ways. But by grafting, which is a form of vegetative reproduction, all uncertainty is eliminated. There is only one parent involved, and the characteristics always come true. Each scion is a piece of the parent tree transplanted onto a new and vigorous stock. When it grows to maturity, scions may be taken off it and grafted onto other stocks, and so on *ad infinitum*, each new individual being exactly like its parent, for the good reason that it and the parent are really one. Thus whenever a new and valuable variety of fruit or flower appears somewhere in the world as a "sport" or mutant, it may be propagated by grafting indefinitely.

Many of our choice varieties of nuts, apples, pears, and other fruits are grafts, vegetatively reproduced through many generations with unchanged excellence, from some original form. The California avocadoes have the following interesting history.

In 1911 a Mr. Schmidt introduced into California a number of avocado scions taken from various Mexican trees. These were grafted onto California stocks producing inferior fruit. All of the scions died except those taken from a certain tree in the town of Atlixco, in the state of Puebla. Hardier than the others, these managed to survive the colder northern climate and to grow into mature trees producing excellent fruit. From these, scions were cut to graft onto other stocks, and thus the succession was continued. At one time every avocado tree in California was the direct vegetative descendant of that single tree in Atlixco. For many years the *United Avocado Growers of California* made yearly pilgrimages to Mexico to pay it homage, festooning its branches and pouring libations around its roots.

Kinds of Grafts

Grafting is the general term for all forms of tissue union. *Budding* is a special form of grafting, wherein buds of the scion are slipped under the bark of the stock. The processes where the entire scion (bud-stick) is united to the stock are called *cleft-grafting, side-grafting, whip-grafting, tongue-and-groove grafting,* and other terms varying from locality to locality. The essential factors of all forms of grafting or budding are: (1) that the cambium layers of stock and scion be brought together; (2) that they be kept together without movement; (3) that the point of union be sealed over with grafting wax or some similar substance to exclude air and possible disease organisms; (4) that the graft be made at the proper time of year (which varies according to the kind of tree, the form of graft used, and the locality).

When these conditions are fulfilled, the graft will be successful, provided, of course, that the trees concerned are graftable in the first place.

Small trees are usually cleft-grafted or tongue-and-groove grafted at a point near the ground or flush with the ground or even under the ground. Larger trees are budded, or top-grafted, as it is often called, in which process buds are inserted into the limbs, thus avoiding the necessity of cutting off the whole tree at or near the ground. By this means one stock can be budded with several different kinds of scions and so be made to bear different kinds of fruit and foliage. On a native pecan stock, for example, all the known varieties of paper-shelled pecans may be budded: Success, Schley, Stuart, Burkette, etc. Where a Stuart bud is put in, a Stuart limb will develop, and where a Success bud is put in a Success limb will develop. Similarly, a vigorous apple stock may be made to produce every known variety of choice apples, as well as pears and quinces.

Natural grafts sometimes occur where two branches (from the same tree or from different trees of the same species) rub against each other. In such cases the movement of part on part rubs away the bark and exposes the cambium layers, which then grow together. Some very interesting grafts may occasionally be found in the woods, even among trees artificially hard to graft, such as the oaks. Cases have been observed where two trees that have grafted themselves together, one decays completely at the bottom yet keeps on living, not needing its own roots because utilizing through the grafted tissues the root system of the other.

Stands of trees of the same species, either in the wild state or in a man-made orchard, are sometimes so interconnected by naturally occurring root grafts that the whole stand may be said to constitute a single tree. Any tree of the stand that happens to be girdled by animals or accidentally damaged in any way benefits by the root grafts and continues living with unimpaired vigor. On the other hand, any disease that attacks one tree may spread through the whole group by these same root connections. Hence when a contagious disease strikes, a prudent preventive measure is to dig a deep circular trench around the affected tree along the drip line or a little beyond it in an attempt to sever all root connections with others of the stand.

Spectacular effects may be achieved by binding together certain branches and allowing them to graft naturally. By this means young trees can be trained into fantastic forms, their limbs shaped to resemble circles, triangles, arches, etc.

Bridge-grafting

Grafting is practiced on girdled trees to prevent death. When a tree is girdled by animals, insects, or mechanical damage, the bark connection between crown and roots is interrupted, and unless the gap is quickly bridged, the tree will die. Grafts form the bridge: one, two, or many healthy twigs inserted under the upper and lower discontinuous surfaces. Over these bridges—or better, through these conduits—flows the life blood of the tree. Year by year they thicken, eventually fusing together, and the damaged tree once again becomes a whole tree.

Essentials of bridge-grafting are these:
1. To attend the tree as soon as possible after damage,
2. To select vigorous healthy shoots, preferably from the affected tree itself,
3. To join cambium of shoots with cambium of damaged tree,
4. To prevent movement of parts.

The scions are cut at each end into a bevel so as to slip under the bark of the host tree. They are bowed slightly outward so that their tendency to straighten will exert pressure on the grafts and hold them in place.

Side-grafting

Side-grafting, also called *inarching*, may be practiced on a tree whose top is healthy but whose roots are damaged, the object being to supply the desirable top with new roots. This most interesting result is achieved by planting one or more seedlings near the tree in question; then, when they have become young whips, by side-grafting them into the trunk of the larger tree. This is done by slightly cutting or scraping the faces of both young and old stems at the point of contact in order to bring their cambiums together; by tying or nailing the whips in place, and by cutting off their tops above the point of graft. If the graft is successful, the young trees gradually come to function as roots for the old tree, whose original roots may then disappear.

In many respects, this process is like grafting an old brain on a young body. Theoretically, any given crown could thus be preserved indefinitely, by continually supplying it with new roots as the old ones become exhausted. The process occurs naturally on all those trees having aerial roots: the mangrove, the banyan, and the tropical figs. By constantly supplying itself with new roots and new points of support a single banyan tree spreads over acres.

Pecan Grafting

Grafted fruit trees are, of course, standard throughout the world, as are also grafted roses and other prized ornamentals. Large nurseries employ grafting specialists who become astonishingly adept at the work. In every section of the country and every part of the world certain grafted varieties predominate: in California walnuts, oranges, grapefruits, almonds, avocados are everywhere; in New York the apple is probably the most commonly grafted tree; in the South it is the pecan. The pecan in Texas is so abundant that it has been chosen as the state tree. Grafted pecans are sold in great numbers by the nurseries, and native trees are grafted or budded extensively. The most common paper-shell varieties in the South are Burkette, Success, Mahan, Western Schley, and Stuart. The brief discussion of pecan grafting that follows will illustrate the process in general, although we must not forget, of course, that grafting and budding techniques are multiple and that for each species there are a few most favored methods.

Small trees (an inch or less in diameter) are usually tongue-and-groove grafted several inches below the surface of the ground and covered with a small mound of dirt. This operation is done during the winter months, and although the whole top of the tree is sacrificed in the process, the scion will grow to a height of 3 or 4 feet by June. Cleft-grafting of small trees is possible at any given height above ground, but is not to be advised because the scion grows so fast that it sometimes snaps off in the wind at the point of union. The union made below ground is much stronger structurally and has the added advantage of preventing the development of adventitious shoots along the stock.

Larger trees are top-grafted or budded. This process takes about a year to complete, being done in a series of separate operations; hence it is necessarily costly, although the increased yield in improved pecans more than pays for the cost in a few years of production. A tree cannot be top-grafted in one operation, and the home-owner should distrust anyone who claims to do so. Many itinerants collect a handsome fee, insert a few buds, and disappear. For his own protection, the home-owner should deal only with a reputable and established specialist, from whom he should exact some kind of guarantee. As an additional safeguard, he should arrange to pay for the work as it progresses, rather than paying for the whole job at the beginning.

The first step in top-grafting a pecan is the cutting back of the top during the winter months. All branches are cut back to within a foot or foot-and-a-half of the trunk, and the upper third or so of the leader is cut off. All cuts should be made on a slant and covered with protective tree paint to promote rapid healing.

The second step is the insertion of buds in the new growth that appears on the lopped-off branches. When these new shoots become about as thick as a man's little finger (by June or July in Central Texas), they are ready for budding. Bud-sticks (scions), each with four or five well-developed buds, are cut off the desired variety of tree and taken to the site of operation wrapped in wet sawdust or wet newspaper. (Bud sticks should be used as soon as possible after cutting; after three days they begin to dry out.) The best-shaped and most vigorous of the new shoots on the stock are selected for budding; the rest are cut off. Into the bark of each of the remaining shoots, at a point about six inches up from its base, an inverted T-shaped cut is made, using a sharp pocket knife. (Grafting knives are made with a specially shaped blade that facilitates the operation.) With the point of the knife the bark is loosened and lifted slightly at the corners of the cut. Next a bud is cut off the bud stick with a small amount of bark and sapwood attached; the bark and sapwood portion is thinned and tapered; then the wood is pryed loose with the point of the knife, and the thin sliver of bark with the bud in its center is inserted under the bark of the inverted T-cut on the stock. The loosened edges of the latter are pressed gently back in place around the bud and secured by a stout string wrapped firmly around the shoot along the length of the cut above and below the bud.

Grafting wax should be smeared over the cuts to prevent drying out of the tender tissues, although many experienced grafters omit its use, relying on the expertness of their fit and tie. The T-cut on the stock limbs should always be made on their outside face so that the branch that develops from the inserted bud will begin growth in the right direction. For the same reason, the buds should be put in with their points up, not down.

The third step is the removal of the strings about three weeks after budding. If the strings are taken off too soon, the graft may not take; if left on too long, they will interfere with the expansion of the branch. At the time the strings are removed, the buds are inspected, and any that have died are replaced (in a new location).

The fourth step is taken during the following winter. It involves the cutting off of all budded shoots just above the point of insertion of the bud.

The fifth and last step is the inspection of buds during the following summer and the trimming off of suckers (shoots that form along the trunk of the tree below the buds).

The buds remain dormant during the first summer and winter, showing no signs of life until the following spring. Because of this, many persons believe them dead, and budders are frequently called back to explain this fine point to their clients, who are impatient to see their new pecans.

Trees begin to bear two or three years after budding. Growth is usually very rapid, and a certain amount of after-care is needed for three or four years in order to prune away undesirable shoots, thin out the center, and remove suckers. Budded trees also sometimes suffer from sunburn because of the sudden removal of the original top and the consequent exposure of the limbs to the sun before the new shoots have a chance to develop. The bark along the upper sides of limbs is frequently killed.

3

Bracing and Cabling

Tree trunks, and tree branches, sometimes split longitudinally. When this happens, the separated parts need to be rejoined and fastened together. Even while still intact, many trees give to the practiced eye clear warning of future splitting and should be supported mechanically in anticipation of the event. As in other phases of tree care, prevention is fairly simple, while repair is costly.

Why does a tree split? Essentially because its trunk, at a certain stage in its growth, divides into two or more parts. The resultant crotch becomes a potential weak spot from the moment of its formation. All the mechanical forces acting on the far-flung top converge upon the central crotch with enormous leverage, while all the agents of decay, given the slighest opportunity, exploit it as an entering wedge. Trunks which do not divide, such as those of most of the conifers and some of the broad-leaved species (the tulip tree, for example), do not split.

Among the trees that form trunk crotches, some, such as the oaks, are so strong and so well constructed, that they very seldom split in spite of neglect, mistreatment, and environmental stress. Others, such as the ashes, the elms, and the mulberries, are by their nature predisposed to splitting and will often do so as they get older and heavier, unless properly braced ahead of time.

The immediate causes of splitting are:

1. Weak wood, such as that of chinaberries, willows, trees-of-heaven, and other fast-growing species.

2. The tendency of the trunk to divide into one or more weak V-shaped crotches, such as those characterizing so many of the elms and ashes, in contrast to the strong U-shaped crotches of the oaks—a tendency that cannot be corrected by pruning.

3. The formation of a multiple crotch composed of three, four, or even more members which could have been corrected by early pruning but was not.

4. The formation of a cavity or cavities at or near the crotch. The rotting away of the strong wood fibers at the place where they are most needed makes splitting almost inevitable.

5. The presence of unhealed and unattended pruning wounds in the crotch region or slightly above it. Such wounds, if large and unprotected by the proper dressing, often crack open and admit the agents of decay, which

Trees with a weak, V-shaped crotch are in ever-present danger of splitting. This tree can be saved by prompt repair measures. The separated portions should be drawn together and secured by threaded rods or bolts and nuts, while flexible galvanized wire cables should be installed higher up among the main limbs.

then weaken the tree internally. Even though the cracks in the exposed wood face of the pruning cut may be so small as to go unnoticed, the resultant decay is sometimes as grave as that accompanying an open cavity.

6. A too heavy superstructure. Some trees, such as the mulberries and the large tropical figs, develop an almost unbelievably dense and spreading crown which at some point becomes too much, in terms of sheer weight, for the single trunk to support. This situation can be corrected by preventive bracing and by a shortening of the branches around the periphery and/or by selective removal of whole branches throughout the crown's interior.

7. A sudden increase in the superstructure's weight, as when the branches become coated with ice or bowed down with snow.

8. Extraordinary stresses produced by high winds.

9. A seasonal increase in weight due to an unusually heavy fruit crop. Even shade trees produce flowers, fruits, and seeds, which, although small individually, may constitute a deceptively large mass in the aggregate.

Total waste of time and material shows up in the amateurish plastering of this tree trunk and the attempted cabling of the two main limbs. A tree unskillfully attended had better be left to its own resources. *Primum non nocere*— First do no harm, should be the motto of the tree surgeon as well as of the medical doctor.

Mechanical assistance given the split or overladen tree takes several forms:

1. Bolts or threaded rods passed transversely through the trunk (or branch) at the point of greatest strain.

2. Flexible wire cables installed high up among the branches to support the two halves of the tree on the principle of opposing forces.

3. Upright supports (usually metal tubes but sometimes wooden beams or masonry constructions) resting on the ground.

4. Guide wires anchored in the soil to a dead man or attached to some adjacent object.

Supports are conveniently divided into *flexible* and *inflexible*, according to the material used. Flexible supports

A Hackberry tree beginning to split at the crotch.

are usually made of galvanized wire cable, sometimes of chains, and, provisionally, even of rope; they generally afford a certain amount of movement to the supported members, in contrast to the inflexible supports, which allow none.

Trees that have not yet split but seem in danger of doing so are easily braced by the use of cables attached to their branches and/or the use of rods passed through their crotch, as outlined.

Trees in which the split has just started may be drawn together, if not too large and heavy, by use of rope-and-tackle or, more conveniently, by use of the light-weight portable hoist now on the market. Provisional rope loops are fastened around the limbs at a distance as high as practicable above the crotch (the higher the attachment the greater the leverage); the ends of the pulling unit are attached to the loops, and pull is exerted until the split halves come together. Threaded rods are then installed through the split portion and cables among the branches. When the job is finished, the provisional tightening accessories are of course removed.

Large heavy trees that have split completely apart may be drawn together by use of pulleys and a winch truck. The procedure is essentially the same as the one just described, with all the pulling and fastening entities being stronger and heavier in proportion to the weight to be lifted.

The important thing in the case of any split, on large tree or small, is to undertake the repair as soon as possible after the damage is discovered. If action is taken in time—meaning within several days or at the most within several weeks—even trees that have split all the way down to ground level can be successfully rejoined. It may seem hard to believe that a tree split down the middle, with each half lying on the ground, can continue to live. Yet so it can, for the problem is a mechanical one, not a physiological one, and the split tree may continue as green and as flourishing as before. This is not to say that splitting is harmless, for the exposed heart wood is immediately subjected to the destructive action of the weather and to invasion by insects and the agents of decay. Besides, of course, instead of an upright tree, you will have two sprawling overgrown shrubs. If the split tree is left too long unattended, new growth taking place in the new position will make its rejoining difficult, if not impossible. The principle is much the same as that of a broken bone: prompt setting makes possible exact realignment and normal healing, while delay hinders both.

If you are unfamiliar with the tree's growth habits, you may attempt to encircle trunk or limbs with chains, cables, ropes, or iron bands, believing encirclement harmless and perforation harmful. Actually, the exact opposite is true. Since the trunk (and every branch and every twig) grows in diameter by adding new layers of wood around the outside (the inside tissues remaining immovable), any permanent encircling chain or band must interfere with such growth and eventually result in death. If an iron band is slowly tightened about the arm or leg, it will first interfere with the circulation of fluids, then crush the underlying tissues. Much the same thing happens with encirclement of the tree. Even though the band or chain, wire or rope may not be slowly tightened, the steady outward growth of the tree against these obstructions produces the same result: in effect, the tree slowly strangles itself. Wooden slats or rubber or cloth cushions inserted under the encircling material do not prevent the strangling process, they merely postpone it. The first rule governing any type of bracing, cabling, or simple attachment to the tree is this: AVOID ENCIRCLEMENT.

Two threaded rods, properly installed in a horizontal plane. Although extensive crotch decay had brought this tree to the danger point, excavation of the decayed wood, insertion of a filler, and installation of supporting rods give it a new lease on life.

To bore holes through the trunk for the installation of rods or bolts you need a collection of bits that are sharp, long, and strong. On a large tree even the long bits may need to be augmented by use of the bit-extension device. When you use this, tighten it very securely to the end of the bit, for if it becomes loose before the boring is completed, both bit and extension will remain irretrievably stuck in the hole. Some trees, such as the oaks, are easily bored; others, such as the pines, elms, and mulberries, tend to gum the bit, and boring becomes difficult. In such cases, it is better to drill a few inches at a time, working the bit in and out to extract all the loose wood which otherwise tends to compact and make difficult both continued boring and insertion of the rods. With a sharp bit, you can drill through even the largest tree with a hand brace. If you use a power drill, you can, of course, progress much more rapidly but you run an increased risk of breaking the bit. To prevent this you should use a stronger bit especially designed for the purpose and should keep working it in and out of the hole to avoid compaction.

The size of the rod to be inserted, and consequently the size of the hole, is directly related to the size of the tree. For very small trees a rod half an inch in diameter is sufficient; for larger trees the size is progressively increased. A 3/4″ rod is adequate for trees two feet in diameter, while 7/8″ or 1″ rods are adequate for even the largest trees.

In some cases, the bolt-and-nut combination is to be preferred; in other cases, the threaded rod. Use of the bolt-and-nut permits extra tightening at the time of installation, and afterward if need be. (Make sure it is a carriage bolt or a square-headed bolt; otherwise during tightening you may be unable to keep the head from turning.) A disadvantage is that all the strain is concentrated on two points, and should the head of the bolt shear off or the threads on the other end strip (an unlikely but not an impossible contingency), there is nothing left to hold. In contrast, the rod, threaded continuously along its length, holds at all points and is therefore stronger and safer; its disadvantage is that it exerts no tightening action but merely holds the parts in place.

One caveat: the threaded rods sold in hardware stores are not designed for tree bracing and will not hold under stress; their threads are not deep enough and are not set at the requisite angle. (They may, however, be used if fitted with washer and nut at both ends.) Specially designed threaded rods may be obtained from arboricultural supply houses (*A.M. Leonard & Sons,* Piqua, Ohio, for example); these have deeper, sharper, and more widely spaced threads with a different angle of attack and need no nuts at the ends.

Where the bolt is used, the hole must exceed it slightly in diameter to permit easy insertion. Where the threaded rod is used, the hole must be slightly smaller than the rod, 1/16″ smaller in some woods, 1/8″ smaller in others. This proportion is important because the rod must be screwed into the hole: if too loose, it will exert no holding effect; if too tight, it *cannot* be screwed in. The right proportion is easily discovered after a few tries. Start the rod by holding one end against the hole and striking the other end with a heavy hammer; screw it in with a pipe wrench, applied at the very end to prevent damage to the threads. Continue screwing until the rod emerges on the other side of the tree. Then cut off the near end of the rod with bolt cutter or with hack saw, flush if desired or with half inch or so left protruding. Flush cutting is preferred when the rods are at a level where you may accidentally strike against any protruding ends; but where above the danger level, a slight protrusion may be preferred because new tissues will be laid down around the protruding ends and so make the connection even stronger.

Where you use the bolt-and-nut combination, fit each end with an elliptical or a diamond-shaped washer with its long axis lined up with the long axis of the trunk (or limb). First cut away the bark under each washer with a chisel and countersink the wood itself slightly so as to allow firm seating and to permit quick healing over. At the nut end cut

The proper way of fastening cable to tree. A lag screw hook is screwed into a predrilled hole, a thimble is fitted over the hook, and the cable is passed around the thimble and spliced to itself. With continued growth the hook will gradually be engulfed by new layers of bark and wood; with still further growth the end of the cable itself will disappear within the tissues of the expanding limb.

the bolt off flush for the sake of looks and/or safety or, if desired, allow·it to protrude slightly as explained in the preceding paragraph. When the threaded rod is used, nuts and washers are not required.

The rods (or bolts) are always installed in horizontal pairs. One rod is useless because it will be broken in short order by the sideways twisting of the only partially secured trunk. Two rods or even three or four are similarly useless if installed in vertical alignment. I once saw a tree with eight 1″ rods neatly placed at 10 inch intervals, one above the other, along the center line of the trunk perpendicular to the split—all neatly broken by back-and-forth lateral twisting, as a wire may be broken by continual back-and-forth bending. To repeat: THE RODS MUST BE INSTALLED IN HORIZONTAL PAIRS. Once installed, no further movement of the split portions is possible. One pair is usually enough but on large heavy trees two pairs may be advisable. Sometimes one pair is installed through the trunk just below the crotch, and another pair through the separate limbs just above the crotch.

When rods are installed through the trunk, cables should be installed among the branches as a matter of course. Where rods are not installed—that is, where the trunk is not split—cables may be used alone as a preventive measure. Whether or not cables should be used depends on whether or not the branches overhang valuable structures or important living areas; the size and heaviness of the tree's crown; the strength of the wood; the presence or absence of decay; and the angle of the branches. In potentially dangerous trees or particularly valuable ones sometimes every major branch is cabled. In exceptionally strong-wooded trees, such as the oaks, even far-spreading horizontal limbs need not be cabled—provided that they are sound.

Where possible, cables are installed on the principle of opposing forces: the branch that inclines to the north is supported by the one that inclines to the south, the one to the east by the one to the west, and so on. The structure of some trees makes this arrangement impossible, for on some, all the major limbs incline in the same direction and cabling is then possible only from the weakest limbs to the strongest ones regardless of their angle. On trees that have a single upright trunk with lateral branches more or less uniformly spaced, such as the pines, the main bole itself serves as the necessary anchor to which any weak, broken, or potentially dangerous side branch must be attached.

The point where the cable is to be attached is a matter of importance. If attached too far down (too close to the base of the branch), it will be subjected to great strain and may not prevent breakage of the branch beyond that point. If attached too far up toward the branch's tip, its holding

A special problem occurs when both trees are leaning in the same direction and the tree needing support is the upper one—in this case the one to the right. Since there is no tree behind it to cable to, it has been made to rest on the lower tree (the one to the left) by means of a strong metal pipe. The cable visible just above the pipe serves to hold the two trees together so that the pipe will not fall away during wind-produced swaying.

Boards, nails, and odds and ends of wire hold this split tree together. While better than many amateurish attempts in that it offers no immediate danger of strangulation, this is obviously a makeshift repair job. The separated parts should have been drawn together and fastened by threaded rods or bolts and nuts.

power will be nullified by the branch's flexibility. The optimum point of attachment is approximately two-thirds of the way along the branch's length, measuring from the base. With a little practice, you can learn to judge this point easily. What is often not understood is that any installed cable will remain always at the same distance from the ground, *not* moving upward as the branches elongate. This means that the two-thirds ratio will be modified with continued growth, and additional cables may need to be installed or the original ones relocated.

Galvanized wire cable is the most practical material for this use, and is obtainable in all major hardware stores. (If not available, light-weight chain may be substituted.) For small trees, small-diameter cable (3/16″ or 1/4″) is adequate; for larger trees the diameter is progressively increased. Arithmetic increase in diameter means geometric increase in breaking strength; thus a 3/8″ cable is very much stronger than a 1/4″ cable and is adequate for all except the very heaviest of limbs. In exceptional cases 7/16″ and 1/2″ caliber may be used, although such large calibers are heavy and unwieldy, especially if the span from branch to branch gets up around 20 feet or so.

Attach the cable to the branch by means of a screw fastener, *not* by encirclement. For small branches the ordi-nary porch-swing screw hook or screw eye may be used, but for larger branches a lag-screw hook 7/16″ or 1/2″ in diameter and 6″ or 7″ long, and with a strong, square, nearly closed hook is preferred. Drill a hole slightly smaller than the diameter of the hook into the branch, and screw the iron in until its hook end comes flush with the bark surface. The alignment of the hole, and consequently of the lag-screw, must be parallel with the direction of pull for maximum holding power; a sideways pull may bend or even break the hook.

The holding power of a lag screw is very great; if properly installed in sound wood, it will never pull out. Continued growth of the tree serves to make the attachment stronger as new layers of sound wood are laid down around the hook, gradually coming to engulf it entirely and, given time enough, even to grow outward along the cable. Formerly it was customary to use the bolt-and-nut combination instead of the lag screw, but this offers no particular advantage. Indeed, it unnecessarily opens up two holes (entry and exit) in the bark surface instead of one and if used on very small branches can actually weaken them to the breaking point.

When both fasteners have been installed, the cable must be stretched from one to the other. Where the cable is small is really a task for three men: two in the tree and one on the ground. But with all the necessary tools and by following all the procedures outlined here, one man alone can do the whole job, however difficult.

Attach the cable to the hook either by splicing or by use of cable clamps. Splicing demands a special kind of seven-strand, soft-annealed cable, sometimes hard to get. Hardware stores more commonly stock a stiffer, springier type (often called aircraft cable) which can be fastened down

Cable in the process of being spliced. A lag screw hook is screwed into a predrilled hole, a thimble is fitted over the hook, the end of the cable is passed around the thimble and spliced to itself.

Threaded rod is screwed into a predrilled hole by means of a pipe wrench applied to one end. If the hole is too large, the rod will not hold; if too small, the rod cannot be inserted. A proper fit calls for a hole 1/16″ smaller than the rod. When the far end of the rod comes out flush with the bark surface, the screwing is stopped and the protruding near end is cut off with hack saw or bolt cutters.

and light weight and the span is short, an approximate length or even a whole roll may be carried into the tree, and measurements, attachment, and cutting effected on the spot. But where the cable is heavy and the span long, it is better to first measure the distance from one hook to the other with a length of rope, than to cut the cable to fit on the ground, not forgetting to allow an extra 10″ or so at each end for making the splice.

Where both hooks are equally accessible, the splicing order is a matter of indifference. But where, as is usually the case, one hook is less accessible than the other, the cable should be secured to this hook first, then the final adjustments can all be made in the more convenient location.

Passing the unsecured end of the cable across a long span can be easily accomplished by making a provisional loop in the free end (utilizing a cable clamp), tying a rope through the loop, and throwing the rope to the desired location. Installing a long cable high up in the branches of a large tree

Iron brace band killing Hackberry tree.

problem. If the cables are preventive only, then they need not be fiddle-string tight, may even be left with a slight sag. If, however, a branch is partially broken or decayed and in danger of falling, or if it needs to be drawn upward or sideways for any of various reasons, then obviously the cable must be made taut.

Amateurish attempt to repair split limb. The rods and the boards constitute a cage that will interfere with the normal expansion of the stem. The boards should have been dispensed with, and the rods should have gone through the tree in a horizontal plane, each to one side of the center. The cable at the top should not encircle the limbs but should be attached to lag screw hooks inserted into predrilled holes.

only by means of cable clamps. In either case, the end of the cable is looped around a thimble and then folded back along its length for a distance of 8″, 10″, or 12″ before being spliced (or tightened down with cable clamps). A thimble in this sense is not a cap fitted over the finger but an oval-shaped piece of metal grooved along its outside. The thimble is used, both to make splicing easier and to prevent the cable from bending too abruptly around the hook, for sharp bends promote breaking. Once the loop is spliced (or fastened) around the thimble, slip it under the hook, and give the hook its final half turn that brings its lip against the branch and prevents the loop from jumping out. If you use a screw-eye instead of a hook (or if you previously screwed the hook down to a perfectly flush position), pry open the pointed end of the thimble slightly to permit slipping it over the eye (or hook), then splice (or fasten) the cable around the thimble in place.

Repeat the whole procedure at the second hook. Things become more difficult here because the cable must be drawn taut. Just how taut depends on the exact nature of the

Tightening may be accomplished by insertion of a turn-buckle between the cable end and the hook or at any point along the cable length, although this involves making extra splices. Open the turnbuckle as far as possible to start with, then after drawing the cable tight manually and making all the splices, close it gradually until the desired tautness is reached. The cable may also be tightened without use of the turnbuckle. If the branches are small, they may be drawn together first by means of ropes and the cable installed in this forced position; when the ropes are released, the cable will tighten. If the branches are too large and heavy to permit such prebending, the cable may be tightened by

to the desired degree of tightness. Cable clamps can then be fitted over the cable end before the hoist is released. (In this situation, splicing is impossible.) If no branch is easily accessible for anchoring the end of the hoist cable, fasten a large cable clamp provisionally at some convenient point along the main cable; against this cable clamp the end of the hoist cable may obtain the necessary purchase. This provisional use of the clamp makes the backward tightening pull of the hoist exactly parallel to the line of the main cable, and so makes easier the fastening of the permanent cable clamps. When the hoist is released, the provisional clamp is also removed.

Orchard trees, bred to bear large fruits in abundance, pay the penalty for their abnormal productiveness by breaking apart. Their artificially intensified yield must, therefore, be accompanied by artificial support measures.

Orchard trees, bred to bear large fruits in abundance, pay the penalty for their abnormal productiveness by breaking apart. Their artificially intensified yield must, therefore, be accompanied by artificial support measures. The simplest and most efficient way of bracing such trees is by means of wooden props. A V-shaped notch sawed into one end of the prop accommodates the branch while the other end rests on the ground at the requisite angle. The orchardist keeps hundreds of props of different lengths on hand for use year after year; after picking the fruit he puts them away to be used again the following season.

using a block-and-tackle or, more conveniently, a portable hoist. Secure the free end of the cable, after passing it through the thimble and over the hook, by a cable drag-clamp or by vise-grip pliers. Grapple one end of the portable hoist cable around this provisional fastener, loop the other end of the hoist cable around a convenient branch in line with the direction of pull, and wind up the hoist drum

For cutting the cable a special Swiss-made cutter exists, but it is a very expensive tool and obtainable only by special order; a bolt-cutter is the most practical substitute. Bolt-cutters are available in all hardware stores and come in

Pecan tree with pipe bracing.

various sizes; if possible, use a large (30″) cutter on the ground and a small one (14″) in the tree. While this cutter makes short work of soft-annealed, seven-strand cable, it works less well on springy aircraft cable composed of many fine wires; with persistence, however, it will chew its way through. If no bolt-cutter is available, you can use a hacksaw as a last resort, or, if you make the cuts on the ground, cold chisel and anvil. For tightening down the clamps the boxed-end wrench is the indicated tool. When working high up in the tree, carry your tools in a small cloth bag with a ring around its mouth to hold it open and a handle to which you may tie a rope for lifting and lowering.

Fruit trees present special cases because they pass through a regular seasonal cycle of little weight, much weight. As the fruit ripens, the load on the branches steadily increases, over the short period of two or three months. Trees growing in the wild have small fruits and resist the strain; but cultivated varieties, selected for larger and larger

fruits, often are unable to hold up under the dramatic weight increase and either split apart at the crotch or lose their branches one by one. A few kinds, such as oranges and other members of the citrus group, are so strong-wooded

Vertical pipe brace under leaning Pecan tree. Where no anchor tree is nearby or where the weight of a leaning tree is excessive, vertical braces are sometimes the only solution. Note the rounded "cradle" at the top end of brace; this follows the contour of the stem and inflicts minimal damage to the tree.

that they seldom break or split. Others, such as peaches, plums, apples, figs, avocados, and even some of the nut trees, such as the English walnut, break easily and need mechanical support.

When such trees are young, their fast-growing, flexible, inside shoots, one from one half of the tree, another from the other half, may be bent inward towards each other, twisted together along their length, and provisionally tied in that position with soft cord; they will then graft together and come to form a natural cable that increases in size and strength as the tree grows and so protects the main crotch from splitting.

Branches present a special problem. It is impracticable to install a wire cable in every branch of a fruit tree, because the fruit, and consequently the weight, tends to be concentrated at the very ends. Wooden props are generally used instead. These props can be made of 1″ boards of varying widths and lengths according to the need. A V-shaped notch is sawed into the upper end of the board to hold the branch in place and the lower end is seated against the ground. Such an arrangement is inexpensive and permits easy and constant adjustment. After the crop is harvested, the props are taken down and stored for use in the following year. Hundreds of thousands of trees are propped in this way in the great fruit-growing central valleys of California.

Trees, whether shade or fruit, that lean markedly to one side and are in danger of falling because of their imbalance, damaged root system, trunk decay, or any combination of these, may be supported by means of a vertical brace—particularly if there is no nearby tree or other object to which they may be cabled. This brace may be a wooden beam, a masonry construction of some kind, or, best of all, a metal tube 3″ to 6″ in diameter, depending on the weight of the tree. Such a tube should have a flange welded across its bottom end and should be seated in a concrete footing. A curved piece of metal 4″ to 6″ broad

Heavy vertical pipe brace for Italian Stone Pine at the Capitol Building grounds in Sacramento, California. Note how at the point of contact the trunk is flaring out, attempting to grow around the unyielding pipe.

An English Walnut tree showing growth split.

An English Walnut tree showing growth split at base of tree.

several inches. They should be filled with plastic asphalt (no tar or creosote) and will normally heal over during the following growing season. Where the splits are unusually deep or long, the trunk may be bored through and braced with threaded rods or with bolt-and-nut.

Transplanting braces on a young Spanish Oak tree.

with its concave surface uppermost should be welded across its upper end, and against this cradle the leaning trunk or one of its outjutting limbs can rest. Where circumstances demand, the tube, rather than being set vertically, may be inclined toward the tree. (Note that use of the cradle does no damage, for, unlike encircling chains or cables, it touches the bark surface over a small area only.)

A special case arises where two trees are growing close together, both are leaning in the same direction, and the tree that needs to be supported is not the "underneath" one but the overhanging one. In such a case, it is obvious that the overhanging member of the pair cannot be cabled to the other. It can, however, be supported by the sound tree by means of a metal tube placed horizontally (or diagonally if need be) between the two, cut to fit so that each end is firmly seated against sound wood. To keep the tube from dropping away when the trees sway in the wind, a cable can be installed between the two just above or below the tube.

Trees that are repeatedly frozen and thawed sometimes split open at one or more points along the trunk. These frost cracks may extend lengthwise anywhere from a few inches to several feet and inward anywhere from half an inch to

While on all trees, the dead outer bark is *always* split by underlying growth (hence its ridges and furrows), the growing inner bark usually keeps pace with the radially expanding wood and remains unbroken. Some trees, however, such as the English walnuts, grow so fast that they split the inner bark, too. Growth splits are easily distinguished from frost cracks because they are always shallow. The same uninhibited growth impulse that produces them favors their rapid healing over, and no treatment is needed.

Recently transplanted trees, small or large, should be braced for several years until their roots have taken hold in their new location. This can be done by using rigid "push" supports like two-by-fours propped against the trunk or flexible "pull" supports like guide wires. Whichever is used, the important thing is to guard against bark damage, to which young transplanted trees are particularly suscepti-ble. If props are used, they should not touch the tree directly but be separated from it by heavy cloth pads or by rubber strips. If wires are used, they should go around the trunk in large, loose loops and should be separated from direct contact by means of similar materials. Small trees can be supported by small wires, attached at the lower end to stakes driven into the ground. Large, heavy trees—and some transplants, especially palms, may be 60 feet tall or more—should be supported with cables rather than with simple wires. The upper end of the cable is attached to the tree in the manner explained above, while the lower end is attached to a dead man (heavy weight) buried in the ground.

The thing to remember is that the bracing of transplanted trees is provisional, not permanent, and the rubber strips, cloth pads, two-by-fours, etc., must be removed after a few years. In every town and city in the United States there are trees showing damage from these bracing devices that we intend to be provisional but forget to remove. Apart from the trees killed by strangulation, there are thousands of others with gaping wounds where wooden or metal props rub against them and thousands with pipes, wires, slats, garden hoses, and miscellaneous materials pressing against them or sticking out from them for the snaring of passers-by, obstruction of continued growth, and antiesthetic clut-tering of the community.

4

Fertilizing

Trees growing in a forest fertilize themselves by continually shedding leaves, flowers, and fruits—sometimes even twigs and small branches, all of which decay and enrich the soil. They are further fertilized by other decomposing plant matter and by decomposing animal matter. In addition, the soil under a community of trees is usually porous, allowing free passage of air and water. Rains are frequent, but the pounding action of rain on unprotected soil is prevented by the heavy leaf cover, and the water filters and trickles down to ground level in the gentlest possible way. Once there, it is prevented from running off by the loose mat of debris and the thick porous layers of humus.

In urban areas, most of these conditions are reversed. Leaves are swept up and burned or hauled away. Many trees are artificially prevented from fruiting; or, if allowed to fruit, the product is consumed or removed from the site. Neither plant nor animal debris is allowed to accumulate. The ground around the trees is either tightly packed by being walked on or is covered with cement, asphalt, or heavy sod, all of which interfere with the supply of air and water to the roots. The water supply, both underground and above ground, is frequently inadequate.

Because of these unfavorable conditions, most trees growing in city areas need to be artificially fed and watered. Some need it more than others, but nearly all need assistance unless growing along a stream or in some abandoned back lot. Horticulturists and landscape architects are engaged in a never-ending search for tree varieties capable of withstanding the difficult urban environments.

Superficial feeding and watering have not proved satisfactory. Food scattered over the top of the ground and water sprinkled on it seldom reach the hungry tree roots below. The water evaporates and the fertilizer is swept or blown away, or both are absorbed by the heavy turf that often surrounds city trees. Hence, a method of feeding that breaks through surface coverings and puts the food and water where the tree roots can get at them is of much greater benefit.

Root Location

It is often said that the roots of a tree extend outward as far as the branches do. Many people, recalling the relatively small root-ball moved with shrubs and transplanted trees, find this hard to believe. In fact, however, the roots of an established tree not only extend as far as the branches but usually much farther—in some cases two, three, four times farther, or even more.

Oddly, those who find it difficult to believe this often accept, without question, the popular belief that the roots go down as far as the tree goes up. This, apart from very exceptional cases, is certainly not true. Ordinarily the roots go down only a third, a fourth, or a fifth of the tree's height, and then only some of them go this deep, mainly the huge anchor roots and, in some trees, the taproot, which often makes a spectacular descent in search of underground water. The pecan, for example, has a long vertically descending tap root which, in some soils, may well equal the tree's height or even exceed it; and the mesquite, in desert conditions, may have above ground only a few thorny switches 6 or 8 feet in height, while sending its marvelous root 75 feet straight downward in pursuit of subterranean water. At the other extreme is the redwood: 370 feet tall with a widely extended but very shallow root system—a giant poised on a disc. Regardless of the anchor root pattern, however, the feeder roots of all species are always close to the surface, for the most abundant and richest food is to be found in the layer of topsoil. The feeder roots of nearly all trees occur within two feet of the surface.

Area of Application

By considering root location, it becomes apparent that fertilizer should *not* be applied:
1. Close to the trunk,
2. Too shallowly (sprinkled on top),
3. Too deeply (more than two feet down.)

The most common error in feeding is to apply the fertilizer immediately around the trunk, doing little if any good and sometimes doing harm, particularly in the case of young, tender-barked trees which are easily burned.

The area in which fertilizer is most effectively placed is *the outer two-thirds of the branch spread and one-third beyond*. Directions frequently given on commercial fertilizers recommend application under the drip-line (the crown periphery). Although this is approximately correct, the area indicated above is better because it is broader.

Manner of Fertilizing

Make small holes throughout the indicated area about 2 feet apart and about 1-1/2 to 2 feet deep. It is usually recommended that the holes be made in a series of concentric circles in order to assure uniform distribution, but this design need not be strictly followed so long as the indicated spacing is approximately observed. The essential point is that a more or less even coverage be obtained, so that one side of the tree is not starved, while the other side gets a double dose. (In cases where a tree is near a building, only the accessible half of the root system can be fed, of course.)

How many holes should you make? Enough to accommodate the required quantity of fertilizer (explained below), which for large trees may be several hundred pounds, for

medium-sized trees 30, 40, 50, 60 pounds, for small trees 5 to 10 pounds, and for very small trees perhaps 1/2, 1, or 1-1/2 pounds.

A number of devices have been developed for making the holes. The simplest and least expensive is a straight, pointed iron bar about 6 feet long and 1-1/2 inches in diameter, which is forced into the ground manually by repeated jabbing. In reasonably soft ground, a strong man can make 100 holes or so in about two hours. Each time the bar is jabbed in the ground, it should be wiggled around to make withdrawal easier and to make the mouth of the hole somewhat larger for the easier pouring of the fertilizer.

In very hard or rocky soil you may find it necessary to use a shorter bar (2-1/2 feet long) and to pound it in with a sledge hammer.

Special earth augers driven by electricity or compressed air are often used by commercial companies where the soil permits. These are faster and easier to use than the bars, and they make a somewhat larger hole with the sides less compacted. They can also make a slanted hole (difficult

While one man makes holes with a special earth auger powered by an electric drill, another puts in the prepared fertilizer mixture. Note the spacing of the holes.

with the bar) which permits subsequent leaching of the dissolved nutrients into a wider area. Where only a few holes are needed and the ground is not too hard, the soil-sampling tube (available at some feed and seed stores) may be used.

Another device utilizes the erosive force of water ejected at high pressure. It consists of a 1/2 inch or 3/4 inch pipe with a small hole in the end, which is gradually worked into the ground, digging the hole and softening and watering the surrounding soil at the same time. Some large companies achieve the same effect in loose and porous soils by using jets of compressed air. Holes made in this manner are subsequently filled with either dry or liquid fertilizer.

Another device, called the feeding needle, or sometimes simply the root-feeder, consists of a tube terminating in a point and much slenderer than the one just described. Near its pointed end it has a hole, and at its upper end a hollow chamber with detachable cap into which you place fertilizer

Using an electric drill and special earth auger for making feeding holes greatly speeds up the process. In soils that are too rocky or too hard, however, the auger cannot be used with any success.

in the form of dry powder or, more often, prepackaged cartridges. After loading the chamber, you screw the garden hose into its side, turn on the water, and the fertilizer is dissolved and carried to the root site, presumably in the right proportions. (Some needles work off hydraulic sprayers with the benefit of increased pressures.) Various modifications of this principle are used, among them a simple yet ingenious siphon device in which the force of water running through the hose draws the feeding solution up from bucket or pail and incorporates it into the flow.

Extremely compacted soils are sometimes loosened by dynamite. Instead of harming a tree, as might be supposed, dynamiting is beneficial by adding nitrogen to the soil, as well as by loosening it.

Amateurs sometimes try to make the holes with a post-hole digger. This tool makes too large a hole and damages too many roots in the process. By contrast, the pointed bar damages roots very little. It is, however, potentially damaging to drainage pipes, the copper tubes of sprinkler systems, and similar objects. An additional reason for not making holes close to the trunk is to avoid injury—whether by bar or drill—to the large, muscular roots that are usually nearer the surface in that area.

Once the holes are made, they should be filled about three-fourths of the way with the fertilizer mixture. If you use dry fertilizer, mix it with approximately equal parts of peat moss or dry sand or loose earth to reduce its concentration. If large quantities are involved, you can mix them conveniently in a wheelbarrow with a hoe and then wheel the mixture around, pouring it into the holes by means of a quart or half-gallon can bent to form a pouring spout. Once in the ground, the mixture should be well watered, both by inserting a hose into each hole and by soaking the complete area, for the fertilizer cannot be absorbed by the roots until it enters into solution.

Since the hole mouths will usually not exceed 2 or 2-1/2 inches in diameter and since they are partially concealed by the grass (which, incidentally, will grow much more lushly around each hole rim because of the fertilizer accidentally spilled there), they cannot be said to disfigure the lawn and constitute a hazard except to spike-heeled shoes. They should, therefore, be left open as long as possible—in fact, should be reopened from time to time by reaming out with stick or broom handle, for the mere making of the holes is beneficial to the tree even though no fertilizer is applied.

Recently a new way of feeding trees and shrubs has appeared on the market that involves neither broadcasting nor hole-making. The fertilizer comes specially mixed and compacted in the form of solid "tree spikes" which are driven into the ground with a hammer around the drip-line and allowed to remain there, gradually dissolving with rain or normal watering practices. The claimed advantage is the ease and rapidity of application and the gradual release of the nutrients under the action of rain and snow. The mixture for evergreens and shrubs is prefabricated as 12-6-6 and for broad-leaved trees as 16-8-8.

Types of Fertilizer

There are as many different opinions about the best kind of fertilizer as there are about the best kind of automobile. Many people will use only horse manure, others sheep manure, others pig manure; some swear by leaf mold, made in the back-yard compost heap; some prefer bone meal; some insist on bat guano from the caves of Mexico, others on sea-bird guano from the rock-ribbed islands off the coast of Peru. Actually, all of these are good fertilizers, and none need be exclusive of the others.

The essential elements needed for plant growth are nitrogen, phosphorus, potassium, iron, calcium, magnesium, sulfur, manganese, boron, copper, zinc, and molybdenum. Most commercial fertilizers contain principally the first three elements, expressed as a proportion, such as 5-10-5, 6-8-4, 10-10-0, etc., indicating the relative amounts of each in the order given. The other elements of the list, called trace elements or micronutrients, were formerly included accidentally rather than intentionally; now, however, they are included systematically.

Each element has a specific effect on plant growth, and the lack of any given one will produce specific and sometimes spectacular abnormalities. Some soils are deficient in iron, some in copper, some in manganese, etc. Whenever a tree, or other plant, is not growing properly and no above-ground cause can be discovered, the first thing to look for is a soil deficiency. Such deficiencies occur with surprising frequency and in circumstances that often seem improbable. Perhaps the maple in your front yard is flourishing while the one in your back yard languishes. Can significant differences exist between two locations so close together? They can and do. Soil composition can change abruptly at any point, and there is no logical reason to expect the soil of the front, back, and side yards to be the same. Sometimes after growing slowly for many years and presenting a sickly and stunted appearance, a tree suddenly takes on a new look and begins to grow lushly and rapidly. What may have happened is that the tree was originally planted in a mineral-deficient area and hence grew poorly until at some point the roots finally grew beyond the deficient area and entered a region where they encountered the missing elements.

Sometimes the exact opposite happens: a tree is planted in a soil where all the needed elements are present and hence grows well during its first few years, but then as the roots extend farther and farther they grow out of their magic

In some soils the punch bar, jabbed into the ground by hand, is preferable to the earth auger. While one man makes the holes, another puts in the prepared fertilizer mixture, using a quart can bent into a pouring spout and refilled from the wheelbarrow.

circle and begin to penetrate mineral-deficient regions. Growth then slows down, and with the exhaustion of the soil of the original area, abnormalities, such as streaked or spotted leaves, may begin to appear.

Many tree abnormalities may be remedied by supplying the right kind of fertilizer. The trick, of course, is to determine which *is* the right kind. Where iron deficiency is indicated, for example, it would be idle to supply pure nitrogen, and vice versa. And where there exists a manganese deficiency, it cannot be corrected by the addition of phosphates.

Fertilizers are useful not only in maintaining a tree in maximum health but also in providing it with a stimulus to hasten healing over pruning wounds or over recently repaired cavities. Some large companies do not undertake extensive pruning or cavity repair unless authorized to fertilize at the same time.

Nitrogen is the element most responsible for maintaining the green color in leaves; also for normal twig growth. In some orchards, cover crops are systematically plowed under to assure its replenishment; in the forest it is replenished naturally in the form of decaying animal and vegetable matter. But the shade tree, particularly the city shade tree imprisoned in a narrow parkway strip between sidewalk and road, is often nitrogen-deficient. Barnyard manure, slaughterhouse refuse, and other organic products are good nitrogen-suppliers; so are sodium nitrate, calcium nitrate, and ammonium sulfate. Leguminous trees, such as locusts, mesquites and redbuds, and certain trees of other families, such as the alder, actually add nitrogen to the soil by means of colonies of nitrogen-fixing bacteria that grow in nodules on their roots.

Phosphorus assists in the maturation of tissues and stimulates root growth. It is particularly important in the production of flowers, fruits, and seeds. Since it normally penetrates the ground very slowly (as contrasted with the rapid leaching action of nitrates), it, possibly more than any other ingredient, needs to be deep-fed rather than sprinkled. Of all the major elements needed by organisms, phosphorus seems to be the one in shortest supply and the one most likely to impose a limit on the number of living things that can subsist on this planet.

Potassium (potash) assists in the manufacture of sugar and starches. It also helps tissues mature properly, and it heightens the color of flowers. Plants deficient in potash may become either too succulent or too brittle.

Magnesium and *iron* are essential to the formation and maintenance of chlorophyll. Where lacking, leaves are yellowish and unhealthy.

Calcium serves a number of purposes, not the least of which is to ''sweeten'' the soil and favor the activities of beneficial micro-organisms.

A number of gardeners insist on mixing their own fertilizer, building it up element by element according to carefully worked out weights and measures. While theoretically this may be ideal, it turns out in practice to be a dry, dusty business—and costly and time-consuming as well. Most of us have neither the time nor the patience to elaborate our own product, and even though we may try it once or twice, we usually end up at the feed and seed store some Saturday morning to pick up the ready-mixed article. Fortunately, most of the commercial fertilizers have been much improved in recent years; like spraying materials, they seem to be moving in the direction of constantly increasing specificity. Special mixtures are packaged for roses, for azaleas, for begonias, and many others; special mixtures exist for fruit trees, and for shade trees, almost species by species. Some lawn fertilizers include as part of the product mix herbicides for broad-leaved weeds and various broad-spectrum insecticides.

Those not satisfied with the commercial preparations can modify them, as I frequently do, by starting out with a 12-8-6 or perhaps a 10-6-4 compound and adding a roughly equal quantity of sheep manure (or in its stead other animal manure or tankage) plus about half again as much of bone meal and, where it seems needed, a small amount of iron sulfate. This mixture supplies the needed ingredients in roughly the right proportions and in such a manner that their action is continuous over a period of time, some taking effect immediately, others more slowly. I have used it with good results for deep-feeding a wide variety of shade trees and recommend it as a good ''general'' fertilizer.

Special Cases

Fertilizing, however, is not always the simple matter it may seem to be. Circumstances alter cases. What benefits one tree may not benefit another, and what works in one locality may not work in another. In some soils, aluminum sulfate needs to be mixed with iron sulfate in order to make the iron available. Often chelating compounds must be added to fix iron in stable compounds and so make it available to the tree roots. Some soils need to be changed from acid to alkaline or from alkaline to acid. Although most shade trees seem to prefer a slightly acid soil (pH value of 5.5 to 7.0), there are numerous exceptions.

Ground limestone will increase the alkalinity of soils, while aluminum sulfate and sulfur will increase their acidity. The pH value of any soil can easily be determined by means of a soil-testing kit costing less than ten dollars; you need only to follow the manufacturer's directions. Such a kit plus a soil-sampling tube are indispensable prerequisites for tree-feeding.

Not all trees respond equally well to fertilizing. Oaks, elms, pecans, walnuts, and lindens usually show a high degree of response quickly. Some species react very slowly, while others may actually be harmed, due to a complication of other factors. The pear tree, for example, may become badly attacked by fire blight when excessively stimulated by nitrogenous fertilizer; hence, it should receive food containing little or no nitrogen.

Only an expert is competent to diagnose abnormalities due to a deficiency of trace elements; and even after the deficiency is identified, an excessive application of the missing element may do more harm than good. The proportions must be exact: micronutrients in over-supply become pollutants.

The whole matter is additionally complicated by inherent physiological differences among trees, even those of the same species that externally may be virtually identical. Biochemical individuality exists among plants as well as among animals, and we may assert with perfect propriety that one tree's meat is another tree's poison. Among trees (and other plants) growing in identical soil there are always a few less vigorous than others, sometimes markedly so. Where no external cause can be found, the explanation would seem to lie in some genetic inadequacy of the plant. Even in nutrient-deficient soil, some species thrive; and in any soil, good or bad, some individuals of any given species prosper while others succumb.

Because of all this, the tendency of horticulturists and plant breeders today is to attempt to find plants suitable to the soil rather than to modify the soil to suit the plants. This procedure, however, is more easily applied to small and short-lived plants than to trees. If you have an established tree in your yard, there is (as yet) no known way to alter its genetic structure. You are left with the alternative of improving the soil.

Amount of Fertilizer

There are a number of formulas in use for determining the amount of fertilizer to apply. One school states that the diameter in inches of tree trunk at breast height should be multiplied by itself and that the product of that multiplication should then be divided by three. Thus a trunk 6 inches across will yield a product of 36, which divided by 3 will give a quotient of 12, which may be read off directly as 12 pounds. Another school asserts that trees 6 inches or under in diameter at breast height (DBH) should be fed at the rate of 2-3 pounds for every diameter inch (thus a tree 6 inches across should receive between 12 and 18 pounds of food) while larger trees should be given 5 or 6 pounds per inch of DBH. The arithmetic involved is very simple: the required quantity is determined and enough holes are made to accommodate it.

Time to Fertilize

Many experts believe the best time to fertilize (for Temperate Zone trees) is in early spring because then new growth is most active, and adequate nutrients must be available to meet the demand. Fertilization in midsummer is less effective, and in late summer it should be avoided, as any new growth stimulated into being at this time stands a good chance of being injured by early frost. Fertilization in late fall or winter, although producing no apparent effect, is believed by some arborists to be the best time of all, for the materials gradually dissolve during the winter months and are on hand in very early spring. Another advantage of late fall or winter fertilization is that you yourself or the people you hire may be less busy than during the spring rush. In tropical and semitropical regions the time of year becomes a much less critical determinant.

A sickly tree or one recovering from an insect defoliation or from mechanical injury of some kind should, however, be fed as soon as the abnormality is discovered, regardless of the season.

Frequency of Application

How often should you feed your trees? Once a year, twice a year, once every two years? The answer, of course, depends on the kind of tree, the climatic zone, and the circumstances.

A tree with good color and vigorous growth need never be fertilized. Why tamper with something perfect? On the other hand, a below-par tree or one diseased, attacked by insects, or damaged mechanically, should be fed abundantly once each year or once every two years until it recovers. After that, it should be fed as needed, until its difficulties are surmounted.

Some trees may need only one feeding in a lifetime to enable them to overcome some temporary ailment. Others may need periodic feeding once a year, or once every two or three years all their lives. As previously noted, trees, even those belonging to the same species, vary widely in their inborn ability to wrest needed nutrients from the soil; some may need no help, some little help, some continuing help.

Soil Improvement

In spite of its usefulness, fertilizing is only a part of a soil-improvement program. If the soil around a valuable tree is exhausted or vitiated, it may need to be dug out and replaced entirely. This can be done gradually over a period of years and, although expensive, is an almost certain method of rejuvenation.

Soils that are too thin or sandy may be improved by the addition of rich, heavy soil. Conversely, soils too wet and with too much clay should be spaded up and mixed with sandy loam or fine gravel. Most soils can be improved by the incorporation of a goodly quantity of humus.

Although we often fail to realize it, the great bulk of a tree is built up from elements not part of the soil at all (carbon and oxygen from the air, hydrogen from water). That is why when a tree dies and decomposes, it adds far more to the soil than it ever drew from it. Trees are not the exhausters of soil they are sometimes represented as being but the most important of soil builders. If the tree built up its substance out of the soil in which it grows, we should expect to find around each trunk a large concavity, deepening and widening as growth continued; instead of that, we find the soil level undisturbed or, if anything, slightly raised by the expanding trunk and intruding roots. Further proof: when a large tree is burned, the water, the carbon, and the oxygen are returned to the air as gas and vapor, while the minerals drawn from the soil during the tree's entire lifetime may be contained within a few shovelsful of ashes.

Yet in spite of the quantitative insignificance of the soil ingredients, their qualitative significance is very great. Without the necessary soil minerals, photosynthesis, respiration, and other life processes of the tree would go on very poorly or not at all. The presence or absence of these minerals and their degree of availability are largely responsible for the differences of vigor among trees having similar heredity.

Organic versus Inorganic

Few controversies run so deep as the one between those who advocate the use of only organic materials as fertilizers and those who draw no distinction between the use of organic and inorganic materials. Organic gardeners, equating "organic" with "natural", accuse all who do not agree with them of poisoning the soil. Dissidents claim that nitrogen is nitrogen and phosphorus phosphorus, whether they come from a "natural" or "artificial" source.

What is an organic compound? Strictly speaking, anything that contains carbon in its structure. Since there are hundreds of thousands of such compounds and since so many of them are found in plant and animal organisms, the belief has gradually grown that plant and animal residues are "natural" fertilizers and that all other materials are "artificial". Over a period of time "organic" has become a synonym of "natural", and both terms have acquired a kind of mystique; organic materials are believed to possess special cosmic qualities no less real because undiscoverable under the microscope. Those of the opposing camp point out that an increasing number of organic compounds can be synthesized and that these artificially produced substances, when applied as fertilizers, cause plants to grow quite as well and to produce as abundantly. To which the organicists reply that the plants only *seem* to grow as well, and that although they may produce as abundantly, they fail to manufacture essential nutritional factors for the lack of which we who eat the plants pay the penalty in terms of various obscure deficiency diseases. J. G. Bennett makes this interesting statement: *"by poisoning the soil, we introduce psychic poisons into ourselves. It is an observed fact that all countries which use a maximum of artificial fertilizers are subject to a maximum of psychic disorders."* *

Organic advocates point out further, and more convincingly, that long-continued use of "chemical fertilizers" causes a gradual deterioration in the physical structure of the soil and, as an additional evil, interferes with the development of normal soil micro-organisms needed to promote soil fertility.

With attention focused on today's problems of environmental abuse as never before, the rift between the organicists and the synthesizers widens and deepens daily. Whether we side with one or the other party, the fact is that, in spite of all the arguments against it, the use of artificial fertilizers continues to increase on a worldwide basis with no discoverable check in sight.

*J. G. Bennett, *Gurdjieff: Making a New World,* Harper & Row, 1973, p. 209.

5

Diseases

Disease has been given many definitions, but the essential meaning is that carried by the word itself. A "diseased" organism is one that is "not at ease"—that is, out of equilibrium, upset, unbalanced, and/or unstable. The concept always suggests some kind of metabolic dysfunction—a physiological disturbance rather than a structural dislocation. An animal with a broken leg is not considered diseased nor is a tree with a broken branch. Nevertheless, structural damage, if unattended, may open the way to disease, and it is usually by changes in structure—at least in plants—that we first become aware of the disease process.

It is interesting to note that while *sickness* and *illness* are virtually exact synonyms (at least in American English), *disease* is not precisely equivalent to either. Just as a man may be sick at his stomach and yet not be diseased, so a sick plant is not necessarily a diseased one. A plant wilting from lack of water is not diseased, but a plant wilting from internal rot very definitely *is* diseased. Thus we work our way towards a definition of the term.

In referring to animal bodies, we say that disease is (usually) accompanied by suffering; but since plants have no nervous system and presumably no feelings and certainly no way of communicating with us directly, we are deprived of this means of making or confirming a diagnosis. We are thus forced to define plant disease through its manifestations, which are:

1. The dying of tissues, called *necrosis,*
2. The dwarfing or underdevelopment of tissues, called *hypoplasia*,
3. The overgrowth of tissues, called *hyperplasia* or *hypertrophy.*

Examples of necrosis are dead twigs, dead leaves, dead branches, dead bark, dead roots, etc. Examples of hypoplasia are chlorosis, or underdevelopment of the chloroplasts in the leaves; small, runty fruit; stunted twig development, etc. Examples of hypertrophy are galls, (cylindrical, disk-like, or globose swellings on leaves and on twigs); and the leaf-curl diseases, which cause grotesque enlargement of part or all of leaf blades.

While a number of things will produce these pathological manifestations in trees, it is generally felt that for the process to merit the name *disease,* damage must be serious, more or less long-continued, and microorganisms must be involved. It is convenient, therefore, for a number of reasons, partly traditional and partly exclusionary, to consider as agents of disease proper only microorganisms and of these only those that are:

1. Infective,
2. Contagious,
3. Destructive,
4. Parasitic.

These pathogenic agents may be divided into five great classes: viruses,* bacteria, fungi, algae, and nematodes. Of these the first three classes are, in reference to trees, by far the most significant, although the last two are receiving increasing attention.

Nutritional excesses or deficiencies may also produce in trees the three manifestations of death, underdevelopment, and overdevelopment (see chapter FERTILIZING), but since they are neither infective, contagious, not parasitic, they are not regarded as agents of disease; that the expression "deficiency disease" has crept into general use indicates, however, that the idea contains a germ of truth. Similarly, while climatic adversities, changes of grade, escaping gas, and other external factors may also produce the same manifestations (see chapter ENVIRONMENTAL DAMAGE AND MISCELLANEOUS TROUBLES), these things are excluded from the present definition. (Why for example, is a bulldozer not "an agent of disease " in spite of the outrageous damage it inflicts on so many trees?)

By the same arbitrary exclusion principle, insects, in spite of the immense harm they sometimes do to plants, are not considered agents of disease proper. They are, however, often associated with disease, either as carriers (*vectors*) or as partners in a symbiotic relationship with one of the pathogenic organisms. (See chapter INSECTS.) Nor, of course, is a porcupine considered a disease, although it may girdle a tree as effectively as any fungus, nor is a moose, although it may destroy tender shoots as ruthlessly as fire blight. Mistletoe, dodder, witchweed, *Rafflesia,* and other parasitical flowering plants, although true agents of disease by almost any definition, are excluded from this chapter

---

*Whether viruses should be regarded as true microorganisms or nonliving bundles of protein is still being debated.

only because of their large size. (For mistletoe, see chapter ENVIRONMENTAL DAMAGE AND MISCELLANEOUS TROUBLES.)

A more logical grouping which contains insects, moose, algae, deer, rabbits, fungi, bacteria, nematodes, mistletoe, hippopotami, and all other plant-predatory organisms is that of *biological competitors,* regardless of size, color, or chemical composition. These are the enemies that trees, and other higher plants, have to face—enemies for the most part so unforesightful that they would destroy the very fount that gives them life were it not for these plants' incredible resourcefulness. Where it is plant against animals, the plant usually wins—not directly but indirectly, by a kind of biological jiu-jitsu, yielding but subtly exploiting the animal's strength for the furtherance of its own ends. Only when it is plant pitted against plant are the trees and other higher forms sometimes vanquished by the bacteria and fungi whose resourcefulness often equals or surpasses their own.

The disease-producing organisms, then, are a comparative handful, classwise, of the tree's many biological competitors, arbitrarily defined as such because they were for so long unknown, invisible, unidentified, and hence mysterious; of overriding importance because of their ubiquity, their virulence, their astronomical numbers, and their extraordinary adaptability, which in turn derives from their short life span, their prolificacy, and their capacity for mutation. They are, to repeat, viruses, bacteria, fungi, algae, and nematodes. Three of them are plants. One—the virus—is "an ultramicroscopic principle." The fifth—the nematode—belongs to the Animal Kingdom. They are discussed in the pages that follow.

Disease is also sometimes defined as "any departure from the normal" and is thus extended to include the mutant forms that appear from time to time. Most mutations do indeed involve profound physiological disturbances that lessen the vigor of the organism and cripple it in its battle for survival; many are lethal. But some mutations are advantageous, and because of this the departure-from-the-normal definition of disease will not do. The definition leaves out of account not only the occasional departures from the normal that confer benefit on the organism but also those departures which neither help nor hinder.

In the first class, we have the mutations that; have given us many important varieties of fruits, vegetables, flowers; and indeed, if there were no "departures from the normal," there would be no evolution. In the second place, we have those innocent and unexplained modifications of structure or physiology which affect the organism neither favorably nor unfavorably in its struggle for existence—an unexpected difference in texture of bark, color of flowers, shape of leaves, habit of growth, etc. The point to be made is that just because an organism is different from the normal, it is not necessarily "diseased." It may be better than the normal, as well as worse. Even parasitism, while usually producing disease, does not always do so: sometimes the host is stimulated into the actualization of potentialities that otherwise would have remained latent and unsuspected.

In practice it is, of course, more important to recognize a disease than to define it. Even the inexperienced can tell a badly diseased tree from a healthy one: its general look of stuntedness, lack of vigor, sparseness and unhealthy color of foliage are unmistakable.

Unfortunately, however, trees so noticeably ill are often beyond saving. It is much more important—and much more difficult—to detect disease just as it is beginning, at the stage where it is still controllable. Apart from obvious cases of necrosis, hypoplasia, and hyperplasia, other symptoms that help in detection are the fruiting and vegetable bodies of the pathogenic fungi, sometimes quite large, such as the fruiting bodies of the shelf fungi, which may reach a foot or more in diameter; also the bleeding of affected parts, the cracking away of bark, the discoloration of wood, the exudation of gum, the emission of odor, etc.

Diagnosis

To discover the cause of the trouble and to prescribe the remedy are the functions of the diagnostician. The actual application of the remedy is the province of the tree-worker, or dendrician, as he is sometimes called. In most cases, the diagnostician and worker are combined in one individual, particularly in small or medium-sized communities where a higher degree of specialization is not possible.

The diagnostician is the most important man of a tree company's personnel. He should have the widest knowledge, the broadest experience, and the keenest eye. In many large cities the arborist-diagnostician offers a wholly independent service, being equally at the disposition of the homeowners and the tree experts but bound to neither. More often, such services are given by representatives of local or state governments, such as city foresters, county agents, or state university extension specialists.

In making the diagnosis the following tools will be found useful: (1) mallet and chisels (1/2" and 1/8" widths) for probing into trunk, branches, or roots; (2) sharp knife for probing, cutting, and slicing; (3) hand shears for clipping off twigs and leaves; (4) short-handled spade or mattock for digging around roots; (5) brace-and-bit or, better, increment borer for testing trunk soundness and bringing out core sections; (6) hand lens for examining infected parts.

With these simple tools, which can easily be carried about in a car, most of the on-the-spot diagnoses can be made. In the case of obscure fungal or bacterial diseases, samples of the infected tissues should be studied under high-powered microscopes.

Viruses

Viruses are "ultramicroscopic principles," also sometimes called "pathogenic particles," "infectious agents," "rogue genes," and other tentative terms in an attempt to describe something we still know very little about.

Viruses are known principally by what they do. They are so tiny that they can be seen only with the aid of the electron microscope; so tiny that they pass through the pores of the finest filter we can fabricate.

Benign tumors on domestic Fig stems. The wood inside these overgrowths is sound, and the tree is healthy. Something, however, perhaps bacteria, perhaps viruses, upset the normal growth pattern of each swelling.

They are responsible for some of our most serious diseases—in animals as well as plants. They cause phloem necrosis in the American elm, tobacco mosaic, aster yellows, raspberry leaf curl, peach yellows. In man they cause measles, rabies, smallpox, and infantile paralysis.

They overwinter within the tissues of the host plant and can be neither controlled nor prevented by spraying. However, since they are often associated with insects and since insects often carry diseases from one tree to another, control of insects means partial control of viruses.

Bacteria

Bacteria are microscopic plants without chlorophyll. Some scientists class them with the fungi, others put them in the Animal Kingdom, others give them a place all to themselves. They are all one-celled organisms, dividing by simple fission to form two distinct individuals. Each of these two divides again to form two more; each of the four divides to form eight, and so on. Since the division is very rapid, it is possible for one bacterium, if unchecked, to produce thousands or millions of replicates of itself in a very few hours. It is the presence of great numbers of these tiny organisms in our blood stream or in the plant body that causes certain types of disease.

Bacteria have varying shapes; those that parasitize plants are for the most part rod-shaped. Some forms possess minuscule tail-like organs (flagella) by means of which they move about in a limited fashion when in liquids.*

Under certain conditions bacteria form into a sphere, pass into what seems to be a state of dormancy, and surround themselves with a comparatively thick wall. In this spore stage they can resist cold, heat, and some kinds of acid for surprisingly long periods of time. It is as spores that they are usually disseminated by wind, water, insects, animals, and men.

Fungi

Fungi are plants of a simple order which have no chlorophyll and hence are unable to manufacture their own food, being dependent upon existing organic matter.

The kinds of fungi that feed upon dead plants (or animals) only are called *saprophytes.* The kinds that feed upon living plants (or animals) are called *parasites.* Some kinds are both saprophytic and parasitic, living on dead tissue until they can contact live tissue.

Examples of saprophytes are the fungi that bring about the decay of old stumps, dead limbs, untreated lumber, etc. Like termites, they are beneficial in that they effect a rapid dissolution of dead wood which otherwise would cover the earth in a few years. They are harmful in the sense that they cannot distinguish between wood we have discarded and wood we want to save.

Examples of parasites are the fungi that cause Dutch elm disease, powdery mildew, shoe-string root rot, etc. Parasites are legion. There are thousands and thousands of different kinds, all so small they must be studied with a microscope. Ordinarily they escape unnoticed except when the damage they do is serious enough to draw public attention to them, and then it is their effects which are seen and seldom the organisms themselves.

*It has recently been demonstrated that in some bacteria the flagella work on a rotary principle rather than in a whip-like fashion, as so long believed. This means that each bacterium, small as it is, is equipped with a propeller driven by a reversible electric motor complete with rotor and stator! (See Scientific American, August, 1975, page 36.)

Heartrot of Apple produced by mushroom *Pholiota* k.

Fungus fruiting bodies on Hackberry tree.

These tiny parasites live upon the leaves, stems, fruits, or other tissues of the host plant, drawing nourishment from it. They produce the various forms of leaf spot, blight, rust, mildew, etc., which are economically of such extreme importance, particularly when they affect cereal plants or fruit trees. They are so small they cannot be dealt with mechanically. Saws, hooks, and shears actually serve to propagate these organisms, for tools used first on an infected tree and then on a sound one serve as a perfect medium for the transmission of disease, unless they are sterilized in between operations.

Fungi are distinguished by their small size, their lack of chlorophyll, their manner of reproduction, and the thread-like structure of their vegetative body. Although usually very small, they are often quite complex, sometimes existing in two totally different forms: vegetative and reproductive. Examined under the microscope, they are seen to be beautifully symmetrical. Small as they are, some of them produce fruiting bodies on a macroscopic scale, such as the common toadstools, mushrooms, and shelf fungi, which may exceed a foot in breadth.

Fungi reproduce by means of microscopic spores. These are blown by the wind, splashed by water, and carried by insects, birds, pruning tools, even on the shoes and clothing of tree workers. They enter a healthy tree through wounds or through natural openings, such as the lenticels of the bark and the stomata of the leaves. Some even have the power to penetrate directly the unbroken tissue of leaf blades. Once inside the tree, they rapidly develop into an intricate system of far-reaching mycelial threads, which digest the tree's tissue as they grow into it. When inside, they cannot be affected by any spray applied to the tree's exterior, except certain systemic fungicides or chemotherapeutants which may be absorbed and translocated to the infection site. Such substances are the objects of intensive research, and it is to be hoped that their applicability can steadily be extended. Unfortunately, however, many fungi attack heartwood or older layers of sapwood where there is little or no circulation of fluids—areas lying beyond the reach of sprayed-on or injected materials.

The whole life of fungi is warfare; observing them we see our own history repeated in miniature. The unceasing struggle between fungi and their hosts is waged with total ruthlessness: all primitive and modern martial tactics are requisitioned, the sole law being to win at all costs. Un-

Direct trunk injection for application of systemic insecticides and fungicides is finding more and more uses. Injected—or rather placed—in shallow holes drilled around the trunk, the substance mingles with the sap flow and is carried to all parts of the tree. In this picture a worker is seen applying *Metasystox R* to a maple for control of aphids. The very newest material to be injected in this manner (although the holes are usually made at ground level) is *Lignasan BLP* for control of the Dutch Elm disease.

folding before us, we see advances, retreats, skirmishes, infiltrations, parachuting behind enemy lines, nocturnal attacks, mass invasions, entrenchment, clearing of trenches with chemicals, ambushes, erection of barricades, sapping, flanking, pincer movements, scorched earth policy. Back and forth goes the struggle: when the fungus penetrates the host's defense, the host must perforce throw up a second

line or perish. And when the host succeeds in blocking the advancing fungus, whether structurally or physiologically, the invader must then develop another strategy. So the warfare goes on, both over the short and the long term. Adaptations are sometimes astonishingly quick—a matter of hours or even minutes; on the other hand, radical, pervasive changes in strategy may take centuries or millenia. The more exactly we try to describe all the fungi-host interactions the more we are driven to the use of martial analogies; the parallel with human warfare overwhelms us. Given the opportunity, should not a great mycologist make a great General?

Algae

Algae range in size from the microscopic diatoms common in both fresh and salt water to the giant kelps from the California coast that may reach a length of 100 feet. They are very widely distributed about the planet, occurring in virtually all the waters, even in the hot springs of the Yellowstone geysers. They are familiar as the green scum that accumulates on bodies of still water; familiar also as the green stain so widely found on the moist and shaded sides of trees, rocks, barns, and houses.

The known varieties of algae—and no one knows how many are still undiscovered—are bewildering, and their total numbers are prodigious, astronomical, incomprehensible. Although they are generally regarded as "primitive" plants, all of them, even the simplest one-celled forms, are capable of carrying on all the complex processes of life associated with higher plants: absorption, photosynthesis, digestion, respiration, growth, and reproduction.

Unlike fungi, algae have chlorophyll in their tissues and hence are capable of manufacturing their own food. The vast majority of them are, therefore, not parasites. In fact, the exact opposite is the case: they are the primary producers of food and oxygen on the planet and without them we probably would not long survive. *All* marine organisms are parasitic directly or indirectly on algae, which alone of all the creatures that inhabit the seas are capable of manufacturing food from inorganic elements.

A small minority of algae, however, *are* parasites. That these forms are seldom mentioned in botany text-books or in agricultural bulletins is due to the fact that most of them are found in the tropics, while most writers of books live and work in the Temperate Zones.

The most important parasitic alga is *Cephaleuros virescens*, familiar to students of tropical agriculture as a troublesome pest of crop plants. This aberrant alga also attacks large trees, causing leaf spots and blotches and sometimes partial or total defoliation, thus weakening the tree and making it more susceptible to invasion by other pathogens. In addition to the leaves, it attacks fruits and stems, producing constrictions, malformations, and even breaks in the bark. It also may combine with certain fungi to form the lichen *Strigula,* which, when superabundant, may damage foliage by smothering it. While confined chiefly to the tropics, it occasionally turns up as far north as North Carolina, and we begin to wonder how often and for how long it has gone undetected.

If it seems strange that a plant capable of manufacturing its own food should take up a parasitic way of life, we need only recall mistletoe, a flowering plant with green leaves capable of photosynthesis, which has done exactly the same thing. Mistletoe, in fact, has gone even farther in that direction, for it has renounced its autonomy and become an *obligate parasite*, unable to live without its host and dying when the host dies, while the parasitic algae are still capable of independent existence when the need arises.

Nematodes

Nematodes are smooth, non-segmented, cylindrical worms found in enormous numbers in the soil, at the bottom of lakes, rivers, ponds, and oceans, and parasitically in the bodies of plants and animals. Adult lengths range from 1/500 of an inch to three feet, the majority lying in the range 1/16 to 1/2 inch. Those that infest plants are generally microscopic in size and for many years escaped detection. Being parasitic, destructive, infective, contagious, and very small, they fit perfectly into the definition given above; they are agents of disease *par excellence.* *

Judging from their astronomical numbers and their very wide distribution, nematodes must be ranked among the most successful of all living things. To give an idea of their numbers and ubiquity, it has been calculated that if all the matter of the globe could be made to vanish except the nematodes, there would still remain visible, in ghostly outline, all the principal geographic features, the mountains, hills, valleys, rivers, lakes, and seas; also the trees, shrubs, and smaller plants and the vast majority of animals, both large and small.

Some nematodes feed on vegetable matter, some on animal matter, some on both, some on debris, saprophytically like fungi, some only on the body fluids of the host. The hookworm, scourge of tropical lands, is a nematode; so is the pinworm, the troublesome parasite of the human rectum. Trichinae, parasites of rats, hogs, and men that produce the dreaded trichinosis, are nematodes. Ascaris, a serious parasite of the hog's small intestine, attaining a length of 6 to 16 inches, is also a nematode.

Called nemas, eel-worms, and round worms, nematodes are known in plant pathology chiefly as parasites of crop plants and of ornamentals, such as narcissus, hyacinth, and phlox; also, of course, as the wide-spread leaf pests disfiguring ferns, coleus, begonias, and other greenhouse plants. Root-knot or root-gall, a nematode-caused infection,

---

*Many insects could also be fitted into this definition , of course, and the placing of them in a separate category is purely and simply a matter of convenience.

attacks more than 500 different species of plants, causing dwarfing, chlorosis, and general lack of vigor.

Less well known is the fact that nematodes often work closely with bacteria, fungi, and viruses, transporting them and sometimes being transported by them, as by the sticky spores of the fungus *Colletrotrichum.* While direct nematode damage to trees is slight (so far as is known), indirect damage via their role as vectors and symbionts is possibly much greater than commonly believed.

Insect Control

Tree diseases are controlled by four methods:
Protection,
Eradication,
Exclusion,
Immunization.

Protection

Protection means prevention, and an ounce of prevention is worth many pounds of cure. Certain practices will prevent the onset of disease. Prominent among these is anticipatory spraying, which by killing spores and by covering tree parts with a protective film prevents many diseases from taking hold. By killing insect eggs as well, the spread of disease by mature insects is also avoided. (Dutch elm disease is perhaps the best-known example at the present time of an insect-carried disease.) Spraying is discussed in a separate chapter.

Equally important is the manipulation of the environment to make conditions more favorable for the tree, less favorable for the disease organisms, or both.

Trees growing in good soil and receiving abundant water are found to be more resistant to disease than trees growing in less favorable situations. Hence the best step in protecting a tree is to improve the soil and to stabilize the water supply.

Similarly, when a tree is ill, applications of fertilizer and water are usually recommended. In some cases, however, fertilizing may be contra-indicated, at least in respect to some of the standard ingredients. For example, while fertilizer high in nitrogenous elements will stimulate trees to outgrow certain diseases, such as most of the cankers, the same materials will make apples, pears, hawthorns, and other trees unduly susceptible to dangerous fire blight; hence the proper fertilizer in this case is one low in nitrogen and high in potash and phosphorous.

Giving the tree plenty of room to grow also increases its vigor. Trees with crowded top or impaired root system cannot develop properly. Sunlight and air should be allowed to enter as freely as possible. While many trees in their juvenile stage are adapted to grow in the shade and some, such as many dogwoods and some maples, thrive in the shade even as adults, most of our common shade trees do best when in full or nearly full sun.

Proper pruning increases the tree's resistance to disease. Every dead or diseased branch removed prevents contamination of the others. Removal of rubbing, overlapping branches prevents the formation of bark wounds. Cutting off jagged stubs closes the door in the face of the enemy. The proper opening up of the tree's center and the judicious thinning of too heavy a top allows the sunlight to enter and provides for quick drying of wet branches—an important hygienic measure because most fungus spores need to be kept moist for several hours before germinating.

Even cabling may be considered a disease-preventive measure, since by forestalling breakage of limbs and tearing of bark, it helps preserve an undamaged bark surface. In short, anything that contributes to keep the tree in high vigor or to keep it structurally intact is a method of disease prevention.

Canker of Southern Live Oak *(Quercus virginiana)*. Where burls form globular swellings, cankers form sunken, depressed areas that slowly spread and, if unchecked, many times result in the death of the tree.

Eradication

Eradication means the elimination of diseased parts. It involves the simple sanitary practices of sweeping up and burning diseased leaves, twigs, fruits, etc.; the pruning out of dead and diseased branches, and the removal of incurably diseased trees. It also involves cavity repair, treatment of cankers, and other surgical measures. It further involves spraying where disease organisms are already present. Such sprays are usually dormant or delayed dormant directed at pathogenic spores (such as those causing leaf blisters and anthracnose) which overwinter in bud scales and on twigs.

Programs of eradication, particularly aimed at removal and destruction of the entire tree, are carried out continuously by the United States Department of Agriculture. An excellent example of such a program is the eradication campaign waged against the European larch canker (caused by the fungus Dasyscypha willkommi). This campaign, begun in 1927, has resulted in the destruction of more than 3,700 diseased larches, thus preventing the spread of the disease to our native stands.

Another form of eradication involves the eradication of alternate hosts. An alternate host is a plant (tree, shrub, or smaller plant) which is as necessary in the life cycle of the pathogen as the tree one desires to save. For example, apple trees are attacked by the cedar-apple rust. The fungus causing the disease spends part of its life on the apple and part on the red cedar *(Juniperus virginiana)*. Destruction of all nearby junipers will interrupt the cycle and so save the apple trees. Some apple-producing states have a law requiring such destruction. It is obvious that eradication and prevention overlap in many respects.

Exclusion

Exclusion (actually a form of prevention) is quarantine. It means that plants from an infected area will not be allowed to pass into other areas. A 100% quarantine would obviously be effective, but the difficulties of enforcement are great and the possibilities of violation, both intentional and accidental, are numerous. Some countries practice no form of quarantine or only the very slackest; others have rigid controls. The same remarks apply to our own states. California, being so heavily committed to agriculture and in particular to fruiticulture, imposes one of the strictest of existing quarantines; from whatever point you enter the state you are subject to painstaking examination.

Many of our tree diseases (and insects) have been imported with logs and lumber. Had exclusion been enforced, we would not now have these problems. Sometimes apparently innocent ornamental plants are carriers of pathogens that later attack trees.

Quarantine is made harder to enforce because of insects and birds (and unco-operative people) that carry pathogens from one place to another. In spite of the strictest controls many diseases continue to spread: the Dutch elm disease is one of the classic examples. First observed in Holland in 1919, it has since spread all over northern and central Europe, wiping out many of the finest elms. In 1930 it made its appearance in eastern United States and since then in spite of all efforts at containment has moved slowly west- ward, decimating our elms. Very recently it has shown up in California, stimulating the state to redouble its efforts at quarantine and eradication.

In some cases, however, quarantines are successful. The serious black-fly citrus infestation of 1949-1954 that damaged so many orange and grapefruit groves in Mexico was prevented from entering our country by very rigid controls all along the border; also by our financial and technical assistance to the Mexican government in the combatting of the plague on native grounds.

Immunization

Immunization means two things: (1) the development of disease-resistant strains so that they may be planted in infected areas with impunity; and (2) the use of chemical compounds that act inside the plant to increase its resistance to disease. Until recently the word was used only in the first sense because direct chemotherapy, although long a theoretic possibility, had stubbornly refused to become a fact.

Development of Resistant Strains — Even in the sense of disease-resistant strains, progress for many years was deplorably slow. Although a considerable amount of work was done in this connection with cereal plants, such as wheat, oats, corn, and others, little was done with trees. The United States Department of Agriculture has long been active in discovering trees naturally immune to certain diseases and in extending them into infected regions, but programs dedicated to breeding resistant strains which hitherto did not exist have lagged behind the times. Within the past ten years or so, however, the situation has begun to change. Tree genetics is a science receiving more and more attention, both on the part of the government and on the part of the large lumber companies, many of which have a multimillion dollar stake in making their trees grow faster and in making them disease-resistant. The pioneer efforts of Luther Burbank and other distinguished men are, at long last, being followed up by large-scale stock-improvement programs; breeding and hybridization are now the object of intense and continuous study.

Immune varieties are often not so desirable in respect to size, beauty, shape, etc., as the susceptible varieties. Also, of course, while immune to a given disease, they may turn out to be highly susceptible to another disease as bad or worse—a susceptibility that sometimes doesn't show up until they are planted in large numbers. Yet the use of naturally immune trees or the development of new strains of immune ones is often the only recourse in the case of uncontrollable diseases. A striking example is the almost complete destruction of the American chestnut by blight and its gradual replacement by the less desirable, but more resistant Asiatic chestnuts. Exactly the same pattern seems to be unfolding for the American elm, one of our stateliest and best loved shade trees: as it succumbs to the ravages of the Dutch elm disease, it is being replaced by the Chinese elm, the Siberian elm, the Zelkovas, and other Asiatic varieties, none of which equal it in beauty but many of which survive.

Use of Chemical Compounds — A provocative word in tree care today is *chemotherapy.* Meaning simply "curing with chemicals," chemotherapy is not a new idea, but the recent developments of it are different from anything ever done before. Although work in this field is just beginning, its progress is undeniable and its promise is enormous. There is hope that trees now considered incurable may in a not-too-distant day be saved by treatment with the proper chemicals. In fact, commercial work to that end is now being done on an experimental basis.

Strictly speaking, curing with chemicals occurs everytime a pruning cut is painted with wound dressing. It occurs everytime roses are dusted with sulfur. Nevertheless, *plant chemotherapy,* as used today, has been given a new and sharp definition: "The control of plant disease by compounds that, through their effect upon the host or pathogen, reduce or nullify the effect of the pathogen *after it has entered the plant.*" Thus the use of chemicals as external protectants is excluded from the definition.

A chemical compound that enters a plant (1) through the leaves by spraying, (2) through the trunk by injection, or (3) through the roots by application to the soil, and is translocated internally to the locus of infection or potential infection where it exercises a therapeutic action is a *chemotherapeutant.* In contrast, a chemical compound which acts on a pathogen before it has entered the host is simply a protectant or a preventive.

Research workers have long been intrigued by the possibility of artificially giving a plant body chemical immunity to disease. If the animal body could be immunized, why not the plant body? The concept was a bold one and attracted much interest, although from the very beginning some botanists challenged the whole idea, alleging that since plants have a less closely knit organization than animals and a much slower, less extensive, and less effective circulatory system and since they do not produce antibodies as animals do, they could not be vaccinated or immunized. The more imaginative workers in the field, however, believed the concept within the limits of theoretic possibility are well worth investigating. Persuaded that since *natural* immunity exists among plants as well as among animals, they might hope to discover the physical basis of this condition and so learn how to induce *artificial* immunity, they pressed ahead with research. The practical difficulties they encountered have been staggering. For many years attempts were made to immunize the chestnut against chestnut blight *Endothia parasitica* and the elm trees against Dutch elm disease; and although many cures were reported, none have stood the test of time. Research has continued, however, and as little by little the pieces begin to fall together, we may say with assurance that chemotherapy has ceased to be a dream and has become a fact. The new science has taken its first few faltering steps; it will inevitably take others.

On trees proper the first positive chemotherapeutic results were obtained by Howard against the bleeding canker disease of hard maples, and by Stoddard against the disease of peaches. The work of these men, already several decades old, showed for the first time that trees, like animals, could be made immune to diseases.

Although the exact mechanism or mechanisms by which chemotherapeutants produce their effects are not well understood, three modes of action have been described. The first is by counteracting the toxin generated by the patho-genic organism. The second is by acting directly on the pathogen, destroying it or greatly reducing its numbers. (Such chemotherapeutants are called *systemic fungicides* and are currently on the market under such names as *Benomyl*). The third mode is by altering the metabolism of the host in such a way that its resistance to the invading pathogen is increased. As a simple example of this, the Verticillium wilt that affects hops and tomatoes may be reduced considerably in severity by augmenting the amount of nitrogen supplied to the plants, and conversely, fire blight of pears and other fruit trees may be abated by the withholding of nitrogen.

As yet no chemotherapeutant has been discovered that renders a plant permanently resistant to disease. To give a plant continuous protection, treatment needs to be repeated at regularly defined intervals.

Two promising and exciting recent developments are these: (1) the discovery that resistant mutants can be produced from a susceptible strain by irradiation with gamma rays, and (2) the discovery that otherwise susceptible plants—in some cases at least—can be rendered immune by treatment with animal antibodies.[*]

From the same research emerge the following results: first, that susceptibility or resistance to a given disease are inborn characteristics of a plant, determined by the presence of a protein that either recognizes or fails to recognize toxin produced by the invading pathogen (bacterium or fungus); second, that apart from this inborn immunity some, perhaps all, plants are also capable of manifesting an *induced resistance* that is uncannily analogous to the antigen-antibody immunological system of animals, including ourselves! The immunological difficulty that seemed insuperable for so many years—the fact that plants do not produce antibodies—is perhaps not insuperable after all. For while not producing antibodies in the strict sense of the word, plants (at least some of them) do produce *phytoalexins:* a new term defined by Gary A. Strobel[**] as "compounds that are formed in a plant in response to elicitors released by certain pathogens and that proceed to inhibit or even destroy the pathogen." The line between antibodies and phytoalexins becomes difficult to draw; it is obvious that the differences, although important, are technical in nature; the principle is the same.

This, then, is another of the many new frontiers. Continued study of immunity, inborn and induced, seems certain to lead to an elucidation of the molecular, chemical, and biological processes involved and thus to make it possible, in a day hopefully not too distant, to prescribe a specific chemotherapeutant for every disease.

Canker on Hackberry limbs. Note the sunken deformed area and the series of elliptical rings as the disease relentlessly moves outward from a central point. Several months after this picture was taken, the tree died.

---

*These startling experiments have involved the eye-spot disease of sugarcane caused by the fungus Helminthosporium sacchari; the antibodies were produces by rabbits. See Scientific American, January, 1975, pages 81-88.

**Ibid.

Antibiotics

Antibiotics may be considered as a separate category, or they may be considered as special kinds of chemotherapeutants. In their method of application, in the way they are absorbed, and in their effects, they are for practical purposes identical with chemotherapeutants. In their origin they are different, deriving from micro-organisms found in the soil.

The discovery of penicillin focused the attention of the world on the importance of soil microflora. From the humblest of created things, from molds growing in the dirt under our feet, have come discoveries revolutionizing medicine. Stemming from the same source, somewhat the same kind of revolution seems to be impending for plant pathology. Since 1942 many thousands of antibiotic materials have been isolated and tested, chiefly for use in human medicine. Of these, very few have been tested extensively for agricultural use, but from these comparatively few some very startling effects have resulted. The present uses, limited as they are, are pregnant with promise.

While chemotherapeutants proper have been found effective chiefly against fungi, antibiotics are effective against bacteria. Some kinds of antibiotics, such as antimycin, exceptions to the rule, are effective against fungi. Other kinds, such as endomycin, are both antifungal and antibacterial.

Antibiotic materials are used in quantities so small that a new kind of spray terminology must be employed. Instead of so many pounds per hundred gallons of water, it is necessary to speak of parts per million (ppm). An ounce and a half of antibiotic material dissolved in 100 gallons of water gives a solution containing 100 ppm. In some cases the proportion is reduced to the almost unbelievable figure of 1 ppm.

Most antibiotic materials are sprayed onto the foliage. Others, such as terramycin applied to peach trees for control of bacterial leaf spot, are injected into the trunk. Materials are absorbed and translocated to the site of the infection or potential infection; hence they are systemic. Antibiotics applied to the soil have yielded negative results: apparently they are destroyed or modified before they can be picked up by the roots and translocated.

Good results have been obtained by applications of streptomycin and mixtures of streptomycin and terramycin against blight infections of apples and pears. Streptomycin has also been used against the walnut blight organism. Cycloheximide (Actidione), a by-product of streptomycin fermentation, has proved effective for the control of cherry leaf-spot fungus. It has also been found to inhibit teliospore formation when applied to cedar-apple galls at 100 ppm.

Not all results are positive. Many antibiotics prove ineffective or actually harmful. Certain materials injure the leaves, others produce cracked or discolored fruits. Many otherwise beneficial materials may be ineffective in low concentrations and phytotoxic in high concentrations.

It is not yet known whether the therapeutic effects are the result of changes induced in the host plant or simply the result of an accumulation of enough antibiotic materials in the host's tissues to prevent the pathogenic bacteria from developing.

The duration of therapeutic effects varies according to the disease. Experiments with pear blight indicate that the effect did not last as long as 14 days when lower concentrations of antibiotic mixtures were used. On the other hand, the terramycin experiments with peach trees gave control throughout the entire season.

Absorption of antibiotic materials through the foliage is not immediate. Rain falling within a few hours after spray application nullifies or weakens absorption. But rain after 24 hours have elapsed has little or no effect.

Experiments are constantly in progress to determine the effect of an antibiotic materials when they are mixed with (1) fungicides, (2) hormones, and (3) cuticle solvents.

The price of antibiotic materials for plants is surprisingly low and will doubtless go lower as production in mass lots increases. It has been calculated that a tree may be sprayed three times at the rate of five gallons a time for a total cost of fifty cents.

Common Diseases

Some of the most common and widely spread tree diseases are discussed in the pages that follow.

Vascular Diseases (Wilts)

Vascular diseases are so called because the part of the tree directly affected is its vascular system, that is, its sap-conduction vessels. The various kinds of fungi which cause these diseases gain entrance into the sapwood through wounds in the roots, branches, or trunk. They can extend themselves sufficiently in the sapwood to clog up the vessels, preventing sap from rising above that point and thus causing the branches immediately above to wilt. This wilting and curling of foliage is the first indication of the presence of the disease; it is so pronounced that *"wilt disease"* is a term often preferred to *"vascular disease."* Although wilting may occur generally throughout the tree, it more often occurs differentially, directly above and on the same side as the infected wound.

Although many kinds of trees are affected by wilt, the fungus that attacks one kind of tree does not necessarily attack another kind; that is to say, most fungi are host-specific. Some trees are entirely immune. As indicated above, the search for the molecular basis of susceptibility and its opposite, immunity, is gaining momentum and holds the promise of eventual control of most or all diseases.

It is now known that the causative fungus will not live in finished lumber made from infected timber, nor will the fungus itself weaken or deteriorate the timber even though it kills the tree. Diseased trees, however, should be salvaged as soon as possible to prevent deterioration from ordinary wood-rooting fungi.

Leaf Diseases

Many diseases attack the leaves alone, without affecting woody parts and without entering the vascular system. These are much less serious than root rot, phloem necrosis, wilts, cankers, etc., but they often sharply retard the growth of the tree, lower its vigor, and consequently pave the way for the inception of some worse disease.

Leaf diseases are caused by bacteria or fungi, which are transported in the spore stage by wind, water, and insects. Upon germinating, the organisms may grow entirely on the leaves' surface, or they may penetrate their inner tissues, drawing out the juices with tiny sucking organs. They spread most during hot, humid weather when little wind is blowing to dry the moist plant. They overwinter in dead leaves and fruit, in cracks along the bark, and in tiny crevices in the ground.

Sanitation — meaning the immediate removal and burning of dead leaves, twigs, branches, and fruits, is important in their control. Preventive spraying is equally important. Proper pruning, which works to keep the tree's interior open for the free passage of light and air, does much to forestall the diseases. Some of the most common kinds are discussed below.

Leaf Spots

Leaf spots are irregularly shaped spots or marks of discolored or dead tissue on the leaf blade caused by many different kinds of fungi. When the area involved is large with indefinite margins, the disease is sometimes called "blight" or "blotch." Leaf spots usually have a dead center of one color surrounded by a dying area of another color. Small black dots on a spot are fungal fruiting bodies; their absence may mean that they have not yet formed, or it may mean that the spot is of bacterial rather than of fungal origin.

Leaf spots are ordinarily of little importance. A certain number occur on all trees at all times. It is only when this number becomes excessive that harm may be done. Under exceptional circumstances they may cause entire defoliation, slowing the tree's growth and lessening its resistance to other diseases.

Whenever it is possible to separate spotted leaves from the others, they should be swept up and burned. If added to the compost heap, they constitute a source of inoculum for the following year.

Studded with thorn-like processes, soft at first but hardening with age, this spherical gall on the underside of a leaf provides food and shelter for the developing insect within. At maturity the insect will emerge, fly about, mate, and seek out another leaf on the same or another tree in which it can deposit its eggs and so keep the cycle going.

Spraying with *Bordeaux* mixture in the spring as the leaves unfold is a preventive. Sometimes several subsequent sprayings are necessary. Sulfur sprays and dusts and copper-lime dust are also used. *Captan* is a recent fungicide that has been found effective. Control of spots is usually more important on fruit trees than on shade trees.

Sooty Molds

Sooty molds, or sooty fungi, cover the leaves of many plants with a black, sooty coating during midsummer. The culprit fungi are closely related to the powdery mildews but distinguished from them by having dark-colored mycelium instead of white.

Rather than invading the inner tissues of the leaf, these fungi grow along the surface, feeding on sugary exudations from the plant or on secretions from attacking insects,

On the surface of a single Avocado leaf are found these thirty or so cylindrical galls. Each gall is caused by a tiny flying insect which stings the leaf at selected points, depositing an egg, or eggs, inside the plant tissues and simultaneously somehow instructing the plant to form the gall, which then houses and nourishes the insect developing within as it metamorphoses from egg to larva to pupa to adult. In this latter form the insect emerges from the gall, flies about, mates, and lays eggs on another leaf to begin the cycle.

principally plant lice (aphids) and white fly. Hence they are not parasitic, although if excessive they harm the plant by shutting out sunlight and preventing photosynthesis, just as soot from factory chimneys does.

Where serious, the molds can be washed off by a strong stream of water, rubbed off by hand (on small plants), or sprayed with *Bordeaux* mixture or dritomic sulfur. Simultaneous spraying for control of the accompanying insects is also necessary.

Powdery Mildew

Powdery mildew is much like sooty molds, except that it forms a white covering over the leaves rather than a black one, and it actually penetrates the leaf tissues with root-like sucking organs.

It is more common on small plants, such as roses, phlox, lilac, and crape myrtle, than on trees, although under exceptional conditions it may occur on these. It causes curling, dwarfing, and death of young, succulent growth, but seldom affects older leaves.

Spores are wind-borne. Preventive spraying with dritomic sulfur or dusting with fine sulfur will give easy control. Raking and burning leaves in the fall is also recommended.

Scab Fungus

Scab fungus is a serious disease of fruit trees, particularly apples, and a disease of lesser severity on some shade trees, particularly willows, in certain parts of the country. It produces definite, nearly circular, slightly raised lesions on the underside of leaves, especially along the veins and midrib; sometimes also on fruits and twigs. On the apple it may cause loss of from 50% to 100% of the crop, and by injuring the leaves it reduces the possibility of next year's crop.

The fungus overwinters on dead and injured twigs and in shed leaves and shed fruits. In the spring the spores are carried by the wind to the developing leaves.

Where serious, the disease needs a more or less continuous program of spraying: an application of *Bordeux* mixture or dry lime-sulfur just as the leaf buds are opening and successive sprayings as needed to prevent secondary infection. Burning of diseased leaves, twigs, and fruits is essential.

Leaf Cast

Leaf cast of conifers (also called *needle cast* and *leaf browning)* attacks such cone-bearing trees as pine, fir, spruce, larch, juniper, and hemlock. It is caused by several different kinds of fungi, each one partial to a particular species. This trouble has been confined to forested areas, doing little damage to the coniferous ornamentals.

Yellow or brown spots or bands form on the needles, followed by fruiting bodies in the form of black pustules. The entire leaf (meaning, of course, the *needle* if pine, fir, spruce, or similar forms, and the flat, overlapping *scale* if juniper or cypress) gradually browns and falls off. Even small twigs may be killed. In some cases only current growth is attacked; in other cases it is the older growth that is infected. Spraying with *Bordeaux* mixture is recommended. Young trees seem to be more susceptible to infection than older ones.

Root Diseases

Some of the most difficult diseases to diagnose and to control are those that attack roots. Since they develop mostly underground, they are usually not noticed until they have become well established. Treatment is, of course, much complicated by the problem of excavating large amounts of soil and of discovering all infected root areas. Too often one is working in the dark, literally as well as figuratively.

Cotton Root Rot

In the Southwest probably the most serious root disease is *cotton root rot.* (Also called Texas root rot and Phymato-trichum root rot.) The cause is a soil-inhabiting fungus (*Phymatotrichum omnivorum*), which gets its common name for its frequent attacks on cotton and its specific scientific name for its omnivorous ability to attack over 1700 known other plants! Surely this fungus should be in the Guinness book of records; it is beyond any doubt one of the most successful organisms nature has ever produced. Only the monocotyledons and some of the crucifers, mints, and verbenas are able to withstand it.

Infected plants suddenly turn yellow, wilt, and die. If the infection is noticed in time, the plants may sometimes be saved by heavy applications of ammonium sulfate to the soil. But once the infection has progressed past a certain point, remedies are unavailing.

The fungus spends most of its time underground, over-wintering in the form of sclerotia. During periods of abundant summer rains, masses of fungus mycelium may appear on top of the ground. Soil can be disinfected with formaldehyde or carbon disulphide, although these should not be used in the vicinity of growing plants.

Shoe-string Root Rot

Another very serious root disease spread more generally over the country is *shoe-string root rot.* (Also called *crown rot, mushroom rot,* and *Armillaria rot.*) Almost as omnivorous as cotton root rot and geographically more ambitious, the causative fungus attacks oaks and maples principally; birch, black locust, apple, larch, chestnut, mountain ash, pine, spruce, poplar, and sycamore less frequently.

The pathogen, *Armillaria mellea,* is versatile as well as ambitious; it can be parasite or saprophyte as conditions demand. This means that it may live on dead stumps and dead roots or may attack a living tree directly. Spores gain entrances into a live tree through wounds in roots or in lower trunk. Once the mycelium has developed (either on a live tree or on a dead stump), it sends out long, black strands ("shoe-strings") that grow through the soil to contact healthy roots of adjacent trees, penetrating and infecting them. Thus the fungus rapidly extends itself, traveling through the air by wind-borne spores and through the ground by black, snaky strands. Caught by this pincer movement, whole stands of trees are sometimes wiped out.

Symptoms are difficult to distinguish from symptoms of other diseases, particularly from those of illuminating gas injury. In cases where the progress of the disease is rapid, the leaves suddenly wilt and become dry. Where the progress is slower, the whole top shows a decline in vigor, the foliage becoming scanty and the branches dying one by one.

The surest diagnosis is made by examining the main roots or the base of the trunk at the soil line or just beneath it. Where disease is suspected, the bark should be cut away. If the fungus is present, it will appear as a felt-like white mass closely appressed to the sapwood. Where the tree is affected on one side only, the fungus will be found on that side. Where the entire top has died, the fungus will be found in complete encirclement.

Once the disease has gained a good start, the chances of saving the tree are remote. If the diseased roots are few, they should be cut back to sound wood, the affected region of trunk should be chiseled and scraped down to healthy tissue, and all cut surfaces should be painted liberally with antiseptic wound dressing. Soil should be dug away from the affected area to allow free entrance of sunlight and air. The tree should be fed and watered generously. To reduce the possibility of further spore infection, the mature fruiting bodies (appearing as honey-colored mushrooms) should be destroyed, although in city conditions these rarely appear.

Destruction of the fruiting bodies—mushrooms, toad-stools, bracket fungi, and similar forms—merely reduces or, hopefully, eliminates spore dissemination; it has no effect on the vegetative body of the fungus—the mycelium—which is the mass of strands that grow through the wood, digesting it as they work their way along. The appearance of the fruiting bodies is actually a sign that the fungus is solidly established—so solidly established that it can afford to expend part of its substance on elaborate reproductive mechanisms. A four, five, or six inch mushroom is an enormous and prodigal structure in comparison with the microscopic spores released from its gills. Just as no nation except a very affluent one can build and launch space satellites, so no fungus except a prosperous one can accumulate the necessary surplus of food and energy to construct *its* launching platforms and to send its billions of spores at hazard into the vastness of space. The appearance of the fruiting bodies does not mean, then, that the disease is just beginning: it means that it is far advanced.

Badly diseased and dead trees—including as much of the root system as possible—should be removed and burned. If another tree is to be planted in the same location, the soil should be thoroughly sterilized with formaldehyde or carbon disulfide or, better still, dug out and replaced.

To prevent underground spread from a diseased tree to healthy ones, a circular trench one foot wide and two feet deep should be dug around the infected tree, and all roots within the trench—both from the sick tree and the nearby healthy ones—should be cut off and sealed with antiseptic tree paint.

Fortunately, the disease does not ordinarily attack trees in high vigor. Those weakened by root suffocation, lack of water, lack of nutrients, insect depredations, or any other cause are its chosen victims. Hence the best preventive measure is the maintenance of vigor by prudent care and adequate feeding and watering.

Investigations have shown that phenyl mercury acetate applied to the soil (at the same strength usually recommended as a leaf spray) will in some cases control Armillaria rot.

Phloem Necrosis

Phloem necrosis is a very serious virus disease that injures or kills the inner bark and consequently the whole tree. In the last four decades or so it has caused severe losses among American elms in the central and lower Ohio River watershed. The disease was first identified as a virus disease in 1938, although reports indicate that it was prevalent in parts of Indiana, Illinois, and Kentucky for many years before this date.

The first symptoms noticed are a thinning and yellowing of foliage. Leaves curl upward along the edges, making them seem narrower and making prominent their lighter-colored under surface. Gradually the leaves turn from yellow to brown and then fall off or hang on in small dry bunches.

Positive diagnosis can be made by examining the phloem (inner bark) and cambium. The phloem shows characteristic discoloration; yellow or golden flecked by brown or black specks, later turning dark-brown and necrotic.

Moderately discolored phloem possesses a faint odor of wintergreen, which may be more readily observed by enclosing a small piece for a short time in a stoppered container. The discoloration and wintergreen odor of the phloem are unknown in any other tree disease. The affected phloem is usually found in root buttresses and lower trunk; less commonly in higher trunk and branches.

No cure or control of phloem necrosis is known. Perhaps resistant strains of trees can be developed. Until that time comes, no elms should be planted in areas where the disease occurs. In other areas it is not wise to plant elms-or any other tree—in exclusive stands, for an epidemic may destroy all. The planting of as many different kinds of trees as possible is highly advisable.

Anthracnose

Anthracnose (also known as ''blight'') is a leaf and twig disease, caused by various kinds of fungi (most of which belong to the genus Gloeosporium). Among the many different kinds of trees attacked are maple, sycamore, ash, elm, poplar, walnut, butternut, hickory, linden, willow, horsechestnut, beech, oaks, cherry, and plum. Each kind of fungus has a preference for a certain kind of tree, although all produce nearly identical systems. The disease is especially severe on sycamore.

Symptoms show up as brown, reddish-brown, or purple spots on the leaves, particularly along and between veins. The spots gradually extend until they coalesce; then the leaf turns brown and falls off. Twigs are also attacked, particularly on the sycamore. Small cankers form, gradually enlarging until they girdle the twig. Above the affected area the twig and its leaves die. Diseased trees show many of these dead twig tips, contrasting sharply with adjacent healthy foliage. Later, as the disease spreads, the whole top becomes brown.

In severe cases the tree may be entirely defoliated. If it has strong recuperative powers, it may put out new leaves, but they too may be destroyed by secondary infection. Repeated defoliations and extensive twig die-back disfigure the tree and weaken it to the point where insects or other diseases may find it an easy prey. While mild cases usually need no control, severe cases demand the closest attention if the tree is to be saved.

Control is by spraying and sanitation. Since the fungus overwinters in fallen leaves and twigs, these should be raked up and burned. Infected twigs that do not fall off should be pruned off and burned. In the South and in California the fungus also overwinters in the spore stage on dormant buds. These may be disinfected by a dormant spray composed of one part of lime-sulfur diluted in ten parts of water.

To prevent infection from neighboring trees, leaves should be sprayed just as they first appear with a copper sulfate solution or with organic mercury formulations. Where epidemics are present, leaves should be re-sprayed with the same solution every 10 to 14 days, according to conditions, the disease progressing most rapidly during periods of cool, rainy weather. A badly infected tree should be fed and watered liberally to help it make a rapid recovery.

Fire Blight

Fire blight is known to every orchardist as one of the most troublesome diseases of apple, pear, and quince. Less well known is the fact that it also attacks many ornamental trees and shrubs, particularly those of the rose family. It has been found on English hawthorn, mountain ash, flowering plum, flowering quince, cotoneaster, cockspur thorn, pyracantha, serviceberry, Christmas berry, rose, spirea, and others.

The disease makes itself known by a sudden browning or blacking of flowers and leaves near twig tips, making the tree look as if scorched by fire, whence the name. Twigs, and occasionally larger branches, die. Sometimes large cankers develop on main limbs or trunk, in which the pathogenic organisms conveniently overwinter. On some plants, such as flowering quince, only the blossoms are affected.

The disease is caused by the bacterium *Erwinia amylovora*. Bacteria are carried by splashing rain, bees, flies, and other insects. Infecting blossoms in the spring, they are rapidly transmitted from one tree to another. From the blossom they travel downward into fruit spurs, twigs, and even the larger branches.

Use of nitrogenous fertilizer on pear trees stimulates the growth of new, tender shoots which are very susceptible to blight. Hence such fertilizer should be used sparingly; similarly, severe dormant pruning of this tree should be avoided.

Control is achieved by pruning and spraying. All diseased twigs should be cut off several inches below the affected area, and pruning tools should be thoroughly sterilized in denatured alcohol or some other solution before being used again. Cankers can be treated surgically if not too extensive. This is done by chiseling out the affected portion and painting the sound wood with bichloride of mercury, followed by antiseptic tree dressing. Where a branch is nearly girdled by cankers, it should be cut off and burned. By the same token where the whole tree is cankered, it is better destroyed.

Some cankers may be cured by painting over without need of excavation. A good chemical paint for this purpose is made of cobalt nitrate (3-1/2 ounces), commercial glycerine (1.7 fluid ounces), oil of wintergreen (3.4 fluid ounces), acetic acid (1.7 fluid ounces), and ethyl or denatured alcohol (27.2 ounces.)

Spraying of blossoms just as they are entering the full bloom stage with a 1-3-50 *Bordeaux* mixture or with a copper-lime dust is recommended. In severe cases two sprayings may be necessary.

Recent developments in the use of antibiotics have shown that agrimycin (a mixture of streptomycin and terramycin) will greatly reduce blight infections on apple and pear.

Cankers

Cankers are caused by a number of different fungi, and they assume different shapes, according to the kind of tree affected. They weaken and disfigure the parts they form on, sometimes killing only the affected limbs, sometimes the entire tree.

Cankers usually appear as sunken, deformed areas on limbs or trunk, often bleeding, sometimes dry. Examination often shows successive layers of dead callus radiating from a center, indicating the yearly attempt of the tree to grow over the infected region and the gradual spreading out of the infection into the adjacent healthy tissue.

Burl on Post Oak trunk in Austin, Texas.

Cankers damage the tree by killing the tissues they are in direct contact with, usually the bark, cambium, and sapwood, and by interfering with the flow of nutrients through the affected region. A canker on a branch will cause it to wilt and die, by gradually shutting off its sap-conduction vessels, but will not affect the rest of the tree unless it works down internally to other parts. A canker on the trunk is more dangerous; if large enough, it blocks the circulation of fluids in both directions, preventing the roots from receiving food manufactured in the leaves and preventing the crown from receiving needed water from the soil, resulting in leaf drop, wilting, die-back, and, if unchecked, eventual death.

The causative organisms are usually wind-borne, gaining entrance into the tree through old stubs, open cavities, unpainted pruning cuts, split bark and mechanical wounds of all types. The disease is usually well established before symptoms appear. In regions where the pathogenic organisms are present even the slightest wound may prove an entrance point; a careless saw cut, a rope burn, a knife thrust, an accidental blow by the lawnmower. Even attempts at control, if unskillful, contribute to spread the invading fungi: experiments have proved that they can be transmitted to a healthy tree from an infected one by use of

Basal burl on Camphor tree (Berkeley, California). On some trees, such as the Camphor and the California Pepper tree, such burls occur so commonly as almost to be considered normal. The cause is bacterial or fungal infection.

unsterilized pruning tools and by tree paint devoid of an antiseptic ingredient.

Exceptionally vigorous trees sometimes outgrow the disease. Where damage has not progressed too far, the tree may be saved by cutting off and burning affected branches.

If on the trunk, main root, or main limb, the canker may be treated surgically. Trees too far gone should be cut down and burned.

Surgical treatment means the excision of the infected area, including enough adjacent sound tissue to insure complete eradication; swabbing of exposed wood with corrosive sublimate; and covering of the whole area with an antiseptic and waterproof wound dressing. All chisels and other tools used in this operation should be sterilized immediately after use by washing in denatured alcohol. A surgically treated limb may be weakened to the point where it needs bracing. Diseased trees should be fertilized and

watered abundantly to hasten callus formation over the affected area.

Recent work in chemotherapy gives hope that some day the cankers may be controlled by chemical injection. At the present time, however, the only significant chemotherapeutic cure is that of the bleeding canker on maples.

Nectria Canker

Some of the most widespread cankers are those caused by species of the fungus *Nectria*. There are many of these species, attacking nearly every kind of broadleaved tree and some of the larger shrubs. The fungus is wind-borne, entering the tree through wounds, insect injuries, frost cracks, etc.

The most usual form assumed by the cankers is that of an open pit showing successive layers of destroyed callus tissue around it, in the form of concentric circles. Because of this appearance, the disease is sometimes called the *target canker;* on birches it is called *European canker.* At certain times of the year small scarlet or reddish-orange pustules (fruiting bodies) are found along the margin of the newly killed bark.

Twin burls on Post Oak. Cause not definitely known. The tree continued alive and healthy for many years, although it has been removed for other reasons since this picture was taken.

Birches seem to suffer most from this fungus. Other trees are seldom killed, although their vigor is reduced and the way is opened for other infections. Maples often outgrow the canker, particularly if given nitrogenous fertilizer.

Sphaeropsis Canker

A number of different kinds of fungi belonging to the genus Sphaeropsis cause cankers on both evergreen and deciduous trees. These fungi usually attack only those trees previously weakened by other diseases or unfavorable environmental factors. Among evergreens the pines (particularly the Austrian, Scotch, Mugho, red, and white) and the Douglas fir and blue spruce are victimized. Among deciduous trees American elm and some of the oaks are the most common victims.

On evergreens, symptoms show up as wilting and browning of foliage at twig tips and deposits of resin along twigs. The lower branches are the most seriously affected. Examination of the needles, twigs, and cones reveals the pin-point, black fruiting bodies characteristic of this fungus.

On deciduous trees the dying and browning start at the top and gradually work downward. Dark-brown or reddish-brown cankers develop on the bark, the wood underneath taking on the same discoloration.

Chestnut Blight

Called "blight" because of its rapid killing action, this disease is really a canker. It is caused by the parasitic fungus *Endothia parasitica* which kills cambium and bark on chestnut trees.

Introduced into our country from Asia in the early 1900's the disease has virtually wiped out the stands of native chestnut in the eastern United States. The loss of the chestnuts is probably the major tragedy of our American woods. The rapidity, completeness, and virulence of the disease's spread is without parallel in the history of our forests. Hope may be taken from the fact that old stumps continue to throw up vigorous shoots which sometimes attain considerable size before the blight attacks and kills them. The search for disease-resistant varieties continues. Chinese and Japanese chestnut have proved highly immune, although unfortunately they cannot compare with the American chestnut *(Castanea dentata)* as a timber tree nor are their nuts of equal value.

First symptoms are a sudden browning and wilting of part or all of the tree's top. Examination of affected branches shows the presence of girdling cankers, which take the form of discolored, sunken areas along the bark. When this is peeled off, yellowish or reddish wefts of fungus tissue are found beneath. Tiny fruiting bodies dotting the affected bark are sometimes visible. When the canker is on a limb,

only the distal parts of that limb are killed. When on the trunk near the ground, the whole top is killed.

Spores, ejected in great numbers, are carried by wind, insects, birds, and water to wounds in other trees (or other parts of the same tree). No control method has been discovered. The same fungus has been found growing with somewhat lesser effect on chinquapin *(Castanea pumila)*, staghorn sumac, shagbark hickory, red maple, and some of the oaks.

Cytospora Canker

Several species of the fungus *Cytospora* produce disease on both evergreen and deciduous trees. Among evergreens the Colorado blue spruce and the Norway spruce are most commonly affected; Koster's blue spruce and Douglas fir less commonly. Symptoms are browning and dying of needles, almost always accompanied by copious exudation of resin at various points along the twigs. (Hence the disease is sometimes called *resinosis*. By cutting into the affected area at the point where it joins healthy tissue,

Burls on trunk of Palm tree.

cankers with their black, pinpoint fruiting bodies can be discovered. Branches are affected differentially, the dead ones often lying in close proximity to the live ones. Dead and diseased branches should be pruned away as soon as they appear, although pruning should not be done in wet weather because it is then that the spores are most easily spread. The making of wounds, even the tiniest, should be very carefully avoided.

Deciduous trees attacked include peach, willow, elm, the Carolina and silver-leaf poplars, and others. Being both saprophytic and parasitic, the fungus frequently bides its time living on dead branches until the appearance of a wound in live tissue affords it an entrance point; hence the importance of periodically pruning out dead wood.

Cankers usually appear first on twigs. Gradually the fungus travels down the stem, invading larger branches and eventually the trunk. Cankers on the trunk appear as brown, sunken areas frequently covered with red pustules. Wherever girdling takes place, the parts above that point die.

Cytospora usually attacks trees whose vigor has been weakened by some other cause. Correction of the environment accompanied by adequate fertilizing and watering will eliminate the predisposition.

Planetree (Sycamore) Canker

The widely planted London plane, and to a lesser extent the sycamore (buttonwood), is attacked by a canker-forming fungus *Ceratostomella fimbriata*. Many thousands of planetrees have been destroyed along the Atlantic seaboard since 1929. Worst of all, the disease seems to be spreading westward slowly, although it has not yet passed the Alleghanies (chiefly because most of the London planes are confined to the eastern states).

The fungus gains entrance through pruning wounds, insect wounds, frost cracks, etc. It is also transmitted in tree paints that do not contain antifungal ingredients.

When the fungus enters the tree, it grows towards the center of the stem. From the center it grows out radially along several lines, forming cankers when it reaches the bark. A stricken tree shows greatly reduced foliage, followed by death of affected limbs or of the entire tree if the canker is on the trunk. Trees may live one to five years after the canker's appearance.

Wood underneath the cankers is characterized by bluish-black (sometimes reddish-brown) streaks. A cross-section of the wood shows the bluish-black streaks in the form of wedges with the apex at the center of the stem.

No control is known. Infected trees should be cut down and burned. In regions where the disease is known to occur, plane owners should be particularly careful not to wound trees and should allow none but arborists of proven competence to do any needed work. Planting of solid stands of

planetrees within a small area should be avoided, as predisposing to the spread of epidemics.

Burls on Pollarded Sycamores (University of California campus, Berkeley). The mechanical action of repeated pollarding seems to be responsible for the resulting knots and swellings.

Norway Maple Canker

This disease, which has destroyed hundreds of Norway maples since first observed in 1938 or 1939, is caused by the fungus *Phytophthora cambivora*. The disease is described as follows by P. P. Pirone, who first isolated the fungus from a host plant in the United States:

An early symptom is a thin crown resulting from a decrease in the number and size of the leaves. Trees die within a year or two following this period of weak vegetative growth. Another, more striking symptom is the presence of cankers at the base of the trunk near the soil line. The inner bark, the cambium, and in many instances the sapwood are reddish brown in the cankered area. Death occurs when the entire root system decays or when the cankers completely girdle the trunk.*

Infection is believed to occur through wounds. Trees in poor vigor or in poorly drained soils are abnormally susceptible.

No cure is known. Dead and diseased trees should be cut down and burned. Trees should be planted only in rich, well-drained soil. Existing trees should be protected against wounding, particularly near the ground line.

Bleeding Maple Canker

This disease is caused by *Phytophthora cactorum,* a fungus closely related to the one causing Norway maple canker and formerly believed to be the same. It attacks chiefly the maples, including the Norway, red, sugar, and sycamore maples; also the American beech, and, according to Fenska, the southern live oak (Quercus virginiana). Pirone found the first case of this disease in New Jersey in October, 1940.

*P. P. Pirone, *Maintenance of Shade and Ornamental Trees,* New York: Oxford University Press, 1941.

The disease is named for its most characteristic primary symptom, the oozing of sap from fissures overlying cankers in the bark. Infected inner bark, cambium, and sapwood develop a reddish-brown necrotic lesion, which commonly exhibits an olive-green margin. These symptoms differ markedly from those produced in trees affected with basal canker. A secondary symptom, the wilting of the leaves and dying back of the branches, is said by one investigator to be due to a toxic material secreted by the causal fungus.**

The disease has been controlled in a number of cases by trunk injection of a chemotherapeutant (diaminoazobenzene dihydrochloride). This substance, an organic dye, counteracts the toxins produced by the fungus.

Witches' Broom

Witches' broom is so called because its chief symptom is the production of many small, closely bunched adventitious branchlets at or near the tips of twigs. It is a disease caused by such different things as viruses, fungi, mites, and dwarf mistletoe, any one of which may infect buds and so bring about the subsequent grotesque growth.

**Ibid.*, p. 249.

"Witches' Broom" on Pine: abnormally dense growth of needles caused by invasion of the buds by mites.

In the Temperate Zones, witches' broom is known to occur chiefly on hackberry and larch, less commonly on serviceberry, honey locust, hickory, birch, butternut, pine, fir, spruce, and hemlock. Damage on these trees is ordinarily small. Since the buds that give rise to the deformation are infected at varying times throughout the year, control by spraying is very difficult. Pruning off the infected tips is the only recommended procedure.

On certain tropical trees, however, witches' broom can be a serious disease. The fungus *Marasmius perniciosus,* for example, attacks the young, growing shoots of cacao (sole source of the world's chocolate), producing the typical broom-like clusters at twig tips and also sometimes attacking flowers and fruit pods. First noticed in 1895 in Surinam, the disease effectively ended the production of cacao in that country. Since then it has spread to Ecuador, Peru, Bolivia, Brazil, Venezuela, Columbia, and Trinidad, causing grave problems for the growers and being one of the principal causes of the ever-higher price of chocolate in the world markets.

Here, too, the only known countermeasure is the pruning away and burning the infected parts. Spraying has been tried on a limited scale, but the chief hope for control would seem to lie in the selection of resistant clones.

Galls

Galls are globular, semi-globular, cylindrical, or disk-like swellings produced on leaf blades, leaf petioles, and/or twigs by the "sting" of parasitic wasps, or by midges, aphids, or other insects, or by the infestation of bacteria or fungi.

Each gall is characteristic of the insect or bacterium or fungus that causes it; and of all the thousands of different kinds, no two are alike. The gall is actually a part of the plant; it is composed of plant tissues and is alive only so long as the plant is alive—plant tissues diverted from their normal development and forced to serve the ends of the parasite.

The galls or tumors on the stems of such plants as blackberries and roses are caused by bacteria. In the cedar-apple rust the so-called "cedar apple" is a single cedar leaf enlarged and deformed by the fungus *Gymnosporangium juniperi-virginianae.** The plant lice *phylloxera* are responsible for leaf galls on grapes and on certain shade trees. Gall-forming midges usually attack herbaceous plants, such as chrysanthemum.

The great majority of shade tree galls are caused by egg-laying insects, especially tiny wasps. They are, if not most common, at least most noticeable on oaks, where they sometimes take the form of balls (called "oak apples") that

*Recent work has indicated that one of the antibiotics, cycloheximide (Actidione), will inhibit teliospore formation of the fungus when applied at a concentration of 100 ppm.

Spherical galls on Oak twig. When an adult deposits a tiny egg within leaf or twig, a process is initiated that causes the plant to produce these peculiar growths. Inside the developing gall is the developing insect, passing from egg to larva to pupa to adult. In this final form the insect emerges through the circular escape hole, flies about, mates, and seeks other twigs or leaves to begin the cycle.

may reach 3″ in diameter hanging from almost every twig or leaf. On certain days of the year small wasps may be seen, by a very acute observer, visiting the oaks, busily engaged in piercing leaf or twig and depositing eggs inside. It used to be believed that some signal from the egg or from the developing larva caused the gall to form in its characteristic shape, but that theory has been overthrown by experiments in which the recently laid egg is killed by insertion of a hot needle (or by some other method) without affecting the subsequent development of the gall. It now seems that simultaneously with the deposition of the egg the adult insect deposits a tiny drop of fluid that is somehow capable of "instructing" the host plant to produce the desired gall. To discover exactly how this is done is one of the most fascinating problems in biology.

As the gall enlarges, the eggs inside hatch into larvae, eat and grow, and complete their metamorphosis, finally emerging as adults through small circular escape holes. From the insect's standpoint, the gall mechanism has proved highly successful. What safer or cosier home could they possibly find? The tree—generous if unwilling host—provides food and lodging, protection and concealment, while the insect inside lives in complete and perfect luxury, having nothing to do but to eat, sleep, and grow. Whether the tree receives any secondary or derivative benefits from this association has never been demonstrated.

If the perfect parasite is one that allows its host to live on with unimpaired vigor, the gall-forming insects may be taken as exemplars. While on smaller plants they may interfere, to a slight degree, with the circulation of fluids, on shade trees they do no discoverable harm. We may infer that imperfect parasites, such as mistletoe that kill or seriously weaken their host are of more recent origin than the perfect parasites, which presumably have gradually arrived at their benign relationship over a very long period of time; thus we gain some idea of the many millenia the gall-forming insects have been going about their business in unbroken cycle: egg, larva, pupa, adult, endlessly repeated.

On hackberries and cottonwoods, galls are usually found on the petioles. On oaks they are usually found on the leaves, in any of many different forms. Nearly every kind of tree is subject to some kind of gall.

Uninformed homeowners discovering galls for the first time often take them as symptomatic of a dangerous disease and may resort to drastic remedies. Sometimes they have the affected tree cut down, misled into believing that they are protecting their remaining trees from infection; sometimes they have it topped; most commonly, they have it sprayed.

Felling and topping are of course useless, since the gall-producing insects may fly to any tree from any point of the compass. Spraying is similarly of very doubtful value, for the adult insect may not come at the time expected, so that to prevent egg-laying, spraying would need to be more or less continuous over a period of weeks or months or the spray material would need to have such long-lasting residual properties as to make it biologically non-degradable and hence environmentally undesirable. To the egg or larva already inside the gall, spraying will, of course, mean no more to it than rain means to a man inside his house.

Some kinds of galls have been found useful to us, particularly the kind occuring on a species of a oak (*Quercus infectoria*), found in Asia Minor, Persia, and Syria. From these galls, called "oak apples", "gall nuts", or "nut-galls", tannin and gallic acid are extracted and used in

Twig galls on Hackberry.

Spherical galls on Oak leaf. This unusual photograph shows ten or eleven galls crowded onto a single leaf. Produced by the tree itself in response to "instructions" somehow imparted by the sting of the adult insect, the galls provide food and shelter for the developing insect within.

Different forms of galls on Oak twigs. These strange swellings are produced by the sting of a tiny wasp. Inserting her ovipositor into the tissues of the tree, she deposits an egg or eggs and also a minute drop of fluid which somehow instructs the host tissues to grow into the characteristic form. The egg inside hatches into a larva which is nourished and protected by the growing gall; gall and larva grow together.

Galls on Hackberry twig. These strange structures are caused by the sting of a tiny flying insect which, while depositing an egg, or eggs, within the plant tissue, simultaneously somehow instructs the host plant to form the gall. As the gall grows, the egg inside develops, metamorphosing from egg to larve to pupa to adult, sheltered and nourished by the plant issues diverted to serve its ends.

tanning, dyeing, and the manufacture of ink. Galls are among the most powerful of vegetable astringents and are also used in medicine.

While the majority of insect galls are benign, bacterial and fungal galls may be much more serious. The most dangerous of these is crown gall.

Crown gall is a bacterial disease that causes tumors or gall-like swellings on the roots or on the trunk near its base on such different trees and shrubs as apple, pear, plum, quince, flowering almond, cherry, sycamore, poplar, maple, willow, juniper, English walnut, chestnut, Arizona cypress, incense cedar, yew, oleander, and euonymus.

The culprit bacterium is *Pseudomonas tumefaciens*, which gains entrance through wounds in the bark. Rather than killing the tissues affected, the bacteria cause them to hypertrophy. As a result, general growth may be retarded, foliage may turn yellow, roots and branches may die. Although no great harm is done on older trees, young trees are sometimes killed.

The only control is prevention. Newly set-out trees should be inspected for signs of galls on stem or roots.

Precautions should be taken to prevent wounding tender bark. Wounds made by the lawnmower in cutting grass are often a focal point of infection. Where the disease is known to be prevalent, only non-susceptible varieties should be planted.

Burls

Burls are another kind of deformation or hypertrophy of tissue, occurring on the trunk and/or major limbs rather than on twigs and leaves. They are globular or semiglobular swellings ranging in size from three or four inches to five feet or more. They develop slowly, growing as the tree grows; solid and woody, they are actually part of the tree, not something superimposed from the outside. The outer bark surrounding them is usually rougher than normal bark. Inside them are found dozens, even hundreds, of dormant vegetative buds; when redwood burls (sold as curiosities up and down the California coast) are kept moist, they begin to send up numerous leafy shoots and can, if properly planted, grow into a new tree.

Trees afflicted with burls, even monstrous ones, may continue to live for many years; exactly how much, if at all, the burl subtracts from the tree's longevity has not yet been determined.

The grain inside a burl is often harder than normal wood and is almost always fantastically twisted and convoluted; slabs sawed from a burl usually show very attractive patterns. Burls form on many trees, such as the common fig, the camphor-tree, various kinds of oak, California buckeye, California peppertree, cottonwood, elms, different species of eucalyptus, locusts, olives, pines, and manzanitas. While many of these are of little commercial value, those forming on mesquite, rosewood, black walnut, and coast redwood are highly prized by cabinet-makers. Black walnuts, especially those graced with a burl, have become so valuable that they are now an object of "tree rustling". The demand for redwood burls is as great or greater: table tops six or eight feet across may be cut from a single redwood burl and are marketed at prices that may run to $2000 or $3000.

A burl originates when a cell (or group of cells) somehow escapes from the normal inhibitions that confine its growth within predetermined channels. Freed of control, the maverick cells begin to divide in all directions, producing the characteristic globular shape. The stimulus leading to this

Spherical galls on Oak twig. When an adult deposits a tiny egg within leaf or twig, a process is initiated that causes the plant to produce these peculiar growths. Inside the developing gall is the developing insect, passing from egg to larva to pupa to adult. In this final form the insect emerges through the circular escape hole, flies about, mates, and seeks other twigs or leaves to begin the cycle.

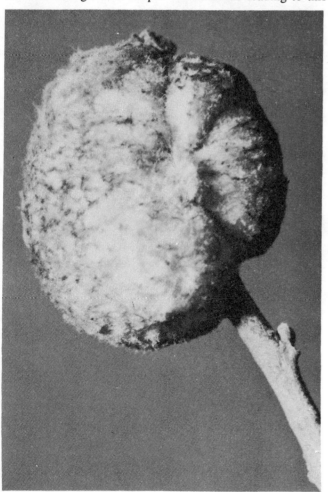

Twig gall on Post Oak tree. Inside are tiny larvae.

abnormal behavior may be any one of several different things or even a combination of them: fire, extreme low temperatures, insect damage, bacteria, fungi, viruses, mistletoe, and mechanical wounding. Pollarding, a pruning practice involving repeated heavy cutting (a form of mechanical wounding), causes burls to form just below the point where the cuts are made and even farther down along the stem. Cottonwoods, sycamores, mulberries, and willows, which are among the most commonly pollarded trees, frequently exhibit these trunk and limb burls. Grapes and tree roses, both subjected to repeated heavy pruning, also develop burls.

Burls are apparently not contagious and seem benign rather than otherwise. If you find one on your tree, there is no cause for alarm. The attempt to cut it off or chisel it away will probably do more harm than good. Cankers (q.v.), however, are a different thing altogether, usually requiring excision and sometimes amputation. If unable to distinguish between a burl and a canker, call in an expert.

6

Insects

Insects—we shall always have with us. There were insects on the earth millions of years before man appeared, and the last living creature on our planet, as it slowly freezes in the heatless rays of a dying sun, will very probably be an insect.

Insects are fitted in many ways to win in the relentless war of survival. Consider their small size, their prodigious numbers, their reproductive facility, and their marvelous powers of adaptation. They can eat anything, including soap and match-heads; in emergencies they eat their fellows or even their own body. They can adapt to anything, even to DDT and hydrocyanic gas. When they fly, they darken the sky. When they go on the march, nothing can obstruct their progress. They have honeycombed the earth, mastered the air, invaded the waters, infiltrated plant and animal organisms. They are omnivorous, ubiquitous, uncountable, indestructible.

In many ways insects are different from vertebrate creatures. Instead of having lungs, they breathe through a series of small openings distributed over their body. (The goal of many insecticides is to clog up these breathing pores.) Instead of having internal skeleton endowed with the power of continuous growth, they have no skeleton at all, or at best only an outer shell which must be shed from time to time as they outgrow it. (If a boy were put into a suit of armor, he would have to change it for a larger one every year or so until he became an adult. The discarded armors of the cicada are familiar discoveries on tree trunks in the summertime.)

The peculiar growth habits of the insects cause us to see them many times without recognizing them. Although "the child is father to the man" and looks enough like him to prove it, who, without foreknowledge, can imagine the maggot as father to the fly? Or the spiny grub as father to the beautiful luna moth? Or the insatiable wood borers to the totally dissimilar adult beetle?

When insects have what is called a complete metamorphosis, they exist in four forms: egg, larva, pupa, adult, each form developing in the order named and each greatly different from the other. When they have an incomplete metamorphosis, they exist in three forms only: egg, nymph, and adult, the pupa stage being omitted.

The growing stage (larva or nymph) is the eating stage in which the insect does most of its damage to plants. The larval form is variously called grub, caterpillar, and maggot. To most of us it is a "worm"—a many-footed, restless, imprudent, and a very hungry crawling thing. For birds, the larva is the piece de resistance.

The pupa is the resting stage. After having eaten himself—or rather; *itself*, larvae are neuters and sex comes only with adulthood—into a stupor, the larva builds a cocoon and curls up for a long sleep. Although apparently a stage of complete dormancy, the pupal stage is actually a time of very important and complex metabolic and structural changes whose end-product is the adult.

Very different from the hungry larva, the adult emerges from the cocoon, flies about, mates, and, if female, deposits her eggs, and dies. Some adults live but one day, some but a fraction of a day. Some have no mouths and cannot eat. Others, such as ants, live on for several years, working, eating, and hoarding.

Insects cause incalculable damage to forests, to shade and ornamental trees, to cut timber, and even to finished lumber. By defoliating trees, they retard their growth, weaken them, and sometimes kill them. By sucking the sap out of leaves and twigs, they produce much the same result. By boring into limbs and trunk, they interfere with sap flow and weaken the tree structurally to a point where it may be wind-thrown; even if it remains standing, it may be ruined for timber. Called *vectors,* they serve as carriers of disease, introducing fungi, bacteria, and viruses into parts where they would not have normally entered. (The infamous Dutch elm disease, for example, is associated with certain bark beetles.)

It should not be forgotten, however, that many insects are helpful rather than destructive: many assist in pollination, many are predators on their harmful cousins, many are neutral, using the tree merely for a perch or shelter. A program calculated to kill all insects without knowledge of their kind and function is misguided.

It is because of this difference among them that one-shot sprays are seldom as effective as a carefully worked out spraying program. On fruit trees, for example, a single spraying often results in less fruit than if no spraying at all is

Courtesy U.S. Dept. of Agriculture
Locust leaf miner *(Chalepus dorsalis thumb).*

done. This happens because the spray kills not only the plant-destroying insects but also the kinds which prey on them. Unfortunately, the destructive kinds, such as aphids, mealy bugs, and various forms of scale, reproduce much more abundantly and rapidly than do their predators. Hence if both are destroyed at the same time, the destructive kinds will reappear first and will remain one jump ahead of the predators for several months, or perhaps several seasons.

The whole economy of nature is so intricately bound up with insects that their sudden and total destruction would (in a few months or a few years) mean the complete disappearance of many plants, most animals and very possibly, man himself.

Insects have many natural enemies that tend to keep their numbers more or less constant. Among these are other insects, birds, reptiles, toads, fishes, bats, numerous small mammals, and some fungi.

Courtesy U.S. Dept. of Agriculture
The European Elm bark beetle *(Scolytus multistriatua).* **This beetle carries the Dutch Elm disease.**

On plants a certain minimum number of insects is virtually the normal state. Only under exceptional circumstances do they become epidemic. In towns and cities, unfortunately, exceptional circumstances always prevail, since trees are always growing under more or less artificial conditions; hence the need for artificial control is greater.

Chewing Insects

In respect to their methods of feeding, insects may be divided into

1. Chewing insects,
2. Sucking insects,
3. Boring insects.

Chewing insects are those that actually chew and eat plant tissue, such as the leaves, the flowers, buds, and twigs. Although their numbers are legion, common examples are the tent caterpillar, the potato beetle, the cutworm, the bagworm, the grasshopper, tussock moth, webworm, cankerworm, coddling moth, leaf roller, leaf miner, sawfly, and so forth.

Since these insects chew up little bits of plant tissue and take them into the stomach, they may be killed by spraying with a stomach poison, either while they are actively feeding or premeditatively before they appear. Before DDT and allied compounds irrupted on the scene, arsenate of lead was the most popular stomach poison and is still used by

Flat-headed borer on piece of Oak. So soft-bodied that it can easily be crushed between the fingers, this extraordinary insect can eat its way through the hardest wood.

many people who distrust the new organic phosphate insecticides. In addition to arsenate of lead, other arsenicals in wide use were arsenate of lime, magnesium arsenate, and Paris green (aceto-arsenite of copper). Cryolite (sodium fluo-aluminate), in both natural and synthetic forms, is sometimes used as a substitute for lead arsenate for the control of the Mexican bean beetle and for codling moth on fruit trees. Since these materials do not kill by contact, their effect is apparent only after a lapse of time, usually 24 to 48 hours after application. This waiting period is one of their disadvantages, for in 24 to 48 hours a hungry grub can consume a large quantity of plant tissue. Other disadvantages are that if insects are not eating or do not intend to eat, as when bagworms have retired into their bag, the poison will have no effect; and if the sprayed plants are rained on or accidentally sprayed with the hose, much of the poison will be washed off and the spraying will have to be repeated. Still another, and more serious disadvantage, of the arsenicals is that they are poisonous to man as well as to insects and must not be used where there is any possibility of children chewing or eating sprayed leaves or fruits. There also exists the inconvenient necessity of washing all sprayed fruits with a neutralizing chemical before eating or marketing—precautions not always observed.

Rotenone and pyrethrum are insecticides that function both as stomach and as contact poisons. Although less effective against some of the toughest insects than lead arsenate, they have the virtue of being harmless to man. Formerly widely used, they were temporarily eclipsed by DDT and company but are now coming back into favor as the extreme hazardousness of their powerful rivals has been convincingly demonstrated. Rotenone is extracted from the macerated roots of derris and cube, (leguminous plants found in tropical regions) and has long been used by indigenous tribes to kill or paralyze fish by the simple expedient of tossing it into the water. Pyrethrum is a powdered extract made from any of several species of Chrysanthemum; one form is popularly known as "Persian powder" and another as "Dalmatian powder." These are the true organic insecticides, earning their right to the name because they are made from living material. By an unfortunate semantic twist, DDT and allied compounds have also, and more generally, come to be called organic insecticides (a shortened form of organic phosphate insecticides). not because they are made from living material—but because, like living things, they happen to make use of carbon as one of the chief building blocks of their molecular structure. This coincidence of terms has given rise to much gratuitous confusion; "organic" has come to have one set of values when used in the phrase "organic gardening" and a very different set when used in "organic insecticides."

The British have recently developed a *synthetic pyrethrin* that has all the effectiveness of the most powerful organic phosphates and chlorinated hydrocarbons with none of their toxicity. Among the advantages claimed for the new product are; (1) its low toxicity to mammals (although highly toxic to fish), (2) its mass-producibility (the English are already talking about sales of 20,000 tons a year), (3) its extreme effectiveness, being 100 times more effective than DDT and up to 30 times as active as dieldrin, (4) its ready degradability. According to recent reports, it is soon to be placed on the market.

Of the organic phosphate insecticides the best known is, of course, DDT, which when it first came out captured the public imagination almost as dramtically as Sputnik or the atom bomb. Now, however, because of its extreme hazardousness and non-degradability, this insecticide is banned in many localities. DDT is both a stomach and a contact poison, paralyzing any insect unfortunate enough to come within its radius of action. Moreover, the insect does not need to be hit by the spray; it is killed just as dead by merely walking or crawling over a DDT-sprayed surface.

So remarkable are the residual effects that when mixed with xylene and triton X-100, DDT forms a spray powerful enough to kill or paralyze elm bark beetles within a few minutes after they land on a twig even though applied as long as ten weeks before. Close upon the heels of DDT are chlordane, lindane, methoxychlor, and others, some of which are still in use, although less widely than before the pollution crisis.

Sucking Insects

Sucking insects are those which, instead of eating the plant, suck out its juices by means of a special beak inserted into the tissues of leaf, twig, branch, flower, or fruit. Common examples are the aphids (plant lice), scale insects, psyllids, mealy bugs, thrips, leaf hoppers, and mites. (Mites are not true insects but for all practical purposes may be treated as such.) These pests, although tiny, occur in great numbers, often causing more damage (shown by discoloration, drooping, wilting, or general lack of vigor in the affected plant) than the chewing insects, whose damage although more conspicuous is not necessarily more serious.

Sucking insects are unaffected by stomach poisons (except systemics, discussed below) because they do not eat the outer surfaces of the sprayed leaves or twigs. They must be killed by contact poisons—sprays which by directly hitting the insect's body produce death by burning, paralysis, asphyxiation, or a combination of these. Since most of the older contact insecticides have little or no residual effect, they must be applied when the insects are present, not before or after, and the application must be repeated whenever the insects reappear. Application of a contact poison thus requires even greater thoroughness than application of a stomach poison: since the sucking insects move around very little, the poison must go to them, whereas the chewing insects often go to the poison.

For many years the best-known and most widely used contact poison was nicotine sulfate, followed closely by rotenone, and pyrethrum, less closely by lime-sulfur, sulfur dusts, potassium sulfide, oil emulsions, and miscible oils. Just as lead arsenate and other stomach poisons were temporarily eclipsed by the advent of the new, powerful organic phosphates, so these traditional contact poisons were similarly eclipsed—and are similarly slowly winning their way back into favor.

Each of these materials has its own method of application, its own temperature requirements, its own dangers. Manufacturer's directions should be followed exactly, for there are many details that must not go unattended. For example, nicotine sulfate is often combined in the same spray with lead arsenate to produce a double-barreled blast aimed at both sucking and chewing insects. When nicotine sulfate is used alone, soap is added as a spreader. But when it is mixed with lead arsenate, soap must not be used.

Of the organic phosphates, DDT, chlordane, lindane, and methoxychlor, already mentioned, are both contact and stomach poisons. Apart from their stigmatization as pollutants, they also sometimes cause injury to plants. Lindane and BHC leave unpleasant residual odors and produce off-flavor taste in many fruits and vegetables.

For about fifteen years *Aldrin* and *Dieldrin* were very widely used as contact insecticides, but recently they too have been blacklisted as pollutants. *Toxaphene*, long considered one of the most effective contact poisons, is also now under suspicion. *Malathion* is still in good standing, although not used as much as in the past. HETP, TEPP, and parathion are regarded as highly dangerous and should never be used near dwellings nor by inexperienced operators anywhere; cases of death from parathion appear in the newspapers with every new spraying season. *Carbaryl*, *piperonyl*, and *diazinon* are among the new favorites.

In recent years new types of materials called *systemics* have been developed. These are substances which, applied locally to some part of a plant, enter its circulation and are carried to all parts of its body, repelling or poisoning insects (systemic insecticides) and killing or inhibiting disease organisms (systemic fungicides). Some of them are applied as granules in the soil around the roots, to be absorbed slowly over a period of time and thus afford long-lasting protection. Others are injected into the trunk; still others are sprayed, being absorbed by leaves and stems. The spraying may need to be repeated every ten days or every two weeks or every month, depending on the plant and the severity and persistence of the insect attack.

Bidrin, particularly useful for the control of elm leaf beetle, is injected into tree trunks by means of driven-in spikes to which a vial with a measured amount of solution is then attached. *Meta-Systox,* perhaps the best-known systemic, is both injected and sprayed. Injection is accomplished by drilling holes around the trunk at intervals of approximately six inches, each hole penetrating inward about two inches and slanting slightly downward. Each spring the holes are filled with the proper quantity of *Meta-Systox* and stoppered with a cork. This treatment is very effective for the control of aphids on maples.

Systemic insecticides act as stomach poisons and kill both chewing and sucking insects, thus obviating the necessity of using only contact poisons on the latter.

Since the toxic material is distributed more or less equally in all parts of the plant, including the fruits, it cannot be used on food crops and should not be used even on non-food plants where there is any possibility of children or pets chewing on the leaves.

Borers

Among the most troublesome of insects are the wood borers. There are many kinds of these, some small, some large, some attacking live wood, some dead wood, some both.

Courtesy U.S. Dept. of Agriculture

Hylurgopinus refipes builds its egg galleries across the grain of the wood.

Like other insects with a complete metamorphosis, borers exist in four different forms: egg, larva, pupa, adult. As adults, most of them are beetles or moths, often quite beautiful and difficult to associate with the eyeless grubs that are the larvae. These grubs are usually white, yellow, orange, or brown, soft-bodied, strong-jawed, growing in some species to three or four inches or longer, in thinness like a pencil or sometimes grossly swollen to the size of a finger. They make excellent fishing worms and form the favorite food of the woodpeckers.

Borers are characterized by the galleries or tunnels they make in the woody part of the tree. Each kind has its own style and tunnel pattern and hence may be readily identified by its work even though no longer present, just as a workman may be told by his chips. Some borers work in the heartwood, some in the sapwood, some in the cambium and inner bark. They eat the wood as they tunnel through it, honeycombing it as termites do. Sooner or later most of them eat their way to the outside, making a round or nearly round opening out of which they eject characteristic frass composed of the semi-digested wood that has passed through their alimentary canal.

When they eat the heartwood and sapwood only, their damage is largely structural, weakening the tree to the point where it may be wind-thrown. The secondary effects are sometimes as bad or worse, for by means of their tunnels other insects and wood-rotting fungi gain entrance to the interior of the tree. Carpenter ants are commonly found in borer holes, enlarging the galleries and preventing healing. When the borers eat the inner bark and cambium directly, they destroy the vital parts and may kill the tree in short order.

A kind of borer common in Mexico makes a single longitudinal tunnel through trunk and limbs on the ash tree very nearly in their geometrical center, deviating from this pattern only to make a perpendicular exit hole for the voiding of frass. Into this hole the Indians pour water until the borer rises to the surface whereupon they dexterously lasso it with a thread. After catching a goodly number, they build a small fire, heat up their *comal* (a frying pan with no raised edge), roast the larvae alive, and eat them with a pinch of salt, a few drops of lemon juice, and, when available, a swallow or two of tequila.

The most important borers, according to the damage they do, fall into two great classes: the flat-headed (Buprestidae) and the round-headed (Cerambycidae). In one or more of their many forms these borers are found throughout the United States, attacking nearly every kind of tree. Each species has a particular tree or trees that it prefers. Moreover, each species prefers its wood in a certain condition. On a fallen tree, for example, each part of the log is attacked by different borers: the still living parts by one kind, the recently dead parts by another, the dry dead parts by another, the moist dead parts by still another.

Both outer and inner bark have been knocked off, and the exposed wood has not been treated. Such an exposed area is a target for fungi and wood-boring insects. In this picture scattered borer holes are clearly visible.

Methods of entering the tree vary. So do the types of wounds. Where the larva bores into the wood from the bark, its tunnel usually remains open behind it, and its presence may be detected by exuded frass and, frequently, sap ooze. But there are many other borers that do not make holes to get into the tree but to get out of it. They get into the tree in the form of an egg, laid within the woody tissues by the long, thread-like ovipositor of the adult female. The egg hatches into a larva which tunnels about in the wood most of its life, finally making an exit hole so that after pupation (which occurs within the tunnels) the adult (which the larva becomes) can escape to the outside world. In many cases the adult itself makes the exit hole. Once outside, the adult mates, the female lays an egg in the same tree or another tree, and the cycle is repeated.

Often the tiny hole made by the female's ovipositor heals over, so that there is no way of detecting the presence of these borers until they have made their exit holes and gone.

Maple tree badly infested by borers. By eating the inner bark and cambium, they seriously injure the tree and if unchecked can cause its death.

In some cases, however, the hole made by oviposition gradually enlarges, serving as an avenue for the discharge of frass and oozing sap, which at once indicate the larva within.

Borers, like termites, are useful when they confine their efforts to dead trees or dead parts of live trees. But when they attack living trees, as they sometimes do, particularly newly transplanted ones or those weakened by environmental damage or disease, they become a matter of considerable concern.

Borer-infested trees show a thinness of crown and a gradual or sudden decline in vigor. Positive symptoms are circular elliptical holes appearing on trunk or branches with exuded frass and sometimes dripping sap which forms a black or brown stain along the bark.

Very tiny white "worms" often found in infected areas just under the bark are not borers. Nor are the holes made by the sapsucker (kind of woodpecker), which many mistake for borer holes. The two may be readily distinguished, however, for the sapsucker holes are very shallow and are

made in even rows, while the borer holes are deep, irregularly located, and almost always made at an angle, indicating the tortuous nature of the tunnels underneath.

Borers have many natural enemies that help keep their numbers in check. Some borers are predaceous on other borers. Certain ichneumon flies parasitize borers, drilling with their slender ovipositor through several inches of solid wood to locate the hidden grub and deposit their eggs along its body. Other parasites and even diseases afflict them, particularly when their numbers become epidemic. Perhaps their most active and indefatigable enemy is the woodpecker, which with his barbed extensible tongue spears them out of their most secret hiding places.

In the forest we must rely largely on these natural enemies to hold the borers in check. But in cities we may practice our own methods of control.

To start with, all dead trees and dead limbs on live trees should be removed and destroyed to eliminate breeding places for the insects. Cavities should be cleaned out and sealed over for the same reason. The trunks and larger branches of newly transplanted trees should be wrapped with special tree-wrap to prevent egg-laying. Trees wea-

Digging out borers in trunk of Maple tree. Sometimes they may be impaled with a wire flexible enough to follow the windings of their tunnels; sometimes they may be dug out with mallet and chisel; and sometimes they may be asphyxiated by poisonous gas or liquid.

kened by disease or unfavorable environmental factors should be fed and watered to build up vigor.

Where already present, borers may be attacked directly. Where their presence is indicated by oozing sap or exuded frass, they may be dug out with mallet and chisel. Where their tunnels are open, they may often be impaled on the point of a piece of wire. Where they cannot be reached mechanically, they can be killed by putting carbon disulfide into their tunnels. Where the tunnel leads downward, an oilcan may be used to squirt in the chemical; where it leads

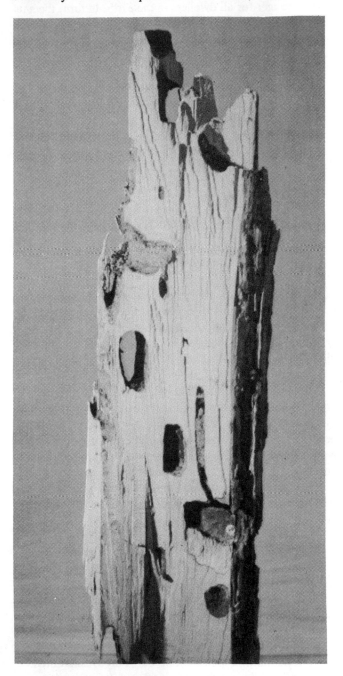

This section of dead sapwood removed from a living tree shows dramatically the results of borer invasion.

upward, a wad of cotton moistened in the fumigant and thrust into the tunnel may be used. In either case the mouth of the hole must be plugged immediately (with concrete, asphalt, putty, cork, or moist earth), for the liquid is so highly volatile that it will dissipate itself into the outside air if not sealed in. Since carbon disulfide is a poison, its fumes should not be breathed; since highly inflammable, it should not be brought close to fire; since extremely volatile, it must be kept in a tightly closed container.

Where borers are very numerous, the tree trunk may be painted or sprayed with an orthodichlorobenzene emulsion, made by mixing 12 parts of orthodichlorobenzene with 1 part of fish-oil soap or common laundry soap and 3 parts of soft water. (Hard water may be softened by adding one teaspoonful of washing soda to each gallon.) This mixture is then diluted in water at the ratio of 1 to 6. It should not be applied to tender branches or to foliage, for it will cause burning.

When borers have affected a considerable area of trunk, it is sometimes better to trace* the entire region, cutting away the loosened and damaged bark and then painting the exposed wood with a solution of cottonseed oil and para-dichlorobenzene crystals in the ratio of 6 ounces for each quart of oil.

Adult borers may be discouraged from laying their eggs by spraying the tree trunks with a 5 percent solution of DDT at the time the insects are active. Where DDT is no longer available, similar preparations may be substituted.

Since borers work mostly in the heartwood and the older sapwood where there is little or no circulation of fluids, they are usually unaffected by systemics, whether injected or sprayed.

Borers below the soil line (very common in peach trees, for example) may be killed by placing paradichlorobenzene crystals in loosened soil all around the trunk about two inches removed from it, then covering with a mound of earth, and uncovering them 10 to 14 days later.

Trees particularly subject to borer attack may be protected with a fine wire mesh wrapped around the trunk. This discourages egg-laying and at the same time prevents emergence of adults from any larvae already present.

Ants

Ants are so frequently found on trees that it is natural to believe them harmful. However, most of the ants that crawl up and down trunks live in the ground, not in the tree. They climb in the tree to milk their aphid-cows (plant lice) and to transfer them from one leaf to another as needed. Wherever large numbers of aphids are found on the leaves, even of the

*For a discussion of tracing, see the chapter Wound Repair.

tallest trees, ants are almost always to be found in attendance. Apart from milking the aphids and moving them about, they have even been observed to defending them from their enemies. The relationship is an endlessly interesting one. Hence, the harm the ants do is indirect rather than direct. If they were not present, doubtless the aphids would be less numerous.

There are other kinds of ants, however, that attack trees directly. One of these is the leaf-cutter (*Atta texana*). Living in the ground, the ants cut leaves off trees and carry them to their nests, sometimes over unbelievably long distances. The leaf-cutter is confined to Texas, Louisiana, and other southern states, where their damage is severest on slash and long-leaf pine. Where given a chance, they will defoliate rose-bushes with relish. In Mexico and farther south, various species of Atta become enormously active, sometimes defoliating an entire tree in a single night.

Control is by destroying them in their nests. This can be done by introducing a fumigant, such as carbon disulfide, as far down into the galleries as possible, using a funnel and a length of 2 inch rubber tubing. If carbon disulfide is used, all the entrance holes leading to the nest must be stamped shut and kept shut. A chlordane solution poured into the tunnels, or chlordane dust sprinkled around the mouth of the holes, is also very effective.

Carpenter ants are large black ants that tunnel into wood, causing a minor amount of damage. They attack telephone poles, fence posts, structural timbers, cut logs, dead parts on live trees, and occasionally live trees themselves. They gain entrance into living trees through cavities, unhealed stubs, cracked and unpainted pruning cuts, fire scars, etc. They also frequently utilize abandoned borer holes, cleaning out and enlarging the galleries.

While carpenter ants do not eat the wood, they tunnel away at it to make room for their constantly growing colonies. They actually live in the wood, not in the ground. They are harmful in that they weaken a tree structurally and provide a potential entrance point for other insects and disease-causing organisms.

These ants can be killed by injecting (into their nests) carbon disulfide, sodium fluoride, arsenical dusts, kerosene, orthodichlorobenzene, or four percent rotenone. When the nests are small, the fumigant carbon disulfide is effective. But where they are large and the galleries labyrinthine, as they usually are, the fumigants are less effective than poisonous powders, such as sodium fluoride or rotenone, which may be picked up by the ants' feet and tracked to all parts of the colony.

Some tropical and semitropical trees and shrubs and various species of ants have evolved a highly interesting symbiotic relationship. The plants produce a peculiar kind of long thorn with a thick, swollen basal portion; the ants somehow find these plants, climb up to where the thorns are, make a small hole near the base, hollow out the body of

the thorn, and move in. As new thorns appear and mature, the ants extend their colony to include them; thus every thorn on the tree (or shrub) is inhabited. The growth of a new branch corresponds to our building of a new subdivision. And imagine the real estate boom in the spring when a jungle of new plants begins to sprout!

The relationship is mutually beneficial, as all good contracts should be. The plant partner provides the ants with shelter—the original tree-house—where few enemies can get them and where they are safe from flooding, an ever-present danger for all dwellers in the earth. In turn, the ants protect the plant from intruders of all kinds. Woe to the browsing animal who takes a mouthful of leaves or the curious human who incautiously examines the plant! At the slightest movement the ants boil out of the thorns and swarm over the invader. What other terrestrial creature of comparable size can move as fast an an angry ant? In a moment they are all over you, biting as they go. The lesson, though brief, is indelibly stamped in, and the next time you encounter one of these interesting trees you give it a wide berth.

Termites

Frequently miscalled "white ants," termites are distinguished from true ants by their white color and thicker waist. They are very interesting social insects (phylogenetically related to the cockroaches) that tunnel through wood, actually eating it and digesting it with the assistance of certain protozoa in their intestinal tract. In our country they are found in most of the eastern and midwestern states and all of the southern states, where the problem of their control is greatest.

There are three main kinds of termites: damp-wood, dry-wood, and subterranean, named in reverse order of their importance. The dry-wood and damp-wood termites do not need contact with the ground and often pass unnoticed until a door-frame crumbles away to powder or a chair collapses beneath you. The most important kind, the subterranean termites, live in the ground, preferably moist ground, attacking above-ground wood under the shelter of mud tunnels which they build as they go along.

The role of termites in nature is the destruction of fallen logs, in which function they are extremely useful. Sometimes, however, they invade dead parts of live trees or rarely the living tree itself. Also, not being able to distinguish between finished lumber and fallen logs, they attack the wooden parts of houses with such persistency that their control (in the South, especially) is a major problem.

In trees, termites are most often found in basal cavities. By honeycombing the heartwood they may weaken the tree until it is overthrown by the wind or falls under its own weight. From the heartwood they sometimes work into the sapwood and even into the bark, both inner and outer. They gain entrance through borer holes, cracked pruning wounds, fire scars, etc. In exceptional cases they build their mud tunnels up the outside of a tree 20, 30, or 40 feet to reach exposed heartwood in a distant cavity.

While termites in timbers are controlled by the injection of poisonous liquids, such methods are not possible in trees. The best procedure is to destroy all mud tunnels, clean out and fill all cavities, dig away the dirt a short distance from the trunk, and destroy dead stumps or other inviting dead wood in the vicinity. It is, of course, advisable to destroy the central nest mechanically or chemically, although this is usually too well hidden in the ground to be found.

In Africa, termites may lay claim to the title of *dominant insect*. They abound there in inconceivable numbers and build giant termitaries that project above the ground 12, 15, or more feet—so strong that a large tree can fall across one of them without breaking it—inside which they live, unseen and unheard, in the most perfectly organized community known in the whole realm of living things. Their destructiveness to man-made objects—timber, furniture, dwellings, cloth, paper—is such that they are credited by many (Elspeth Huxley, for one) as being the principal cause for the inability of the Africans to produce any advanced or long-lasting civilization. (South Africa, lying in a colder zone, is largely free of the most destructive species.)

Pill-Bugs

Pill-bugs, or sow-bugs, are tiny crustaceans related to the crayfish, not insects at all, although often thought to be by those who do not stop to count legs. They are found in or near damp, rotting vegetation. Particularly prevalent in the south, they do considerable damage to young plants. On trees they are often found under loose bark and in cavities, where the combination of darkness and dampness is ideal for their activities. Like termites, they seem actually to eat wood, sometimes even half-rotten boards, although they are not, of course, comparable to termites in destructiveness. They may be tricked into eating poison bait or may be sprayed with various burning and repelling solutions.

Red Spider

Red spider, one of the most common pests, is neither spider nor insect. Yet by any other name it would be as harmful, sometimes causing serious damage to trees and shrubs, both deciduous and evergreen. In hot dry weather it attacks evergreens with particular severity. Leaves become blotched and yellowish and gradually drop off. The mites may sometimes be controlled by washing with a strong

Plant lice on Elm leaves. Under favorable conditions their numbers rapidly become astronomical. Normally, however, their natural predators keep them at a level easily tolerated by the plant.

stream of water. When that proves ineffective, they may be sprayed with lime sulfur, rotenone, pyrethrum, tetraethyl pyrophosphate, malathion, or a proprietary miticide such as Aramite, Ovotran, or Dimite. Dusting with finely divided sulfur is also effective.

Beneficial Insects

Spiders (not insects but inhabitants of the same microcosmos), although frequently found on trees and other plants, neither chew their leaves nor suck out their juices. Strictly carnivorous, they use plants merely as a place to spin their webs or make their nests. When you see a leaf rolled up in a curious manner suggesting the work of an insect, you may find inside a spider instead, safe within a silken nest, resting, incubating eggs, or waiting for an incautious passerby. By eating harmful insects, either by pouncing on them directly, like the wolf spider, or by snaring them in their webs, spiders must definitely be entered on the positive side of the ledger. In a single state, perhaps even in a single county, many tons of insects are consumed each day by the noiseless, often invisible, and much-maligned spider. And he who kills an insect does more than kill a unit: he also kills the 1000 or so first-generation descendants which that insect would have produced, and the millions of third-generation descendants, and all the uncountable progeny that, unchecked, would build up in geometrical progression until, in a few weeks or a few months the total mass could not be made to fit in the limits of our solar system. Such is biological control, and such are the herculean labors of the unsung spider.

The harvestman, or daddy-long-legs, is often found on plants and under loose bark on trees. It does no known harm to vegetation; on the contrary, it apparently eats plant lice and mosquitoes and hence is definitely beneficial.

The praying mantis is one of our most interesting and ferocious predators, feeding on live hornets, spiders, grasshoppers, or anything else that comes within range. It is one of the gardener's most loyal friends. All who have seen Edwin Way Teal's classic photographic sequence of a praying mantis fighting—and killing—a black widow spider will remember it; those who have not seen it should look it up immediately.* In Japan the natives tie the mantis to their bedsteads by means of a long, silken leash to catch and frighten away mosquitoes.

Ladybird beetles, also called ladybugs and lady beetles, although celebrated in the nursery rhymes that everybody knows, deserve also to be celebrated in a major poem. At least as remarkable as Niagara Falls, Mount Everest, the Grand Canyon, or any other of the various natural wonders, they do more toward the control of harmful insects than all the insecticides man has yet compounded. Indefatigable workers, both as larvae and adults, they consume a staggering number of scales and aphids. The most notable example is the citrus industry in California, saved from total destruction by the importation of the modest little lady beetle from Australia with no desire for headlines but an insatiable appetite for scale. On nearly all trees where scale and plant lice are found, these beetles, in one form or another, are almost certain to occur as co-tenants.

Fumigation

Some insects are killed by fumigation rather than by spraying. Commonest fumigants are hydrocyanic acid gas (in the form of sodium, potassium, or calcium cyanide), nicotine (in the form of liquid, powder, or paper), naphthalene (used as a powder or a solid and evaporated slowly over an electric hot-plate or some similar heating device),

Grassroot Jungles.

and sulfur. Of these the first is the most dangerous to handle and also perhaps the most effective. A customary practice is to place a large, gas-impermeable bag over an entire tree (usually citrus, short trunked and globose), release hydrocyanic gas into its interior, and let stand a specified interval. Although for many years this procedure was nearly 100% effective, in the course of time certain scale insects appeared which were immune to the gas, and these became progenitors of resistant lines. When such immunities are discovered, the only thing to do is to initiate a different kind of treatment and to continue shifting about from one remedy to another as the occasion demands, matching our intelligence against insects' adaptability.

Materials used to fumigate the soil are calcium cyanide, paradichlorobenzene, carbon disulfide (sometimes spelled bisulfide), ethylene dichloride emulsion, tear gas (chloropicrin), naphthalene flakes, dichloroethyl ether, and methyl bromide. Of these the only one poisonous to the plants themselves is tear gas, which also happens to be the most complete and effective soil fumigant. Wherever it is used, the soil should not be used for planting until two or three weeks later. Each of these substances has a special use, a special manner of application, a special dilution, and a special time of use, according to the plague to be controlled and the locality in which it occurs. Manufacturer's directions should be closely followed; county agents can sometimes be of help. (The special use of fumigants in connection with insect holes in trunks and limbs is discussed in the section on borer control.)

Banding

Banding is a moderately effective control measure against certain climbing insects. It consists of placing a ring or band of sticky material around the tree trunk so that the insects are trapped in it when they attempt to climb up, just as flies are trapped on flypaper.

The banding substance is sold under various proprietary names in feed and seed stores, department stores, garden centers, etc. On trees with thick bark it may usually be applied without bad effects, but when smeared on young or thin-barked trees it has been observed to injure sometimes to kill them. These ill effects can be obviated by first wrapping the trunk with burlap, then applying the material onto this. The band should be 6 or 7 inches wide and should be renewed from time to time as the bodies of the entrapped insects accumulate.

Banding is effective only against those insects that climb up from the ground, and then not more than perhaps 50 or 60 percent. It is, of course, valueless against flying insects or those that float through the air suspended from silken strands or those that pass from the branches of one tree to another.

Trees banded with sticky substance to prevent the passage of insects. This measure has a limited effectiveness against some crawling insects, none at all against flying insects. The bank should be made sufficiently wide so as not to be too easily bridged. Application of the material to thin-barked trees is not recommended.

Whitewashing tree trunks is also an old-time remedy against climbing and boring insects. Formerly widely practiced in this country, it is now used only to a limited extent. In Mexico it is still almost universally applied to fruit trees and valuable ornamental specimens; every orange, lemon, grapefruit, and avocado tree is meticulously whitewashed from ground level up to four or five feet. Whitewash may be made by dissolving 10 pounds of lime, 2 pound of salt, and 4 pound of rice flour in 10 gallons of water. Popular belief credits it with the killing of insect eggs in bark crevices and the discouraging of climbers and borers. Many entomologists, however, believe it ineffective. Perhaps its most important function is the protecting of trunks from the heat of the sun. Experiments have shown that bark temperatures under a light-reflecting surface may be as much as 20 or 30 degrees lower than under a dark, light-absorbing surface. The trunks of young fruit trees in California, instead of being whitewashed, are protected by enclosure within a white cardboard or plastic loose-fitting container.

Attractants

Attractants—substances produced in some cases by flowers and in other cases by female insects to draw the males to them—have been effectively used as baits to lure insects into traps, where they can then be destroyed mechanically or chemically. Various kinds of lights are similarly used as lures.

Sterilization

Sterilization of large numbers of males and their subsequent release at mating time is another ingenious technique. When the sterile males mate with expectant females, these, deceived into believing their reproductive function performed, refuse the advances of any later-arriving fertile males; no offspring are produced, and the line begins to die out. This method has been phenomenally successful with some species, the screwworm (larva of Lucilia macellaria) being the best-known example.

Third-Generation Insecticides

Those who look with horror on the organic phosphate insecticides and the chlorinated hydrocarbons—which together constitute what has fittingly been called the second-generation insecticides—advocate no spraying at all or, if that is not possible, a return to the comparatively innocuous first-generation insecticides—to the pastes, the glues, the nicotines, the sulphurs, the hellebore, pyrethrum, and rotenone in common use thirty, forty, and fifty years ago.

A promising alternative, however, is the development of *third-generation insecticides:* natural substances produced by plants and/or insects themselves which may be turned against the insects in a kind of biological jiu-jitsu. A number of these materials have already been synthesized and hence are producible in any desired quantities.

Most promising of these substances are growth hormones that can be used to upset the insect's normal development. Some of them accelerate growth, aging the insect prematurely; some retard it, throwing the insect out of phase with the host plant's cycle of flowering and fruiting; some keep the insect permanently in larval form, preventing adulthood and reproduction. The great advantages of these natural substances are their harmlessness to other forms of life and the strong likelihood that no insect species could ever develop immunity against them. Perhaps one day not too far in the future insect control will become much simplified because of their use.

The search for new insecticides goes on at an ever-accelerating pace. Will the perfect insecticide ever be formulated? Is such a thing possible? It would have to be harmless to animals and humans, harmless to plants, applicable, by choice, either externally as a spray or internally (by injection) as a systemic, endowed with long-lasting residual action while on or in the plant and then after, say, a month or two obligingly breaking down into innocuous and recyclable constituents. What glory to the chemist who first elaborates such a compound: imagine a spray that would knock out the noxious insects while leaving the beneficial ones untouched! With the pace of technology being what it is, anything seems possible. We already have selective herbicides—chemicals that sprayed onto a lawn leave the grass unharmed but destroy the weeds. Twenty years ago this would have been dismissed as an impossible dream—like Major Hoople's self-shearing grass that would grow two inches high and then break off. And day by day these herbicides are increasingly refined in the direction of more and more specificity. Already there is one intended to destroy Bermuda grass while leaving adjacent and intertwined grasses unaffected. Admittedly not perfect, nevertheless it is a first step toward controlling that tenacious invader.

Dipel is a case in point—a step in the right direction. Although a biological rather than a chemical insecticide, it has the predicted insect-specificity. It is a dried preparation of bacterial spores—"6.75 billion viable spores to the gram," according to the manufacturer's guarantee. The *organism, Bacillus thuringiensis,* has been preselected because of its affinity for caterpillars, including tent caterpillars, elm spanworm, fall webworm, bagworms, and gypsy moth larvae. *No other kind of insect is affected.* When water is added to the powder and the solution is sprayed on shrub or tree infested with leaf-eating caterpillars, it functions as a stomach poison. The caterpillars are not harmed by the external contact but when they ingest the sprayed leaves, the spores germinate—perhaps half a million or so to each mouthful—and begin to develop at the expense of the host. Within a few hours the caterpillars stop eating, curl up, and like the bystander in Bret Harte's verse who received a chance blow in the pit of the stomach, "the subsequent proceedings interest them no more." Here is a truly selective insecticide of the best kind: plant-harmless and environmentally safe.

7

Spraying

Spraying is the most controversial part of tree care. Powerful arguments can be marshaled both for and against it. While pruning, bracing, wound dressing, soil improvement, and other activities are universally accepted procedures, with opinions differing only in regard to details of technique, spraying, both as a practice and as a concept, has almost as many opponents as it has champions.

Why this sharp division of opinion? Because spraying is a very complicated business, not a simple, straight-forward matter like sawing off a branch or inserting a lag screw hook. It is a complex equation in which many factors must be weighed against each other, and making a decision is far from being easy and automatic. To spray or not to spray is a choice which must be made in each case that arises, and the conscientious sprayer may be excused if, even with the spray gun in his hand and the nozzle pointing toward the target plant, he, like Hamlet, has his moments of irresoluteness.

Like land-clearing, lake-draining, river-damming, etc., spraying interferes with the balance of nature, which, even though not seeming so, is always in a state of delicate equilibrium. Although such interference is often desirable, its consequences are not always foreseeable. An activity that seems completely innocent may invite sudden calamity. The remedy may prove worse than the disease, may in fact aggravate the disease.

Among the factors to be evaluated before applying a spray are the following:

Temperature,
Humidity,
Wind,
Compatibility of spray ingredients,
Correct dilution of spray material,
Kind and stage of insect or fungus to be controlled,
Kind and condition of plant (annual, shrub, or tree being sprayed),
Date of last spraying and possibility of harmful residue,
    Proximity of other plants, buildings, automobiles, and the possibility of damage,
Potential danger to spray operators, residents, passers-by, pets, birds, squirrels, etc.

Proper evaluation of these factors, and others, demands broad knowledge and careful appraisal of the total situation in any given case. It is impossible to lay down a general rule to fit all sprays and all plants. Each type of material has its peculiar temperature, humidity, and compatibility requirements. Each species of plant has its idiosyncracies. Each instance of spraying is a unique event, and a decision taken today may run counter to one taken yesterday.

The issue is further complicated by the pollution problem. Today as never before the antisprayers are organized and highly vocal. Spraying programs formerly taken for granted are now subjected to minute scrutiny by conservationists and environmentalists—and are often vetoed.

The Case for Spraying

Supporters of spraying take the position that the coating of their shrubs and trees with an insect repellent or disease inhibitor is a natural defensive measure, that they do it for the same reason they build a fence around their plants to protect them from trampling and browsing by stray animals, that it is a private, not a public, affair.

They scoff at the notion that chemicals are "unnatural" and harmful, reminding us that water and air are chemicals, too; that plant and animal bodies—including our own—are nothing more than aggregations of chemical compounds temporarily fixed in more or less stable form; that every substance, every process, every reaction, that we have knowledge of, involves chemicals in one form or another. They point out that many of medicine's most valuable and sophisticated drugs are only synthetic copies of compounds originally manufactured in plants; that plants themselves wage chemical warfare both against the insects that seek to destroy them and internecinely, plant against plant, poisoning the soil around their roots to prevent the encroachment of competitors; and that if plants set us this example, why should we not follow their lead?

Broadening their argument, they point with pride to the elimination of malaria throughout the world as a consequence of the intensive DDT spraying campaign and to the very great reduction of other plagues as a direct result of the war waged against ticks, bedbugs, roaches, flies, and similar carriers.

They adduce the pre-eminence of the United States in agriculture, our capacity to grow thousands of tons of food, forage, and textile crops on land formerly ridden by disease and harried by insects.

What the world needs, they allege, is not less but more spraying. If back in the 1840's the Irish had the facilities for spraying that we have today, they could have avoided the potato blight that decimated their population. And very likely our native chestnut trees could have been saved if we had known as much then as we do now. Look at the Dutch elm disease: where adequate spraying programs have been carried out, this disease has been prevented. Islands of immunity have been established in the very center of the hardest hit regions. What more convincing proof do you want?

At a time when the world's population is exploding and the need for food is greater that ever before (they continue), it is madness to talk about discontinued spraying. Who is not familiar with the plagues of locusts mentioned so often in the Bible? And what old-timer doesn't recall the grass-hopper invasions of our own Midwest in the 1930's? Even leaving the insects out of the picture, the fungi, the bacteria, and the viruses do enough damage to keep thousands of spraying crews busy day and night. The fungi alone are responsible for the yearly loss of a quantity of food suffi-cient to feed *300 million people.* To suspend spraying, or even to curtail it substantially, would mean pronouncing a death sentence on uncountable millions throughout the world. Our chemical manufacturers, far from being the agents of destruction and pollution they are misrepresented to be, are spearheads of progress, bearers of hope, emis-saries of good, in a world increasingly menaced by the spector of the Four Horsemen of the Apocalypse.

Finally, and devastatingly, they cudgel the antisprayers with all the *argumenta ad hominem* used against the propo-nents of laissez-faire in all countries and in all ages. Not to spray, they tell us caustically, is to take the easy way out. It is to do nothing, to sit idly by while Rome burns; it is to regress, to deny the efficacy of study, effort and the capa-bility of technology to solve problems. It is, bluntly put, merely ignorance justifying indolence.

The Case Against Spraying

The opponents of spraying take issue with every single one of these contentions and then add a host of arguments of their own. It is not ignorance but a broader and deeper understanding of the problem that makes us oppose spray-ing, they begin. Neither is it indolence, for we work hard—harder than the sprayers—in the attempt to find other methods of combatting insects and diseases.

Spraying is self-defeating, they assert. Once begun, whether with a backyard shrub, a single tree, an orchard, or a forest, it has to be continued. Worse, it has to be intensified: every year larger quantities and stronger con-centrations must be used. New strains of insects and fungi appear that are resistant to the original spray material; this must be applied in ever-stronger doses or must be replaced by some other substance, which will then follow the same pattern. Furthermore, since spraying kills all insects, both those that happen to be injuring the plant and those that prey on these, a second generation of the destructive kinds, freed of their predators that reproduce more slowly, may soon build up in even greater numbers than before.

It is not true that spraying is a private, rather than a public affair, they hasten to add. Before the perfection of the organic phosphate insecticides and the chlorinated hydro-carbons (which came into general use during and after World War II), people used soaps and glues, sulphur dusts and nicotine compounds, hellebore, pyrethrum and roten-one, *Bordeaux* mixture and lime-sulphur, and spraying was, in effect, a simpler and much less dangerous pro-cedure, a kind of backyard, private-affair activity practiced by the comparative few.

But the invention of new, powerful chemicals and the greatly stepped up tempo of their use changed the whole picture. Spray materials are no longer applied with a small hand-sprayer, bush by bush: they are shot from the nozzles of giant machines the size of fire engines or tossed up to the top of the tallest tree by enormous blowers revolving at high speeds; they are ejected by trucks, tractors, trains, heli-copters, and airplanes.

The new materials do not obligingly break down and go away as did their predecessors nor are they limited in their effects. Originally believed toxic only to insects, they have turned out to be toxic to other life forms as well—including ourselves. Worse, they have turned out to be cumulative and long-lasting. Worse still, they have been carried by wind and water to virtually all parts of the globe and have found their way into the bodies of virtually all living organisms.

When DDT (continue the antisprayers, warming to the work) can be found in the livers of fish caught in the sea three thousand miles from land and in the eggs of birds that never leave their remote island outpost, how can spraying possibly be regarded as a private and not a public affair? Have not ecologists taught us to regard our planet as a kind of Noah's ark or a gigantic space-ship and ourselves as crew members and to understand that whatever happens to one member of the crew affects the welfare of all? Have not they taught us that all forms of life are interconnected, linked together in a web of complex pattern; that the streams, rivers, lakes, seas, belong to all; that the plants, animals, desert, brushland, forest, are the common heritage of man-kind; that pollution cannot be localized; that all borders are artificial; that one man's backyard in somebody else's front yard; that there is no such thing as an isolated action; that when a forest burns everybody suffers, and when a lake dries up, all thirst; that when a species becomes extinct, the world is impoverished; that we live, biologically speaking, in One World?

Spraying (continue its opponents), even assuming that it controls a given plague, often harms plants as much as the plague itself would have done. Sometimes it burns and discolors the leaves or produces spots and shot-holes in them; sometimes it results in canker, die-back, blight, or complete defoliation; sometimes it kills outright. Many a misguided homeowner, alarmed by his plants' declining appearance, has redoubled his spraying efforts, not realizing that *it is the spray itself* which is producing the symptoms of disease. Thousands of shrubs and trees have suffered severe burning as a result of unskillful applications of arsenicals, kerosene, and the various oil preparations.

Bordeaux mixture, lime-sulphur, and many of the newer chemicals spoil the appearance or degrade the flavor of the fruits and vegetables they are supposed to protect. Like drugs administered to people, spray materials frequently accomplish their objective only at the expense of undesirable side-effects. MH-30 (maleic hydrazide), so much in demand a few years ago by tobacco growers for preventing the growth of suckers and increasing yield, has been discarded by many because it renders the leaf deficient in flavor. Even antibiotics, useful in so many ways, can be harmful, damaging leaves and cracking and discoloring fruits, when applied in improper concentrations or when not perfectly matched to the plant. Even plain water, sprayed or sprinkled onto a plant in full sun, may cause burning of the foliage. All this by way of showing that spraying is by no means the panacea it is often touted to be.

Such are the effects on plants. The effects on human beings are equally serious (continue the spraying opponents). Who can say how many strange illnesses and premature deaths are not due to contamination by spray materials? We know that many toxic materials ostensibly intended "for insects only" kill birds and small animals as well. Why should we consider ourselves immune? In case after case, a new chemical is put on the market with the assurance of perfect safety, only to be withdrawn five, ten, fifteen, or twenty years later when its full potentiality has come to light. DDT, now prohibited throughout most of the nation, is the best-known example; *aldrin, dieldrin, chlordane,* and *heptachlor* have also been banned.

Powerful and untried chemicals should be considered guilty until proven innocent—and to obtain this proof many years of careful experimentation are usually needed. Poisons have always been dangerous; they are doubly so today. Why? First because with many of the new poisons the effect is delayed, insidious, and cumulative. Consider DDT, slowly accumulating in the fatty tissues of the body without one's knowledge, then, when weight is lost and tissues are metabolized, making its presence known by serious illness or death. Second, because in spite of the publicity given their potential dangerousness by *Silent Spring* and a host of similar books, in spite of warnings by health authorities, in spite of the manufacturer's own explicit directions, many

users of spray materials are unbelievably negligent, failing to take even the most rudimentary precautions. At a time when people are increasingly distracted, hurried, and anxiety-ridden, it is totally unrealistic to assume that they will use chemicals wisely and carefully.

In the early days of spraying, arsenicals poisoned operators and by-standers with predictable regularity. To the hazards of these have been added the horrors of DDT, HEPT, TEPP, parathion, aldrin, dieldrin, rothane, lindane, chlordane, methoxychlor, and many others, which, when not killing or disabling directly, often eventuate in cancer or other imperfectly understood maladies. And most of these poisons, mind you, *are actually used on food crops!*

As if all this were not enough, the chemical industry has now come up with *systemic poisons*—substances which when sprayed on or injected into a plant will be translocated internally to all parts, providing present and future protection (from a few days to a few weeks). There are now on the market systemic insecticides (*Metasystox* being the best known) and systemic fungicides (*Benomyl).* The plant—animal, shrub, or tree — is poisoned from the inside! Triumph or tragedy? For John Muir, who learned to eat the leaves of .50 or so kinds of trees, it would be a tragedy. For Cesare Borgia and contemporaries who tried repeatedly (but tried in vain) to sprinkle poison around the base of fruit trees so that it might be taken up by the fruits which could be then opportunely presented to their enemies, it would be a triumph.

Spraying (warn the antisprayers, their eyes shooting fire), has become a wide-spread vice. Like smoking and drinking, it is promoted by those who stand to gain by it as something desirable, necessary, and socially acceptable. Hypnotic advertising makes sprayers feel that each time they poison an insect or squirt spray on a blighted leaf they are doing their bit for their country and for the world at large. Manufacturers, distributors, vendors, all nourish the myth of imminent destruction by hordes of hungry insects—if their product is not promptly and consistently used. Pest control operators—many of them unscrupulous enough to crawl under a house with a rotten board and a vial of termites concealed about their person, later to be exhibited as proof of infestation—are everywhere growing rich by battening on the public's artificially induced fears. Exposed to an unceasing barrage of propaganda—in newspapers, in magazines, on the radio, on television, on billboards—few consumers fail to be convinced. After years of this treatment, people come to look upon all insects as their hereditary enemies, and the reach for the spray-can or the dust-gun becomes as automatic a response as the reach for the cigarette pack. In short, spraying has become big business, running up annual totals of hundreds of millions of dollars, and those who profit from it, oblivious to ethics and regardless of long-term consequences, exert every effort to encourage and intensify its practice.

Biological control, aver the antisprayers, is far and away preferable to any form of chemical control. Biological control is nature's own method. It puts the shark in the sea, the hawk in the air, the wolf in the forest and the lion on the plains, everywhere and always pitting the carnivore against the herbivore, the predator against the herd. In the world of insects, biological control gives us the praying mantis, the ladybird beetle, the aphid lion, the dragonfly, the syrphid flies, the ground beetles, the ichneumon, braconid, and chalcid wasps, and many others. These are the carnivores of the insect world that prey on or parasitize the insect herbivores, keeping their numbers in check.

Too few of us realize that although a small minority of insects are harmful to our interests, many are helpful and many are simply neutral. Indiscriminate spraying that fails to take into account the equilibrium existing among them does more harm than good. How did the world wag on before spraying was invented? By biological control which always asserts itself, sooner or later. When the normal equilibrium is upset, as it sometimes is for any of several reasons, and the (from-our-standpoint) harmful insects break out in epidemic numbers, the predators are never very far behind. In a month or so, or sometimes a season or so, the pursuing catch up with the pursued, and normal equilibrium is re-established.

What saved the citrus industry in California, threatened with total destruction by the cottony scale? Not spraying, but the importation from Australia of 500 or so of a species of ladybird beetle. What saved the orange groves of Mexico back in the early 1950's, menaced with the infamous black fly? Again not spraying—although an intensive campaign was mounted and the trees and the soil were drenched with uncountable gallons—but the cultivation and propagation of a tiny parasitic wasp. What saved the Mormons from starvation when their first hard-won crops in the Utah desert were faced with total destruction by the Rocky Mountain crickets? Not spraying, for no spray was available and none could have acted that fast and that efficiently, but suddenly appearing flocks of seagulls which fell on the crickets like the wolf on the fold. Everywhere in nature a biological equilibrium exists, an equilibrium that misguided spraying programs more often upset than reinforce.

What conclusions are we to come to after so much conflicting testimony?

First, it seems clear that spraying has proved its usefulness many times over—in ogy, in agriculture, and in arboriculture; and that, properly understood and properly practiced, it is an integral part of tree care.

Second, it seems equally clear—painfully clear—that spraying has been and continues to be grossly abused; that enormous quantities of deleterious chemicals have accumulated in our soil, air, and water; that biological control, wherever possible, is always preferable to chemical control; that the warnings of environmentalists must be heeded.

Like fire, firearms, automobiles, atomic energy, or any one of a thousand other things, spraying has vast potentialities for evil as well as vast potentialities for good. The problem is whether we, its inventors and users, are sane enough to make proper use of it.

Main Uses

In tree care, spraying is resorted to for the following purposes:

1. The attempt to control injurious insects.
2. The attempt to control bacteria, fungi, and viruses.
3. The attempt to control extraneous growths, such as lichen, Spanish moss, ball moss, and mistletoe.
4. The attempt to inhibit or stimulate growth of the entire plant or some of its parts.

Point (1) is discussed further in the chapter *Insects.*

Point (2) is elaborated in the chapter *Diseases.*

Point (3) and (4) are discussed below.

Point (3) Some trees, particularly in our southern states, become so heavily covered with lichen, Spanish moss, or ball moss as to need spraying.

A lichen (symbiotic combination of alga and fungus), is not a parasite; it merely clings to the tree, as it clings to a rock, deriving its nourishment independently through the photosynthetic power of the constituent alga. It can, however, harm the tree in the rare cases where it occurs so abundantly as to interfere with its lenticels (breathing pores). (Many oaks in a state of declining vigor are heavily scaled with lichen.) It can be killed by spraying with a lye solution (3 parts of lye to 100 parts of water) when the tree has shed its leaves, or, in the case of evergreen oaks, just before the buds open in the spring. Where spraying is not feasible, the limbs can be cleaned by scraping with a wire brush.

Spanish moss and ball moss (or "bunch moss", as it is sometimes called) are also epiphytes, not parasites, but they too may do harm where they occur overabundantly. The same lye solution spray or sometimes an arsenate of lead spray is effective, burning them to death, although the withered remains hang on the tree for a year or so afterwards. (These interesting plants are discussed more fully in Chapter 11, *Environmental Damage and Miscellaneous Troubles.*)

Point (4) Hormones are chemical substances that accelerate or retard certain aspects of plant growth. One of the most commonly known hormones, practical and spectacular in its results, is the weed-killer, 2,4-D. Sprayed directly onto the plant, this material kills by causing such an overstimulation of growth that food cannot be absorbed rapidly enough to accommodate the new demands. Since its introduction, other herbicides have been elaborated, all in the direction of increasing specificity.

Other hormones of great interest and extreme practical importance are those that assist in the formation of new roots on a cutting or a transplant (chiefly indolebutyric acid), those that accelerate fruit production without the necessity of pollination, those that restrict the formation of fruit (much used in California for spraying olive trees and mulberries when they are lawn or street specimens), and those that enable a tree to retain its fruit until maturation. Most of these are applied by spraying.

As important as choosing the correct spray material is the timeliness of its application. Fungal and bacterial diseases are far more easily prevented than cured. This means that the spray material must be applied *before* the spores have an opportunity to penetrate the leaves. Usually, as in anthracnose prevention, application is made just as the new leaves begin to appear. If subsequent rains wash off the material, the spraying should be repeated.

Spraying for insect control is equally difficult. Sometimes there is an interval of only two or three days when the target insect is active. If the spraying is not done at that time, it is often wasted. Spraying before is like firing ahead of the duck; spraying later is like firing behind him. Bagworms are a good example. They must be sprayed when actually eating the leaves. Spray applied before they appear deteriorates and loses its effect; also unprotected new growth may appear. Spray applied when they have finished feeding and are retiring into their cocoons affects them no more than rain affects us inside our house. Control of the plum curculio is another example. Once the egg is inside the developing fruit, all subsequent spraying is useless.

It was precisely to overcome this difficulty that the organic phosphate insecticides and the chlorinated hydrocarbons, most of which have long-lasting residual effects, were developed. DDT, originally believed to be the insecticide to end all insecticides (and all insects) could in some cases retain its lethal qualities weeks or months after application. But DDT has run into so much trouble that most states have banned its use. Strains of insects appeared which were unaffected by it. Plants were sometimes damaged by it. Birds and other small organisms (and some not so small) were killed or severely harmed by it. The same extraordinary residual effect which was supposed to make it the most favored of insecticides ended up making it the most feared. Since the same thing was and is true of other of the new potent insecticides to lesser or greater degree, it is evident that the factor of timeliness has not been eliminated, as was hoped, but remains as one of the chief problems of spraying.

The newest attempt to overcome the problem is the invention of systemics, mentioned above and discussed more fully in Chapter 6, INSECTS. Whether the systemics will follow the pattern of the organic phosphates and the chlorinated hydrocarbons—first acclaimed with rejoicing, then banned in horror—remains to be seen.

Technique of Spraying

The basic idea in spraying is to cover all parts of the tree with a protective film that either (1) kills insects and fungi that may be present or (2) repels those that may come later or (3) performs both functions. "All parts of the tree" means the trunk, the branches, the twigs, both upper and lower surfaces of the leaves, the flowers and fruit, if any; and sometimes even the ground itself.

While thoroughness is essential to successful spraying, this does not mean that the tree must be saturated until the spray runs off. Saturation merely wastes spray material without increasing effectiveness. What is needed is to wet all parts uniformly and thoroughly and then to stop.

Regardless of the thoroughness of coverage, the spray material sometimes runs off as fast as put on, particularly on smooth, waxy foliage. Hence "spreaders" or "stickers" are added to the solution to break up surface tension and make the material cling to the leaves.

Some of the most-used spreaders and stickers are soap flakes (or liquid soap), fish oil, calcium caseinate, resin, glue, common flour, and billboard paste. Glue, at the rate of 1 ounce to 100 gallons of water, is an excellent sticker. Used a little stronger, it actually sticks down some of the smaller pests, such as red spider, and kills them by immobilizing them, as fly-paper kills flies. Common flour, used at the rate of 2 to 4 pounds per 100 gallons of water (2 or 3 tablespoons per gallon), is perhaps the safest of the spreaders, producing no chemical reaction with any of the spray ingredients. Oil emulsions, while good spreaders, may in the growing season cause burning and destruction of bloom on ornamentals.

While it is good to know how sprays are prepared and mixed, most people today buy the product ready-made. Virtually all the proprietary brands come already mixed with the necessary spreaders and stickers. Some present-day substances bear this reassuring clause on the label: "With activators, spreaders, stickers, penetrants, and in-plant compatible vegetable oils." A number of them are also "fortified with trace elements—iron, zinc, and manganese—for greener leaves and more vigorous fruits and blossoms".

If you use a hand-sprayer, you may obtain thorough coverage by working around and around the plant, moving the nozzle from side to side and up and down in such a manner that both upper and lower leaf surfaces will be covered. By climbing on a stepladder you will be able to reach all parts of small trees not exceeding 12 or 15 feet in height.

Only power sprayers are adequate for large trees. Power-spraying should be done on days when there is no or little wind. Some operators wait for the first stirrings of a

The big advantage of the hydraulic spray rig is that although stationed in the street (or any other fixed point) it can send through its long hoses with undiminished pressure a stream adequate to cover all parts of large trees hundreds of feet distant.

breeze, then spray *against* it, claiming that in this way the foliage is more effectively wetted on both sides and from all angles. Very windy days are always to be avoided, since the spray material gets completely out of hand and may be carried three or four blocks from the site.

If you use a power-sprayer or hire one used in an urban area, you must be prepared for complications. Like loud noises, encroaching spray material may be considered a disturbance of the peace and a violation of the rights of others. Neighbors may allege, truthfully or untruthfully, that they are allergic to the materials, that it makes them ill, or their children, their guests, or their pets ill, that it contaminates the water in their swimming pool, that it poisons their food, ruins their party, damages their shrubbery, stains their house, or spots their automobiles.

To such complaints there is of course no answer, for legally they may be sustained. Even before the pollution crisis, spraying was a delicate matter; now it is an explosive one. Before doing any kind of tall-tree spraying, the proper thing to do is to get permission from the neighbors and to ask them to close their windows and move their cars. Tender plants likely to be affected can be covered with canvas or a plastic sheet. If the tree to be sprayed is in a park or near a busy thoroughfare, sometimes a small area around it can be roped off to exclude pedestrians.

Mechanisms

All power sprayer operators should wear a mask, for repeated inhalations of toxic materials can have serious consequences. Even contact with the skin should be avoided. The hands should be protected with rubber gloves, and hands, arms, and face carefully washed with soap and water after each exposure. Spray that accumulates on a street or sidewalk should be washed off as soon as possible to prevent possible damage to children or pets playing in it.

Sprayers work on the principle of hydraulic pressure: the same principle that makes a jack raise a car, brake shoes close against the brake drum, and blood spurt from a wound.

In all sprayers, air pressure is built up in a tank containing liquid. By mechanical means the air is compressed; the air pushes against the liquid, and the liquid is forced out through a tiny orifice which may be opened or closed at will. The greater the pressure the more forceful the flow from the orifice. The orifice (nozzle) is so made that it may adjust from a solid stream to a fine mist. All power sprayers have an agitator to keep the solution thoroughly mixed. In hand-operated sprayers the whole tank is agitated manually.

Small three-gallon tanks, pumped manually, are made to be carried about on the back or slung over the shoulder.

Although designed principally for small plants and shrubs, they can be used on trees up to 10 or 12 feet.

Wheelbarrow sprayers, also pumped manually, have a larger tank capacity and build up somewhat greater pressure. For trees, however, their limits are approximately the same.

New types of small sprayers continue to appear—everything from hand atomizers of quart capacity in various styles to the "trombone sprayer", claimed by its manufacturers to be adequate for trees up to 25 feet. There is even an electrically operated sprayer, with or without cord.

For large trees only large power sprayers are adequate. Some of these are mounted permanently on a special truck and equipped with hoses and nozzles almost as formidable as those of the fire department. They can throw a solid stream 80 feet into the air that breaks up into a fine mist and floats over all parts of the tree. With a tank capacity of several hundred gallons and hoses 200 feet or so long, a rig

With the hydraulic rig stationed in the street the spray operator can move about freely over a large area, directing and controlling the powerful stream at all times and reducing his own exposure to a minimum.

of this type can supply spray enough to cover all the trees around a residence while remaining parked in one place in the street.

The rival to the hydraulic sprayer is the mist blower. In these machines the spray materials are let into a powerful stream of air through nozzles that break up the material into the size of fog particles. Agitation of the topmost leaves of the tree by the air stream is a measure of the effectiveness of the operation. The finely dispersed spray particles filter down on the foliage like mist. The big advantage of the blower is that it is able to use the spray materials in more concentrated form, economizing on water and consequently on weight, time, and labor. Its big disadvantage is that it must be positioned directly under or to one side of each target tree, unable, of course, to send the mist through hoses. It is this limited maneuverability that prevents it from supplanting the hydraulic rig entirely.

Partly offsetting the limited maneuverability of big blowers is the recent introduction of knapsack blowers. Weighing 30 to 40 pounds, gasoline-powered with a 3 H.P. motor, and having a tank capacity of 2 to 3 gallons, these devices are very effective for fogging shrubbery, hedges, and small or medium-size trees. Some of them even have twin tanks: one for liquids and one for dusts.

Many gardeners prefer dusting to spraying. Dusters range in size from quart atomizers to the knapsack blowers. On the smaller kinds, the dust is ejected by manually moving a plunger back and forth or by turning a crank. Dusting is more suited to small plants, hedges, and shrubbery than to trees, and should be done when there is no wind. The material most commonly applied as a dust is sulphur.

When, instead of a backyard garden or three or four isolated trees, the target is several hundred acres of cropland or part of a forest, no device can equal the airplane in rapidity and economy of application, whether of spray or of dust. Crop dusting by airplane has become standard practice in many parts of the world, and skilled pilots travel about from region to region, selling their services like Swiss mercenaries of old. Both spraying and dusting by air have been successfully used to combat such forest pests as the gypsy moth, the hemlock looper, the catalpa sphinx, and the spruce budworm. The application of herbicides by low-flying airplanes in Vietnam and the consequent defoliation and death of hundreds of square miles of trees is, technologically speaking, one of the outstanding achievements of that ill-starred war. Ecologically speaking, it is memorable as a Horrible Example.

Parting Advice

Spray as little as you can. Do not spray because it is the fashion or because your neighbors do or because you saw it done on television or because some passing quack has knocked at your door and tried to convince you that it should be done. Whether you spray yourself or hire it done, be sure the reason is a sound one and be sure there are no alternative methods of control.

If you must spray, try to use materials that leave no dangerous residues. Ask for biodegradables and non-pollutants, and even if you cannot get them, make your wishes known. When enough people start insisting on these substances, they will be manufactured, and the others will begin to disappear. Remember, it is *your* environment and your children's environment that is being contaminated.

Do not deal with itinerants. Deal only with a reputable arborist who is able and willing to take responsibility for his work. If in doubt, consult with your county agent or your state experiment station. If there is an ecology center or a conservation club or a bird-watchers group near you, check with the people there; a different perspective is always valuable.

8

Climbing

Are climbers, like poets, born rather than made? It often seems so, for while some men have a natural aptitude for climbing, others never lose their awkwardness, their slowness, or their tendency to giddiness. Or are we all born with the ability, losing it as we grow up because we fail to exercise it?

Whatever the explanation, tree-climbing is today one of the lost arts. A tree-climbing adult is a rarity; out of a hundred men an employer solicits from an agency, he may count himself lucky if he finds one who can climb.

This state of affairs is unfortunate, for tree-climbing can do wonders for us, both physically and psychologically. It is recreation in the purest form—every bit as exciting, as stimulating, and as rewarding as mountain-climbing, perhaps more so. Compressed into minutes are the sensations that mountain climbing yields only after hours of painful toil. All the exhilaration and the danger and the sense of immediacy are there; all the wonderful changes of perspective, all the sense of triumph. As a bonus, you do not have to drive 300 miles or so to get to your base of operations nor spend weary days preparing your gear. Trees are everywhere, and tree-climbing is a glorious, unsung sport.

To be a good climber you must be strong (particularly in the arms and shoulders), agile, sure-footed, and fearless; you must have steady nerves, the equilibrium of a tightrope walker, and an intuitive and unfailing judgment of space and distance. You must have a quick eye for seeing and a sure hand for grasping, must be unaffected by heights, must be able to move about quickly and nimbly from place to place, from one side of a tree to the other, from top to bottom and bottom to top.

You can, of course, climb just for climbing's sake: this is the pure approach. Or you can climb the tree in order to work on it: this is the utilitarian approach. Oddly, there are people who like to climb and who also like to work: for these happy few the tree offers a degree of fulfillment seldom attained in this disjointed world.

When a boy, I spent most of my spare time climbing trees; no pastime intrigued me more. Today I make my living climbing, and I love my work. Trees have become the primary fact in my life, and although I might write a thousand books in praise of them, I should never do them justice. Thoreau remarked that whatever one is obliged to do for a living, one comes to hate. This is not true in my case. For me climbing trees is work in the economic sense only; psychologically it is pure pleasure—as much now as the day I began it.

I envy the natural climbers; the squirrels, the cats, the bears, the monkeys, and all others of the happy arboreal tribe. Only birds have greater freedom and more fun. Not being able to fly, I have contented myself with climbing, and not having a tail, I have learned to use a rope. Not that a good climber needs a rope: he no more needs it than a good walker needs a crutch. In a sense a rope takes away part of the thrill, by taking away most of the danger; in another sense it adds to the thrill by enabling you to swing in great arcs from limb to limb or to drop vertically 100 feet or so and then to stop abruptly with your feet just brushing the ground.

If you decide to climb just for the fun of it, fine. But if you decide to work at the same time, you may be surprised to find your enjoyment intensified. Remember, though, that working in a tree is much more exhausting than working on the ground. Almost constantly in a strained position, reaching upward or far to one side to achieve proper flush-cutting of branches that emerge from parent limbs at every conceivable angle, hanging in mid-air from a rope, carrying an armamentarium of tools suspended from your waist, unable to relax for more than a few fugitive moments snatched here and there, you are an extraordinary physical specimen if you can keep up a good pace for eight hours at a stretch. Few men can work at peak efficiency for eight hours even when on the ground freely moving about; how much harder to do so when clambering up and down a tall tree! Difficulties, danger, and fatigue increase in direct proportion to height. While small trees are like play and medium-sized ones something in the nature of an appetizer, it is the really tall trees (over 75 feet) that bring the climber alive. The taller they are the more he yearns to climb them, for the same reason that the most inaccessible mountain peaks call most strongly to the mountaineer. Yet fatigue and danger are the inseparable companions of challenge and exhilaration, and the prudent worker soon learns that three or four hours a day are enough in the really big ones. If you are still climbing at 50 or 60 years of age, as some exceptional individuals are doing, it is because you learned long ago that he who climbs and runs away may live to climb another day.

The climber must be skilled in three things: climbing in the tree without any mechanical aids, climbing with ladders, and climbing with ropes. Different kinds of trees demand different techniques. The Southern Live Oak (*Quercus virginiana*), for example, is probably the world's easiest tree to climb in: it has a low crotch, many branches disposed with great regularity like ready-made handles, and long, horizontally spreading limbs of great strength on which one can walk about as surely and safely as on a ten-inch plank. In such trees a ladder is rarely needed, and ropes are more in the way than helpful.

On the other hand there are some trees, such as American elms and pecans, whose habit of sending out long, slender limbs at 45 or so from the trunk and bare of lateral branches along most of their length, makes them both difficult and dangerous to climb in. Such trees are best worked by a combination of ladders and ropes.

Ladders

The longest practical ladder is 40-feet, made in two sections with a necessary overlap of 4 or 5 feet so that the total utilizable length is only about 35 feet. For most trees, however, this length is sufficient, particularly for working the long, out-hanging, lower limbs so difficult to reach from the inside of the tree. All extension ladders should be equipped with a pulley and a stout rope to assist in raising and lowering the upper section. When the ladder is in place, it should be tied to the limb it is resting on and also tied at the bottom, particularly if it is standing on concrete. Special safety shoes are now manufactured for fitting on the bottom of the ladder uprights; these are usually provided with two attachments, one a corrugated rubber surface for holding on concrete, the other sharp points for digging into soil.

You should have at your disposal a number of ladders of different lengths: short ones of 8, 10, 12 and 15 feet and the longer ones of 20 feet which may be joined together to form the extension ladders. Short ladders are useful in a number of places where long ladders will not fit; they may even be hoisted up into the tree to help scale difficult spans and may be placed horizontally from limb to limb to serve as a catwalk or as a seat for reaching an inaccessible cavity. The ladder used should be securely lashed to the tree and may be made more comfortable by a plank laid along its length. With a little ingenuity, you can discover many uses for small light ladders up in the tree.

Special light-weight aluminum ladders flared at the lower end and tapered to a point and equipped with a hook at the upper end are in use by outdoor billboard advertising servicemen; these come in various lengths and may be adapted to use in certain trees.

The greatest elaboration of the straight ladder is the fire-truck ladder, quickly and safely extensible to unheard-of lengths, and more recently the shorter extension ladders with a revolving base mounted on a truck and now widely used in cities for servicing street lights, hanging Christmas decorations, etc. More and more similar types of motorized extension ladders are coming into use by tree companies, being particularly useful for working park trees or those along city streets. The disadvantage of a ladder mounted on a truck is that there are a number of places where the truck cannot be taken; many residential trees—perhaps the majority—grow in side yards or back patios where mechanized equipment cannot enter.

Stepladders are useful for working in small trees or on the lower branches of large trees. The stepladder has the advantage of permitting access to limbs too slender or too weak to support the weight of straight ladder and worker. It has the disadvantage of being unstable in lengths over 6 or 7 feet, especially when used on soft or uneven ground.

Scaffolds

The idea of the stepladder with its convenience and mobility has inspired inventors to evolve from it various kinds of scaffolds and movable platforms. In certain cases where there are many large trees close together on reasonably level terrain, a rigid scaffold made of metal tubing and mounted on castors may be found useful. This may be rolled about from tree to tree, and from its top level the long outspreading limbs so difficult to climb on and too high for ladders may be easily worked. In most cases, however, the rigid scaffold is not practicable; too much time is consumed in assembling, disassembling, and moving it. To get around this drawback various kinds of adjustable scaffolds have been invented, some mounted on wheels; some, better still, on truck beds, the best of which works on the principle of the scissors jack, folding upwards or downwards by hydraulic action and thus giving instant access to all parts of a tree up to its maximum height (usually not over 30 feet).

The most remarkable elaboration of the adjustable scaffold idea is the *Industrial Monkey* or *Cherry Picker* which consists of a long mast-shaped boom with a small platform at the top enclosed by a railing where the worker stands. Mounted on a truck, the boom is raised and lowered hydraulically, telescoping back on itself like the piston of a hydraulic jack; moreover, it may be swung about in a complete circle whose radius is the boom extended at any given length. Both the swinging and the up and down movements of the boom are controllable by the worker on his platform and/or by the driver of the truck. This apparatus is a godsend for reaching hard-to-get-to places and is particularly useful in the removal of dead trees which are often too dangerous to climb in. From his platform on the

Experienced climbers develop astonishing skill. Using the ladder only to get into the superstructure or to work some of the lower horizontal branches, they move about among the top branches with squirrel-like agility. The unfit are quickly eliminated.

end of the boom, the worker may cut a tree down piece by piece in the most difficult situation with perfect safety for himself. The advantages of such a machine are at once apparent. The disadvantages are:

1. Its cost, prohibitive to all except the largest companies,
2. Its comparative rarity and hence the high cost and difficulty of repairs,
3. The fact that its use is limited to places where the truck can be driven, thus excluding many trees on fine lawns.

Its main applications are for line clearing and the care of city street trees.

Ropes

While ladders and scaffolds and movable booms are excellent aids for the climber, they are at best only accessories. The one indispensable piece of climbing equipment, in all except small trees, is the rope. With the rope, you can go anywhere in any tree, quickly and safely, without mechanical aids of any kind and without assistance from anyone on the ground. You hang from the rope as a spider hangs from its thread; and just as spider cannot be knocked off a perch to the ground, always saving itself by the omnipresent thread, so the tree worker correctly tied cannot be knocked to the ground. You may be knocked loose from your perch, but you will remain hanging in the air, unless the rope breaks or unless the whole tree falls over. The advantages of the climbing rope are many:

1. You are always safe,
2. You can work faster and better, all or part of your weight being sustained by the rope and both your hands being free,
3. You can move about faster in the tree, dropping from one level to the other without having to go to the ground to move a ladder,
4. You can use the trailing end of the rope to pull up tools as needed,
5. No expensive investment is involved, the cost of the rope being minimal,
6. No extra man is necessary on the ground to move truck or ladder.

The most common kind of climbing rope is 1/2″ manila in lengths of 80 to 100 feet. To use it the worker first climbs to the highest part of the tree, passes one end of the rope through a sound, strong crotch, fastens that same end about his body, and then ties it back around the line dangling from the crotch to the ground ("ground line"). Thus he is suspended by a rope encircling his waist and passing over a point above, and may move up or down the rope freely by paying out or taking up slack. The special kind of knot that makes such movement possible is called the "taut-line hitch" or the "Monkey knot" or the "traveling knot." It is formed in such a manner that when pull (the worker's weight) is exerted on it, it will not slip, but when under no strain it can be slipped forwards or backwards with ease.

Tied thus, you may hang freely in the air working with both hands, or you may stand or sit on a limb with the rope partly supporting you. Beginning at the top of the tree, you work gradually downward, always keeping the safety rope tight, or almost tight, giving you just enough slack to be able to work with freedom. As you move about in the tree, you run the taut-line hitch up or down, so that the rope is always ready to catch you up short in case you should fall, just as if a man were standing on the ground holding the free end of the rope, paying out line as you descend and taking up the slack as you climb upwards.

The taut-line hitch is a remarkable discovery; for the tree climber it is the most useful knot in the book. (It also can be used in steeple-jacking, for lowering oneself over cliffs, for descending into mines, etc.) It is tied by passing the leading end around the ground line in a clockwise direction to form two complete tight loops, the second below the first; then by forming two more clockwise loops also around the ground line but at a point above the first two, with the difference that each time the leading end is brought around the ground line to complete these loops, it must pass under the bight (now forming the connection between the two sets of loops). Hence the completed knot consists of four tight loops side by side around the ground line (which runs through all of them like a stick through four doughnuts). Counting from the top downward the loops of the correct hitch are tied in this order: 3, 4, 1, 2; that is, the top loop was the third to be tied, the second from the top was the last to be tied, etc. From the completed knot, the leading end should remain sticking out 10 inches or so and should have a figure 8 knot tied at its end to prevent it from accidentally slipping through the loops of the taut-line hitch, should that ever become loose. This free end is also sometimes useful for carrying about a paint bucket, a saw, or some other tool.

The most dangerous moment in using the rope is at the beginning: the first ascent of the tree, when you must carry the rope up to the top to crotch it. In this climb, since you are not tied on, you must be doubly careful. You may use the ladder to get into the main branches, but from there on you must climb the tree. In so doing you should try to stay as close to the trunk as possible. In trees with a straight, slender bole and many branches like pines or cottonwoods, the climbing is simple, but in trees of divided bole or of bole so huge that it cannot be embraced, the climb up is difficult. You can help yourself by throwing the rope over limbs 8 or 10 feet above your head, pulling yourself up to that point, throwing the rope again, and so on successively. Once the rope is crotched at the top, your difficulties are over, and your descent is as gentle as the fall of snow.

Ascending by the rope elevator. The other end of the rope (in this case two ropes have been used for extra safety) is tied to a truck which is carefully pulling the man up. This is unorthodox but it's fun. When the climber gets to a working station, he will tie the loose end of the rope (visible just beneath his feet) across the ground-line by means of the taut-line hitch. Thus protected from falling, he will be able to let himself down or pull himself up at will. Both hands will be free for working at all times.

In very large trees of divided bole, you may find it necessary to re-crotch the rope several times for greater convenience in working. To do this, get as near as possible to the new crotch before untying your safety rope and seat yourself in a safe place or better still tie yourself to a limb with another, shorter rope that can be carried about for that purpose. Then untie the safety rope, pull it out of the original crotch, and pass it through the new crotch. In very large trees, you may prefer to take up two climbing ropes instead of one. In this way you not only double your margin of safety but also facilitate your climb up by remaining suspended from one rope while relocating the other. The use of two ropes also comes in handy when you find yourself in an awkward position where you must remain for several hours, as in repairing a cavity; by use of both ropes, each running diagonally upward on either side, you can stabilize your position.

At the end of the day the safety rope should be pulled out of the tree, coiled up, and put away out of reach of moisture, oil and grease, and cutting edges. Even if the work is not finished when quitting time comes and you wish to leave the rope in position to facilitate re-climbing, prudence counsels that it is better not left in the tree overnight. Pranksters may cut it half way through, children may injure themselves trying to climb up it; rain, fog, or mist may wet it, and of course instead of returning the following day as planned, you may be delayed indefinitely.

You may fasten the rope to your body in any of several ways. One way is by tying a large double bowline at a point about 5 feet from the end, and slipping into it, one loop passing around the waist and the other around the buttocks. Although many tree workers use this simple tie, it is objectionable because the rope tends to cut into the flesh, particularly if you are forced to remain suspended in the air for any length of time.

A far more comfortable rig and a safer one is a type of leather harness specially manufactured for the purpose. This harness fits about the waist and around each thigh with strong, broad straps; at the front in the center it has a large metal ring to which the rope is tied (at a point about 2-1/2 feet from its end, leaving enough line to form the taut-line hitch with its trailing tail). The harness should be equipped with several smaller rings around the waist strap on which tools can be hung or tied. There are several variations of the harness, one of which is the "bos'n's chair" a short board lodged in a loop of rope to form a seat while working long in one postion.

In large trees the harness and the safety rope should never be removed, except for re-crotching, until you return to the ground. The United States Park Service Department has a rule that any man untying his safety rope before touching the ground in any tree is subject to fine, or in aggravated cases, to dismissal. Although it may be a demonstration of skill and courage to work in a large tree without a safety rope, it is neither sensible nor efficient to do so. By use of the rope the worker accomplishes more and tires himself less, feels safer and is safer.

Climbing Spurs

In some of the eastern states, the use of climbing spurs on living trees is prohibited by law. In other parts of the country, however, many tree workers continue to use them, as a matter of convenience, in spite of the damage they do.

Foot spurs for ascending telephone poles have been with us for a long time, and for that purpose no one can deny their usefulness. They have a similar usefulness as climbing aids in dead trees or in living trees that are to be removed, but they should not be used in any other cases, except perhaps on unusually tall eucalypts or pines devoid of side branches and unclimbable by any other means.

Spurs are harmful to the living tree in that they open unnecessary wounds which then become potential infection points; they are particularly to be avoided in regions plagued by epidemics. While it is true that where no disease is present, the small spur wounds, longitudinally oriented, heal over quickly, it is also true that many of the wounds, rather than being small, are long, tearing gashes; moreover, disease organisms, although not present at the time, may move in later; may, in fact, be carried long distances from diseased trees to healthy ones on the spurs or clothing of itinerant workers.

Workers who climb with spurs are generally unskilled in the use of ropes; hence they are at a disadvantage in the deliquescent-type tree with its open crown and spreading branches. Not only do they inflict hundreds of unnecessary wounds but they cannot move about in the tree with the ease and rapidity of the experienced rope climber. Incidentally, not all the wounds are inflicted on the tree: by a sudden slip many a worker has impaled leg or groin on the sharp points of his own spurs.

Clothing

When climbing you will find it convenient to wear special clothing:

1. Shirt and pants of strong, heavy khaki that do not tear or rip easily and loose-fitting enough to permit free movement in any position;
2. Close-fitting bill cap that the wind will not blow off (a hat with brim will catch on every twig in the tree);
3. Heavy shoes or boots of the army type that cover the ankle, having thick rubber soles that give an absolutely slipless grip (a thin sole tires the foot quickly on ladder rungs or on small limbs, while slick leather soles are out of the question);

4. Heavy leather work gloves, which save the hands many a cut, bruise, and rope burn.

Even in hot weather it is better to keep the shirt sleeves buttoned at the wrist, for the bare arm is easily scratched by rough bark and torn by stubs. In cold weather a sweater covered by a loose-fitting jacket is perhaps the best dress. Pants, shirt, and jacket can be fitted with special pockets for carrying tools, for your hands are busy enough with the climbing, and everything that can be carried in pockets or suspended from the belt is a help. Special tool bags, like the riveter's bolt bag, that may be slung over the shoulder are useful accessories.

In selecting clothing, choose it strong and heavy enough to give protection and yet light and loose-fitting enough to permit maximum mobility. Of all the articles of clothing perhaps the shoes are the most important. Beginners often try wearing tennis shoes. In spite of their rubber soles, these are impractical in tree work, for they offer no protection to the toes, which may be crushed by a falling limb or cut by axe or chain saw, and after long standing on a ladder or in narrow crotches they become instruments of torture. The best shoes, to repeat, are those of heavy leather with iron toe and thick rubber soles; in the tree the extra weight is no disadvantage.

9

Pruning

If you are a homeowner and fortunate enough to have trees in your yard and able and willing to care for them yourself, pruning is that phase of tree care by which you will find yourself more and more engrossed.

If you are a tree surgeon, you will have already discovered that pruning is the staple of your trade, occupying perhaps 75% or 80% of your time. The first tool you buy and the last one you sell is a saw.

A tree is planted only once; it is cut down only once; it is sprayed occasionally, as the need arises; it is braced once or twice during its life, if at all; it is fed perhaps four or five years, perhaps never; but it is, or should be, pruned at least once a year throughout its life.

What is pruning? And why should a tree be pruned at least once a year? Despite its importance, few subjects are so widely misunderstood.

Pruning means cutting—with saw, knife, or shears. But it does not mean just random sawing and snipping here and there, nor is it synonymous with topping (also called decapitation or dehorning)—a barbarous practice justifiable only in very special cases. Pruning is directed, purposeful cutting toward a predetermined end. It is selective removal, for a specific purpose, from tree, shrub, or herbaceous plant, of twigs, shoots, branches, major limbs, or roots. The removal of a single twig is an instance of pruning; so also is the cutting back of a root, as in the creation of a bonsai specimen; so also is the cutting off of a shrub or a tree at ground level, provided that the intent be regeneration and not simple felling.

The purposes of pruning are multiple:

Pruning for Safety

Any tall, overhanging object is potentially dangerous. Statistically speaking, trees fall over and branches break off more or less continually. During high winds breakage markedly increases; during cyclones it becomes spectacular.

Even without winds, limbs can break off and trees can topple over. Dead branches are particularly treacherous, but even live and apparently sound boughs can break off, sometimes with no discoverable cause. The California Valley Oak is noted for that habit. Sometimes, without warning and when no breath of air is stirring, a major limb breaks off and comes crashing down.

Toppling trees and falling branches cave in roofs, flatten automobiles, injure and kill people. Insurance companies foresee such contingencies and generally include them as one of the protected risks. Cyrano de Bergerac was killed by a falling beam. By the cruellest of ironies, one of my college chums, who several times enacted Cyrano's role in amateur theatrical representations, was killed by a falling oak limb on the day of his graduation.

All dead branches, large and small, should be removed as soon as possible. All unusually long and heavy horizontally growing branches should either be braced (see Chapter 3) or lightened or both. (Lightening is accomplished by heading back the branch—also called "foreshortening"—or by removal of some of its side branches.) All unusually tall trees should be headed back to an appropriate lateral. Note that heading back to laterals is not the same as dehorning: heading back preserves the tree's beauty of form while simultaneously reducing its hazardousness; dehorning, by cutting off all major limbs at an arbitrary level, destroys the tree's natural symmetry and encourages the rapid growth of a jungle of weak, adventitious shoots.

Since pruning for safety is very nearly synonymous with control of size, the problem can be avoided altogether by planting varieties which by nature grow only to small or moderate heights. If however, your home already has a large established tree, pruning for safety should be one of your main objectives.

Pruning for safety applies to smaller plants as well. Although no one is crushed by falling shrubs, many eyes are injured by sharp dead stubs negligently left among them, hands and legs are scraped and scratched, knees are impaled, and abdomens occasionally punctured. Sharp, woody stubs are particularly dangerous in areas where children play. For maximum safety: no stubs among the shrubs,

Pruning for Sanitation — Dead branches not only endanger persons and property underneath; they also endanger, in a different sense, the tree itself. Dead wood invites termites, borers, and carpenter ants, which, after destroying the non-living tissues, may sometimes attack living parts. It also invites wood-rotting fungi of various kinds, which in some cases similarly pass from dead to living tissues. The bark protects the tree's underlying tissues in much the same way as the skin protects ours; and just as our skin constantly strives to maintain the integrity of its surface, so the bark strives continually to reestablish an unbroken surface, growing back together where disturbed. A dead branch, or a broken-off branch, or an improperly sawed-off stub prevent the normal process of healing over. The bark surface interrupted at that point, insects and wood-rotting fungi gain access to the tree's indefensible interior. Dead branches also serve as a home and breeding site for many other kinds of vermin which may be objectionable even though they do no harm to the tree: roaches, earwigs, spiders, mosquitos (in little pockets of water), centipedes, millipedes, slugs and snails; and, when the branches are large and tend to produce cavities, frogs, rats, snakes, opossums, and even larger animals.

If dead branches do so much harm, how do uncared forest trees survive? As a matter of fact, many forest trees are blown over or destroyed by insects or wood-rotting fungi long before completing their potential life-span; most of those varieties which attain such amazing longevities, as the pines, firs, and redwoods, have a protective resin in their tissues which inhibits decay. Our cultivated varieties, chosen for beauty of form and color or for production of fruit, could not long survive in the intense competitive conditions of the forest, where every cubic inch of space becomes a battleground and every nutrient a prize to be fought over.

Pruning for Stimulation of Growth — Many people believe that the more severely a plant is pruned the more lustily will it grow. That this is true in some cases cannot be denied: the grapevine and the peach tree ''live by the knife'': annual pruning means annual harvesting. But fruit production is a special case (discussed below). Most shade trees are more harmed than helped by unduly severe pruning.

The normally growing tree maintains a balance between root growth and shoot growth. Sometimes half of the tree is underground and half in the air; sometimes, as in certain desert trees, three-fourths or nine-tenths may be underground, iceberg-like, with only a few thorny switches above the surface. Sometimes, as with the palms, the greater mass seems to be in the air, the roots, although very numerous, being uniformly slender. In any case, a definite balance is struck depending on the kind of tree and the exigencies of its environment. Pruning, whether of the roots or top, disturbs that balance, and the affected tree will almost at once take steps to restore it.

When a tree or shrub is severly cut back, it suspends all other activities and grows a new top as quickly as possible. From one point of view, this is not so much stimulation, as replacement. From another point of view, it is true stimulation, for the new growth often surpasses in lushness and vitality the old that it replaces. Many declining shrubs may be completely revitalized by a drastic cutting back—even down to ground level. Some trees can similarly be helped

The white ring is new tissue growing from the edges toward the center over a large pruning cut. Complete healing-over takes years, however, and in the meantime the exposed wood, not having been protected, has decayed completely away, leaving a gaping cavity. Moral: flush-cutting, while the indispensable first step in proper pruning, needs to be followed up by periodic applications of wound dressing plus inspection by an expert to detect incipient decay.

by this radical treatment, particularly when the upper parts are old, decayed, or non-vigorous; in such cases the vice of decapitation becomes a virtue of rejuvenation.

But stimulation is also produced by much less drastic pruning—and without the disfigurement that accompanies

Broken-off or improperly sawed-off stubs like these are unsightly and, if at or near head level, dangerous to passers-by; moreover, they invite wood-boring insects and wood-rotting fungi, and they prevent the healing-over process that should take place and would take place if they were cut off at their base, flush with the lines of the trunk.

Tree butchery, not tree surgery. Not pruning so much as amputation, this clumsy procedure is a measure of last resort, to be used only in the attempt to save a tree that is dying at the top.

also channels the energies of growth toward the tree's periphery. Although the stimulating effect of this kind of pruning is often noticed, its causative mechanism is seldom understood. But this is simplicity itself: elimination from the society of branches of those weak, inferior members which, photosynthetically inefficient, consume more than they produce.

Pruning For Appearance — Pruning is an art as well as a science, and the properly pruned tree—since art's perfection lies in concealing itself—should from a distance show no evidence of the handiwork that made it what it is: it should from all sides present a graceful, symmetrical shape and a nearly unbroken surface of foliage. When you stand under it and look up, you should see—if it is an elm, ash, birch, willow, or any other of the deliquescent type—an open, loosely enveloping hemisphere of green lattice-work through which air passes freely, supported by a clean, spare scaffolding of branches with no dead or criss-crossing members. If it is a fir, spruce, cedar, deodar, or any other of the excurrent type, you should see a clean, straight, mast-like bole from which graceful, springy branches, freed of all accumulation of dead twigs and needles, radiate evenly and harmoniously, the whole central cone open to air and light. Such an uncluttered interior is not only esthetically pleasing and structurally sound; it also permits quick drying after rains and so discourages the growth of fungi, and it prevents an excessive build-up of insect populations for whom a leafy, heavily shaded central area often serves as a refuge.

Practice of the technique described above will tend to produce this ideal form. Experience will give you the ability to anticipate results, and the final degree of excellence will depend partly on the tree's co-operativeness and partly on your own artistic sense. Special effects are always possible.

decapitation. In the healthy, well-shaped shade tree, where excessive height is no problem, pruning should be limited to the removal of dead branches, criss-crossing branches, inward-pointing branches, weak secondaries, and adventitious shoots (suckers). Such pruning not only eliminates those branches esthetically and structurally undesirable, it

Outstanding examples of topiary art. Repeated clipping of growing points has produced these unusual bell shapes. Among the species that best lend themselves to this treatment are yews, privets, and Laurel Figs.

Occasionally you may wish to train a tree into an asymmetrical form or may desire it to grow at a certain angle or in any various abnormal shapes or positions. With certain kinds or trees, as yews and arborvitae, you may wish to try topiary effects—once the most popular of all gardening pursuits. Possibilities are limitless.

Few activities are more esthetically satisfying than working with plants. When Keats wrote ''A thing of beauty is a joy forever,'' he might well have had in mind a tree. Congreve was a landscape gardener as well as a dramatist; so was Pope; and Edgar Allan Poe in *The Domain of Arnheim* and its pendant *Landor's Cottage* eulogized the delights of landscaping in the manner difficult to surpass.

Pruning for the Production of Fruit — This is a special study and not within the scope of this book. Very briefly, it can be said that each kind of fruit tree is pruned in a different way; each has its own season and its own pecularities. Where some, like the peach, thrive on radical annual pruning, others, like the avocado, would not bear under such treatment. Dead and diseased branches should be pruned away as soon as discovered; the interior of the crown should be kept reasonably open to admit the free passage of light and air, and fruit spurs (short, wiry shoots that bear fruit year after year, occuring on some trees, as the apple, but not on others) should not be cut off. Since the load of fruit the tree must support is often very heavy, special attention must be paid to supplying a strong scaffolding of branches. From the time the tree is first set out, it should be trained to have a short, stout trunk with branches appearing in staggered order, the first one, two, or three feet from the ground and the remainder at intervals of a foot-and-a-half to two feet. Long, spindly branches should be headed back or eliminated entirely. Where the shade tree should have a spreading, more or less open structure, the fruit tree should be as small, compact, and concentrated as possible. With its strong wood, small sturdy branches, short trunk, dense spherical crown, and prolific fruiting habit, the orange tree is as close to the ideal as it is possible to get.

Pruning for the Removal of Extraneous Growths — Sometimes a tree is parasitized by mistletoe, which attacks branches and/or trunk (occasionally even roots); sometimes it becomes involuntary host for the hanging Spanish moss

Outstanding examples of topiary art.

(Tillandsia), bunch moss (also Tillandsia), or other epiphytes, which, although not drawing sustenance from the tree as mistletoe does, nevertheless may harm it by occurring in such large quantities as to reduce the amount of light and air reaching its vital tissues. Sometimes its branches may be covered by excessive quantities of true moss (Bryophyta) or overgrown by lichens. Sometimes it may be entwined by a vine which, growing beyond permitted limits, usurps its place in the sun and so gradually smothers it to death. The removal of these extraneous growths is more a clearing out process than pruning in the strict sense of the word; yet since the two activities so often go together, I include it here. (For more detailed discussion of such growths see the chapter "Environmental Damage and Miscellaneous Troubles", Chapter 11.)

Balance

Trees always tend to grow symmetrically, and the pruner should, in general, strive to maintain that natural shape. Symmetry is not only pleasing esthetically, it is also physically necessary to the tree. Why? Because by facing in all directions the foliage can absorb the maximum amount of light available, both direct and reflected. And because an erect, branch-bearing trunk, which is the pattern the tree has developed over millions of years, is most stable when the branches are evenly distributed on all sides. If a tree has from the sapling stage been subjected to strong wind pressure from one side only, it can adapt to the stress, grow in a bent position, and produce branches on the leeward side only. But if a large tree grown under normal circumstances is suddenly deprived of one or more major limbs on one side only, it becomes unbalanced and in high winds may fall over. Thus balance is definitely a factor to take into account when contemplating the removal of any large, heavy limb.

Thinning

Thinning is a special and very important part of pruning. It means the selective removal of branches or twigs from a given area with specific intent to reduce the weight load appreciably and permit more light and air to pass through the foliage without disturbing the overall appearance. This *mini-pruning*, as we may provisionally define it, is an activity requiring skill and patience, and we who are always in a hurry seldom find time for it. Stubbing off a large limb is a much faster and more impressive operation than the meticulous removal of overlapping twigs, one by one. The first is a noisy and showy technique, punctuated by the whine of chain saws, the crashing to the ground of heavy limbs, and the shouting and gesticulating of a crew of workers; the second technique is quiet, totally unspectacular, and usually executed by a single man. It would not be difficult to correlate pruning techniques with the spirit of the times and the genius of the race: crude "dehorning" with early settlers wrestling with a raw land; single-twig removal with the reduced land area and the exquisite taste of the Japanese.

The properly pruned tree should show little external evidence of the work that made it what it is. Its silhouette should be pleasing, graceful, and symmetrical, and its inside should be clean and open. Since art's perfection lies in concealing itself, the many hundreds of saw cuts that contribute to produce such an effect go unnoticed except to the eye of the expert.

Thinning has two special applications: the first where a tree obstructs a view and one wishes to see through it without destroying the beauty of its lines; the second where a tree with long, drooping sprays of foliage needs to be lightened to prevent breakage. The view-opening application is in particular demand on hillsides where trees on the lower levels (often belonging to the neighbors) tend constantly to close off the line of sight. The second application involves weeping willows, birches, Siberian elms, various kinds of eucalypti, California pepper trees, and other species characterized by long, graceful, drooping branches. On some of these, the slender, attenuated, downward-hanging branches may attain a length of 25 or 30 feet; and with continued growth there comes a time when they interfere with free passage under the tree or when the supporting limbs seem in danger of breaking. Called upon to remedy the situation, an unskilled pruner is likely to do one of two things: shear off the ends of the descending twigs at some arbitrary level as if cutting an inverted hedge, or stub off a major branch somewhere up in the tree's scaffolding. Either operation destroys the beauty of the tree: the first by giving it a crew haircut, the second by mutilating it permanently.

The skilled pruner will do neither of these things. Beginning where the foliage is thickest, he will remove twig by twig, branchlet by branchlet, eliminating all overlapping and duplicating material, and leaving the dominant sprays intact. In this way the weight of a branch may be reduced by a fourth or a third or sometimes even by half. Thus lightened, it rises upward, no longer interfering, no longer in danger of breaking, and at the same time preserving all its natural beauty.

Thinning follows the same principles as pruning on a larger scale. Weak, secondary, sparsely leaved twigs and branchlets are cut away. Where branchlets overlap, the weakest or least desirable are eliminated, the strongest and best shaped allowed to remain. Where all seem of equal value, half or a third may be removed on the basis of simple alternation. Towards their tips branches multiply by forking: where the two prongs of the fork lie side by side, either can be cut off, but where the fork is vertically aligned—that is, where one prong is above the other—it is always the lower member that should be cut off. (This is because the lower member of a fork is weaker structurally and susceptible to breakage if its stronger twin is cut away at the crotch.)

The most suitable tools for thinning are the short-handled curved pruning saw, loppers, hand-shears, and pole-pruners of various lengths. The closer you can get to the branches, the more easily and efficiently you can do the work; tall step-ladders are useful here. All cuts should be clean and flush.

Thinning is a time-consuming operation. Many hours of loving hand-work can go into a small tree or even a large shrub. If you do the work yourself, be prepared to devote many week-ends to it; if you hire it done, expect to find it expensive.

Time to Prune

Many believe that a tree should be pruned only in the winter, when dormant. This belief is a carryover from the days when pruning was synonymous with severe topping ("Dehorning"); in such cases dormancy is indeed the indicated season. But as we have seen, pruning means far more than topping, and when practiced scientifically and artistically can, with certain exceptions, be done at any time.

Since in the Temperate Zones growth occurs most rapidly in the first few weeks of spring and since healing is a form of growth, it follows that pruning cuts made just before spring will begin to heal over almost immediately, and conversely that cuts made in late summer will have to wait until the following spring before healing can begin. On most trees, however, a difference of a few months is not a serious matter, and in practice pruning crews work all year around.

Dead wood, of course, is insensitive to seasons and should be removed as soon as it is noticed; it is, incidentally, easier to detect when the tree is in full leaf.

Some trees, such as birches, walnuts, maples, and yellow-wood, will bleed profusely if pruned when dormant or in early spring. These, in direct opposition to popular belief, should be pruned only when in full leaf.

Desert trees follow a different pattern, growing rapidly when moisture is available and suspending growth when it is not. Tropical trees, subject to very heavy rainfall throughout most of the year and to days and night of roughly equal length and knowing no seasons as we understand the term, grow in flushes of irregular duration. They do not, therefore lay down a single growth ring per year in their wood as Temperate Zone species do, but lay down two, three, four or more rings per year. Pruning of such species is obviously not correlated with the seasons.

Wire Clearing

Wire clearing poses a special problem, involving the removal of branches that are touching, or about to touch, or in danger of falling on, telephone or power lines. Often this work is done by the utility companies' own crews. More and more, however, the companies are contracting the work to tree specialists, partly because they can do the work faster and more efficiently and partly because they treat the trees with more consideration, thus avoiding difficulties with property owners, who justly protest against the mutilation of their trees by unskilled hands.

As homeowner you are not likely to have occasion to do your own wire clearing. However, understanding the procedure will enable you to protect your interests.

There are four types of wire clearing:
1. Topping,
2. Side-pruning,
3. Drop-crotching,
4. Directional pruning.

Topping shears off the whole top of a tree to prevent it from touching overhead wires. This treatment destroys the natural lines of the tree and consequently most of its beauty. Moreover, it has to be repeated frequently because of the jungle of new shoots that rapidly spring up from the cut-off stubs. It is the method most commonly practiced by unskilled workers, particularly in small towns, where public opinion is less articulate in protest.

Side-pruning means the removal of all branches, both large and small, on whichever side the wires happen to go through. It is, in effect, "vertical topping" and no more to be recommended than horizontal topping. It leaves a one-sided tree or at best one with a gaping hole in it, unbalanced both physically and esthetically.

Drop-crotching means the pruning back of large center branches to outward-pointing laterals, in an attempt to make

Difficult to resolve is the conflict between trees and overhead wires. Skillful pruning permits the wires free passage without marring the appearance of the tree. In this case the pruning was obviously not skillful.

the tree grow away from the wires. Although better than (1) and (2), its necessary cutting of large limbs opens up areas of possible decay.

Directional pruning is the best method of all, from the stand-point of the tree; also the one that requires the least follow-up. It means the judicious removal of small branches in order to open up adequate but not excessively large paths for the wires; also the anticipation of future growth by the skillful pruning of neighboring branches in an attempt to train them to grow away from the wires. It is the intelligent tailoring of the tree to the wires with benefit to the latter and no disfigurement to the former.

Branches Over Roofs

When a tree and a house are close together, special problems in pruning arise. Branches keep on growing and begin to rub against the shingles; major limbs break off in winds and knock holes in roofs; the trunk sways in the wind and damages the roof and walls even though special apertures have been designed for its accommodation; the roots enlarge and crack foundations. With continued growth (and trees cannot stop growing) there comes a point where the house must be modified or the tree removed. The attempt to fit the two together is not good for either. If you are contemplating designing you home to include a tree somewhere within its roof-line, *don't.*

Special considerations obtain in the cases where branches overhang but the trunk is distant. When kept within proper limits, branches over a roof add beauty, interrupting the severity of the straight edge, and making even the drabbest of roofs a thing of interest; at the same time they contribute significantly to the cooling of the building. The built-in advantage of the deciduous tree is that it puts out leaves in the spring and summer, furnishing you with shade precisely when you need it, and then sheds its foliage upon the advent of cold weather precisely when you find the sun most welcome. Evergreens, lacking this built-in feature, should not be planted in any location where their winter shading might prove oppressive.

The inconveniences of branches over roofs are the possibility of their breaking, the probability of their scraping, and the certainty of their filling the gutters with leaves. But breakage can be prevented by proper cabling, gutters can be screened to keep out leaves, and scraping can be obviated by proper pruning.

Proper pruning does not mean the ugly stubbing off of branches at roof edge. It means rather the flush-cutting of all smaller, downward-pointing branches and branchlets that are touching or are likely to touch, in the attempt to train the tree to grow upward away from the roof, bearing in mind that during high winds the branches may swing through arcs of five or six feet or more.

Deciding which twigs or branches to remove is the first step. The second step is learning the specific technique of cutting. The third step is learning which tools to use and how to use them. Theory, application, implementation.

Technique of Cutting

How, specifically, should a branch be cut off? If it is a small branch, one cut will do. If it is a large, heavy branch, at least two cuts are needed, sometimes more. When a long, horizontal branch is cut from the top side, it tends to split; when cut from the bottom upward, it pinches the saw. Both of these difficulties can be avoided by making three cuts: two diagonal, one from each side, forming a "V" with the apex at the bottom, and the third from the top down. A branch so cut will break away cleanly. Extra long, heavy horizontal branches should be cut off in several sections, each section allowed to fall freely where possible or secured with a rope and lowered carefully where something breakable is underneath.

Vertical branches are more dangerous than horizontal one because you cannot always judge which way the branch will fall and because the base end, with all the weight of the branch above it, may fall straight down against your leg or into your abdomen. Such branches, if large, should be pulled in the desired direction by a rope attached near the top before the cut is begun. For a clean jump-cut the "V" technique just described can be used. On very large boughs a notch can be opened up, as in felling, on the side towards which the piece is expected to fall.

The most important cut is the final one—the one which shears off all protruding vestige of the cut-off member. Put another way, all final cuts should be flush cuts. The twig should be cut flush with the branch it arises from; the branch flush with the bough, and the bough flush with the trunk itself. Flush means precisely that; this is a case where almost right is wrong. If a five-inch stub is left or a four-inch stub, or a one-inch stub or even a half-inch stub, the cut is not a good one. A stub is harmful for several reasons: (1) it is unsightly; (2) if it continues to live, it sends out numerous thickly clustered adventitious shoots that do not harmonize with the natural lines of the tree; (3) if it dies, it prevents the living tissues around it from growing together and so serves as a kind of drawbridge over which insect and fungal enemies may enter into the heart of the fortress.

Flush-cutting is more easily described than executed. Because branches are thicker, tougher, and harder at the base, the pruner's natural tendency is to make the cut at a point four or five inches away from the base, thus leaving an undesirable stub. And because branches issue from the parent limb at all angles, it is often difficult so align the saw blade in the correct position so that no stub or lip will be left. This is particularly true when using a pole saw and when the branch to be removed is high up in the tree. Even

This large pruning cut, naturally pointed at the top, should have been artificially shaped into a point at the bottom; had the cut been thus streamlined, the healing process would be occurring more rapidly. As it is, healing is beginning (note the slowly advancing white ridge of new tissue at each side), but it is taking place so slowly that the exposed wood, unprotected by paint, is cracking and hence admitting decay organisms into the interior.

professionals may make 10% to 15% of their cuts incorrectly in a large tree. In using hand-shears, loppers, or the pruning hook, flush-cutting should similarly be observed. If you want perfection, position the shears so that the cutting blade is always against the part of the tree that is *not* being cut off.

Lowering Branches

Small branches may be permitted to fall freely. Large branches, however, often behave unpredictably and in the interest of safety should be roped and tied before cutting. The natural support to tie to is another branch, preferably an overhanging one so that the rope can be pre-tightened and

there will be no slack to take up when the cut is completed. If no convenient overhanging or lateral branch is available, you may be forced to tie the branch to itself; this can be done by intentionally leaving a stub for the anchor, then cutting the stub off and letting it fall free. Care must be taken, particularly if using a chain saw, not to saw through the rope; also to tie the rope in such a way that it will not foul. The simplest and most effective knot for attaching a rope to a branch is the timber hitch. The other end of the rope, after being passed over an adjoining branch or through an overhanging crotch, can be secured by several turns around a third branch or any other convenient anchor. No knot need be tied in this end, for the friction of the rope passing with its several turns around the anchor branch is sufficient to support the weight of even the heaviest cut-off pieces, provided (of course) that the free end is held in the hand and paid out gradually as the piece is lowered. Where there is a projecting roof edge or a power line or some other obstruction, you will find it useful to attach one or even two lighter ropes to the mid portion of the branch to guide it as it is lowered, in which case, of course, you will need a helper on the ground.

For light-or medium-weight branches, the anchor rope should be half-inch Manila hemp 50 to 60 feet long (twice these lengths in very tall trees). Hemp ropes are light, strong, and easy to tie and untie. Exceptionally heavy limbs may be tied and lowered with 3/4 inch nylon rope, which has the advantage of being very strong and also of being elastic, absorbing shock in any free fall and thus less likely to break. Its disadvantages are its stiffness, its weight, and the difficulty it poses in tying and untying knots. Nylon ropes of small diameters may be used for guide ropes but, although strong, should not be used for anchor ropes as they cut into the bark and are difficult to hold. Wire, wire cables, and chains are all unsuitable materials for tying and lowering.

Healing

Properly made cuts heal over with the passage of time. Healing—which means the laying down of new tissue—proceeds from the edges of the wound toward the center; the exposed face of the cut, often elliptical, more often circular, is gradually covered over by growth taking place on all sides, so that the wound, if observed in a sequence of time-lapse photographs, appears as a slowly closing circle. Some tropical trees, because of the greater abundance of living, unspecialized cells distributed throughout their interior, are able to regenerate callus tissue directly from the exposed wood face, as well as from the edges of the wound. This may occur to a limited degree even on some Temperate Zone trees—pecans, for example. Small cuts may heal in one growing season, larger ones may require three or four years, while still larger cuts—say eight inches or more in diameter—may take a dozen years or more.

Painting Wounds

With every pruning cut, the tree's interior tissues are exposed and hence subject to attack by the legions of fungal and insect enemies normally kept at bay by the unbroken bark surface. Decay of the exposed wood occurs very rapidly in some species, very slowly in others. Unfortunately, many of our most highly prized species, such as the oaks, belong in the first group; and with these the matter becomes something of a race between the rate of healing and the rate of decay. Large cuts on susceptible trees need to be covered over with some protective film to keep out fungus spores and to repel insects. What is needed is a kind of substitute bark, which, among its other remarkable properties, repels invaders both chemically and mechanically, as well as insulating against heat and cold. Many materials have been tried for this purpose, ranging from orange shellac to strips of cloth tacked across the wood face. The most commonly used material, however, and the most practical one, is paint. Special tree paints are now widely sold in nursery supply houses, discount houses, and hardware stores; most of them are made of an asphalt base and are often advertised as being "acid and alkali resistant" and as containing "an antiseptic ingredient."

In color the paint is usually black or brown; if too thick for easy application it may be thinned with linseed oil. House paints are not recommended for use on trees, nor are creosotes or heavy tars.

On small and medium-sized trees you will find it convenient not to begin painting until you have finished all of the pruning, for if you paint as you go along, you will almost certainly rub against the painted surfaces as you move about in the tree, ending up with as much paint on yourself as on the pruning wounds. This problem can be avoided by painting from the ground with a brush fastened to the end of a long pole. On large trees it may be necessary to paint the higher cuts as you make them.

Large cuts that take many years to heal should be repainted as often as needed. Even though protected by paint, the wood face of a large cut often cracks open as it dries; these cracks should be filled up and covered over with a heavy asphaltum-asbestos compound such as those used for sealing leaky roofs.

Pointing

To accelerate the healing process over a large pruning wound it is sometimes advisable to "point" the cut at both ends. The theory behind this operation is that since the sap flows lengthwise along the trunk and along all of its branches, it will pass more easily around an interruption that enters the flow gradually than around one that obstructs it transversely. Hence large, circular cuts should be shaped to a point at both ends—meaning, of course, in the direction of the sap flow; put another way, they should be streamlined. This is a case where, paradoxically, the excision of a certain amount of sound tissue makes possible the more rapid laying down of new tissue along the whole length of the wound. The operation is performed by chiseling away the outer and inner bark at the wound down to a firm wood surface; the wood itself need not be cut into. Small and medium-sized cuts heal over so rapidly that pointing is unnecessary.

Tools

For pruning herbaceous plants, a pair of hand shears is sufficient. For shrubs you will need, in addition to the hand shears, a pair of long-handled shears (often called "loppers") and a small, curved pruning saw with backward-pointing teeth for the heavier material. For trees you will need loppers, a pruning hook (also called "twig pruner," "branch pruner," "pole pruner"), an assortment of hand saws, and, for the larger branches, a small gasoline or electric chain-saw.

The pruning hook is a shearing device mounted on the end of a pole and actuated by a cord; it is indispensable for heading back the small flexible branches around the tree's periphery out of reach of the hand and too springy to be sawed with a pole saw. The hook may come mounted on the end of an 8, 10, or 12 foot pole, or it may be built up to any desired length by means of coupling sections, usually of six-foot lengths. Poles are normally of wood, now often of fiberglass, sometimes of aluminum, although these are dangerous in the proximity of power lines. Although lightweight, the poles quickly become heavy, especially in the longer sections. Any length of over 12 feet is unwieldy and should be avoided.

Lengths of 7 to 9 feet (including hook) are the most practicable, particularly if working horizontally or diagonally. The effective length of the pruner is increased by use of the step ladder or straight ladder where possible. The cutting quality of the hook varies widely from brand to brand, and the mere fact that a store stocks a certain kind is no guarantee of excellence. Some brands are made of such inferior material that the cutting edge chips or bends after a few days of use; others are of such poor design that one wonders how they continue to be sold. The good pruners are made of high quality steel and are so constructed as to confer a mechanical advantage, multiplying the hand pull on the cord by a factor of three, five, or more. The best I have found in more than thirty years of looking is the *Florian Ratchet-Cut* pole pruner, made by the *American Standard Co.* of Plantsville, Connecticut. With this ingenious tool, branches up to two inches in diameter can be neatly cut off with little effort. The principle involved is analogous to the acceleration of a falling body: each equal-force pull on the cord produces an effect greater than the preceding one, and all the pulls are cumulative. The same revolutionary cutting concept is built into the two-handled, conventionally shaped, two-foot long, lopping shears, manufactured by the same company. These pruners are as much fun to use as a well-designed golf club, and for all those who are obsessed with quality tools, as I am, they represent a source of perpetual joy.

The saws used in tree work are not the same as the saws used in carpentry. Carpenter saws are meant for sawing dry wood and have a different over-all shape, a different handle, smaller teeth, and a narrower set. Tree saws, used primarily in green wood, are thicker and sturdier, have larger teeth with wider spaces in between them, and considerably more set. They are of two main types: those with teeth pointing away from the operator, cutting, as does a carpenter's saw, on the push stroke, and those with teeth pointing towards the operator, cutting on the pull stroke. Both types are useful in tree work—the push saw when you can get above the branch and put your weight behind each stroke, and the pull saw when the branch is above you or to one side where pushing is difficult and ineffective. The professional has a large assortment of both types, of varying lengths, widths, and shapes; the homeowner should have at least one push saw and two pull saws.

While the cutting edge of the push saw is straight, the cutting edge of the pull saw must be curved, for it is the curve that makes the teeth bite in. These curved saws, available in most hardware stores, garden shops, and in special supply houses, can be bought with needle teeth or wedge teeth; I prefer the latter type. Those purchased in stores usually come equipped with a slender handle, 8, 10, or 12 inches long, graspable by both hands. Although such handles are adequate for small trees easily accessible from the ground level or from the stepladder, the saw's effectiveness can be increased by removing the factory handle and attaching another of your own making: preferably a straight piece of spruce about 28 to 30 inches long, 1-1/2 inches wide, and 7/8 of an inch thick, with rounded edges. To attach the blade, simply saw a slot in one end of the handle, drill two holes to line up with the holes in the saw, and secure with 3/16 inch stove bolts, equipping head and nut ends with large washers to prevent crushing of the wood. Through a hole drilled in the other end, attach a loop of cord, which will serve to hang the tool around the wrist or over a convenient branch stub.

Thus equipped, this saw has a number of striking advantages: it is light-weight and may be used all day without producing fatigue; it may be grasped with one hand or with two hands at any point along its length; when held at the end with one hand, it more than doubles the length of the arm, giving you a reach of six feet in any direction (30 inches of arm, 30 inches of handle, and 12 to 14 inches of blade). By being able to transfer it quickly and easily from one hand to the other and by taking into account the width of your shoulders and your ability to bend from the waist in any direction, it makes you master of a sphere 14 feet in diameter; from a central position you can reach virtually any part of a small tree.

The ideal blade to put on the end of so useful a handle is a quality piece of metal 16 inches long (including the part that goes into the slot), 1-1/4 inches wide at the base end, 3/8 of an inch wide at its tip, formed into a gentle curve, with an even, regular taper from base to tip and a row of business-like backwards-pointing teeth, seven to the inch, along its inner edge. A blade with too much curve will not do: instead of cutting smoothly, it will bounce and see-saw in the cut. Long, needle teeth are to be avoided because they bend and break easily, do not cut as well, and are more difficult to sharpen. (Sharpening, incidentally, is better entrusted to professional shops which have machines that keep all the cutting angles uniform.) Saws with a blunt, wide end are to be avoided because a narrow, tapered end is needed for starting cuts in tight places.

For larger trees and heavier branches, similar curved saws are available in longer and wider dimensions, with five teeth to the inch instead of seven, and of sturdier construction throughout. These can be mounted on poles of any desired length, most commonly 6, 8, or 10 feet. When working high in the tree, the six-foot handle is the most practicable; longer handles become tiring and get in the way of side branches. When working across long spans or from the ground, the longer handles are often useful. Any handle much over 10 feet, however, becomes impracticable; if of wood, it tends to break; if of aluminum or even fiberglass it quickly becomes heavy; and at the very end of a long pole you can seldom exert the required pressure. The 18 and 24 foot sectional poles sometimes advertised may look good on paper but are almost totally unusable.

A special type of curved pull saw is manufactured for cutting palm fronds. This has a 12 to 14 inch handle and a 20 to 24 inch blade with long, widely spaced teeth and extra deep gullets to prevent clogging by the fibers. Here, too, handles of different length may be adapted as needed.

The blade of the push saw should be about 20 to 22 inches long, of good heavy material so as not to bend under pressure, with 5, 5-1/2, or 6 teeth to the inch. The handle should have no projecting ears along its back side, as the carpenter saw handle does, for these get in the way when the saw is used in a reversed position. Hard rubber handles, if available, are preferable to wooden handles because they do not break when the saw is dropped, as it often is. For larger limbs and tough knotty stubs, a larger push saw is manufactured with a 30 to 32 inch blade and 4-1/2 teeth to the inch. Among professionals this was known as the "bull" saw or sometimes "the bull-of-the-woods." Although mechanical saws are making this tool obsolete, it is still convenient to have around for those occasions when the machine fails.

Chain saws are now, of course, almost universally available. For those who, like myself, grew up in the woods working 10 to 12 hours a day with axe and cross-cut saw, the chain saw is a kind of perpetual miracle. When using one, I feel for it a respect bordering on awe; even when not using it, I can sit and admire it for hours at a time. The progression from notched flint through straight saw, curved saw, circular saw, band saw, chain saw is indeed wonderful. How many thousands—millions—of man-hours were spent in the drudgery of back-and-forth sawing! And how many of us stood and watched the buzz saw at work without imagining the possibility of flattening the disk, shifting the axis to one side, and mounting the teeth on a movable chain which could be lengthened indefinitely!

The first chain saws were heavy, unwieldy, two-man affairs with a handle and an oiling device on the far end. Although a very great improvement on the older types of log saws (which worked with a reciprocating motion, like manual sawing), they were still not quite perfect. One thing more was needed: the elimination of the second man. This was done by shortening the bar and taking the handle and the oiler off the far end, leaving it completely exposed; this modification gave us the saw as we know it today—the most ingenious, fantastically efficient, and deadliest machine ever taken into the woods.

The open-end, one-man saw is small, light, easy to transport, easy to use, and extraordinarily versatile. It may be operated in any position: upside down, sideways, diagonally. It will cut a log crosswise, lengthwise, or at any angle.It can tear its way through the toughest stumps and crotches, turning into useful chunks pieces otherwise unsplittable. Its open end permits starting a cut anywhere and permits the free movement of the bar inside log diameters larger than its own length, thus making possible the felling of a 20-inch tree with a 10-inch bar. It also permits cutting with either upper or lower bar edge or with the point itself, useful in plunge cutting in the special cases when you want to cut away a tree's interior before breaking its back or in cutting holes through posts or beams for fence-building or other purposes.

The saw serves equally well for felling, bucking, and limbing, and with the aid of a guiding device recently developed, even for sawing a log into boards. It can be suspended from the high climbers waist and carried up into the leafy top of a 200-foot spar. It can be used to cut off a tree an inch or so above ground level, or even to cut it underground, root by root, once the dirt has been dug away. With this marvelous machine, one man can cut a standing tree into firewood lengths, section by section, as fast as a helper can roll them to one side and stack them. He can buck the fallen log, whether lying freely on the ground or entangled in brush, into any lengths, cutting indifferently from the top down or the bottom up without need of wedges or jacks. If skillful enough, he can cut a tangled pile of branches, of all thicknesses and all lengths, into firewood without touching a single stick with his hands, simply rolling, tilting, and kicking them into position with his feet, within fifteen minutes reducing a hopeless tangle into a neat pile of uniform lengths.

The chain saw has been a godsend for farmer, rancher, camper, tree surgeon, and forester, permitting one man to do the work of ten. All over the world it has revolutionized logging techniques. Few mechanical devices have spread with such rapidity: chain saws are now marketed in every major city of the world; in our country they are sold in hardware stores, garden shops, sharpening shops, discount stores, even in service stations and drug stores.

In addition to the gasoline-powered saw, which is by far the most popular type, there are also electric and pneumatic chain saws. The air-driven saw has the unique advantage of working under water and is therefore the indicated tool for maritime construction companies. The electrically driven saw is steadily increasing in popularity, spectacularly so within the last few years, as the energy crisis has made people fuel conscious. Although less powerful than the gasoline version, the electric saw possesses several significant advantages. It is quieter, easier to start and stop—and therefore safer—requires no mixing of fuel, and very seldom needs to go in for repairs. Principal disadvantages are that it needs to be plugged into a source of power and hence entails the dragging around of a long extension cord, which can easily become entangled in brush. Both homeowner and tree surgeon, however, are almost always within easy reach of an electrical outlet, and the dragging of the cord is something you can get used to. If a generator is taken along, the electric saw can be used even in the woods. Builders and construction companies use it widely, and motor home owners find it ideal. For the homeowner whose activities are limited to cutting off branches intermittently and to cutting occasional firewood, I recommend the electric saw. It can lie around unused for years and be ready to go the moment you pull the trigger.

10

Wound Repair

Cavity repair is possibly the most attention-catching phase of tree care. The very fact that the whole field has come to be called "tree surgery" indicates that in the public mind the chisel, gouge, and mallet have pre-empted the center of attention and the part has given its name to the whole.

But had that appellation not been bestowed on arboriculture in its infancy, it might not have stuck, for today things are different. It was in the 1910's, 1920's, and early 1930's that cavity repair attained its heyday—became, in fact, something of a fad, with the very wealthy competing with each other for the services of those arborists who could provide them with the largest and most ostentatious filling.

In recent years, however, cavity repair has suffered an eclipse—in part because the Great Depression of the '30's destroyed its economic base and in part because the more enlightened among the arborists gradually came to realize the exaggerated nature of their pretensions. Where formerly hundreds, even thousands, of dollars were spent on the meticulous excavation, spraying, swabbing, bracing, draining, and filling of a single large cavity in a prized tree, the tendency today is to treat the stricken tree with "benign neglect," writing it off as a casualty and spending available funds on setting out younger, intact specimens. And today's tree workers, proficient in the use of chain saws and climbing spurs and geared to fast take-downs, instant disposal of brush (via chippers), and fast get-aways, have little or no training and less interest in the slow, laborious excavation and filling of extended cavities. Definitely, the state of the art is in decline.

This state of affairs is to be lamented, for while it is true that many trees are not worth repair and many are beyond repair, it is equally true that many others, particularly large, noble, well-shaped oaks (peculiarly subject to heartwood decay) more than justify all the time, trouble, and expense necessary for their restoration.

What is a cavity? A cavity is any hole, large or small, on trunk or limb, occurring in the sapwood or heartwood or both. A perfect tree presents an unbroken bark surface continuous from roots to twigs, and so long as the bark remains in that condition, no cavity can ever develop. But whenever the bark is skinned, cut, bruised, or burned in such a manner that the wood proper is exposed, the affected area becomes the site of a potential cavity. Bark wounds—

and this includes, of course, all pruning cuts—are not themselves cavities, but they often open the door to the development of cavities.

Cavity filled with concrete in live Oak tree. Note sections dividers inserted to prevent cracking due to expansion and contraction. Note also how the filling is slightly recessed so that the new callus growth will be able to grow over it rather than being impeded by it.

Serious crotch cavity correctly filled with concrete. Note the callus tissue forming around the edges. Note also the way the filling is carried up into all the affected limbs.

Crotch cavity correctly filled. Note the formation of callus tissue around the edges, representing about four years' growth. Note also the section dividers and the pointed shape of the cavity at its lower end. The affected limb must be securely supported by cables.

Wounds, then, are of two kinds: (1) bark wounds, involving damage to the inner bark, and (2) cavities, involving decay of the sapwood or heartwood or both.

In this book when bark wounds are mentioned, it is the *inner bark* not the outer. While the outer bark is useful to the tree in protecting the underlying living tissues against extremes of heat and cold, some insects, and some mechanical damage, it is not itself alive, and its loss is much less serious than is the loss of the living inner bark. (See section *Structure and Physiology*.) An exception to this rule is the very thick, nonflammable outer bark of the redwood which must be accorded equal status with the inner bark, as having enabled this tree to survive the hundreds of forest fires that have threatened it during its millenary existence.

Generally speaking, cavities are more dangerous than bark wounds, since they indicate deeper penetration of decay. But this does not mean that the latter are to be taken lightly, for a tree will die if a continuous encircling band of the inner bark of its trunk is knocked off, cut off, or otherwise destroyed, even though its sapwood and heartwood remain intact. Under no circumstances should bark wounds be dismissed as unimportant; they not only open infection into the heart of the tree but imperil the most vital part of the whole organism, the cambium layer itself.

The repair of bark wounds and cavities is facilitated by the fact that trees, like many other living things, have the power of regenerating lost parts. Wounds in trees heal much as do wounds in animals: by the formation of scar tissue. The difference is that in trees the growth of new tissue is

One way cavities get started. This tree split at the crotch, leaving a wound and a stub, which were uncared for. Insects and decay organisms have now attacked the tree at these points, and its days are numbered.

The California Valley Oak is one of the few trees whose sapwood rots away faster than its heartwood. Note the sound core of heartwood remaining after the decayed sapwood has been excised. In this condition the tree resembles a hollow tube loosely fitted over a post. If decay continues to progress, the tree's mechanical problem of how to hold itself upright will become critical.

chiefly from the edges of the wound (where the living cambium is present) toward the center, the woody heart being inactive, whereas in the animal body scar tissue forms from the bottom of a wound as well as from the sides.

(In many tropical species and in a few Temperate Zone species, such as the pecan and some of the oaks, so much embryonic tissue is distributed throughout the sapwood that regeneration is sometimes possible directly from the ex-

Deep central cavity in Oak trunk. Whether this tree should be cut down, repaired, or left to its own resources depends on how much the owner values it.

regenerative faculty that the cork oak repeatedly rebuilds its entire bark surface after each commercial stripping.)

Many persons believe, quite naturally, that any tree with a large hole in its trunk is not worth repairing because it will probably die or fall over in a few years anyway. This is not necessarily true. While obviously an intact tree is better than a damaged one, the damaged tree may sometimes live on for many years. In fact, it can make virtually a complete recovery—slowly, if unattended, more rapidly if properly taken care of. The part of a living tree that decays is usually the heartwood, and the heartwood is, fortunately, physiologically inactive; and while the heartwood is important to the tree structurally, giving it greater strength and rigidity, it is not indispensable for this purpose. Engineering principles show that a given amount of material is more effectively distributed in the form of a hollow tube than as a solid rod; thus a hollow tree, consisting only of a thin sapwood shell, may, if the shell is sound, be unbelievably strong.

To those who are still unconvinced that a hollow tree may survive and may rebuild itself, both with and without help, I recommend the examination of any fine large oak tree—and there are thousands of them throughout the country—which was properly attended, say, fifty or sixty years ago and which is today alive and well and showing every promise of living another hundred years or so. I also call to their attention a cavity 50 feet high and 30 feet in diameter in the base of a living tree: the incredible hollow redwood tree in Piercy, California, 250 feet tall, 2000 years old, and still living and growing in spite of having had its center burned out 300 or so years ago—a tree with a complete store inside whose walls are the tree's living sapwood shell.*

Repair of Bark Wounds

Treatment of a bark wound is relatively simple. Using a sharp knife or mallet and chisel, cut back the bark edges around the damaged area into the form of an ellipse with its long axis parallel to the direction of sap flow, cover the freshly cut edges with orange shellac to prevent drying out, and paint the exposed sapwood with antiseptic tree paint. This procedure is often called *tracing*.

When the wound is so shaped, the healing-over process is accelerated. Why? Because sap can flow more easily around

posed wood as well as from the cambium at the sides of the wound. Little islands of new tissue, each forming its own new layers of woods and its own paper-thin bark, begin to appear on the face of the wound. With continued growth, these gradually coalesce until, assisted by the normal healing process from the edges of the wound, they completely rebuild the damaged surface. It is because of this unusual

*To enter this store, you walk down a short flight of steps, enter through the yet unhealed portion of the fire scar, and stroll about at your leisure inspecting the merchandise. Moved by impulse, you walk to one side and lay your hand against the store wall and are startled to feel a slight but perceptible movement as the tree above sways in the wind. You look up apprehensively through the charred, narrowing, natural chimney and realize with a shock that the whole enormous bulk of the living tree stands straight above you.

although preservative of dead wood, are toxic to live tissue and may be carelessly brought into contact with it. Specially prepared tree paints, obtainable at most garden shops, feed and seed stores and are made with an asphalt base and usually contain fungicidal and antiseptic ingredients.

Ordinary pruning cuts are, of course, bark wounds and should be painted if they exceed two or three inches in diameter. Large cuts (8 inches or more across), besides being painted, should be shaped in the manner described above. Beginners often object to such shaping, arguing that

Mammoth cavity properly repaired and filled in this horizontally growing Pecan. Note how the filling is rounded to follow the natural contour of the trunk; how it is recessed slightly to permit new tissues to grow over its edges; and how it is laid in brick-like sections, which both improve appearance and serve as expansion joints.

Proper tracing of bank wound. Note the alignment parallel with the stem's axis, the pointing at both ends, and the adequate application of wound dressing. Such a properly dressed and shaped wound will heal over rapidly.

an ellipse than around a square corner, just as air flows more readily around a modern streamlined car than around the old-fashioned box type.

Painting of the exposed wood is necessary to prevent its decay before new callus tissue can cover the wound. If the exposed area is large, it should be repainted every six months or every year, as the paint weathers off. Ordinary house paints are not satisfactory for this purpose, nor are paints containing creosote or carbolineum, since these,

The unattended stub in the center led to crotch decay which in turn resulted in the splitting off of the limb to the right. Installation of cables would have prevented the split, while flush-cutting of the stub and treatment of the decayed area would have promoted healing.

it doesn't make sense to make an already large wound larger and thus open up additional areas to potential infection. Experience shows, however, that the properly shaped cut heals over more rapidly than the unshaped cut; thus all the ground apparently lost is recovered. The process is something like sacrificing a pawn in order to take a piece, or like falling back a bit in order to advance more strongly.

Principles And Purposes of Cavity Repair

Treatment of cavities is more complex than treatment of bark wounds because:

1. Decay may spread upward, sideways, and downward for considerable distances,
2. Most of this decay is not visible from the outside,
3. The work of cleaning out and repairing must often be done from a small opening of living tissue which is easily injured by careless blows of mallet or glancing cuts of chisel.

Cavities originate, as we have just seen, as a result of bark destruction by mechanical wounding, pruning cuts, broken-off branches, insect ravages, fire damage, etc., they enlarge

as the exposed wood decays or is eaten by wood-boring insects. Wood decay is caused by various kinds of fungi, which grow best when supplied with air and water. Exclusion of air and moisture usually brings about the retardation, and sometimes the complete stoppage, of the decay process. Thus the chief purpose of cavity repair is the prevention of decay, or its retardation if already begun, by artificially rebuilding a protective surface—a kind of synthetic bark—at all points where the original surface has been destroyed.

Other purposes of cavity repair are:
1. To provide a firm surface over which the new roll of callus tissue can grow and so to encourage the rapid closing of wounds,
2. To strengthen the tree by internal bracing of the cavity, where needed,
3. To eliminate breeding places for roaches, mosquitoes, ants, and vermin of all kinds, large and small,
4. To improve the tree's appearance.

What a contrast between the treated and the untreated cavity! In the first case you have an aperture properly cleaned out, properly drained, properly braced, properly painted, and if need be, properly filled, with all the processes of deterioration checked and the processes of regeneration facilitated. In the second case you have a tree with a gaping, unsightly hole in its side, dripping, oozing,

A long narrow cavity properly filled and almost covered over by new tissue. In a few years more the filling will no longer be visible, and the tree will exhibit no signs of the major operation it underwent.

Improperly prepared cavity. Note that on each side the concrete filling is separated from the living, growing region by a vertical band of dead wood. This indicates one of two things: (1) before inserting the filling the lateral excision of dead wood was not carried to its proper limits, or (2) careless use of hatchet, chisel, and mallet damaged the tender living strip contiguous with the edge of the original excavation, which then died back for four or five inches along its entire length. Unfortunately, this type of damage does not show up until weeks or months later.

and foul-smelling due to the products of decay and the accumulation of standing water, a site of infection and a kind of skid-row hotel for frogs, owls, snakes, possums and lesser vermin, preying and preyed upon. If the age-long controversy between *laissez-faire* and intelligent intervention were to be decided on the strength of this one example alone, it would be a controversy very soon ended.

Cavity repair includes both the open-cavity and closed-cavity techniques. Both procedures are scientific, both are commendable, each has its legitimate use. The procedures are supplementary, not mutually exclusive, as adherents of one or the other method sometimes allege. At times the open-cavity technique is indicated, at times the closed-cavity technique, according to the nature of the problem. Not infrequently the methods may be combined in the same operation: the lower half being treated as a closed cavity, the upper half as an open one. Every cavity is different; each one is a challenge to the ingenuity of the surgeon.

Specifically, open-cavity procedure differs from closed-cavity procedure in that the cavity is left open or unfilled in the first instance, while in the second instance it is filled with some solid material, such as concrete, wood bricks, rubber strips, or various asphalt-sawdust preparations. In all other respects, the two procedures are the same. The preparatory steps of cleaning out, bracing, draining, and shaping, correspond point for point. In open-cavity technique only the final step, the of inserting the filler material, is omitted.

The advisability of using solid fillers has from the beginning been a controversial issue, and the development of the open-cavity technique originated as a reaction against the abuse of heavy materials, particularly concrete, which have sometimes proved unsatisfactory. In general, a cavity is best left open in the following cases:

1. When the cavity is very shallow and the exposed wood still sound,
2. When the cavity has nearly healed over so that filling would necessitate reopening it, in which case more harm than good might be done,
3. When the cavity is long and narrow and does not catch water,
4. When the cavity is situated at a joint or on a branch subject to frequent movement and cannot, for one reason or another, be made sufficiently rigid to prevent the filler from cracking or pulling away from the edges,
5. When the tree involved is in a declining condition and shows little promise of forming good callus layers,
6. When the tree involved is a short-lived or soft-wooded species,
7. When the tree involved does not, for any other reason, justify the expense.

In all other cases, cavities should be filled. Particularly, they should be filled:
1. When they are large and deep and in a valuable tree,
2. When they are so located as to catch and hold water,
3. When they occur in a major crotch (assuming that this can be properly braced so as to prevent movement) or near the ground line where further decay may mean destruction of all or part of the tree.

Technique Of Cavity Repair

Specifically, the repair of cavities involves the following steps:
1. Removal of dead and badly diseased wood as far as possible,
2. Correct shaping of the aperture at bark level,
3. Painting of exposed wood surfaces and shellacking of exposed cambium,
4. Provision for drainage,
5. Internal bracing,
6. Filling.

Removing Dead And Badly Diseased Wood

In the early days of tree surgery it was believed that *all* diseased wood should be removed; and acting on this doctrine many a conscientious surgeon chiseled away, termite-like, at a tree's interior until the tree toppled over. Such uncompromising excavation is no longer resorted to, for it is now known that the mycelial threads of the decay-producing fungi run many feet from the center of decay in all directions, invading even apparently sound wood, and that *complete* eradication is mechanically impossible. In many trees, particularly in the oaks, layers of sound wood and layers of rotten wood often alternate throughout the cavity in such a manner that the attempt to dig out all the rotten wood would mean sacrificing so much of the sound that, in times of wind stress, the tree might well fall over. Thus while in a tooth it is both possible and necessary to clean out every speck of decay before putting in the filling, in a tree such asepsis, although no less desirable, is neither possible nor—fortunately—necessary. What must be done is to strike a bargain between the ideal and the practicable. This means that the water-soaked and most badly diseased wood should be carefully cleaned away down to a reasonably sound surface of firm wood.

It is natural to suppose that if part of the rot is left inside, the decay process will continue after the cavity if sealed over. Doubtless it does to a certain extent, but once air and water are excluded, the process is greatly retarded. Examinations (both autopsies and biopsies) of cavities that have healed over on their own show that decay is in many cases almost completely arrested, even though pockets of water and bits of rot are sealed up inside. Much depends on the kind of tree and the kind of attacking fungus. Some wood-rotting fungi are more benign than others, and some trees are more resistant. On the other hand, some fungi, among them the infamous *Trametes pini,* bane of the conifers, are so determined that apparently nothing can stop them. Once the right kind—or the wrong kind—of fungus spore comes along, it will find its way into the tree's interior through the tiniest microscopic crack, and despite the best efforts of the arborist.

The only feasible thing, then, is to get out the worst of the decayed and punky wood and to establish a seal as nearly air-tight as possible over the rest. In the case of open cavities, where no water is caught, no seal is attempted, the wood is decaying very slowly or not at all because it is kept dry by exposure to the air.

In excavating dead and diseased wood, the tools used are hatchets, wood chisels, gouges, wooden mallets, various kinds of scrapers and smoothers, and long-handled scoops or spoons for pulling out the debris from the bottom of pockets. Where the exposed wood is dry and hard, electric drills are used with specially designed bits to accelerate the excavation. (Attempts to drive gouges and chisels by compressed air have not yet been perfected.) Skillful use of the chain saw by an operator experienced in plunge-cutting will eliminate much hand labor.

All tools must be kept sharp—an old truism so seldom observed. Hatchets (even axes) may be used to advantage where the cavity is large enough to permit. Near the edges, however, where dead tissue meets live tissue, only chisel, gouge, and mallet should be used, and these as carefully as possible, for a chance blow of the mallet on the tender living tissues or a chance cut with the chisel or even an outward prying movement where the living edge serves as a fulcrum will kill the tissue at that point and so cause new callus development to begin farther back.

Shaping The Cavity At Bark Level

Correct shaping, as for simple bark wounds, means bringing the upper and lower edges of the cavity to a point so that the completed figure, as seen from the outside, looks like an oval or an ellipse with its longitudinal axis parallel with the direction of sap flow. When a cavity occurs on the trunk itself, its long axis should be vertical—unless the trunk is leaning, and then the cavity should follow the angle of lean. When a cavity occurs on a branch, it should conform to the branch's angle of inclination. If the affected branch grows at an angle of 45 degrees, the longitudinal axis of the cavity should tilt at that same angle. If the branch grows straight outward, the axis of the cavity should be horizontal. If the branch curves upward or downward throughout its affected area, the cavity should follow it in its twistings.

The purpose of this conformation is, as explained above, to accelerate the healing process. Since sap flows lengthwise up and down a stem, the lines of the cavity must accommodate themselves to this current, entering it gently, like a wedge, rather than intercepting it abruptly, like a barrier. When the bottom and/or top of a cavity is left square or even broadly round, the flow of sap, (in sapwood, cambium, and phloem) makes its way around these blunt corners at a slower rate than when the top and bottom are shaped to a wedge-like point.

Note, however, that these remarks apply only to the outside of the wound, at bark level, where the healing callus tissue is to form. The inside of a cavity may be left in any shape—square, rectangular, round, or irregular—although for sake of convenience it is generally cut to the same shape as the outside. To prevent the filling from working loose and falling out, the hole itself should be larger than its surface opening.

Painting And Shellacking

When a cavity can be cleaned out down to a firm wood base showing no farther evidences of decay, the wood surface should be scraped and smoothed and painted. The paint should be applied liberally and allowed to dry before insertion of the filler. It should have an asphalt base to make it waterproof and should contain a fungicide to discourage further decay. Creosote is an excellent wood preservative, and although it should not be used on bark wounds, as explained above, because of possible damage to living tissue, it may profitably be used in the cavity's interior. If there is any doubt about the antiseptic and preservative qualities of the paint, apply a preliminary coat of *Bordeaux* powder dissolved in linseed oil. The preparation of this is simplicity itself: simply mix the powder and the oil together until you get a paste thick enough to promise effectiveness but not so thick as hinder easy application. After letting this dry for several days, repaint the whole area with an asphalt-base paint; if this should also have antifungal ingredients, so much the better.

If the interior of the cavity is beyond reach of the brush, or if you have been forced for one reason or another to leave some of the decayed and spongy wood inside, spray it thoroughly with *Bordeaux* powder dissolved in water. Since spraying forces the material into cracks that brushing cannot reach, some arborists consider this an indispensable preliminary treatment for *all* cavities. However, if the cavity's interior is easily accessible and if you have been able to work down to a surface of sound wood showing no cracks, application of the *Bordeaux* by painting would seem preferable to spraying because the brush, heavily impregnated with the linseed oil, (which would clog most sprayers), guarantees superior penetration.

Some arborists, not content with painting the wood, go so far as to cover it with roofing paper to prevent the filler (usually concrete) from touching it. Since moisture often condenses on the inner face of a concrete filling, the roofing paper is an additional guarantee against subsequent decay. A further elaboration is to cut grooves into the back of the cavity in a pattern resembling (very appropriately) the venation of a leaf, complete with midrib and lateral veins, in such a manner that any water accidentally entering will roll down the lateral veins into the midrib and down the midrib to the bottom of the cavity whence it is conducted through a drain pipe to be discharged outside the tree.

How far to go in the way of these refinements depends on the value of the tree and the disposition of the owner. Obviously, the more the care the greater the protection. In most cases, however, particularly in small and medium-sized cavities, spraying and/or painting of the wood before inserting the filler are precautions enough.

In the case of the open cavity, use of antiseptic paint is doubly important. Although such cavities do not have the protection of a seal, they have the advantage of being open to inspection at all times and being accessible for periodic cleaning and repainting.

A supplement of painting is shellacking. Orange shellac, obtainable in paint or hardware stores, should be applied to all newly cut bark and cambium surfaces. Usually cut into during the enlargement or final shaping of the cavity, these tissues are extremely tender, drying out and dying back for a distance of 1/2 to 1 inch from the edges of the cut. If, however, they are covered with shellac within a few minutes of being exposed, they do not die back; hence new growth can start from that point rather than farther away, and healing over will take place more quickly.

Providing For Drainage

Since it is important that water should not stand in a cavity, you should bore a hole in the bottom of the pocket and insert a short length of iron or copper drain pipe. Such a hole serves not only to drain out any water present at the time of excavation but also to provide an exit for any moisture entering subsequently. While theoretically no such moisture should enter, sometimes it does, seeping in around the edges of the fill, condensing on the inner face of the filler, or percolating down from above through some small undiscovered or later-occurring hole.

To find the exact bottom of a cavity is sometimes difficult, for pockets of decay run sideways and diagonally at various angles. You can run a probing instrument in the form of a long, slender rod down the mouth of the cavity to attempt to locate the bottom, transfer the measurement to the outside, and bore a hole at the estimated level. Sometimes you will need to bore several holes, each one a little farther down, before locating the bottom of the pocket. When the bit brings out sound wood only, you may be sure the cavity has ended and the next hole above is the true bottom.

Many times it helps to wash out a cavity with a garden hose equipped with high-pressure nozzle. The quantity of muck that can be flushed out through the drainage holes is astonishing. During the flushing operation the hole or holes should be reopened from time to time with bit or probe to prevent clogging.

The drain pipe should be slightly larger than the hole so that it may be driven in tightly. It needs to enter the sapwood only a short distance, 1-1/2″ or 2″. If it enters too far, protruding beyond the bottom of the pocket, it will not drain properly. Since healing occurs only at bark level, there is no danger that the inner mouth of the pipe will be sealed over by growth from the inside of the shell. Make the hole with a slight upward slant, so that the pipe may slant downward. The pipe should protrude 5 or 6 inches so that the drip will not run down the bark, discoloring and often

injuring it. Protruding drain pipes close to the ground may be dangerous for children playing nearby and in such cases should be shortened or covered in some way.

Copper is considered the best material, although sections of ordinary iron water pipes are often used. In case a cavity has several diverging pockets, a drain pipe should be installed at the bottom of each.

Bracing the Cavity

Small cavities in sound wood need no bracing. Even large cavities, if surrounded by 4 or 5 inches of strong, healthy sapwood, rarely need bracing. But in many cases decay has progressed so far that the surrounding shell of sapwood often measures less than 4 inches, sometimes only 2 inches or less; at some points decay actually bursts through the shell so that the cavity may have two, three, or more openings.

In such cases some kind of internal bracing is indispensable for two reasons:
1. To help keep the tree from breaking at that point,
2. To prevent the walls of the shell from pulling away from the filling.

Of course, if decay has eaten too far into the trunk, the tree might better be cut down. But if the shell is reasonably sound and the variety a desirable one, then bracing, filling, and fertilizing will do much toward saving the tree.

The decision whether to brace or not depends on a combination of factors: the kind of tree and the shape, size, and location of the cavity. Some trees (such as oak) are much stronger than others (such as box elder, chinaberry, tree-of-heaven, or catalpa). A three-inch shell in an oak might be strong enough to make bracing unnecessary even though the whole heart were gone; while a three-inch shell in a box elder would hardly warrant confidence, braced or unbraced. Again, a long narrow cavity seldom needs bracing, being naturally strong and healing over very rapidly, while a wide, deep cavity almost always should be braced because of its tendency to open up farther and its slowness to heal. A cavity in a major crotch, even though only medium-sized, should be braced because of the great strain it is continuously subjected to. Moreover, supplementary supports in the form of cables should be installed at a point above the crotch. (See Bracing Chapter 3).

Internal cavity bracing may be done in several ways:
1. If the surrounding sapwood is strong enough and thick enough, install lag screw hooks, connect them with short lengths of galvanized cable and draw the cable tight with a turn-buckle. Obviously, only a large cavity will afford working room for this operation.
2. If the sapwood shell is too thin to permit the use of lag screw hooks, or if the cavity is too small to permit

High limb cavity, properly filled. The work here is complicated by the fact that too much excavation may weaken the limb to the point of breakage; also because swaying with the wind tends to fracture the concrete. If possible, the limb should be tightly cabled to several others.

working inside, bore a hole from the outside entirely through the tree and install bolt and nut. Fit both head-end and nut-end of the bolt with oval-shaped washers, and countersink these below the bark surface so that scar tissue may cover them. By adjusting the nut, the walls of the cavity can be prevented from buckling outward.

3. Instead of bolt and nut, the threaded rod (an untapered rod threaded along its entire length) may be used. Bore a hole, 1/16″ smaller than the diameter of the rod, entirely through the tree. Using a pipe wrench, screw the rod in the hole until it begins to emerge from the other side, then cut the remaining portion off with a hacksaw.

Advantages of the rod are that it does not need to be countersunk nor pre-measured to fit. Its disadvantage is that, while holding tight enough, it does not draw up.

Whichever type of brace is used, the principles involved are the same. Short cavities may demand one brace; long cavities two or more. Braces are usually installed transversely (but not necessarily side by side), sometimes diagonally.

Filling The Cavity

If the cavity has been properly excavated and shaped, its filling presents no special difficulty. Usually it will be larger on the inside than on the outside. When it does not have that natural shape, it should be artifically reshaped in order to prevent the filler from falling out. Put in soft and malleable, the filler spreads out inside the cavity and after hardening cannot work out of the smaller opening. (The same principal is used by a dentist as he drills away at a tooth to make the inner pocket larger than the surface opening.) Where the mouth of the cavity is bigger than its interior, the exposed wood surface should be studded with partially driven–in large-headed nails or shingle tacks before the filler is installed. When the filler hardens around the protruding nails, it will be securely held in place, even though the mouth of the cavity faces downward.

The essentials of installing a filling are:

1. To put the filling in as tightly as possible so that it will not fall out or be forced out by subsequent growth.
2. To make the seal—that is, the union between the filler and the edges of the wound—as nearly airtight and watertight as possible.
3. To bring the face of the filling out, radially, to a point flush, or slightly less than flush, with the cambium layer in the edge of the surrounding wood shell. If the filling is carried outward past this point—flush with the outermost bark surface, for example, as is common in amateur operations—more harm than good is done, for the all-important cambium layer is then plastered over and kept from growing.
4. To carry the edges of the filling, laterally, to a point within 1/8″ of the live cambium in the surrounding shell. If more distance is left between the edge of the filler and the edge of the cambium, the intervening sapwood, even though sound at the time of filling, will often decay or develop cracks that allow air and water to enter behind the filling.

If the cavity is an old one and scar tissue has already begun to grow around its edges, following the shell around on its inner face as it sometimes does so that, curiously, the tree comes to possess a double structure (bark on the outside and bark on the inside, with layers of sapwood back to back) the cavity might better be left unfilled. Much depends on how far the inward rolling of callus has proceeded. If the process has just begun—that is, if only the edges of the aperture are covered by a callus roll of perhaps 1″ or 2″—the cavity may still be filled. In this case, however, the completed filling should not extend outward, radially, so far as to cover the slowly forming roll of callus. Stopped at the proper point, the filling will not be flush with the extrapolated circumference line, but recessed.

What is the best kind of filler? This is a question not yet answered. Many kinds of materials have been used: wooden blocks, rubber strips, asphalt and sawdust preparations, magnesite compounds, sand, adobe, etc. An early treatise on the subject, in the time of George III of England, recommends a mixture of lime, rubbish, sand, wood ashes,

and cow manure. Amateurs often nail sheets of tin or zinc over cavities. Even plaster of paris molded around wire mesh has been used. Temporary coverings include sections of roofing paper, sheets of cardboard, wooden slats, split-open oil cans, and mail-order catalogues.

The perfect filler should be inexpensive, obtainable everywhere and at all times, quickly and easily installable, light in weight, strong and durable, semiflexible, resistant to insect invasions, waterproof, unaffected by heat and cold, and as nearly harmonious as possible with the physical and chemical properties of wood. Such a material has not yet been discovered, although some of the magnesium or magnesite compounds approximate the ideal very closely.

At the present time, despite its disadvantages, concrete continues to be the most widely used filler. Its advantages are:

1. It can be manufactured at any given place and in any desired quantity,
2. Its mixing requires no special skill, no heating, no waiting to cool,
3. It is inexpensive,
4. When mixed as dry as possible, it can be pressed and patted into every kind of corner and pocket without falling or slumping,
5. It hardens quickly into the desired form,
6. It is permanent,
7. It is invulnerable to boring insects and bored little boys with hatchets,
8. When properly smoothed and painted (black, usually), it is highly presentable.

Its disadvantages are:

1. It is inflexible, not accommodating itself to movement of the surrounding shell; hence violent movement of a filled limb (or trunk) may crack the concrete or break the limb (or trunk) at that point,
2. It is heavy, adding undesirable weight to a weakened part,
3. It expands and contracts at a different rate from that of the surrounding wood; hence cracks tend to open up at the interface where the two substances meet,
4. It is cold, so that moisture often condenses on its inner face.

Judged by popularity of use, concrete's strong points continue to outweigh its drawbacks, most of which can be overcome by judicious supplementary measures. It is best used in small cavities or in cavities near the ground, where there is little or no movement. Large cavities high up in the tree where swaying of branches or trunk is expected should be strongly braced internally to prevent the edge of the wood from pulling away from the concrete.

To make concrete for use in tree cavities, make a dry mixture of two parts of sand with one part of cement in the quantity desired. After mixing thoroughly in the dry state, add water a little at a time and continue mixing. For mixing small quantities, a mortar board and a mason's trowel are sufficient. For somewhat larger quantities the top of a metal garbage can, inverted, is ideal; its raised rim prevents the water from escaping. Still larger quantities may be mixed in a wheelbarrow with a hoe and then conveniently wheeled to the site. Many lumberyards and hardware stores now sell "mortar mix," a preparation containing sand and cement already mixed in approximately the right proportions. The convenience of this premixture more than justifies its expense; you need only add water, following the described procedures in all other respects.

When the mixture reaches the point where a ball of it kneaded with the hands will just hold together, it is ready for use. The error of the beginner is to make the mixture too wet, in which condition it will run out of all cavities, except those with their mouths uppermost. But when just moist enough to hold together, it can be molded, like putty or plastic wood, and made to fit into corners and follow curves.

You can place the mixture in the cavity with trowel, scoop, or your hands. Build up the filling a little at a time, pressing, tamping, and smoothing, and working it into all corners and pockets. If the cavity is more than 10 or 12 inches in diameter, the concrete face should be scored at intervals of 4 or 5 inches, both horizontally and vertically, and narrow strips of heavy roofing paper or asphalt shingles should be inserted. The horizontal strips should be slanted slightly downward so that water does not enter; as an additional precaution against that possibility the scoring should penetrate into the filling somewhat less than its total thickness.

The strips, often called "section dividers," may be put in place as the filling is built up, or may be put in after its completion, by scoring the face of the concrete with the point of the trowel to the desired depth. A filling so prepared gives the impression of bricks joined by mortar. Not only is this brick effect more attractive than a solid concrete slab but also, and more importantly, the flexible strips provide for a certain amount of play and serve as expansion joints, even though they may not extend through the full depth of the filler. Any cracking that occurs in the inner continuous portion of the concrete is interrupted by these expansion joints and thus does not show up on the face. A peculiar feature of the joints is that when scar tissue begins to grow together over the filler, it often grows more rapidly along the joint lines, forming little tongues of callus that follow the dividing strips and outrun the rest of the growth.

In this properly executed basal cavity the excavation has been carried down into the ground and upward into each limb as far as the decay had progressed. Note the section dividers. Note also how new growth is proceeding all around the periphery of the filling.

Successful filling slowly being covered by new callus tissue, which grows from the edges toward the center. In 8 to 10 years more, the concrete will no longer be visible and with each passing year the woody covering over it will become thicker.

Properly filled cavity, laid in sections and pointed at both ends. Not the tree surgeon's signature, the skewed appearance is simply the result of following the irregular course of the underlying decay.

After the concrete is thoroughly tamped and pressed and the section dividers are put in place, the face of the filling is smoothed by use of a small trowel or, better, by a foundry slick (also called cavity slick). This last is a specially designed, miniature trowel, flat and pointed on one end and rounded like a spoon on the other—a very handy tool for smoothing and pressing any filling, large or small. However dry the mixture may seem to be, moisture will ooze out of it when polished with the cavity slick, and a smooth, slick finish will be obtained.

When the concrete is mixed as described, it may be put into nearly all cavities, whether they face upward, side-

ways, or downward, without the use of forms. In the case of very wide cavities facing directly downward, however, some difficulty may be experienced, and boards may have to be nailed or tied temporarily over the cavity's mouth to hold the filling in place. Another solution is to use a piece of heavy screen wire or wire mesh, placing the edges within the cavity and inserting the mixture through the ends or through an opening cut for the purpose. After the concrete hardens, the wire may be left in place and covered up by an additional thin layer of wet cement. In such cases, section dividers cannot be used.

inches thick, built up across the mouth of the cavity, exactly as described above, but supported at the back by a platform of boards wedged and nailed in for that purpose. Thus the rear face of the filling, instead of resting against the inside wall of the cavity, rests against the board backing, the distance in between being converted into a dead-air space.

This arrangement has the virtue of bringing the concrete into contact with the tree around its edges only and of reducing considerably the added weight. It also makes drainage easier and provides a means for subsequent spraying and disinfection of the cavity's interior (through the drain pipe), if this should be necessary.

Basal crotch filling correctly executed. Note section dividers; also note new growth forming all around the filling's periphery. The standing water at upper right is witness to the tightness of the seal.

Small cavities may be filled solidly. Larger cavities, particularly when both large and deep, need not be filled to their total depth—indeed, should not be so filled, because a huge, heavy mass of concrete only adds unnecessary weight and comes into contact with the surrounding wood over an unnecessarily large surface area. Contrary to general belief, concrete in a tree does not make it stronger—may in fact make it weaker by providing a fulcrum on which the tree may break apart.

Instead of a solid filling, a "facing" (shell or facade filling) may be used. The facing is a mass of concrete 2 or 3

Very clumsy job of cavity-filling. The excision was not pointed at the top nor was it carried into the ground. Careless use of mallet and chisel at the time of excavation caused die-back of the tender tissues along the edges. The concrete was improperly divided into sections and improperly secured on the inside.

Home-made attempt at cavity-filling. Screen wire has been tacked across the cavity's face, and some kind of plastic material has been smeared on it. Since moisture accumulates behind this improvised covering and has no chance to dry out, decay is progressing rapidly, and worms abound. Better to have left the tree to its own resources.

The board backing must be put in place very securely; otherwise the pressure exerted on the concrete by the slowly advancing scar tissue will dislodge it. The boards should be

of good, sound wood, painted and firmly nailed or bolted together against supporting back crosspieces. The ends of the boards should be inserted into grooves cut in the tree's sound sapwood. If the cavity has internal brace rods (as it should have if large and deep), the backing may conveniently rest against these. Wedged-in rocks or bricks also make a good backing for the facing, in some cases a better backing than boards.

The completed filling may be painted black for the sake of appearance. Lampblack mixed with linseed oil, which both thins and imparts luster, is suitable for this purpose; black enamels, obtainable in most paint stores, are equally suitable. Those who find black objectionable may try gray or brown enamels or a mixture of the two in an attempt to approximate natural bark color.

A further refinement is to bevel slightly the edges of the concrete where it abuts the section dividers, thus enhancing the bricklike design.

Tin Facing For Special Cases

Where only the center of a large wound or large pruning scar is decayed and the surrounding wood is, although dead, still sound and hard, its removal many times seems almost unwarrantable, and the natural tendency is to dig out only the decayed center and replace it with a concrete plug. Such a procedure is of little value, however, for almost always the sapwood between the edge of the filler and the rim of the newly forming scar tissue decays before the healing process can be completed. The wider the spread of intervening sapwood the longer it takes the new tissue to cover it and the greater its probabilities of decaying.

Hence there is need to remove even sound tissue (at face of cavity, for a depth of 1-1/2″ to 2″) so that the edge of the filler may be brought into proximity with the edge of the live cambium, or with the rim of the scar tissue. When only 1/8″ or 1/4″ separates the cambium (or the scar tissue, if already formed) from the filler, the former is sure to grow over the edge of the latter during the first subsequent growing season. This is precisely the thing desired: once the new callus tissue has managed to grow over the edge of the filler all around its periphery, even though ever so little, an air-tight seal is achieved, and the success of the repair is assured. Thereafter, even though scar tissue may delay two years, three, five, ten, or fifty, in growing entirely together over the filling, the tree now presents an unbroken surface to the environment through which, hopefully, neither insects, fungi, air, nor water can pass.

Sometimes a large pruning cut, even though just made and perfectly sound, is treated in much the same way. Anticipating the inevitable cracking of the exposed wood surface and its subsequent penetration by fungus spores, some arborists excavate the entire cut to a depth of 1-1/2″ or 2″ and replace it with a concrete facing. Others prefer repeated paintings of the cut with a heavy, asphalt-based material. Still others first paint the cut, then loosely tack across its face a piece of burlap or canvas painted on both sides, thus hoping to keep out fungus spores until scar tissue shall have covered the wound.

Choice among these different methods, all aiming at the same goal, is contingent on the value of the tree, the rate at which it decays, and the rapidity with which it forms scar tissue. An alternative method which I have developed and used with success on a wide variety of trees consists of (a) excavating the decayed center, if such exists, and either filling or not filling it, as the condition demands; (b) painting all the exposed wood; (c) covering the entire area—that is, the exposed wood face including its excavated center, if any—with a piece of galvanized roofer's tin, covered with tree paint on both sides, cut to the exact size and shape of the area, and tacked in place by a series of closely placed tacks all around its periphery, so that at no point is there more than 1/4″ of exposed wood between the edge of the tin and the live callus tissue. (If the cut is a recent one, read "edge of wound" for "live callus tissue".) The tin should be thick enough to resist pressure but not so thick as to be difficult to cut and handle. Perhaps the best size is 1/64″ (No. 28 in tinner's terminology). It can be bought in large sheets and cut into the desired shape on the spot by the aid of tinner's shears and a paper template, which if fitted over the affected area first will readily determine size and shape.

This method of installing a facing offers some striking advantages:

1. It is quickly and easily accomplished and hence is less expensive than a full-fledged concrete filling,
2. It leaves intact large areas of sound wood which are often necessary to the tree for support,
3. It hinders further decay and furnishes a base for new callus tissue quite as effectively as a concrete filling or facing can do.

When tacked securely into place and carried out to the very edge of the wound, it is as quickly grown over as concrete or any other substance. Once new tissue has grown over its margins, it is 100 per cent airtight and watertight. It will never fall out or be dislodged or crushed. Being galvanized and painted, it will not rust or deteriorate. It will not crack, as concrete often does.

Such use of tin is, to repeat, limited to facings only—that is, in those cases (a) where an intact wood surface is to be covered, and (b) where a partially decayed wood surface is to be covered, the decay occurring chiefly in the center with the surrounding sapwood being still relatively sound and hard. The tin covering should *not* be used where the exposed wood is decayed all the way across the face of the wound; in such cases, the conventional concrete filling, either solid or facade, is preferred.

Use of Earth Filling To Promote Rooting

Large central cavities in a trunk that extend downwards to ground level are better filled with earth than with concrete. In many such cases the tree sends out, from any adjacent callus tissue, exploratory adventitious roots that enter the cavity and often grow down through it to establish badly needed new anchorage in the ground. When such a cavity is filled with earth, the downward growth of the roots is greatly facilitated, whereas a concrete filling totally prevents the process.

Filling with earth presents no difficulty when a completely intact woody cylinder encloses the cavity through all or the major part of its length, but if decay has burst through the shell at one or several points, forming a long open gap or various discrete mouths, the earth will tend to escape, especially when wet. Such escape can be prevented by insertion of tin flashing; this, however, should not be used if it is seen to wall off from the cavity's interior any of the embryonic regions from which the adventitious roots might develop, and often it is precisely from the growing edges of gaps and mouths that such rootlets do form. It should be obvious that if no adventitious roots have access to the cavity, either because no adjacent callus tissue is present or for any other reason, the use of earth as a filler becomes pointless.

Such a cavity had better be filled with concrete or some other solid material. Similarly, if the cavity does not extend all the way to ground level, use of earth is not recommended, since the adventitious roots will not be able to make contact with the soil and any water that may enter will be unable to escape, thus contributing to further decay.

Consider carefully the value of a tree before undertaking extensive cavity repair. If your tree is old, in a declining condition, or of a variety not particularly desirable, you would probably do better to remove it and plant a young, thrifty tree instead of spending money on expensive repairs. The choice is much the same as whether to repair an old car on its last legs or to buy a new one.

On the other hand, small cavities even on old trees are profitably repaired if the tree is otherwise in good health. Very large cavities may be repaired if the tree is:

1. Valuable intrinsically, historically, or sentimentally,
2. Vigorous enough to be able to callus over the filling, at least partially,
3. In no danger of falling over or breaking off at the point of weakness.

The ideal, of course, is to prevent the development of cavities by proper pruning and dressing and to prevent the enlargement of existing small cavities by their prompt repair.

If you undertake the repair work yourself, follow the directions carefully and, if possible, call in an expert for

This picture shows the most common mistake amateurs make when attempting to repair a cavity. The concrete has been carried radially too far outward instead of being recessed beneath the edge of the inner bark layer. As the tree continues to grow, it will push against the filling rather than growing around it, resulting in three unfavorable consequences: (1) growth will be impeded, (2) the concrete will be cracked and partially or totally forced out, (3) the interface between concrete and tree will become a danger zone where insects and fungi can obtain access to the tree's interior.

consultation. If you hire the work done, deal only with a reputable arborist and get his written declaration of what he proposes to do, the approximate cost of doing it, and the dates on which he will return to make inspection. Do not deal with itinerants who will almost certainly cheat in one way or another and who will not be around for redress.

Because they are comparatively short-lived or weak-wooded, or both, the following species are not recommended subjects for extensive cavity filling:

Black Locust
Boxwood
Chinaberry
Crape Myrtle
Dogwoods
Lombardy Poplar
Magnolias
Mountain Ash

Ornamental Cherries
Panicled Goldenrain Tree

Paper Mulberry
Peaches
Plums
Redbud
White Birches
Yellowwood

The following trees are recommended for cavity filling only if otherwise exceptionally healthy:

Apples
Black Oaks
Box Elder
Catalpa
Chinese Elm

Poplars (other than Lombardy)
Royal Pawlownia
Silver Maple
Tree-of-Heaven
Willows

11

Environmental Damage and Miscellaneous Troubles

As an animal travels about from place to place, it runs every kind of risk and exposes itself to every kind of danger. It may roll off a cliff, fall in a hole, get trapped in quicksand, stick a thorn in its foot, or drown in a flood. Since a tree cannot travel about, it would seem to be spared such blows of fortune. But however quietly it stays in one place and minds its own business, it is no more exempt from misfortune than is the animal. A tree need not move to come into collision with objects; objects will seek it out even though it install itself in the heart of the forest.

The kinds of mechanical and environmental damage that can befall the tree are beyond belief. If in the woods, moose, deer, and porcupines chew its bark off, beavers fell it, insects bore into its heart, termites honeycomb it, giant vines strangle it in their deadly caresses, fire consumes it, water undermines it, lightning splits it into a thousand pieces.

If in the city, the risks it is exposed to, although different, are no less perilous. As it stands along a city street, asking for nothing, bestowing the blessing of its shade and beauty on all with god-like impartiality, it would seem to be the one object in the world without enemies. Yet its enemies are legion. Some, like insects and fungi, pursue it with malice aforethought here just as relentlessly as in the forest, attacking roots, trunk, branches, twigs, leaves, and fruit, without quarter or respite. Others, born of the artificial urban conditions, may be subsumed under three heads: ignorance, neglect, indifference. Lawnmowers nudge and bump it with the manly good will of one outdoorsman to another. Bulldozers salute it *en passant,* carrying away half its bark surface with every fraternal backslapping. Automobiles scrape and bump it and occasionally wrap themselves around it in incontainable outbursts of camaraderie. High-loaded trucks break off its branches in fugitive nocturnal caresses. Electric wires burn its leaves and branches. Sweet-faced cherubs carve and hack on it affectionately with knives and hatchets. Frustrated garbologists dump cement, cinders, kerosene, crankcase oil, weed-killer residues, and related soil-building products around its roots. Storms break out its crown or split it down the center. Sadistic and untrained tree butchers tear and jab it with the climbing spurs of telephone lineman and encircle trunk and branches with unyielding iron bands that, with continued growth, slowly and inexorably result in strangulation.

Nearly everything around the tree is an actual or a potential enemy. It lives on only because of its strength, its adaptability, and its capacity for self-repair. Some of the principal environmental hazards are discussed below.

Fill

One of the worst disasters that can befall a tree is to have heavy fill suddenly dumped around it. As the tree grows up from the sapling stage, its roots become adapted to a certain soil level. Through the soil they receive air, water, and food. Uncountable millions of microorganisms live in that medium, directly or indirectly assisting the tree in its life processes. Whenever the soil level is changed—either made higher or dug lower—the roots, and consequently the whole tree, feel the effect.

In cases where absolutely necessary, the grade level may be lowered or raised without ill effect if done gradually. "Gradually" means over a period of years. While a tree cannot adapt to sudden changes, it can adapt to gradual ones. If soil is gradually taken away and roots exposed (as often happens on the banks of streams), new roots will develop underneath. If soil is gradually added, particularly in first one segment, then another, the existing roots will have time to adjust themselves to the new condition.

But if the roots are *suddenly* exposed or *suddenly* covered over, damage is almost certain to result. Fill is even worse than exposure, although both are bad. Large quantities of dirt dumped around a tree suffocate it by shutting out the passage of air and water to its roots and by interfering with the indispensable function of soil micro-organisms. The harm is done, not so much by placing the dirt close to the trunk, but by spreading it out over the entire root region (roughly comparable to the branch spread).

The extent of harm depends on the kind of tree, age of tree, type and amount of fill. Some species, such as the post oak, are quickly killed by even small quantities of fill. Others, such as the southern live oak and the American elm, can survive several feet. Young trees are much more

Struck repeatedly by the lawnmower, this young Mimosa tree is in danger of dying. This type of damage is inexcusable, since all that is needed to prevent it is any kind of simple guard: stakes pushed into the ground or a rubber door-mat loosely wrapped the trunk. Young trees with tender bark are those that suffer the most from hit-and-run lawnmower accidents.

adaptable than old ones. One of the most remarkable survival feats on record is the case of the coast redwood that had 40 feet of fill dumped around it during a road-building project and that (as revealed by excavation in a later road-building program) managed to send out from the trunk a whole new root system 40 feet above the first, adapted to the altered soil level.

The least harmful kind of fill is loose, highly porous soil permitting the passage of air and water. The worst kind is heavy, tightly packed clayey soil, a few inches of which are enough to kill less resistant species. The remedy is to use no fill, or if absolutely necessary, to use the most porous type possible (gravel, sand, sandy loam) and to the minimum depth. Where financial resources permit, a system of horizontally laid tile pipes, 4 or 5 inches in diameter, may be installed in a thick bed of gravel and the whole covered with the minimum amount of fill needed to make a presentable yard. Each pipe should communicate with the surface by

means of a short elbow joint and should have drainage holes cut at intervals along its lower portion. Air, water, and food can all be supplied to the roots through the surface openings; these can be covered with heavy screen wire or hardware cloth to prevent passage of large objects.

Impervious Coverings

Everything said about fill applies with even more force to concrete slabs, blacktop, or any other kind of impervious surface-covering material. The fact that many kinds of trees can grow in rocky soil—some even showing a distinct preference for it—should not mislead us into believing that we can build concrete patios around our trees with impunity. Again it is a question of adaptation. Trees growing on the rocky mountainside are adapted to that terrain from the beginning, but trees growing in the backyard in soil usually rock-free and partially cultivated and enriched are almost

What it means to be in the wrong place at the wrong time. Too close to the backing and turning automobiles and unprotected by any type of guard, this tree is repeatedly struck by trucks and cars. No sooner does new growth begin to cover the wound than it is knocked off. Unless help is forthcoming, the trees will remain in this state.

The sign ("Reserved for Ladies and Their Escorts"), fastened to this large Elm many years ago, is slowly being engulfed by continuing radial growth. In five or ten years, perhaps, it will no longer be visible, having been entirely overlaid by new tissue.

certain to feel the shock of any sudden blockage of the normal surface layer.

Some tree species, such as the ubiquitous tree-of-heaven, can grow anywhere, rooting in the tiniest cracks between concrete alleyway and building side, maintaining themselves, and growing to maturity there in spite of lack of water, lack of a root aeration, and lack of everything else ordinarily deemed essential. But very few species possess such versatility. Most kinds need room for trunk and root expansion, ample root aeration, and more or less regular watering. Oaks, walnuts, and pecans, although deep-root-

ed, and other good trees less deeply rooted, are easily injured by impervious soil coverings placed around them. Many thousands of fine, large trees have been killed by the proliferation of shopping centers into wooded areas and the consequent laying down of thousands of square feet of blacktop for vehicle parking and maneuvering. The irony is that many of the shopping center architects *want* to preserve the trees, or at least some of them, realizing that their beauty and their shade are irreplaceable assets. Very few, however, make provisions for underground watering and aeration of the trees (as explained above) and few are able to hold back the contractors who seem to insist on carrying the blacktop as close as they possibly can to each tree. Worse still, many builders, before pouring the blacktop, spray the whole area with herbicides to prevent subsequent sprouting of weeds and/or Bermuda grass. Nothing is more common—or more distressing to watch—than the year-by-year decline of the shopping center patriarchs, their roots shut off from air and water by the far-stretching impermeable asphalt cover, and—salt in their wounds—any moisture they might still be able to wring out of the imprisoned soil contaminated by the herbicides so thoughtlessly added.

Some species are more resistant to this sort of thing than others, and young trees are more resistant than old, long-established ones. Where no weed-killers have been sealed in, some trees have even been observed to grow and prosper under these seemingly insuperably adverse conditions.

This fine Pecan has been killed by the laying down of an impervious asphalt covering all around it. The small uncovered circular area, marked by the raised concrete curb, cannot admit sufficient air and water to supply the far-ranging roots. While some kinds of trees are quickly killed by such a covering, others seem unaffected. Mulberry, Laurel Fig, Chinese Elm, and Tree-of-Heaven are among the most resistant species.

Apart from the tree-of-heaven, mentioned above and an exception to all rules, the trees that do well are the Chinese elm *(Ulmus parvifolia)* and the laurel fig. Regardless of the species, however, much depends on the availability of underground water. Where the water table is high, the roots may be able to contact the capillary fringe and thus obtain all the water they need. In some cases, paradoxically, an impervious blacktop may actually assist the tree by preventing excessive evaporation of circumjacent water. All moisture rising (by capillarity) from a high water table is trapped beneath the asphalt and so kept available to the thirsty tree roots which may often grow 150 or 200 feet in all directions in search of it.

Since under such conditions, the air supply to the roots is likely to be seriously impaired, it seems probable that the species that can survive are those possessing an unusually efficient air-conduction system by means of which aboveground air can make its way to the farthermost roots. Indeed, the Chinese elm is exceptionally well equipped with lenticels, little rust-colored islands of which stand out conspicuously up and down trunk and branches.

(The same effect may be observed when traveling along a paved highway through a desert region: plants close to the highway are green, turgid, and flourishing because their roots have access to the moisture accumulating beneath the concrete slab, while all the others, as far as the eye can reach, are stunted and often leafless, the underground water that rises through the loose porous soil escaping to the atmosphere before the roots can utilize it.)

Harmful in another way are rock or concrete wells sometimes built around a tree trunk either for ornamental reasons or in an attempt to keep a rising grade level from touching and presumably damaging the trunk. Such protection does little good, for the feeder roots are not close to the trunk but out under the branches (and often much farther out); consequently, that is the area needing protection from fill, as mentioned above.

If constructed too near the tree, the rock or concrete well will sooner or later interfere with the normal expansion of the trunk. That trees grow only when young and that upon reaching maturity they stop growing and, like people, remain at a fixed size during the rest of their lives is a widespread fallacy. Actually, of course, a tree continues growing as long as it lives: its stems elongate at their tips and enlarge in diameter with every passing year. Ignoring this simple fact, or overlooking it, we build our sidewalks, our garages, and our rock wells too close to a trunk which in time may expand to two, three, or four times its present dimensions.

Since two objects cannot occupy the same place at the same time, concrete and trees are inherently antagonistic. Sometimes the tree wins and the concrete loses in the struggle. Unless unusually thick, a concrete ring touching a trunk is almost certain to be cracked by the enormous

The construction of streets and sidewalks and the consequent cutting of roots always imperils adjacent trees, which thus are deprived of a large part of their anchorage and their water-absorbing system. Whether a tree so damaged can continue to live and whether it can stand up in subsequent high winds becomes a gamble.

pressure exerted during the growing season. Where the tree is only flanked, not encircled, its roots bear the brunt of the defense. The heaving effect of large lateral roots is well known to all who have seen their sidewalks crazily tilted or their patios upthrown or even their house foundations cracked; cottonwoods and elms are the most formidable in this respect. But the battle is an uneven one, and the forces of civilization often win. For the tree lover only one rule is safe: no large slabs of concrete near your trees.

Wire And Cables

As explained in the Chapter BRACING AND CABLING, there is a special way of attaching objects to trees—by insertion, not by encirclement. But since few people besides tree experts are familiar with this method, it follows that trees continue to take a lot of punishment from wires, cables, chains, ropes, and everything else that can be wrapped around or wedged into them.

Fence-builders see the tree as an oversized, conveniently located post and nail to it or wrap around it with all the gusto that accompanies an unexpected windfall. Everyone looking for some place to attach clotheslines, swings, hammocks, hanging flower-pots, etc., seizes on the tree as a

heavensent natural anchor. Even telephone and power companies press trees into their service, fastening all manner of insulators and direction-changing devices to their branches and even using them as anchors for their poles. Road-building, house-building, and house-moving crews loop chains and cables around trees to secure their equipment. In short, the tree, being the most solid object at hand, is utilized by all for every possible supporting, anchoring, or pulling need.

Chains, cables, or heavy ropes sliding around trunk or branch sometimes slip the bark and cut into the wood. Left in place, they do even more harm, strangling the imprisoned member as it tries to keep on growing.

Wires wrapped around trunk or limbs and forgotten often cause subsequent strangulation. If the wire is thin and the tree vigorous, the separated portions sometimes manage to grow around the obstruction and join on the other side. But if the wire is thick or wrapped doubly and the tree is in poor vigor, the tissues are in many cases unable to unite and death by strangulation ensues. If you have any wires, cables, bands, or ropes encircling your trees, remove them at once. (Parts of wire already embedded in the tree are best left in, for by pulling them out new wounds are opened.) If you wish to attach clotheslines, hammocks, etc, to the tree, do so not by encirclement but by using lag screw hooks as explained in Chapter 3, BRACING AND CABLING.

Low Temperatures

A tree is considered *hardy* or *not hardy* according to its ability to withstand cold. Trees are hardy in relation to their natural environment, otherwise they would not be there. But a tree that is hardy south may not be hardy north; hence if it is planted north of its natural range, it often needs to be artificially protected during cold weather, or it will be injured, perhaps killed. A tree that is hardy north will obviously not be harmed by cold if moved southward, although it may be harmed by the heat, the dryness, altered day-night relationship, or other factors of an unfamiliar environment. Many tender trees are damaged or killed by unusual cold waves penetrating their territory.

Even trees well adapted to northern latitudes are sometimes damaged by cold. Although normally matured tissues on cold-adapted species can survive many hours of continuous freezing, new succulent growth formed during "Indian summers" (periods when hot weather is unseasonably prolonged) or forced into being by late-summer fertilizing may be destroyed by low temperatures; this includes buds, twigs, and even small branches. For this reason such late feeding should be avoided, as should severe shearing back of shrubbery or evergreens just before the advent of cold weather.

Another type of injury is the *frost crack*—a longitudinal split which appears on trunks (and sometimes limbs) when sudden thaws follow freezing temperatures occur. These open with a loud report, like the sound of a gun being fired; they may be a foot or a foot-and-a-half long or even longer, several inches deep, and half an inch or an inch wide. Although they usually heal over during the following growing season, they may reopen during the second winter. The interior of the split should be protected with tree dressing. If the crack shows no indications of healing or if it reopens for several years in succession, a threaded rod or bolt-and-nut may be installed at that point.

For many cold-adapted species, a certain number of hours of low temperatures per year are necessary for their proper functioning. Fruit trees that are adapted to high latitudes often fail to flower and/or to set fruit when moved southward. This curious fact remained a mystery until carefully controlled experiments proved that in some species vital biological processes can be triggered only by a minimum number of hours of low temperatures per year. The temperature *pattern* is also significant. For some species the vital factor is the simple accumulation of the number of required hours, even though these come intermittently, spells of cold being interrupted by spells of higher temperatures; for other species the low temperatures need to be continuous for certain minimum periods. Many

of these patterns are not yet worked out; possibly it is their non-observance that explains many plants' erratic behavior, not only when moved out of their natural range but sometimes even within it.

Ice And Snow

Ice and snow do a limited amount of damage to trees every year, and in some years they do an excessive amount. Obviously greater in the North, the damage is not unknown in the South where intermittent penetration by exceptional cold waves injures and sometimes kills many fine specimens; In Dallas, for example, thousands of trees were damaged when freezing rains fell over Texas in the winter of 1949-1950. The damage is caused by the accumulation of ice and snow on the branches and limbs until they break under the unaccustomed weight.*

Ice is worse than snow, for it is solid and it clings, while snow may be blown off or shaken off by the movement of the branches in the wind. Evergreens, although in full leaf, often suffer less than broad-leaved trees because their structure allows them to bend with greater flexibility, and the peculiar arrangement of their branches permits the upper to rest upon the lower and the lower upon the ground.

The only preventive measure against ice and snow damage is adequate cabling and bracing. Fifty or seventy-five dollars spent on cabling might save hundreds of dollars' worth of subsequent pruning and, even more important, might easily prevent loss of the whole tree. In regions where ice and snow are frequent, the planting of brittle trees should be discontinued and the planting of strong-wood species encouraged.

Hail

Severe hail storms damage trees, stripping off the leaves, injuring the bark, and sometimes destroying the season's fruit crop. Damage on old trees with thick trunk- and branch-bark is limited to the leaves and twigs and, of course, fruit, if any. Younger trees with tender bark are damaged along their whole length, every hailstone leaving its mark. A week or so later the damaged bark falls off, exposing the wood, usually along areas 3 or 4 inches long and 1 to 1-1/2 inches wide. A young tree may show many scars of this description, alarming the inexperienced home-owner and sometimes puzzling even the expert.

*Apart from ice and snow, the only other things that weight down branches to the point of breaking them off are the fruits they themselves bear and the animals (or humans) that climb on them. The passenger pigeon is said to have alighted on trees in such numbers as to break off every branch. An old-time tall-tale tells of a hunter in the early days of this country who found so many wild turkeys perched in a tree that it took him all day to shoot them. When he finally finished the job and turned to look for his wagon, he found it dangling fifty feet in the air. Relieved of its load of turkeys, the tree had gradually straightened up, taking the horse and wagon, which he had tied to one of the branches, up with it!—Applied to the passenger pigeon, this story would very nearly be true.

Little, if anything, can be done to protect against hail damage. Young trees can be partly protected by covering with canvas or netting of some kind, although hail generally falls so suddenly that you won't have time for even this protection. Fortunately, damage to twigs and leaves is not severe, and the bark wounds are small enough to heal over very rapidly. On scars large enough to warrant it, paint the exposed wood. Protect against loss of fruit by adequate insurance.

In tropical regions, where totally unexpected, hail often falls with a violence unknown in the gelid North. Stones egg-size or larger fall as if hurled by a mighty hand, stripping every leaf on every tree and killing every exposed animal. When the storm passes, dead birds, rabbits, squirrels, possums, lizards, snakes, and other animals may be found in surprising numbers; and for many weeks afterwards the path of the storm, often rectangular, stands out starkly—a block of desolation within a frame of luxuriant green.

Lightning Injury

Trees are lightning's predestined victims. In every electrical storm of any magnitude occurring where trees exist, one or more is virtually certain to be struck. Although dry wood is an excellent insulator, living trees are moist with their own sap, and they stand with their feet in the water; moreover, they are usually the tallest objects around. They are, consequently, nearly ideal channels for the earthward conduction of the lightning bolt.

Isolated trees are more likely to be struck than those in a forest; and of those in a group the tallest is the most likely victim. Trees along the banks of streams are struck more often than those in drier situations. Trees near a house are sometimes struck, to the possible salvation of the building. It is notoriously unwise to take shelter under a tree during storms—yet people continue to do so. The danger is double: from lightning and from falling limbs in case of high winds.

Some species are more likely to be struck than others. Preferred victims seem to be oak, elm, pine, tuliptree, poplar, and ash. Some of the shallow-rooted species, such as maple, are seldom struck; on the other hand, the shallow-rooted willow and cottonwood are often struck, possibly because of their association with streams and rivers.

Many of us have seen lightning-damaged trees; some of us have seen the actual striking. Lightning does freakish things: when the bolt falls, it may utterly destroy the tree, destroy only part of it, or merely burn off a strip of bark. When I was a boy, lightning struck a large cottonwood in the lot adjoining the family home, utterly demolishing it and flinging branch and trunk fragments all over the neighborhood. One large splinter flew in my bedroom window and embedded itself in the wall a foot or so from where I lay sleeping.

Bark stripped off up and down the whole length of the tree by lightning stroke. Since this specimen is young and vigorous, the formation of new bark over the wound is rapid. Painting of the exposed wood to prevent insect and fungus attack is recommended.

Most struck trees are blasted from the top all the way down to the ground along one side in a strip that varies in width from six inches to a foot-and-a-half. The discharge seems to follow the grain, whether straight or spiraled. The damage is caused partly by actual burning and partly by exploding steam generated in the tissues by the extremely high temperature. Sometimes the tree is totally riven, as by a blow from a giant axe; sometimes it seems to explode, throwing fragments in all directions, like the cottonwood just described; sometimes no damage is apparent until a few weeks later, when the bark begins to fall off, exposing the wood.

Some trees are killed by one blast, others can withstand repeated strikings. Nearly all the oldest specimens among the Sequoias, particularly the isolated interior redwoods, have been struck many times during their thousands of years of growth, surviving with their great regenerative vigor these blows of fate as well as countless forest fires, drouths, floods, insect hordes, and other adversities.

Valuable specimen trees should be protected with lightning rods. The installation is simple and inexpensive. You can do it yourself or have it done by a qualified arborist. The materials may be ordered from A.M. Leonard & Son of Piqua, Ohio, or from some other tree-supply house. Drive a six-foot, pointed copper-iron rod into the ground near the tree's base; attach a braided, half-inch copper wire to the top of the rod and run it straight up one side of the trunk, fastening it at intervals with broad flat staples or flat bands secured by copper nails driven into the wood; fray out the end of the wire so that it opens up conically, and let it project upward a foot or so beyond the topmost twig. As the tree grows taller, splice additional wire on at the upper end. If the tree is an oak-like type with no central bole, run the wire up along the branches to the highest possible point, then fasten a long, stout two-by-four somewhere near the top in an upright position so that it projects beyond the canopy, and run the wire up it. Although no lightning rod is 100% effective, the possibility of eliminating or lessening the danger is attractive enough to make the installation worthwhile.

After a tree has been struck, it is wise to wait a few months to see whether or not it will live before spending money on its treatment. Sometimes the roots are killed by the blast, in which case recovery is impossible. If the roots have not been killed and the above-ground damage is not too great, the tree may well recover. Where recovery seems possible, feed and water the tree generously, peel and scrape away the dead bark, and paint the exposed wood with a liberal application of tree dressing. Support damaged limbs by cabling. If the tree continues to live, it will rebuild its destroyed bark surface in the years that follow. Since the wounds are usually long and narrow, such rebuilding is accomplished more rapidly than might be supposed.

Wind Damage

High winds probably take as great a toll of trees as any other natural agency. They twist off limbs, snap off the main bole at any weakened spot, or blow over the entire tree. To protect other plants, trees are planted as windbreaks, but what can be planted to protect the trees themselves? Only other trees, it being obvious that trees in a group withstand wind better than trees individually.

High winds are serviceable in that they break off branches that have grown disproportionately long and blow over weak and decayed trees that should have been removed six

The shearing effect of wind. Since the prevailing winds blow from the left in this location, the tree grows only in the lee of the protecting boulder.

Trees sheared and shaped by the prevailing winds, which in this photograph blows from the right.

months before. Winds—and termites—are nature's instruments for the disposal of trees that are no longer useful. Unfortunately, however, the wind sometimes takes the good with the bad. If trees possessed consciousness and memory and the capacity to fear things that have not yet happened, they would doubtless regard the wind as the Grim Reaper—a most unwelcome intruder that too often mistakes his target.

Prevention is better than cure. Wherever possible, plant strong-wooded species that do not break and split easily. Favor trees with a naturally strong "U" crotch, after the manner of the oaks, or try to train existing trees to have this form. Whenever possible, avoid the "V" crotch, which elms and ashes tend to develop, and above all the weak multiple crotch, where with continued growth each member pushes against the other, often with resultant splitting even without wind. Other things being equal, plant trees in the lee of other trees or houses, and so locate them, taking into account the prevailing winds, that if they are blown over, they will fall where they do the least damage.

If your tree is large, cable together all major limbs, (See Chapter 3, BRACING.) Leaning trees or shallow-rooted trees may be cabled to other trees. Trees with large trunk cavities particularly need this type of anchorage. Prune your trees judiciously. (See Chapter 9, PRUNING.) Cut back long, spindly branches one-third or one-half their length. Lower the crown in top-heavy trees. Prune to distribute weight equally all around the trunk, for a one-sided tree is more likely to be blown over than a well-balanced one.

An apparent exception to this rule is the case of trees that have grown up in regions where strong winds always blow from the same direction. Such trees are permanently deformed: their branches all on side and all pointing in the same direction and their boles permanently bent. Exposed to the buffetings of the wind from the sapling stage upwards, these trees have developed an exceptionally strong root system and are less easily blown over than straight, well-balanced trees grown in a more or less sheltered location. Such are the uses of adversity.

When winds rise to hurricane proportions, even the forests are not immune. In 1921 a gale traversed the western part of the Olympic Peninsula in Washington, cutting a swath 30 miles wide and 70 miles long with a total destruction of more than 5 billion board feet of timber. In 1938 a hurricane hit New England, flattening more than 3-1/4 billion board feet of timber, damaging 150 miles of telephone line, blocking 1000 miles of foot trails, washing out roads, and creating fire hazards in an area of several hundred thousand acres. Hurricanes have periodically denuded the peninsula of Yucatan, while their damage to the complementary peninsula of Florida has been hardly less severe.*

Unfortunately, very little can be done to prevent such catastrophes. At one time, and perhaps still, some of the state forests of Czechoslovakia were protected by great lines of baffles (fence-like panels) 40 feet high and 30 feet wide—a sort of glorified snow-fence. Reliable observers report this construction surprisingly effective.

*See Lafcadio Hearn's *Chita, A Memory of Last Island* for a dramatic description of the fury of a hurricane unleashed on a small island off the tip of Florida.

Sunburn

Incredible as it sounds, trees may be affected by sunburn. Incredible, because we are taught that plants seek the light, and because trees are the shelters we get under to protect ourselves from sunburn.

But with sun, as with everything else, it is possible to have too much of a good thing. Too much sun and too little water, if long continued, will kill any tree. When water is continuously transpired through the leaves and none is taken in by the roots, the tree is gradually desiccated. Although it may shed its leaves in an effort to preserve itself, even so, when drouth and heat are too prolonged, it dies.

This type of injury, although sun-induced, is not sunburn proper. Sunburn proper, or sunscald, refers specifically to the injury done to bark tissues by direct exposure to the sun. A tree may die of desiccation without having its bark actually burned. On the other hand, it may die of sunburn although receiving and transpiring abundant water.

There are four different cases in which sunburn occurs:

1. On newly transplanted young trees whose tender bark is exposed to hot sun before they develop a protective crown of leaves;

2. On northern trees transplated southward to regions of more intense sunlight;

3. On topped trees whose branches are suddenly deprived of their umbrella of shade;

4. On trees habituated to dense side-shade suddenly exposed to the sun by the removal of adjoining trees or of a protective building.

Note that in all such cases it is the suddenness of the change that does the damage. Like other plants and like animals, trees can adapt themselves to many things if changes are made gradually, but they cannot adapt if changes are made too suddenly.

When sunburn is severe on the trunks of young trees, it sometimes kills them. On large trees that have been topped, sunburn damage is usually limited to destroying the bark and cambium on the upper side of the limbs. To prevent these various kinds of damage, observe the following precautions:

1. Whenever possible, transplant trees in rainy, cloudy weather.

2. Wrap trunks and major branches of all transplants with heavy crepe paper or loose burlap or whitewash them.

Waxed milk containers, slipped over the stems of newly set-out trees, protect the tender bark from sunburn and also from rabbit damage. The wax is distasteful to the rodents and they will not gnaw through it.

In California, orchardists protect the stems of very young trees with a paper milk container from which both ends have been removed, simply slipping the container over the top and letting it rest on the ground.*

3. Protect transplants overhead with a semitranslucent canopy, such as those used in nurseries.

4. In regions of intense sun, spread out the pollarding of a large tree over a period of two or three years.

5. Do not trim trees (or shrubs) severely just as the rainy season is ending and hot cloudless weather is beginning. (This advice is particularly applicable to California, with its Mediterranean climate, the rains falling in the winter months and the summers practically cloudless.)

6. Feed and water sunburned trees in order to stimulate new growth. Scrape away dead bark and paint all exposed wood with appropriate tree dressing.

Dust, Soot, Smoke, and Smog Damage

Trees may experience two kinds of suffocation: suffocation of the roots by water or fill, and suffocation of the leaves and stems by soot, dust, or other foreign material accumulating on foliage and bark. The leaves, particularly on their lower surfaces, are covered with thousands of tiny openings *(stomata)* through which water vapor and gases are exchanged. Similarly, the bark is studded with openings *(lenticels)* through which air and water vapor may pass in and out. When either or both of these organs are clogged up, the tree suffers; in extreme cases it dies.

Trees growing in the forest seldom experience this type of suffocation. Dust, soot, and smoke are virtually unknown there, and frequent rains keep the leaves washed.

In a city, however, conditions are just the opposite. Dust is everywhere and is kept in a state of constant agitation by the unceasing traffic flow. Even when rain gives temporary alleviation, three or four hours afterwards the traffic dries the thin mud crust and churns it into dust. Trees along unpaved streets are commonly more white than green.

In industrial areas, factory chimneys belch out uncountable cubic feet of poisonous gases daily. When atmospheric conditions are just right—or just wrong—the gases, visible and invisible, and their particulate residue (soot), instead of being borne away by air currents and gradually dispersed, settle down like black snow on all objects underneath. The factories of Pittsburgh have long been notorious for their soot deposition. In Edinburgh, Scotland, the trains that puff noisily through the very center of the city so blacken the building fronts that the sale and rental of scaffolds (for cleaning the stonework) has grown to be an important business.

*This also serves to prevent rabbit damage to the tender stem: the rodents are repelled by the wax on the container and will not chew through it.

People living in such areas often suffer severe respiratory discomforts and diseases. Should we not expect trees to suffer similarly? They do, although their troubles do not often make headlines. Soot sometimes accumulates on leaves to such an extent that the tree dies or is seriously affected. The harm is done in three different ways:

1. By clogging the *stomata* and *lenticels,*
2. By reducing the amount of light reaching the chloroplasts and hence reducing the tree's ability to manufacture food,
3. By direct poisoning with sulfur dioxide gas.

Unfortunately, you can do little to prevent the accumulation of dust and soot. Obviously, if you live on a paved street in a quiet residential area your trees have the advantage over those in dusty districts or near factories. By using a hose, you can wash dust off small plants and shrubs and off the lower branches of trees. You can also wash off soot, although to a lesser degree.

Trees with a waxy, shiny coating on their leaves are less affected by dust and soot than others. The poplar, the ginkgo, the tree-of-heaven, the black acacia, and the eucalyptus are some of the best for planting in unfavorable locations.

Ironically, while the smoke and soot of industrial city factories is beginning to come under control, contamination from internal combustion engines, each unit insignificant in itself but staggering in their totality, is increasing daily.

The incompletely burned products from the millions of automobile exhaust pipes include such plant-harmful substances as carbon and olefinic peroxidases. The blanket of smog that envelops many large cities slows the growth rate or kills outright many flowering plants and destroys the epiphytic lichens that frequently mottle tree trunks; in fact, there is increasing evidence that it damages many species of trees, even large ones, formerly believed immune. When an aerial survey by the Forest Service in November, 1969, showed *161,000 acres* of conifers dead or dying in southern California, authorities were unanimous in attributing the damage to Los Angeles smog.

The magnitude of the global pollution problem is at last making us realize that whatever injures plants injures us too, directly or indirectly. Recent energetic action by environmentalists has begun to produce results in the form of decontamination of chimney emissions, obligatory installation of catalytic converters on automobiles, and, most recently of all, the banning of the fluoride propellants in aerosol cans that are believed potentially dangerous to the atmosphere's ozone layer.

Mistletoe

In warmer parts of the country, one of the most harmful of parasites is mistletoe, an interesting and attractive plant

Mistletoe growing on Hackberry trunk and limb. The wood is weakened by the parasite, and affected limbs break off under stress conditions.

in its own right but a most undesirable guest on your lawn trees. Mistletoe sends its *haustoria* (roots) directly into the live tissues of the host tree, absorbing water and minerals and other needed elements. Although green and active photosynthetically, mistletoe cannot live in the soil. It must live parasitically, or semi-parasitically, and trees are its chosen victims. At the point of attack, the tree branch (or trunk) swells, sometimes to two or three times its normal size, and the bark assumes a curious scaly appearance; beyond that point the branch atrophies and often dies.

Where the parasite abounds, trees are found with many short bare limbs, each terminating in a knobby swelling. These, the work of mistletoe, might have been seized upon by the ingenious savage and pressed into service as mankind's first clubs. Many branches twist and turn, shooting off at tangents, in what seems to be an effort to escape the parasite by veering from their normal course. (Such con-tortions are caused by the deformation of tissues at the point of infestation.)

Many hundreds of tree species are parasitized by mistletoe. Particularly susceptible are elms, hackberries, ashes, mesquites, and desert ironwood *(Olneya Tesota);* pecans and walnuts somewhat less; oaks still less, although this varies with the species. The blackjack oak is rather commonly victimized, the post oak seldom, the southern live oak almost never, the California Valley oak sometimes yes, sometimes no, possibly depending on the soil in which it grows. The rarity of mistletoe on oak trees in Europe and Asia is the basis of many superstitions among primitive peoples of those continents. As the bringer of good or bad luck, the symbol of this or that, it is as exceptional and portentous an occurrence as an eclipse or an earthquake. Sir James Frazer in his anthropological classic *The Golden Bough* tells the story in detail. (The "golden bough" refers

Mistletoe growing on Maple branches produce tumors.

crown and part of the trunk, and all new growth should be carefully watched to guard against reinfection. Wrapping of infected areas with black plastic sometimes prevents resprouting.

New infections are caused by birds, which, eating the plant's attractive white berries, carry the sticky seeds from twig to twig in their beaks or on their feet and/or feathers, or deposit them with their droppings; arboreal animals may also be carriers. Even without animate carriers, infection spreads by the viscid seeds falling from higher to lower branches and sticking, there to germinate and take root.

Mistletoe grows slowly but very tenaciously. On an incense cedar with an estimated age of 450 years the principal mistletoe mass is believed to have begun its growth 425 years ago, attacking the tree when this was barely 25 and staying with it, like the Old Man of the Sea on Sinbad's shoulders, ever since. Some infected trees can live on for many years, although with weakened vitality and usually with spoiled beauty. Branches are not only deformed but are also so weakened and so weighted down by the very heavy globular masses that they often break off.

In Australia, experiments have been made to test the extent of mistletoe's damage to eucalyptus trees. Radioactive salts injected into the trunks were traced by Geiger counters and found to have lodged 100% within the mistletoe masses, thus indicating the absorptive and pre-emptive powers of the parasite.

No effective chemical or biological remedy has yet been found. Promising results have been obtained by (1) spot-

to the limb of an oak tree with a sprig of orange-colored mistletoe growing on it.)*

Mistletoe may be removed mechanically by sawing, cutting, or breaking it off. It is most conveniently removed by sawing, since some large masses, which come to weigh as much as 100 pounds, develop semiwoody stems of considerable toughness. Removal of the aerial parts, however, does not usually kill the plant, which soon sends up new shoots from the haustoria embedded within the host. Once the parasite has firmly established itself, it travels through the host tissues and becomes capable of sending up shoots at points several feet from the place of original infection. Hence all small infected branches should be removed entirely, and large ones as well if their loss can be esthetically afforded. Severely infected trees should be cut back radically, even though that means losing the whole

*Could the Dracula legend have been inspired by the spectacle of mistletoe sucking the life out of its victim? Before dismissing this as speculative fantasy, we should recall and review the intimate relationship existing between trees and early men and the mythologial and symbolic significance attached to all natural objects. Consult Sir James Frazer, Claude Levi-Strauss, *et al.*

Mistletoe mass on Cedar Elm *(Ulmus crassifolia).*

Walnut tree heavily infested by mistletoe. Virtually all the greenery in this picture is mistletoe. Its vitality sapped, the dying tree is able to put out only a few hundred leaves of its own at lower right.

Mistletoe burl on Mesquite *(Prosopis juliflora)*. Although the aerial shoots of the parasite have been scraped off, the internal parts continue to live, weakening and deforming the tree.

spraying with various weed-killers and similar preparations, and (2) injecting chemicals into the host trunk in an attempt to destroy the internal parts of the parasite. Although encouraging, the work has not yet passed the experimental stage.

Dwarf mistletoe, much smaller than common mistletoe, its visible parts sometimes protruding only 1/2″ or so, attacks conifers in the western states, particularly in the Rocky Mountain area, damaging millions of dollars worth of timber. It is also implicated in the production of "witches broom" on many species of broadleaved trees.

Epiphytes

Although mistletoe is the only arboreal parasite of any consequence in the Temperate Zones, there are many other plants growing on trees that are commonly mistaken for parasites. These include bromeliads, lichens, liverworts, mosses, ferns, certain kinds of climbing cacti, and even orchids. It is important to become acquainted with the principal kinds of these so as to avoid the very natural confusion that ensues.

Any plant that uses another plant (or some inanimate object) merely as an anchor for supporting itself but that draws nothing from it in the way of nourishment is an *epiphyte,* not a parasite. Lichens, liverworts, and mosses, the small fry among the epiphytes, are often overlooked, but the bromeliads, the ferns, the orchids, and others are too bizarre, too conspicuous, and frequently too beautiful to fail to be noticed. These larger epiphytes (also called *air-plants)* generally have small wiry roots that grip their support very

The effect of mistletoe on a Pecan tree. At each point where the parasite invades the host a large swelling results, often followed by atrophy of the distal portion of the affected limb; hence the numberous short branches each with a ball at the end. Such may have been man's first clubs.

firmly and that, like the holdfast of a seaweed, will usually break before relinquishing their hold. A few moments' examination suffices to show that these tendril-like roots are attached only to the outer surface of the support plant, not penetrating its interior as do the haustoria of mistletoe.

Further observation reveals that they grow on telephone and light wires as impartially as on tree branches. Since epiphytes draw nothing in through their roots (excepting some epiphytic orchids which have specialized root structures for the absorption of water), they are dependent for moisture on whatever they can absorb through their leaves from rain, snow, fog, and dew, and dependent for needed nutrients on dust particles that float through the air and on various plant and animal (chiefly insect) residues that accumulate in their tightly massed structure. All of them have chloroplasts and are photosynthetically capable of manufacturing their own food, provided they receive the needed amounts of water and minerals—always very small and consequently almost always available.

Bromeliads

Largest, most bizarre, and most widely distributed of the epiphytes are the bromeliads. Like the orchids and the ferns, this strange group of plants includes terrestrial members as well—the pineapple being the best known. And with their long, pointed, barbed, leathery leaves, protected with thick waxy cuticle, and arranged in a tight rosette, they much resemble pineapples, although most of us, whose experience is limited to buying the fruit in the super-market or, worse still, dumping it out of a can, will not be helped by the comparison.

The commonest bromeliads in the United States are the "ball moss" (or "bunch moss") and the "Spanish moss" found perched on or hanging from many of our southern trees, in particular the southern live oak. Although "ball moss" is not oranmental and tree surgeons are paid considerably sums year after year to remove it, "Spanish moss" adds interest to its anchor plants, so that the same tree surgeons that are paid to remove its unattractive cousin are commissioned to drape *it* around the boughs of favorite patio trees. Few things, indeed, are more beautiful than a majestic Louisianian or Mississippian live oak with its wide-spreading boughs festooned with the long sweeping tresses of this interesting bromeliad, swaying voluptuously with every slightest breeze and turning marvelous combinations of gray and green when wetted by a passing shower. What would Hopkins, who was fascinated by "shook foil," have written about the soft glittering sheen of this undulant bromeliad?

But to see the bromeliads in their full glory it is necessary to visit Mexico, Central America, and other hot countries of much precipitation. In such places they attain their greatest size and exhibit themselves in greatest profusion, not infrequently being more attractive than the anchor plant itself, growing upon it so profusely as to exclude it from sight, and also from light and air and hence to interfere with its growth and in extreme cases to bring about its death. For this is the evil of epiphytes: although not parasitizing trees, they sometimes grow upon them so thickly as to smother them or by their great weight to break off their branches.

Such epiphytic excesses are, however, confined to the tropics. Even in our southern states, where the bromeliads most abound, they seldom occur in such numbers as to harm the support tree. Where considered objectionable, they may be pulled or scraped off. On a large tree heavily infected this may keep three or four men busy for an equal number of days. The "ball moss" in particular, which grows in tight little clumps ranging in size from a thumbnail to John

Sullivan's fist, takes hold not only along the trunk and main limbs where it is easily reached but out among the twigs to their extremest tip where it must be carefully and tediously pulled loose by hand.

Lichens

Lichens are extremely interesting plants found growing on rocks, fallen logs, old buildings, and the trunks and branches of trees. They make themselves visible as small, irregularly shaped, grayish-white or rust-colored patches or splotches closely appressed against trunk or rock. When wet, their color may change through various shades of gray, green, orange, and red.

Since they are so frequently found on tree trunks, many people believe them parasitic, or at least symptomatic of some obscure disease. Actually, lichens are neither parasites nor fruiting bodies of fungi nor colonies of insects nor any one of the many other things for which they are commonly mistaken: they are combinations of alga and fungus growing together in a partnership mutually beneficial. The algal member of the symbiosis contains chlorophyll (giving the plant its greenish color) by means of which it manufactures food for the common store, while the fungal constituent provides the structural supporting network. The partnership has proved a very successful one, for lichens exist throughout most of the world, even on rocks in Antarctica! Poetically labeled "time's stains", lichens are believed to be among the oldest of living organisms, both phylogenetically and individually; some single specimens are believed as old as or older than the redwoods and the bristle-cone pine. Sometimes they occur as long, drooping filaments (Old Man's Beard), sometimes as fleshy, flower-like lobes (reindeer moss), more often as scaly incrustations on rocks and tree trunks. When examined closely, they are seen to be beautiful little plants, intrinsically of the highest interest, while ecologically they are indispensable in that they colonize desolate areas where nothing else will grow, and by slowly crumbling the rock substratum and catching and holding dust particles they prepare an exiguous soil bed for other members in the long line of plant succession.

Lichens are harmless to trees, except in the rare instances where they occur in such superabundance as to interfere with the lenticels on the bark. Where considered objectionable, they may be scraped off with a wire brush or killed by spraying with arsenate of lead. Ordinarily, however they add interest to the tree on which they grow, and for those who are attracted by miniatures, form a microcosmos complete within themselves. Called by John Ruskin, "the first mercy of the earth," they soften the rock, populate the wilderness, and lend venerableness to the gnarled and twisted trunk.

Moss

Mosses are small green plants often found along stream borders and on tree trunks. Various other small plants superficially similar in appearance and growing in the same habitat, such as algae, lichens, liverwort, small ferns, and even small bromeliads, are often loosely grouped together and mistakenly called "mosses."

The true mosses, members of the phylum Bryophyta, are rather easily distinguished, however, and are well worth a few hours of study. They are living cushions, green, soft, and velvety. Unlike lichens, they cannot stand extremes of heat and drouth, although some of them survive such emergencies by passing into a state of suspended animation. On the contrary, they thrive in cool, moist, shady places: near streams, on decaying logs in the forest, on shingles where the sun is not too intense and the rainfall is frequent (in Jalapa, Veracruz, the red-tiled roofs are beautifully softened with moss); and, as every Boy Scout knows, on the north side of tree trunks; hence their usefulness in orienting oneself when lost in the woods. Why on the north side? Because there they are exposed to less sun and so retain whatever moisture they receive from rain or snow for remarkably long periods in their porous absorbent reticulated structure. As we travel equatorward, of course, we observe the sun declining less and less to the south, until, on that great circle itself, we see it passing directly overhead. Here the Boy Scouts and the Junior woodchucks have to orient themselves by the constellations or in some other way, for no moss grows on the north side of the trunks— indeed, no moss at all is found except in the thick of the forest where deep shade permits its growth and then no one side of the trunk is favored over any other. Still farther south, in the southern hemisphere, the winter sun *(their winter sun)* declines to the north rather than to the south, moss reappears on tree trunks—on the south side—and orientation again becomes possible.

Moss on tree trunks does no known harm, being neither parasite nor saprophyte, growing upon the tree as it grows upon rock. It is rather an adornment than otherwise, and there seems to be no legitimate reason for removing it.

Ferns

Although most kinds of ferns are terrestrial, some are epiphytic, growing on tree trunks and branches as do orchids and bromeliads. Like other epiphytes, these manufacture their own food, using the tree only as a perch; hence they do no harm unless occurring in such numbers as to crowd out leaves—a most unlikely possibility. In addition to the epiphytic forms, some terrestrial ferns also grow on trees: in the crotches when these accumulate a layer of debris thick enough to make rooting possible or in decaying cavities where the presence of water, the decaying wood,

English Ivy *(Hedera Helix)* will cover a house—or a Palm tree. Forming a heavy mass with semiwoody stems, it does little harm when confined to the trunk of the host tree. The real damage begins when it climbs up among the leaves and shuts these out from light and air.

and the accumulation of litter combine to approximate soil conditions or even along the main branches, when horizontally inclined, where exiguous layers of soil sometimes build up by the activity of lichens and mosses. In the tropical forest a single giant tree may be a complete botanical universe in itself, twined about with vines and creepers and bearing on its massive boughs a bewildering variety of algae, lichens, mosses, ferns (both epiphytic and terrestri-

Wisteria vine on gum elastic *(Bumelia lanuginosa)*. Notice how the vine at the bottom has become almost as large as the trunk of the tree and how its numerous convolutions have begun to exert a certain strangling action. From the Westeria, however, and most other Temperate Zone vines the damage to the host results not from strangulation but from light-exclusion: the exuberant canopy of the vine is depriving the tree's foliage of light and air. (Several years after this picture was taken the host tree died.)

al), orchids, bromeliads, mistletoe, and sometimes even other trees,

In our less exuberant Temperate Zone habitats the presence of ferns on trees is a rare enough phenomenon that we should rejoice over it. Along the northern stretches of our Pacific Coast where precipitation is so heavy, and particularly in the Olympic Peninsula, beautiful aerial gardens of mosses and ferns abound; a tree crotch 50 feet in the air may be a Kew Garden in miniature.

Vines

Vines, although neither parasites nor epiphytes, are bad for a tree. Sometimes a tree may live for many years in spite of infestations of mistletoe and heavy burdens of epiphytes, but it can be killed within three or four years by the unchecked growth of certain vines.

Because they derive no nourishment from the trees to which they cling, the common vines are not parasitic; neither are they epiphytic because they have roots in the ground rather than in the air. A vine uses a tree simply and purely for support, and it grows equally well against a house or a fence, on a wire trellis, or on a telephone pole. It damages a tree in a negative rather than a positive sense— not by drawing anything out of it but by developing its exuberant canopy of leaves over the tree's own canopy and thus excluding from it the light and air it needs for proper functioning.

Certain vines more limited or more open in their habits of growth may grow upon a tree without killing it; others, including some of the ivies and the dominating mustang grapes, exert so strong a smothering effect as to bring about death in a few seasons. Even when they do not kill, they stunt; hence all vines must be considered potentially injurious to trees and should be removed from them, at least down to the first significant crotch. While on the trunk itself our common Temperate Zone vines do no direct harm, they serve as a hiding place for insects of all kinds and, by conserving moisture may facilitate wood decay where bark injuries are present. If you prize your trees, the best rule is: No Vines.

Some tropical vines, usually called *lianas,* which ascend a tree by twining rather than by clinging, exert a positive strangling action which interferes with the downward translocation of fluids, thus slowing the growth of the support tree and sometimes killing it. Some of the lianas become so thick and muscular that at first sight the tree seems to be caught in the coils of an enormous boa constrictor. As the tree trunk continues to expand in girth and the coils of the liana tighten by their own continuing growth, a fierce struggle for survival develops. If the tree is weakened by insect defoliation, fire damage, or some other cause, the vine may win and literally strangle its victim to death. But when the tree is vigorous and otherwise undamaged, it usually emerges the victor, growing around the vine and engulfing it. Where trees of the same species are growing nearby, it is possible that these supply the tree with nourishment via natural root grafts during its long struggle with the vine.

Girdling Roots

All exogenous tree stems, including twigs, branches, main boughs, and the trunk itself, expand in girth as long as

Girdling root. As tree and root both continue to grow, the tree is slowly strangled. When the girdling root is underground, the cause for a tree's slow decline and sometimes death often passes undetected.

Wild grape vine on Oak trunk. While this type of vine exerts no strangling action, it harms the tree by foliage competition, reaching up for the light and often overshadowing the host plant to the point where it stunts it or even kills it.

they live. Given the principle of their construction, they cannot help doing so; they have no choice. Hence when a wire or cable is wrapped around any part of an exogenous tree—and this includes all kinds except palms, yuccas, and similar monocots—the encircled stem gradually expands against the obstruction and thus brings about its own strangulation. (Except in the cases where it manages to grow around the encircling band and engulf it.)

The same effect is brought about even more strangely in the case of girdling roots. A girdling root is a root that somehow grows out of its normal position and wraps itself around the taproot or around one of the large lateral roots or around the trunk itself near the ground line. In such a case the root functions like an encircling wire, with the difference that the root and the trunk *both* increase in diameter, until a point comes when the root may completely strangle the tree.

Girdling roots are frequently caused by the nursery practice of potting small trees in metal cans. When kept too long

This huge girdling root is beginning to strangle the tree. This strange form of suicide is not uncommon and, when it occurs underground, often goes undetected.

in such containers the roots become hopelessly twisted and tangled; when planted such a tree may fail to grow for many years or may even die; of those that do grow, many sooner or later find further growth impeded by one or more girdling roots. Girdling roots are also caused by poor planting practices: the roots crammed into a hole too small for them so that they intercross and wind around each other. A third cause is unfavorable environmental conditions, such as proximity to a street, a rock wall, a building foundation, inducing the roots on that side to double back on themselves in search of more favorable feeding areas.

Since roots often form natural grafts, you may wonder why girdling roots do not do the same. Sometimes they do, and in such cases the problem is solved: trunk and root fuse together, and no strangulation results. But often they do not—and why they do not is one of the strangest unsolved problems in tree behavior.

The only remedy for girdling roots is to remove them with saw, axe, or mallet and chisel. When such roots are below ground level, they are, of course, harder to discover. When a tree is in a declining condition from no visible cause, the possibility of a girdling root should not be overlooked. In some cases the taproot may be strangled two or three feet under the surface by an erratic side root.

Chlorosis

Chlorosis is a condition characterized by the paling of normal dark-green foliage to a much lighter green or yellow or even white. It is initiated by a variety of causes, such as excess lime in the soil, low soil temperatures associated with an unusually cold spring, or excess soil water, which in turn may be due to poor drainage, prolonged rainy periods, or simple overwatering. These environmental conditions prevent the necessary nutrients from reaching the tree roots or make them unavailable for absorption and utilization.

The pattern and intensity of the yellow coloring in the leaves serve as clues to help us divine which nutrients are in short supply. Sometimes the insufficient element is nitrogen, sometimes it is magnesium, sometimes it is one of the micronutrients; most often, perhaps, it is iron.

Nitrogen deficiency can be corrected by punch-bar feeding with a good general fertilizer in the proportions of 6-10-4 or 5-10-5 or, if the deficiency is unusually severe, with 20-10-5 or some similar proportion, heavy on the nitrogen.

Iron deficiency can be corrected by root fertilizing with iron sulphate, or, for quicker results, by foliage spraying

1. Move the tree,
2. Move the driveway,
3. Correct the iron deficiency by foliar spraying or by trunk injection, as indicated above,
4. Acidify the soil by the addition of sulphur.

Any soil consistently too alkaline can be acidified by the addition of sulphur or aluminum sulphate. Chlorosis is an abnormal condition and should be corrected as soon as possible. Pale green or yellowing foliage is a distress signal of the most unequivocal kind; no foundering ship ever ran up a more plainly worded appeal for help.

Bleeding And Slime Flux

Many trees bleed or drip from pruning wounds and/or bark injuries. Some, such as most of the oaks, the ashes, horsechestnut, basswood, the eucalyptus, and others, seldom or never bleed. Other species bleed slightly but soon cease to do so. Others, such as mesquite, hard maple, birch, walnut, yellowwood, and American elm, bleed profusely. Although in most cases the bleeding does no serious harm to the tree (except as discussed below), many homeowners are disturbed by it, and the sap drip frequently falls on sidewalks, parked automobiles, and other objects, making objectionable stains.

Unfortunately, little can be done to control bleeding. Trees that are natural bleeders will bleed even out of correctly made pruning cuts painted over with the best of paints, while trees that are not natural bleeders will not lose a drop out of the ugliest stub. The profuse bleeders should not be pruned when dormant but only when in full leaf. This antibleeding technique, although seemingly a reversal of the natural order of things, works because a tree in full leaf requisitions most of the sap flow to maintain turgidity in all those thousands of unfurled rapidly transpiring leaves, while a tree that has shed its foliage is transpiring nothing and consequently has its vessels fully charged and under pressure, ready to leak at the slightest wound. This does not apply to nonbleeders, which can be pruned any time.

When the sap drip from a wound falls directly onto the ground, it does little or no harm. But when the wound stands in such relation to the branch or trunk it occurs on that the drip or ooze runs down these, it often produces what is called *slime flux*. Slime flux is unsightly, malodorous, and harmful to the tissues it flows over.

There are two kinds of flux: (1) brown slime flux, which originates in the heartwood sap,* and (2) alcoholic slime flux, which originates in the sap of bark and sapwood. Although the two kinds may occur together, more commonly only one kind is found at a time.

---

*Although the cells of the heartwood are dead, they are, in many species, filled with resins, tannins, and other metabolic by-products, often under high pressure. In this sense only is it possible to speak of "heartwood sap"—not in the sense of a circulating medium.

With continued growth an erratic, girdling root will exert a strangling action on the base of the trunk and in extreme cases kill the tree. Such a root should be cut off.

with liquid iron (ferrous sulphate) or by trunk injection with ferric phosphate. The latter is accomplished by boring a series of downward-slanting 1/2″ diameter holes around the trunk at intervals of 6″ or so (on a smaller tree fewer holes, of course), each hole penetrating 1-1/2″ or 2″ into the sapwood, and by inserting a ferric phosphate capsule into each hole, letting it dissolve there and be carried upward in the sap flow.

Chelating compounds added to the soil greatly facilitate iron absorption. In a convincing experiment with chlorotic pin oaks, iron sequestrene (a chelating compound) mixed in the upper six inches of soil brought about the appearance of new, healthy leaves at branch tips within three weeks.

Plants vary greatly in their chemical responses. Sweet gum *(Liquidamber)* and silk-oak *(Grevillea)* are so sensitive that they commonly become chlorotic when growing near a concrete driveway or concrete street: the lime that leaches out of the concrete alkalinizes the soil just enough to inhibit the tree's ability to absorb existing iron. Under such conditions and for such plants all the iron in Brooklyn Bridge placed in the soil might prove unavailing. The remedy is to:

As the sap issues from the tree, it is a more or less clear liquid, but the starches and sugars it contains attract large numbers of bacteria, fungi, yeasts, and insects, which rapidly ferment it into a white, foul-smelling solution. The acids and aldehydes in the solution are toxic to the tissues they flow over, destroying bark and cambium.

Treatment is difficult. If the flux comes from a pruning cut or bark wound, this should be properly shaped so as to facilitate rapid healing. (See Chapter 10, WOUND RE-PAIR.) If it comes from the bottom of a filled cavity, this should be reopened for further treatment, and a drain pipe should be installed. In stubborn cases it may be necessary to char the face of the wound (if large enough to permit this) with a blow torch (being careful, or course, not to let the flame come near the surrounding living tissues) and to seal it repeatedly with heavy coats of asphaltum.

Recent experiments indicate that persistent bleeding of elms, and to a lesser extent of other trees, is often caused by a bacterial disease to which the name ''wetwood'' has been given. This disease affects either sapwood or heartwood or both together, producing fermentation and resulting in high pressure which forces the sap out through pruning cuts and bark wounds. Sometimes the infected sap is carried up into the branches where it may cause curling, drooping, wilting, and even loss of leaves.

To combat this condition, bore an upward-slanting hole in the tree below the place where the flux is coming out and install a short length of 1/2'' pipe (copper or iron) to carry the drip away from the trunk. The hole should pass through the heartwood and well into the sapwood on the opposite side—in other words, almost completely through the tree. Insert the pipe just far enough so that it will seat firmly; if inserted too far, it will not drain the sap that accumulates in the region through which it passes. The hole-and-pipe treatment, while not a cure, prevents drip injury to the trunk and usually prevents the toxic sap's being carried up into the branches. Note that the pipe has three functions:

1. It relieves internal hydraulic pressures and so stops bleeding from inconvenient locations;
2. It diverts and discharges the sap drip in such a manner that it does not fall directly on stem tissues;
3. It prevents the drainage hole from growing together, as it otherwise would soon do.

To avoid installing the pipe at head level, where it may be dangerous to passersby, or higher up where its drip may be inconvenient, you might try installing it at ground level or even slightly underground, where in some cases it has been observed to perform its functions equally well.

Injury By Animals

When we think of animal injury to trees, we think at once of insects; but we should not forget that quadrupeds, and even some birds, also inflict a certain amount of damage.

In the woods, deer and moose damage or kill seedlings by trampling and/or browsing. Deer, moose, antelopes, rabbits, squirrels, and porcupines chew the bark, sometimes entirely girdling the tree, especially in the winter when little food is available. Bears also inflict heavy damage on trees in their search for honey, not only breaking off branches by their great weight but sometimes ripping a hollow tree apart with their powerful claws. Just for the record, we should not neglect to mention elephant damage; in the few places where these great beasts survive they treat trees with all the gentleness of a bulldozer, snapping the small ones off and trampling them into the ground, pushing over even medium-sized trees to reach the fruit or foliage, and making long treks of hundreds of miles to get at a stand of tropical almonds *(Terminalia catappa)* from which they strip and eat the bark, presumably because of its high calcium content. Giraffes also do a considerable amount of browse damage, pruning the thorny Mimosa trees around the top in a way that would do credit to the tree surgeon. (Are there any tree surgeons in Africa?)

In urban areas most of these animals are of course ruled out—but not all of them. In the northern parts of our country, in the Rocky Mountain areas, and even in the densely populated eastern states, animals tend constantly to encroach on civilization, as civilization has encroached upon them. People living in suburban areas or on farms are sometimes surprised, particularly in times of prolonged cold and snow, to find deer tracks around their bark-stripped trees.

Squirrels, rabbits, and field mice are common in most urban areas. Squirrels in particular seem to be everywhere. They chew off tender bark, bite off twigs, and crack or harvest all the nuts they can get to. In the South they are regarded as a plague by all owners of pecan trees, who have invented some interesting guards to keep them off, in the shape of bands of tin wrapped around the trunks, flared out at the top like lamp-shades, after the manner of rat guards on ship hawsers. Squirrels and possums live in tree cavities. Although they seem not to enlarge the cavities, they often prevent the mouth of the hole from growing together by their constant entering and leaving.

Dogs frequently damage plants and young trees with their urine. They also are not above chewing the bark, which they often do from boredom or frustration or revenge when tied. For the urine problem, various chemical preparations are on the market to be sprayed on the tree or sprinkled around it with the intention of repelling sniffing dogs. If there are many dogs in the neighborhood and your trees are young and easily damaged, the most certain protection is to build a small wire cage around each tree.

Cats are fond of sharpening their claws on tree trunks. Older trees with thick bark are little affected, but the young smooth-barked trees, which are the ones the cats always seek out, may be seriously damaged by repeated clawing.

The bark on this elm is being chewed off by a pet dog. Where animal and tree are locked up in the same enclosure, the tree often falls victim to the animal's frustrated chewing and scratching.

Although woodpeckers are highly beneficial birds in the economy of nature, the sapsucker is the black sheep of the family. Perching on the trunk, it makes even, horizontal rows of holes, making the tree look as if some one word one had been firing at it with a machine-gun. The bird eats the inner bark and the cambium, then returns day after day to eat the insects that accumulate around the holes and to reopen these when necessary. It is known to attack over 200 different kinds of trees, causing serious damage and in some cases even death. The simplest control measure is to hang, by two- or three-foot cords, light-weight, silver-colored pie plates from the branches up and down the tree's length. These are inexpensive, easy to hang, easy to replace, and by twirling and shimmering with the slightest breeze, they effectively frighten the woodpecker away.

Fortunately the incisions are slender and vertically aligned and hence heal over quickly, but it is always possible to have too much of a good thing. Loose wrapping of the trunk with burlap or with wire mesh (don't forget to loosen it as the tree grows) is an effective deterrent.

Birds do most of their damage to fruit trees, eating the crop before we have a chance to. The choicier the fruit, the more they seem to like it. On many trees they eat the seeds, and on some the buds. However, the good they do by eating harmful insects so far outweighs the bad that we could easily afford to plant extra trees exclusively for their benefit.

It is sometimes believed that woodpeckers injure trees by drilling their nesting holes in them. Actually, they drill only into already rotten or semi-rotten spots. Most of their time is spent hopping up and down the tree, not looking for new places to drill holes but searching out and eating wood-boring larvae.

The one woodpecker definitely pernicious is the sapsucker. This tireless bird goes from one tree to another making horizontal rows of shallow holes from which the sap almost immediately begins to flow. The bird is believed to eat (or is it drink?) the exuding sap, and to eat the insects that are attracted to it. By making many holes all in neat horizontal rows, up and down trunk and branches—and by revisiting periodically to keep them open—the sapsucker seriously damages and sometimes even kills trees of many different species. Of the trees that survive the severe bleeding, most (once the bird goes away) quickly heal over the small wounds.

Paint Injury

Some kinds of paints can damage or even kill trees, particularly young ones with tender bark. Certain paints with an oil base will kill smooth-barked species, such as hard maple and sycamore a foot or less in diameter, if applied in a complete circular band. Creosote, an excellent preserver of dry wood, should not be used on live trees, as it kills inner bark and cambium very quickly. You may use it sparingly to treat the inactive center of an old pruning cut or the exposed heartwood of a cavity, but keep it away from the margin of live tissue. Avoid paints with tar or tar derivatives, which are usually toxic to tree tissues.

Of the various preparations on the market for banding trees (to help control insects that crawl up from the ground), some contain toxic ingredients. When used on old trees with thick outer bark, they do no harm. Some persons, however, scrape this outer bark off to make application easier, sometimes down to the quick, and use of the material then becomes dangerous. Young trees with thin, tender bark are, of course, even more susceptible to injury. If you have occasion to band young trees, first wrap the trunk with burlap or some similar material, then spread the substance over this.

Most commercial tree paints have an asphalt base with some fungicidal ingredient added. Asphalt—not the same as tar—is completely harmless to the tree. Roofing compounds made of asphalt mixed with asbestos fibers should not be used for painting pruning cuts because they form a thick surface that impedes the escape of bubbles of air and liquid from the cut and sometimes actually contribute to decay. They may, however, be safely and conveniently used to fill small holes, either alone or mixed with sand.

Sometimes good paints are made harmful by the addition of toxic diluents. Petroleum oils should never be used for this purpose—certainly not kerosene. Turpentine is acceptable, being itself a vegetable product, but the safest thinner of all is linseed oil. *Bordeaux* powder dissolved in linseed oil is the preferred material for painting cavity interiors.

Pine oil, widely used by veterinarians for painting dehorning wounds and even flesh wounds, is an excellent tree paint. Orange shellac is recommended for painting exposed cambium and inner bark tissues at the edge of pruning cuts or newly opened cavities.

Formerly unacceptable because of their lead content and still dubious because of their oil base, house paints are not recommended. Even latex paints, containing neither lead nor oil, and non-injurious, are not appropriate for living tissues.

Salt-Water Injury

Trees living near the ocean are sometimes injured by blowing salt spray. Trees on the beach itself, such as palms, sea-grapes, and the Monterey cypress, are of course acclimated to saltiness of the air and saltiness of the soil—in fact, can hardly live without the salt. But those living farther back and not normally receiving salt spray through the air are injured when it does accidentally reach them. This occurs rarely, of course, only during exceptionally strong and prolonged winds. The hurricane of 1939, for example, carried salt spray 100 miles inland over much of New England, damaging trees and shrubs over a wide area.

The damage shows up as a discoloration of foliage, followed by shedding of leaves and terminal die-back of new shoots. If it occurs in the wintertime, buds may be destroyed so that spring leafing out is considerably delayed. Tender plants may be killed. The harm is done by the "drawing action" of the salt, which extracts so much water from leaf and twig tissues that they shrivel and die. Because of their thick bark, trunks and large limbs are usually unaffected.

Against such an eventuality there is no control and no protection possible for trees. Smaller plants may be moved inside or shielded in some way. Damaged twigs should be clipped off.

Illuminating Gas Injury

Escaping gas is a common cause of tree injury. Poor construction of gas mains or their breakage or gradual loosening of their joints by heavy traffic makes possible a seepage of gas that is very toxic to tree roots.

Where the leak is slight, symptoms show up as a gradual yellowing and dropping of foliage and the gradual dying of branches near the top. Where the leak is large and sudden, the symptoms are easier to diagnose. The foliage of all affected trees turns yellow almost overnight, branches die back rapidly; and if no relief is given, the bark becomes loose and fungus growths may appear on the trunk.

There are two ways of confirming the diagnosis: (1) by the odor test, and (2) by the tomato plant test. Where the soil is saturated, the gas odor may be very strong. If not noticeable on the surface, punch several holes three or four feet deep into the ground and sniff at the mouth of each hole.

If you still cannot detect any odor, try using a tomato plant, which is more sensitive than the human nostrils. Dig a hole about two feet deep in the suspected area and set a potted tomato plant inside, cover over tightly with a board or some other object, and leave for 24 hours. When the plant is removed at the end of that time, its stems will be bent sharply downward if any gas is in the soil. (The bending is not wilting but a tropism in response to the ethylene factor in the gas.) If the plant is unaffected, you may be about 98% certain that there is no escaping gas in the vicinity. If tomato plants are not available, sweet pea or carnation plants may be substituted. These react to gas differently: buds do not open, and open flowers close.

If the tree is not too far gone when the leak is detected, you may save it by taking the following steps. First, ask the gas company to repair the leak immediately. Second, dig a trench on the side of the tree nearest the leak and replace vitiated soil with new soil. Third, punch holes all over the root area and blow out gas with compressed air. Fourth, flood the whole root area with water to help wash away toxic materials. Fifth, prune out dead branches and cut away dead or diseased roots. Sixth, feed the tree to encourage the development of new roots.

Where a tree has been killed by gas, it should be removed roots and all, and the ground should be thoroughly spaded up and allowed to stand idle several months before anything else is planted in the same place. Gas leaks occurring in the winter when the ground is frozen will kill nearby trees in short order, since the gas cannot leak through to the surface.

Arborists are frequently called upon to determine the price of a gas-killed tree, their services being sought some-

The frightful pace of erosion and the trees' valiant effort to prevent it are both dramatically evident in this photograph. With more rainfall there would have been more trees, and with more trees there would have been no erosion. Paradoxically, it is in semidesert regions where water flows in stream-beds only rarely but then with great force that erosion wreaks most havoc.

times by the gas company, sometimes by the homeowner. Through the years various methods for fair determinations have been worked out. One method in use was that presented in Richard R. Fenska's TREE EXPERT'S MANUAL. The American Society of Consulting Arborists, a new and actively expanding organization, has prepared its own Tree Evaluation Formula which is becoming the national standard. By working closely with Insurance Associations and with the American Bar Association, the ASCA has very recently arranged to double the value of killed or damaged trees involved in legal disputes. For the settlement of such disputes the testimony of ASCA members is legally acceptable *a priori,* while extra-officially it carries so much weight that the gas companies are often disposed to accept their evaluations without quibble.

Injury Due To Lack of Water

Perhaps the commonest cause of tree injury is lack of water. Plants, like animals, must have this precious liquid or they cannot live. Water is a unique substance, endowed with the most extraordinary physical and chemical properties. Where it does not occur, as on the moon, we may be certain that life does not exist. If we were to hierarchize inanimate substances and crown one of them king, it would surely be water.

In plants, water serves multiple functions. Physically, it makes up the bulk of their beings, and without it their tissues shrivel and die. It is the solvent in which nutrients and metabolites are dissolved, and the circulating medium by means of which they are transported up and down the stems. It makes possible some chemical reactions by its very presence, catalytically, and it enters into other reactions as an essential element; without it neither photosynthesis nor respiration nor any other life process would be possible.

The largest and finest trees occur in regions of abundant rainfall: in our northeastern woods, in the Ohio River basin, along the Pacific Coast, in the tropical rain forests. Contrariwise, the poorest and most stunted specimens occur in the desert regions. Abundant water means not only large trees: it means also green healthy leaves and full tops, while lack of water means shedding of leaves and dying of branches.

The most usual cause of lack of water is, of course, sub-normal rainfall. When rainfall is less than normal over any given region, trees suffer. Their suffering may be alleviated to a greater or lesser degree by artificial means, but it cannot be relieved entirely. Although irrigation is a blessing, it is not the same as rain, for rain washes the foliage, cleanses the very air, and envelops the tree in a revivifying cloud of humidity.

City trees sometimes suffer from lack of water even when rainfall is abundant. This may happen:

1. When surrounded by asphalt, concrete, or other impervious substances,
2. When roots are cut or damaged by street-building or house-building, and the reduced root system is unable to absorb and transmit the required quantities of water for the unimpaired top,
3. When roots are damaged by toxic substances in the soil,
4. When roots are covered by non-porous fill,
5. When roots are covered by heavy sod,
6. When the contour of the land is altered so that water runs off before it can soak in.

The remedy in each of these situations is to change the existing condition and to furnish the tree with an adequate supply of pure water. Trees may be effectively watered by making holes in the root area with a punch bar or a soil auger and applying water directly into them. This method is particularly valuable where heavy sods are present. The same result with less effort can be obtained by using the water-spike, now on the market under a variety of trade names. This is simply a hollow tube 1-1/2 or 2 ft. long with a connection for attaching the garden hose at one end and several perforations at the other. Push the perforated end, which is also pointed, into the soil, at a convenient spot 3 or 4 feet from the trunk, turn on the water very slowly and allow it to trickle continuously for as long as the tree seems to need it. Curiously, this method, called "drip irrigation," has proved in many cases superior to the administration of large quantities of water—and much more economical. For these reasons it is coming into intensive use in semidesert regions where water is at a premium.

If for any reason the spike method cannot be used, water can be supplied directly from the surface, as it is of course by nature via rainfall. Slow soakings two or three times a week are better than sudden floodings. Sprinkling is of little value, for where there is heavy ground cover, practically no water gets to the tree roots.

Signs of water deficiency are leaf scorch (browning of leaves around the edges), leaf wilting, new stem wilting, sparseness of foliage, appearance of dead twigs, premature shedding of fruits, leaves, or twigs, and, in extreme cases, stagheading (appearance of large dead branches in the top).

A tree can be killed by too much water as well as by too little. Where there is a clay substratum, water from above may be unable to drain through and may accumulate to such a degree that the roots are unable to receive their required air supply; hence they may be said to drown, in very much the same way as an animal drowns. Adequate aeration is indispensible to plant roots, and if the water content of the soil is suddenly and significantly increased, affected trees may die before they have a chance to adapt to the changed condition.

Tree left standing on stilts as the soil is slowly eroded around it.

Before erosion carried it away, the soil covered the two outcurving roots visible above the horizon.

The frightful pace of erosion and the trees' valiant effort to prevent it are both clearly evident in this photograph. With more rainfall there would have been more trees, and with more trees there would have been no erosion. It is in semidesert regions where water flows in stream-beds only rarely but then with great force that erosion wreaks most havoc.

Chemicals in The Soil

Certain chemicals accumulate in the soil to such an extent that tree roots are poisoned. The accumulation may be sudden or gradual. Some of the most common contaminants are salt, kerosene, motor oil, calcium chloride, cinders, and more recently, weed killers.

Salt in large quantities is sometimes carelessly spilled near trees. Ice-cream freezers are emptied, and even sand piled along the parkway may contain salt that leaches down to the roots. In the colder parts of the country salt is often sprinkled on driveways in an attempt to prevent ice formaton. In shopping centers it is used in large quantities for the same purpose, to the detriment of what few trees might have survived the original bulldozing and blacktopping and the subsequent bumpings or scrapings of errant automobiles.

Home-repair jobs on cars often result in the emptying of kerosene, motor oil, or gasoline in the tree root area. Calcium chloride, used on unpaved roads to help keep down dust, may be washed into the tree root region, causing severe damage. Unweathered cinders or "clinkers" may be harmful if piled around trees, because of the toxic ingredients gradualy washed down to the roots.

The increasing use of weed killers has caused damage and death to numerous trees. Some of these substances are designed to kill brush as well as weeds, and many users, failing to distinguish between the two, end up killing their own trees or those of their neighbors. Many nasty back-fence quarrels have originated over this issue, and the tree expert is often called in to give his opinion. Ammonium sulfamate, painted on or bored into stumps or unwanted trees, sometimes finds its way into nearby desirable trees, either through root grafts or by creeping through the soil or by direct spilling or thoughtless rinsing of containers.

In orchards or other places where trees are sprayed frequently over a period of years the poisons contained in the spray may accumulate in the soil to such a degree that toxic effects are produced. This is particularly true in certain soils, such as sandy loam, and particularly noticeable in shallow-rooted species, such as our common fruit trees, because of the greater accumulation of poison in the soil's upper layers. Damage to apple trees as a result of the accumulation of arsenicals in the soil was noted and commented on as early as 1908.

Repeated or excessive spraying with the organic phosphates and the chlorinated hydrocarbons—that is to say, DDT, BHC, chlordane, aldrin, dieldrin, methoxychlor, parathion, and others, all household words by now—results not only in damage to the above-ground parts of the tree but also in the build-up of long-lasting toxic residues in the soil. Whether these harm the tree by direct action or by interference with the life of the soil micro-organisms or by both is not definitely known. It is the task of the research chemist to develop new materials equal to these in effectiveness but non-toxic to plants and higher animals (including us) and non-accumulative in the soil.

Damage By Fire

Fire and trees are incompatible elements and should never be brought together except in the fireplace. Most of us are aware of the great losses sustained annually because of forest fires. Fire and wind are the tree's most fearsome enemies; worse, they usually work together, the wind fanning an otherwise innocuous spark into a conflagration, and the fire, once started, creating its own wind. Forest fires are stupendous catastrophes, for apart from the millions of board feet of timber destroyed there is always the accom-

Many years ago a fire damaged one side of this trunk near ground level, killing the bark and burning its way deep into the interior. The photograph shows how the healing process occurs: new growth slowly building up from the sides and the gaping wound slowly closing. Still visible at the time this photograph was taken, the charred heartwood will in the space of years be completely covered over by new layers of wood and bark.

panying destruction, sometimes irreplaceable, of smaller plants and animals and often the permanent ecologic upsetting of very large areas.

The worst forest fire in history was the holocaust of 1910 which destroyed in northern Idaho a stand of Western White Pine equal in area to the state of Connecticut; the whole world seemed to be burning. (For a dramatic description of this disaster see Donald Culross Peattie's *A Natural History of Western Trees*.)

Even city trees are occasionally damaged by fire. When leaves or trash are burned near them, the foliage is singed and the branches damaged. Sometimes unthinking unfeathered bipeds build a fire directly against the trunk, killing the bark and cambium over a wide area. Cases are known where a fire built at the bottom of a hollow tree to smoke out a possum has resulted in the burning of the whole tree, the central cavity forming a perfect draught, like a chimney, and the dry wood on the inside serving as tinder.

Where houses burn down, surrounding trees are often damaged. Those very close to the fire are usually killed, those farther away are burned on the proximate side. Damaging heat usually carries much farther than the flames proper, so that even trees that seem to be out of range may be injured.

Burnt branches should be pruned back to the nearest live lateral. Twigs that are only lightly singed should be given time to come out again before clipping off. Burnt bark will usually fall off, exposing the sapwood, which should be painted with wound dressing. Where the bark is damaged but fails to fall off, it should be removed surgically. Badly burned trees should be fed and watered to hasten new bark growth over injured areas.

Bullet Damage

Trees are preferred backdrops for target practice. Who has not nailed a paper target to a tree trunk or laid a bottle in a crotch or on a branch as a test of marksmanship? While bullets may ricochet dangerously from a boulder, they conveniently enter the tree's substance and remain there. From our standpoint, this is all to the good. From the tree's standpoint, the matter looks a little different. While most trees are friendly and co-operative and don't mind a social broadside or two, all agree that you can have too much of a good thing.

The trees in the Argonne Forest had an even tougher time of it. Caught between the fires of the Germans and the Allies, they were shot, shrapneled, blasted, bombed, and literally blown to fragments. As they lay dying, their only consolation was the knowledge that their destroyers now had no place to hide. No cases of lead poisoning were reported.

Atom Bomb Damage

This is one kind of tree damage I hope none of us ever has occasion to see. Nevertheless, it exists and for completeness' sake should be included. Trees near ground zero are utterly destroyed. Those farther away are blown over by the high wind and burned by the heat; those still farther away are only burned.

Trees and other plants whose tops were destroyed in the Hiroshima and Nagasaki bombings quickly sent up a marvelous secondary growth—an unbelievable luxuriance of vegetation which soon recovered the desolate landscape and gladdened the heart of the survivors like a benison. This totally unexpected and of course unprecedented effect was apparently due to atomic radiation of the plant roots.

12

Removals

The removal of small trees offers no special problem. If you are a homeowner, able and willing, and have some small tree you want removed, you might tackle the job yourself for the sake of the pleasure the use of the axe and saw can bring. With chain saws making the axe obsolete, we forget how much fun hand tools can be.

But as trees increase in size, their removal rapidly takes on the aspects of a major project. Difficulties increase in direct proportion to the size of the tree and the occurence of obstacles and in inverse proportion to the equipment, skill, and experience of the man doing the job. Remember that a tree two feet in diameter is not twice as big as a tree one foot in diameter; it is four times as big. This geometric rate of increase is responsible for many miscalculations.

In communities not large enough to support a professional tree organization, tree removal is usually considered a construction project and is handled by contractors having the necessary equipment. In large cities, however, where difficulties and obstructions multiply (buildings, power lines, people, traffic), tree removal becomes a highly specialized problem which construction companies are glad to turn over to the experts.

Which trees should be removed? Those that are:

1. Dead,
2. Dangerous,
3. Crowding other, better trees,
4. Diseased to the point of threatening contamination of others,
5. In the way of buildings, roads, etc.,
6. Undesirable for any of a variety of reasons.

Many people refuse to take down any tree, however scrawny or however badly placed; they would turn a highway out of its course to save a single tree. This attitude is understandable when interpreted as a reaction against the wantonness and stupidity which destroyed half a continent of virgin timber. Yet certain individual trees must be cut down, however much we love trees collectively. A tree diseased to the degree that it becomes a menace to others must come down. A tree in any way dangerous or detrimental to the public interest should go; others can be planted in its place in more desirable locations. Trees growing in clusters, unless unusually picturesque, should be thinned out. It is the obligation of the tree expert to point out all dangerous, diseased, or undesirable trees to their owners and to recommend their removal.

If you have a large tree you want removed, you should be cautious about the man you deal with to do the job. You should select someone with the necessary equipment, the proved ability, and the financial responsibility to cover any damage that might occur. You would also do well to get the contract in writing, specifying whether the tree is to be cut off or dug out, whether it is to be hauled away or cut into firewood, and fixing strictly the liability in case of damage. Many misunderstandings arise which might have been obviated by a written agreement. The tree worker, for his part, should be glad to sign such a contract, since it protects his rights in addition to fixing his responsibilities. The removal of a large tree, although costing perhaps only $200-$300, always involves potentially a much higher amount; a tree falling on the house could easily mean a major repair job.

Preparations and Precautions

In the area where the tree is to be felled, all breakable objects underneath should be moved aside, and an adequate space should be roped off so that nobody comes strolling along at just the wrong time. It might seem unnecessary to mention so simple a precaution, but when dealing with the race of preoccupied and clock-driven city dwellers, no precautions are too obvious to be taken. If not forcibly shut out, people will walk under a tree although the branches are crashing down on all sides, and they will drive their cars under a tree that is in the very act of falling.

Where possible, it is better to have utility lines taken down before beginning the operation, for they are easily broken and make difficulties multiply. Telephone and light companies are usually glad to co-operate in this matter; all that is needed is to notify them a few hours in advance.

Techniques

Felling a tree in the woods is a comparatively simple matter. One takes the lay of the land, estimates the tree's

The open-end, one-man chain saw is the greatest single improvement in the long history of tree-cutting. Since it can be turned in any direction, it is equally useful for felling, bucking, and limbing; moreover, its light weight makes possible its use in the tops of the tallest trees.

height, makes the undercut, then the back-cut, and crash, she's down.

Removing a tree in a city is something entirely different. Growing in the narrow space between houses or entangled in high-voltage power lines or overhanging busy streets, such trees must be removed limb by limb, piece by piece. Free-falling is out of the question—first, because there is simply not enough room, second, because the impact of the huge bulk striking the ground breaks paving, shatters windows, and cracks foundations.

Some removals are performed under conditions little short of the impossible. Imagine taking down a 150-foot redwood in a postage-stamp backyard hardly 10 feet by 10.

The invention of the light-weight, open-end, one-man chain saw has taken the headaches out of tough removals. Where formerly a tree could be sectioned down only by roping and hand-sawing, which took days or even weeks, it is now removed in a matter of hours with less effort and fewer men. The modern crew is highly streamlined, consisting simply of one high-climber and one or two ground

men. The equipment needed is one light truck for loading brush—or better still a chipper for shredding it into sawdust, two or three coils of rope, a few hand tools, and, hero of the drama, a razor-sharp power-packed chain saw with an insatiable appetite for wood.

Sectioning

A man straps on his spurs and walks up the tree, hand saw in his scabbard, chain saw hanging from his belt. Coming to the first branch, he cranks up his machine and saws it off neatly, flush with the trunk. Walking upward a few feet, he cuts off another; leaning to one side, another, and thus proceeding he works his way up to the top. In the meantime the ground men are busy cutting up the brush as it comes down. For this they too use a chain saw, reducing the largest branches to manageable size in seconds.

Finally the branches are off, and the real show begins. The ground men drive off to dispose of the brush, and the high-climber remains alone on top of a towering mast 75, 100, or 150 feet tall.

What can one man, alone, accomplish against this tremendous spar? You call up to him and tell him to come down until his helpers return. He answers cooly that he will have the tree on the ground before they get back.

The roar of a chain saw can be heard for blocks and invariably draws a crowd. Some come running to protest against the noise, but of those who come to gibe, most remain to praise. Tree removal is a dramatic spectacle; the sight of a man risking his life 100 feet in the air silences complaints and elicits admiration.

Alone on the top of his mast, the man drives his spurs in deep, settles back comfortably against his safety belt, cranks up his saw, and in a high-pitched scream of power neatly slices off a two-foot chunk. When only a shred of bark remains uncut, he stops the saw, gives the piece a gentle push, and sends it hurtling downward to a picked spot at the base of the tree. With a satisfied grin, he hangs the saw on his belt, slides down a couple of feet, sinks in his spurs anew, cranks up, and cuts off another two-foot chunk, pushing it out into space to follow its fellow.

So he proceeds, sectioning the trunk piece by piece with masterly skill. His accuracy is that of the experienced bomber. He needs no more than a small area 4 by 4 feet at the base of the tree; each chunk falls exactly where he intends it to. The operation is un-believably swift; the trunk disappears as if by magic. There are no ropes, no lost time, no false moves. Just the whine of a chain saw and one broad-shouldered husky working his way downward calmly and confidently.

When the helpers return with the truck, there is nothing for them to do. The man is on the ground, taking off his spurs and lighting up a cigarette. All that's left of the tree is a pile of wood cut into usable lengths and ready for splitting.

Log being winched up on truck with skidboards. This is the simplest and most inexpensive loading device.

Gone are the expensive winch trucks of yesteryear, gone are the eight-foot cross-cut saws—the "misery whips" of our fathers—gone are the large, heavy coils of inch rope, gone the six or seven supernumeraries standing around holding rope ends.

Unfortunately, however, this brilliant new technique, while the perfect solution for fir-like trees having a straight central bole, works much less well on other trees. Trees of the East, South, and Midwest are built on a different plan—quite unlike the pines, firs, and redwoods of the Pacific Northwest, where the practice of aerial sectioning seems to have originated. Oaks, elms, ashes, maples, and other hardwoods flare out at the top like an unraveled rope, the trunk proper dissolving into a multitude of branches that bend upward and outward at all possible angles. Sectioning is much more difficult on these, and high climbers adapted to walking up a straight, mast-like trunk, are at a disadvantage here, where spurs and climbing belt are of little use. Such spreading trees are worked most conveniently by the experienced rope-climber. While the chain saw remains the most useful tool, the sectioning technique must be modified to meet the circumstances.

Umbrellaing

When long, spreading branches overhang houses, fences, prize shrubs, garden statuary, or power lines there is noth-

ing for it but to revert to the use of ropes. Tying, cutting, and lowering, piece by piece, old-fashioned though it may be, is sometimes the only way. One way of speeding up the process is by tying a rope near the end of a given limb, passing the other end through a high crotch in the center of the tree, cutting the limb at its base *on the under side,* and pulling the rope with truck or winch. By this means the limb is lifted free of the obstacles and pulled toward the tree's center, from which position it may easily be lowered to the ground or, if too long, cut into sections while still hanging. This method, which reverses one's natural impulse to cut a branch on the top side and let the point fall first, is a highly ingenious way of clearing obstacles; many times every limb on a wide-spreading tree may advantageously be cut in this way: the whole tree folded upward as you fold up an umbrella when its tip is on the floor.

Another interesting technique is *high-lining.* Where a tree to be removed is surrounded by valuable objects underneath that cannot be taken away, the branches can be cut off piece by piece and sent via the high-line to a preselected distant point. This is done by securing one end of a stout 3/4 inch rope to the top of the tree and the other end to a distant anchor at or near ground level (another tree or a post or a truck) so that the rope slants diagonally downward. Sliding back and forth on this high-line, by means of a metal eye attached at one end, is a smaller rope 6 to 8 feet long. This is fastened to whatever branch is to be cut off, and as it slides down the high-line (which must be kept reasonably taut), it carries the cut-off branch over all objects underneath. Gravity powers the operation; the short rope is retrieved after each trip by means of a long slender line kept permanently fastened to it. In this way all the branches can be aerially transported away from the danger zone; even the upper part of the trunk, cut into small lengths, can be similarly handled, the high-line being moved down, of course, before each cut. The lower, heavier part of the trunk will need to be handled in some other way, possibly by sectioning it and tying it to itself as it is worked down, step by step.

Free Falling

Where a tree has room to fall, as on a vacant lot, felling it in one piece is of course the fastest and easiest way to get it down. If space is limited in a sideways sense, the branches may have to be cut off first. Remember, however, that when a tree is completely delimbed, it becomes very dangerous, falling with a great thud and jar, whereas when it is felled entire, the resistance of the air to the foliage (if present) slows down the fall considerably and the branches striking the ground first act as shock absorbers. A large tree in full leaf may fall against a house with surprisingly little damage, but a bare trunk stripped of branches strikes with the impact of a wrecking ball.

The veteran lumberjack, disdaining ropes, can fell a tree in any direction by using only saw, axe, and wedge—even against its natural an provided this not be too great. This is done by chopping or sawing out a notch on the side of the trunk in the direction of the fall, then sawing from the opposite side on a line with the notch. If the tree is leaning in the direction of the notch, it will begin to fall before the saw cut is completed. If it is plumb, it will need to be nudged over by forcible insertion of a wedge from the sawed side. If it is leaning away from the notch, it will need to be straightened by insertion of several wedges of increasing diameter. In all cases the notch must be made first, and the saw cut from the back side must never sever the trunk entirely. If tree trunks were quadrangular, they could be sawed from one side only and the notch could be dispensed with. But since they are cylindrical, they are thickest at and near the center; hence a strip of holding

The two-man chain saw with an oil reservoir at the far end was the first to be invented and is still used occasionally on exceptionally large trees. However, the one-man saw that may be fitted with different length bars not only offers much more maneuverability but also frees the second man for other tasks.

Log being cut with two-man power saw. Although the wood is extremely hard, the cut will be completed within a matter of three or four minutes. By hand it would take an hour or two. (Live Oak, *Quercus virginiana*)

wood (often called a hinge) must be left in that region. If the hinge is too far from the center, it becomes so narrow (due to the rapid reduction of trunk diameter) that it may be unable to prevent sideways tipping, while if the trunk is cut through entirely, no hinge at all being left, it escapes from control and may fall in any direction; many men have been killed by making this simple mistake. Why not saw from *both* sides and leave a strip of holding wood exactly in the center? In that case the tree would not be able to fall in any direction—neither sideways nor backwards nor forwards; since the saw cut is narrow, the slightest movement of the tree would make the severed portions abut and movement would cease. If the hinge were wide and strong enough, such a doubly sawed tree could remain standing indefinitely and would soon begin to grow back together around the edges. In summary, the roundness of the trunk makes notching indispensable: the notch means that the strip of holding wood will perforce be left near the center and at the same time it permits the trunk to fold on itself as it begins falling.

Wedges, driven in by a sledge hammer, exert great lifting power and are adequate to force over most small and medium-sized trees. For the very large redwoods and Douglas firs, the hydraulic jack is often used instead of the wedge. To use the jack an auxiliary notch with parallel sides is made on the side opposite to the felling notch, and after the back-cut has been made in the usual way, the tool is placed in the notch and jacked up. Refining on this principle, hydraulic felling wedges are now manufactured, eliminating the need for the sledge hammer.

Bottoming

Free-falling, then, and sectioning from the top downward are the two standard ways of taking down a tree. Are there any other ways? Strange though it may sound, there is another way, and since it exactly reverses the normal procedure of topping, its inventor—who happens to be myself—has decided to call it "bottoming."

This technique can be practiced only when there is another tree or trees of equal or greater size near the tree to be removed. In this case a rope is tied around the top of the tree to be felled, and the free end is passed through a high crotch or around the trunk of one of the adjacent trees and down to the ground where it may be securely snubbed and paid out as needed. If two or three trees are nearby instead of one, the tree can be secured in the same fashion to them all, providing even better control of the operation. With the tree-to-be-felled thus fastened at its top, it may be sawed through at the bottom; since it is not going to fall, no notching is needed, although a degree of wedging may be necessary to prevent pinching of the saw. With the bottom cut off and the tree still in an upright position, all that remains is to begin sectioning it in the desired lengths. After each cut the severed piece is pushed to one side and the tree is lowered by slacking off on the ropes, while always keeping the trunk as perpendicular as possible. Thus piece by piece the tree is cut down—or cut up, rather—with the worker standing on the ground in perfect safety. Provided that the necessary anchor trees are present and the ropes are strong enough, even quite large trees can be cut in this way.

Ropes

Since ropes must be used, although now to a much lesser extent than formerly, it is necessary to develop skill in their use. Extraordinary properties inhere in a simple length of rope; a good case can be made for including these twisted fibers with fire and the wheel among mankind's most important inventions. Extensible, retractable, flexible, a rope functions like an elongated arm. With it you can control an object with precision at 20, 30, 40, 50 feet, even though it may pass out of your line at sight; and by taking a few turns about a convenient anchor, you can support very heavy weights with negligible exertion. Few, if any, more versatile tools exist: without ropes, the sailor, the cowboy, and the tree-rigger would have never been.

For use in trees different-sized ropes are needed: light lines of 1/4″ diameter for pulling up and lowering tools; 1/2″ lines for securing, pulling, and lowering smaller branches, and 3/4″ lines for the large, heavy sections. Manila—strong, non-kinking, and long-wearing—has long been the most popular kind of rope. In recent years, however, ropes made of synthetic fibers are also coming into extensive use: esterlene and polypropylene for throwing lines and support ropes. Nylon ropes also have much to recommend them: they are weather-resistant, elastic, and unbelievably strong. Their elasticity makes them the indicated choice where any sudden jerk is to be anticipated, as when a heavy limb or trunk section must fall a few feet before the rope catches it. The undesirable feature of nylon is that it is stiff, heavy, and difficult to tie; also that it tends to melt and even catch on fire when subjected to severe friction.

It is convenient to have ropes of different lengths, say of 40, 50, 75 and 100 feet. Rope ends should be taped, never tied in knots, for a knot at the end will hang up in the most inconvenient and unexpected places, as when running through an overhanging crotch or tangling in brush on the ground.

A good knot is one that will hold securely and is easily tied and easily untied. Most useful in tree removal are the timber hitch and the double half hitch. The slip knot, too, has its place, as when you must throw a rope around an inaccessible branch, pull the end to you with a long-handled pole saw, tie the knot at a distance, and then pull it tight. In such cases, it is well to tie *two* slip knots, one ten inches or so behind the other, at the same time leaving a two- or three-foot tail so as to eliminate all danger of the knot's coming loose as you pull it tight. Two ropes may be joined by means of the square knot; remember, however, that knots along any rope that must run are to be avoided whenever possible.

Ropes should be inspected frequently for wear, which often occurs on the inside where fibers rub against each other. Inspection is easily accomplished by untwisting the strands at different points along their length. All worn, frayed, or weathered rope should be discarded. At the end of the day all ropes should be carefully coiled, the kinks worked out, and the knots untied.

Poles and Hooks

Useful accessories to ropes are poles for pushing and hooks for pulling. Mounted at the end of a long aluminum pole, the hook is admirably suited for guiding descending branches. The push-pole can be fitted at its business end either with spike or two iron straps projecting in the form of a V. For greater efficiency, hook and pusher can be combined in a single head; this should be attached to a light yet strong aluminum pole 10 or 12 feet long. The disadvantage of aluminum is that it is dangerous in the vicinity of power lines; to get around this, some manufacturers offer collapsible poles with an insulated section near the worker's end.

The push-pole, when strong enough, is sometimes used in connection with a peavy in a special way to form a combination tool called by lumberjacks a "killig." The killig is made by placing one end of the push-pole as high upon the trunk as possible and placing the other end against the peavy about a foot or so above its business end. The point of the peavy is stabbed into the ground or into a tree stump, if one is conveniently by, and pressure is then exerted by the worker at the handle end. Thus a lever of considerable force is formed: as the peavy pivots slowly forward in a vertical plane, the push-pole is forced diagonally against the tree, which, if properly sawed, can usually be felled where desired. While these methods are effective with small or medium-sized trees, large, heavy trees are best pulled over with a rope, chain, or cable attached to a trunk or, if in the woods, to a tractor.

13

Structure and Physiology

A tree, like a rosebush, a cornstalk, an orchid, or a sunflower, is a plant, resembling these other plants far more than it differs from them. In all essential points a sunflower and an oak tree are alike: both consist of a spreading root system, an upright stem, and a multiplicity of leaves; both produce flowers, fruit, and seed; both are nourished by the same elements; both respond in similar ways to their environment; both reproduce according to the same mechanism; both live their appointed span and die. Actually, in the eyes of the botanist, the oak tree is less highly evolved than the sunflower, and the redwood is far less advanced than the dandelion.

Yet in spite of all this, trees remain differentiated from other plants in several important respects. In an artistic, inspirational, and practical sense trees belong in a world apart. They are the predominant feature in any landscape. They pre-empt the eye of the beholder and by their very size force themselves upon our attention, while smaller plants are passed unnoticed or crushed underfoot.

Trees are distinguished from other plants mainly because of their size, their hardness, and their longevity, although none of these factors belongs exclusively to them. Some kinds of bamboo and many kinds of vines grow as tall as or taller than most trees; some kinds of shrubs possess parts equally hard and woody; the humble lichen may live longer than the oldest tree. Nevertheless, it is the combination of these three factors—size, woodiness, and longevity—that makes up our conception and definition of a tree. Few other plants can approach the life span of the oaks, frequently exceeding 500 years, or of the slow-growing yews, the Douglas firs, the ancient olives of Spain, Portugal, and the rim of the Mediterranean, to say nothing of the immensely old *ahuehuetes* (cypresses) of southern Mexico, the California redwoods (the coast redwood attaining 2000 or 2500 years and the interior redwood or Bigtree perhaps 3500 years), and the recently discovered bristle-cone pine, oldest of them all, with a life span exceeding 4000 years. No other plant can equal in size and dignity the towering tulip trees, the firs, the pines, the eucalypti. What other plant can spread itself out like the Indian banyan-tree, a single specimen forming a small forest, or what plant can soar upward with the amazing verticality of a redwood or a eucalyptus, just missing the 400-foot mark? No other plant can equal in hardness or durability the ebony, the locust, the hickory, the mesquite, the *quebracha,* the lignumvitae, and many others.

Among the various definitions of a tree essayed by various writers, none is perfect, although most of them convey the idea approximately. To mention a few:

A tree is a woody perennial.

A tree is a plant of at least 15 feet in height with a single trunk.

A tree is a perennial plant with woody stem and boughs.

I propose a fourth definition: *a tree is a plant that stands of itself and can be climbed in.*

Many vines may be climbed *up* but not *in;* nor do they stand of themselves. Many shrubs and reed-like things grow tall but cannot be climbed in. But once a plant has acquired the necessary size, shape, and rigidity to permit men (or boys) to climb about in its branches, then it is unequivocally a tree.*

From the time they germinate until the time they die, trees are inescapably rooted to one spot. Except in the relatively few cases where gardeners transplant them or the even rarer cases where a river may undermine a small island and carry them downstream to some new lodgment, trees never move. Their cradle, their nursery, their playground, their workshop, their marriage bed, their grave, are one and the same spot. Hence they are, far more than animals, creatures of their environment. In a sense they are a living incorporation of their environment and cannot be understood unless the environment is also understood. But while tied to the physical environment and developing according to its generosity or niggardliness, at the same time they work ceaselessly to modify it and often do so to an astonishing extent. Roots shatter boulders and feed upon the rock fragments, thus initiating the long, slow process of soil-

---

*According to this definition, the thick-stemmed, unbranched, rosette-crowned plants like the papaya and the palms, however tall, are not true trees. While exclusion of the palm will provoke cries of protest from many who may regard it as the very prototype of the tree, there are a number of convincing reasons, apart from the one just given, for placing it in a different category. Note too that this practical definition cuts across formal boundaries, *including* qualifying Gymnosperms as well as qualifying Angiosperms while with equal impartiality *excluding* all the structurally unsuited forms, dicotyledonous (the papaya, for example) as well as monocotyledonous.

building. Forests engender their own storms, then store the rain in the vast intertwining network of their roots, releasing it slowly to form the multitude of streams that give rise to the great rivers of the world. Trees in groups break the fury of winds, and even individual trees in a field, by providing shade and hence lowering the temperature, create gentle ascending and descending air currents.

A tree* is composed of a root system, a central stem or trunk, a series of ramifying and graduated boughs, branches, and twigs, a canopy of leaves, and a reproductive system consisting of flowers, fruits, and seeds.**

Roots

The root system has four functions:

1. It anchors the tree in the soil,
2. It draws in water and dissolved minerals needed for growth,
3. It serves as a storehouse for the accumulation of surplus foods,
4. It serves as a launching pad from which new shoots can be sent skyward when the above-ground parts are destroyed.

Roots divide and ramify like branches; and just as leaves are found most abundantly at or near twig tips, so the tiny root hairs are found most abundantly at root tips. The large muscular roots occurring near the base of the tree serve mainly as conveyors and as anchors, while the rootlets and the fine root hairs (in function strikingly like the villi of animal intestines) provide the actual contact between tree and soil. Through these millions of root hairs many gallons of water are absorbed daily out of the ground and conveyed—by a mechanism as yet imperfectly understood—up through the trunk and out to the very tip of the most distant twig, there to be used by the leaf in its fabrication of food, and to be transpired into the air. Unbelievable as it seems, more water is evaporated over a square mile of forest than over a square mile of ocean. (Think for a moment of the overlapping arrangement of leaves and their thousands upon thousands of surfaces.) Through these same rootlets dissolved minerals pass into the body of the tree to participate in its intricate chemistry, but in quantities so small that the largest tree when burnt yields only a disproportionately small pile of ashes.

It is often said that the pattern of a tree's root system corresponds to the pattern of its branch system, that where a branch goes so goes its subterranean counterpart, a root,

and that the roots extend through the soil fully as far as the branches through the air. This notion, however, is too simple. While there is a general resemblance between the above-ground and the below-ground parts, there is nothing like a one-to-one correspondence. Although the root system, like the branch system, ramifies and tends to spread out more or less radially from a common center, individual roots are highly erratic, growing sometimes straight ahead, sometimes veering to right or left, sometimes doubling back on themselves. And rather than extending outward as far as the branches do, the roots usually extend much farther—three, four, or five times farther, freed as they are (by lying in the soil) of the mechanical difficulty that confronts the branch of supporting a constantly increasing weight from a distant support.

Do the roots go downward as far as the crown goes up? This depends on the kind of tree. Many species, such as the redwoods, have no tap root at all, their roots spreading outward in the form of a flat shallow disk. Others, like the pecan, do have a long descending tap root which, at some growth stages, may equal or even exceed the height of the above-ground portion. Still others, such as the mesquite and other desert-resistant legumes, may, iceberg-like, have enormously developed roots, descending 75 feet or so in search of water, while above ground they put up only a few thorny switches.*

According to their root structure, some trees are easily uprooted, toppling over in strong winds; others cannot be pushed over by bulldozers. In all cases, however, whether a tree has a taproot or not and whether its anchor roots are deep or shallow, the majority of its feeder roots are to be found within a foot or foot-and-a-half of the surface, for it is here that the soil is the richest and the aeration the amplest. (This explains why when a tree is fed, the fertilizer is placed in holes made at a depth of about a foot or foot-and-a-half, not at a depth of four, five, or six feet nor merely spread about the surface.)

In addition to food and water, roots must have air. In most species the air-conducting system that runs up and down the length of the tree is so poorly developed that little air reaches the underground parts via intake through leaves or stems; the roots must make up the deficit by direct absorption of the air that works down through the soil particles. (Some species, such as cypress *(Taxodium)* with its light, highly porous wood, have a much-improved air-conduction system and hence can send their roots through unaerated mud and water.)

A tree that grows up in a given locality has its roots adapted from the beginning to that particular kind of soil and to the amount of air and water available. When the grade level is changed—either raised or lowered—the tree

---

*Palms, yuccas, papayas, and similar rosette-forms excepted, as explained above.

**Excepting Gymnosperms (pines, firs, cedars, redwoods, and other conifers) which' although producing seeds have no flowers or fruits as the terms are commonly understood.

*In such regions you dig for firewood and climb (go up to head-springs) for water.

Multiple trunks of the tropical Fig. The original trunk is to the left; each additional stem began life as an adventitious root growing downward from a branch. When such a root touches the ground, it at once enters it and begins to function as a normal root, while at the same time its above-ground portion thickens to form an enormous supporting post, each of which may become an independent trunk or all of which may fuse together.

suffers; if the change is too abrupt, it dies. Trees are often harmed by building projects that change the contour of the ground. Unfortunately, the kind of fill used in such cases is usually the kind dug out to make basement excavations—a heavy, clayey, non-porous soil through which neither air nor water can pass—the very worst kind possible. Tree roots so covered are literally suffocated; the tree's slow decline and eventual death is the inevitable result, unless the tree is young and vigorous enough to develop new roots near the new surface.

Downward growth of adventitious roots. Ramifying and interlacing, these strange processes grow rapidly under moist conditions, more slowly under dry conditions, eventually making it to the ground and at once striking root.

Roots are important as soil binders and soil conditioners. Their fine network is a primary factor in preventing wind and water erosion over much of the earth's surface. The roots hold the soil; the cast-off leaves from above decay to enrich and mulch it. The roots also work incessantly to build the soil as well as to bind it. Mechanically, they split rocks, their filament-like tips entering the tiniest crevice, then expanding with resistless pressure. Chemically, too, they work at soil-building, enzymes produced by the grow-

*The nutrients which occur in soil as unweathered minerals and organic remains represent the principal capital of soil fertility. From this, plants receive a periodic income of soluble or available nutrients as they are released through the action of chemical and biotic (independent of the tree) agents. If the soil solution is not sufficiently supplied with certain nutrient elements, plants may feed directly on soil particles and derive nutrients from the exchange material or minerals. This 'solid-phase feeding' is facilitated by the close contact of root-hairs with the soil particles and by the excretion of carbonic acid. Solid-phase feeding is especially common to forest trees.'' Wilde: *Forest Soils and Forest Growth*. (Chronica Botanica, 1946.)

ing tips dissolving fragments of the hardest rocks as stomach enzymes break down the fibers of the toughest meat.*

Roots form normally at the base of the seedling; they also form, by a kind of built-in polarity, at the basal end of a cutting. But under exceptional circumstances, they can form at all sorts of unexpected places. Adventitious roots (as we call those that occur in any extra-normal position) may develop from higher points along the stem, as they do regularly on corn stalks, from branches when they touch the soil and sometimes even when they do not, from callus forming around wounds, particularly along the interior of a cavity that has filled with debris, from leaves (in certain species), and even from fruits.

The chinaberry, hackberry, and other species not infrequently produce adventitious roots that grow downward through the tree's own decaying center. When such a root makes it to the ground, it establishes itself, stiffens and enlarges, and comes to constitute a new trunk that replaces,

Although roots usually grow downward and stems upward, that pattern can be reversed. When light is applied exclusively from below, stems will grow toward it; and when trees grow on the side of a mountain, part of their root system grows upgrade. In extreme cases, as when a tree is found growing at the bottom of a narrow ravine with steep sides, many of the roots will grow straight upward.

Adventitious roots of Chinaberry *(Melia azedarach)*. Developing from callus tissue forming around the edges of a wound, these roots grew rapidly downward, entering the soil where shown and constituting a natural anchor to replace—just in time—the tree's own decaying center.

Precariously perched on the very edge of an eroding cliff this tropical fig tenaciously holds on, sending its roots down to distances three and four times its height to penetrate the earth in search of water, nutrients, and anchorage.

just in time, the old decaying one. Thus can root and trunk exchange roles.

The banyan-tree of India and various other tropical species of the versatile fig genus carry this principle one step farther and with remarkable results. On these trees adventitious roots regularly develop from the underside of branches, grow downward until they make contact with the ground, then thicken to form post-like supports that enable the tree to extend itself over very wide areas. At one blow these extraordinary trees have solved two seemingly insoluble problems: the mechanical problem of how to support its branches in the air from an increasingly distant anchorpoint, and the logistical problem of how to supply the constantly receding tips with water and dissolved nutrients. Some of the Indian trees cover acres, a single tree, by this process, coming to consist of a multiplicity of trunks, the original one often indistinguishable from the others, all of which began as adventitious roots. While the height to which a tree can grow is strictly limited by the physical difficulty of supporting its enormous superstructure against the push of the wind, there is no similar theoretical limit controlling the sidewise extension of the banyan. Since the tree is continually providing itself with new supports as it spreads and since it is continually renewed by each adven-

Seeds of Sitka Spruce, germinating on top of this cut-over arborvitae stump, sent some of its roots down into the rotting interior and others downward around the outside—a spectacular reminder of the fact that as much of the tree, or more, may be underground as aboveground.

will produce adventitious roots when dirt is banked up around it or when flood waters rise around it. Indeed, the height of flood waters and the different stages by which they rise can be calculated to a close approximation by observing (after the waters have receded) the various levels of adventitious roots on the trunks of the willows that line the stream bed.

Reversing the roles, the roots of many species are capable of producing leaf-bearing shoots when accidentally exposed to the air; this may be observed on an overturned tree that has part of its roots in the ground and still functioning and part sticking up in the air. Even without the stimulus of over-turning, some species, such as hackberry, silver-leaf poplar, and jujube, regularly send up leaf-bearing shoots from any of their roots that happen to be close to the surface.

The phenomenon of shoots from roots and roots from shoots and all the other interchangeabilities that occur in plants is a direct manifestation of *totipotency,* a nice, precise word signifying that every cell in the plant body contains within itself all the genetic capabilities for producing any part of that body. All that is needed is the necessary stimulus, or, to speak more exactly, the necessary release from the inhibitions that have kept it confined in a certain mold. How could the matter be otherwise? Since all cells in the organism are derived, by a process of equipartite division, from an original single cell (zygote), why should not each cell contain exactly similar genetic material and hence all the potentialities of forming any tissue or any organ needed?

Roots become active in the spring several weeks before the upper part of the tree shows signs of life. In the warmer parts of the world they continue to function throughout the year, and even in the extreme North they seem to become sporadically active during intermittent thaws. If it were not for the roots' initiating activities, the buds would not open, leaves would not unfold, and new twig growth would not begin. That they are able to function more or less spontaneously is due to the vast quantities of reserve food stored in their tissues. Only because of these ample stores can they initiate activity in the spring and only because of them can they begin to throw up new shoots when the above-ground parts have been destroyed. But however vast the reserves, they will be exhausted sooner or later if no leaf-bearing shoots are allowed to develop. If you cut down a tree and are dismayed to find it sending up shoot after shoot from the stump, you need only arm yourself with patience. Just keep cutting off the new shoots as fast as they appear, and the root system will be driven closer and closer to exhaustion and will finally die of inanition. Only green leaves (or their counterparts, green stems) can manufacture food. The image used by Victor Hugo in *Bug Jargal* of a large tree growing by the edge of a waterfall (in a lightless cavern, to boot!) and perpetually putting out new shoots by virtue of

titious root that enters the ground at a new point, why should not a single tree cover an entire province? Some of those in India give the impression that they are attempting to do so.

Other trees may develop adventitious roots under special circumstances. The branches of willows and certain other species will sprout roots if covered by soil; the trunk, too,

Adventitious roots on a tropical Fig. When it reaches the ground, each root thickens and forms a post-like support enabling the branches to continue their outward spread. A single tree may thus come to consist of multiple trunks.

the water by which it was surrounded yet with its leaves torn off as fast as they appeared by the rush of water falling obliquely across it is false: no tree could grow, or even long sustain itself, without the agency of food-producing and tissue-building leaves.

Trunk

At first sight, the stem or trunk would seem the simplest part of the tree, being merely a post to hold the top in the air, merely a connecting link between roots and branches. Actually, however, its structure is as complex as that of any other part of the plant body, its apparent simplicity concealing a variety of functions compressed within the smallest possible space.

To begin with, we might ask why the trunk is round (more properly, cylindrical) instead of square, rectangular, ovate, triangular, or any other shape. A forest of I-beams or two-by-fours is within the realm of possibilities. Why, then, are trunks so consistently cylindrical? Why do branches, twigs, flower stems, petioles, roots (except where flattened by penetration of rock crevices), all follow the same cylindrical pattern?

The nature of the growth process in a tree makes the cylindrical form virtually inevitable. If you start with a group of cells dividing impartially in all directions and endow them with a built-in tendency to grow toward a light source that comes chiefly from above, you can hardly help ending up with a cylinder. Since any growing point will expand in all directions unless pushed or pulled to one side or the other by preferential forces, it follows that the result of such uniform and omnidirectional expansion will always be a sphere.

It follows also that if the expansion is restricted to one plane, it will become a circle, and if it elongates along a preferential axis, it will become a cylinder. Thus a drop of

The erosion-exposed root system of this Juniper is a dramatic reminder that half, or sometimes more, of a tree's bulk is to be found underground. Growing near the California coastline, the tree resembles some marine monster ready at a moment's notice to scuttle back into the water.

water on a waxed surface forms into a sphere, a drop of ink on a blotter spreads out into a constantly widening circle, and a tree stem, growing radially by the laying down of concentric layers in one plane while simultaneously elongating along a preferential axis, becomes a cylinder. Regarded in one way, a cylinder is an elongated sphere; taken another way it is a series of superimposed circles. Thus it is that the tree trunk, expanding radially by division of its cells, *automatically* assumes the familiar cylindrical shape from which flow so many advantages and at the same time so many inconveniences.

The roundness of trunks makes them natural roller bearings and so helped early man to transport the monoliths that make up Stonehenge and the huge blocks of stone that constitute the Pyramids. That same roundness, however, causes perpetual trouble for sawyers, who have been forced to develop special skills for the cutting of prisms from cylinders.

The advantages of the cylinder are many. In the first place, it contains more volume in proportion to its surface than any other elongated form; that is why we, imitating the tree trunk, make water pipes cylindrical, as well as steam pipes, natural gas pipe lines, tin cans, hot water heaters, and countless other structures intended for the containment or conveyance of liquids and gases.

Secondly, for sustaining weight the upright cylinder, solid or hollow, is the most efficient structure known; that is why in building we make so much use of pillars, columns, shafts, and cylindrical underpinnings. A sheet of paper fashioned into an open roll and secured with a rubber band can support the weight of a heavy book, whereas held out flatly it can hardly support itself. In young trees, shrubs, and herbaceous plants the strongest elements of the stem are distributed evenly around or near the outside, while the interior remains pithy or in some cases hollow. No other arrangement of a given amount of material could make the stem so strong; the same amount of material recast into a solid rod or a solid or hollow prism would be unable to sustain the same amount of weight. In large trees the heartwood, which is a by-product of growth, is not needed mechanically; witness the old trees whose heartwood may have rotted out entirely and yet which are capable of

The bearded Fig tree, so named because of the adventitious roots growing downward from the branches. When it reaches the ground, each root thickens and forms a post-like support enabling the branches to continue their outward spread to great distances. This photograph is unusual in that it shows the tree at one of the rare moments when it is bare of foliage.

supporting an enormously heavy superstructure; this is possible only because the remaining sound wood is arranged around the periphery.

In the third place, the cylindrical form gives the tree a certain protection against mechanical injuries to the bark. Since the vital parts of the trunk—the phloem and the cambium—are arranged in a ring near the circumference, complete destruction of this layer means death to the tree. This region would be more easily destroyed by animals rubbing against it or chewing on it or by various forms of human abuse if the shape of the trunk were quadrilateral, triangular, or anything else but round. Any blow falling on a flat side is likely to extend itself across the entire area, while any blow falling on a curved surface strikes it tangentially, affecting only a small part of the whole. A heavy animal rubbing against a flat side of a young or thin-barked tree would almost certainly destroy the tender tissues along that whole face,. Such operations would kill the tree if it were quadrilaterally trunked. It is easier to plane a flat surface than a curved one, and to girdle a round trunk

demands a conscious effort. Men who set out to kill trees by girdling often fail because they leave part of the circumference uncut, not realizing that through a single continuous *vertical* strip of inner bark, though ever so narrow, the life of the tree can be sustained until new growth can repair the damage.

The trunk is composed of outer bark, inner bark (phloem), cambium layer, sapwood and heartwood (xylem), and vascular rays, each part having a definite and distinct function.

Outer Bark

The outer bark is former inner bark converted into dead tissue by the activity of cork cells that exclude from it the water of the stem interior. Of all parts of the trunk the outer bark is the least important, composed as it is of dead tissue, cracked and molded into characteristic forms by the pressure of the constantly expanding trunk. But "least important" is not the same as "unimportant." The outer bark serves as a kind of buffer between the interior parts of the

Adventitious root of **Hackberry** *(Celtis laevigata)*. Developing from callus tissue at under right edge of wound, this root grew downward through the tree's decaying center, anchoring it in the soil and helping prevent wind-throw.

sycamore, creamish on the eucalyptus, a beautiful pink on the madrone. On the majority of trees, however, the outer bark forms into characteristic furrows, ridges, bosses, or excrescences that serve as one of the chief means of identification.

As an additional protection some trunks are studded with thorns which, in some cases, may grow directly from the inner layers of the bark where the dead merges with the quick; those of the sand-box tree *(Hura crepitans)*, for example, reform in the same spot no matter how many times they are cut off. The smooth, light-green bark of the silk-cotton tree *(Ceiba pentandra)* is a veritable armamentarium of strong, wicked, rose-like thorns, belying its tender appearance. The bark of most trees is nonflammable; if you throw it in the fire, it will char and gradually crumble away but will not burst into flame. That of the redwoods is very thick, as much as two feet on some species, and surprisingly fire-resistant, by virtue of which many of the giant trees have survived hundreds of forest fires throughout their secular existence.

Clearly visible in this piece of Oak wood are the mature stem's primary divisions: heartwood, sapwood, inner bark, and outer bark.

trunk and the outside world. Often thick, sometimes corky, it protects the trunk from mechanical injuries, from the teeth and claws of animals, and from insect damage. It also protects the tender inner bark and tenderer cambium from the direct rays of the sun and, to a certain extent, from cold. As it weathers off or is worn off, it is constantly replenished on the inside by the activity of the cork cambium, a layer of embryonic cells between outer and inner bark. (Not to be confused with the vascular cambium layer lying between inner bark and wood, presently to be discussed.)

On some trees, as the sycamore, the eucalyptus, the birch, and the madrone the outer bark does not long remain attached to the trunk, falling off in shreds or tube-like sections (although in older trees a clearly marked segment of outer bark builds up along the lower part of the trunk). The trunks of such trees are slick and smooth, white on the

In the bark furrows and fissures of all trees, countless micro-dramas take place. There insects hunt and are hunted, eat and are eaten; hatch, mate, die, rest, sleep, grow, spin cocoons, pupate. The hunting wasp finds the deep furrows of the oak a favorite hunting ground. The ichneumon fly drills through two inches of bark and wood to deposit its eggs in the burrows of the sawfly larvae. The cicada leaves its shed skin on tree trunks throughout the world.

Formerly discarded as valueless, bark is being increasingly used in industrial products. Bark mulch is common in gardens, and crushed or ground-up bark is now often mixed with wood chips in the manufacture of particle-board and similar materials.

Inner Bark

The inner bark, or phloem, together with the cambium layer that gives rise to it, may be considered the most important part of the trunk, since when a small horizontal band of it is cut away, the tree dies. Every other part of the trunk may be damaged without fatal consequences: the outer bark may be scraped off, the heartwood chiseled out, even the sapwood riddled; but once a thin encircling strip of phloem is destroyed, the tree is doomed.

The phloem must be continuous from roots to crown; it is the vital link between top and bottom. In importance it may be likened to the aorta, jugular vein, or spinal cord of the animal body. The phloem stream is the river along which travels the food that is fabricated in the leaves. When it is severed or obstructed, the roots, unable to receive needed aliments, exhaust their reserves and die; and as the roots go, so goes the tree. Thus to the girdled tree death comes not from the top down but from the bottom up. A girdled tree may remain unaffected for six months; a year, sometimes two years or even more, depending on the reserves of food stored in the roots. Leaves, twigs, branches, and trunk continue in perfect health. The roots continue to draw up water, the sapwood conveys it to the leaves, the leaves manufacture the needed food, and the phloem carries the food downward to nourish all parts of the plant body—downward to the girdle, that is, but not farther. The stream being interrupted, it diffuses into the sapwood and is carried upward again, there to begin the incompleted cycle anew. Since from the girdle downward no food is received, the root system must struggle on as best it can, drawing on its reserves as long as they last; then suddenly it dies—dead of starvation in the midst of abundance. Still connected structurally with a healthy top, it is cut off from receiving the produce of that top. When the roots go, the top goes too, killed not by starvation but by lack of water, for although dead roots can, wick-like, draw up water when immersed in it, they cannot, of course, forage for water in semidry soil nor can they produce the millions of root hairs needed daily for normal functioning.*

Trunk of a Sycamore tree.

Such is the strange history of a girdled tree, which we sometimes mistakenly expect to die in a matter of days or weeks but which does not do so for the reasons just presented. Sometimes the tree does not die at all but lives on in apparent defiance of all the laws of logic, botany, hydraulics, and common sense. Such seemingly mysterious survival is due to one of the following causes:

1. The roots of the tree make a natural graft with roots of a nearby tree of the same species and hence receive everything they need via that channel
2. New shoots come up below the girdle, sustaining life for the roots and enabling them to continue to supply the top
3. The girdling is imperfectly done, a narrow vertical connecting strip being left somewhere around the circumference

*A girdled branch or twig, however, will not die. Such an affected shoot becomes in effect an involuntary parasite on the tree, receiving water and minerals through the intact sapwood but contributing nothing to the general welfare.

The accumulated food surplus, unable to pass the girdle, stimulates the cells around the distal end of the severed rim to exceptional activity, and a new phloic cylinder begins to grow in an attempt to bridge the gap and rejoin the separated portions.

4. The severed bark portions manage to grow back together before the root's reserves can be exhausted
5. New bark-connecting links are built up from the exposed ends of the vascular rays.*

Where the tree is effectively girdled, however, and where none of these salvation mechanisms exist, the tree is doomed to a certain death. Interestingly, such a tree frequently produces its most abundant fruit crop in the season immediately following the girdling. Teleologically, this is sometimes interpreted as Nature's supreme effort to reproduce the species when the individual is doomed. Rationalistically, it is explained as the utilization in flowers and fruits of all the energies and materials that could not make their way to the roots. As an expedient intended to make a non-bearing tree bear, girdling is without an equal. When the largest, and the slothfulest, of my avocado trees refused year after year to bear, I finally decided to girdle it. Cutting the girdle early in February, I had the satisfaction of eating the fruit in September—larger and more delicious avocados that I had ever believed that unco-operative specimen capable of producing. Since I was not attempting to kill the tree but merely make it bear, I was careful to keep the girdle narrow, trying to stay within 1/2" to 3/4" range of tolerance, and was rewarded by seeing the severed portions rejoin completely by the middle of December.**(Had I been trying to kill the tree, I would have cut a girdle 3" or 4" wide and would have snipped off all shoots appearing below it.)

In thickness the phloem occupies a relatively small part of the total trunk diameter, a tree two feet through having a phloem layer ranging in thickness from 1/4" to 1" according to species. As the tree grows, the phloem layer increases somewhat in thickness, although that increase is insignificant when compared with the enormous increase of xylem (sapwood and heartwood). On the other hand, even though the phloem layer is disproportionately thin, its total volume is always larger than it seems, since it occupies the arithmetically most favored location on the very rim of the expanding cylinder. The reason for the great discrepancy between the thickness of the phloem and the thickness of the xylem is that the older layers of the phloem are continuously being converted into outer bark which in turn is continuously being sloughed off or worn off by attrition, whereas the older layers of the xylem cannot be sloughed off or worn off, forming as they do on the inside of the trunk rather than on the outside. They do, however, become inactive, stop functioning as sapwood and assume the passive role of a heartwood which remains in place because it has nowhere to go.

* This is very unlikely in Temperate Zone trees but occurs commonly in tropical or semitropical species. The trunk of the cork oak, for example, can be completely stripped of its investiture along its whole length and yet go on to produce a new one.

**Avocados do not shed their leaves until March, at the time when new ones are beginning to appear. Hence, for all practical purposes they are evergreens, growing throughout the year.

Only when decay gains an entrance into the tree's interior and starts destroying the heartwood do the porportions between functioning phloem and functioning xylem fall into their proper perspective. With all the heartwood eaten away, the tree, stripped down to essentials, becomes a hollow shell: a thin band of inner bark enclosing a thin band of sapwood.* It is noteworthy that in young stems, where growth is most active, the proportions are reversed, the phloem composing, by volume, a larger part of the stem than the xylem.

Most trees are exogens**—that is, they have the phloem arranged in a definite ring on the outside of the cambium layer and hence are enabled to expand continually in girth—indeed cannot help doing so—as long as they live. Exogens include both broad-leaved trees such as oak, elm, ash, cottonwood, linden, maple (dicotyledonous Angiosperms) and evergreens, such as pine, fir, spruce, cedar, redwood, cypress (polycotyledonous Gymnosperms). In contrast, the endogens, consisting of tree-like forms such as palms and yuccas and many smaller plants, are so constructed that their phloem and xylem tissues are scattered throughout the stem. These plants have no cambium layer and no continually expanding phloem band around their periphery; hence they do not grow in girth after reaching a certain size. This peculiarity of construction deprives them of the unlimited-spread potential inherent in the exogens and also of any possibility of ever healing over their wounds; in compensation it confers on them one important advantage: they cannot be killed by girdling. The trunk of the palm may be ringed like a table leg turned on a lathe, yet, if not cut so deeply as to fall over, the plant will continue to live.

The inner bark of exogens has a number of interesting uses. It is often eaten by animals, particularly during protracted snows when no other food is available. The bark of the birch was used by the American Indians to make canoes. The bark of one species of oak gives us our cork; that of other oaks gives us tannin. Bark of the paper mulberry is used, or was used, by the Chinese in the preparation of high quality paper and by the Polynesians for the making of mats and articles of clothing.

* So stripped down, the tree can continue to function perfectly and can, because of the mechanical principles mentioned above, continue to support, if well-balanced, all the weight of its enormous superstructure composed of many dozens of heavy boughs, themselves sound and solid. This affirmation should not, however, be construed as implying that a hollow tree is as good as a sound one. It merely points up the engineering excellence of the over-all design and the large margin of safety built into it. Obviously a sound tree is to be preferred to a decayed one, just as a sound tooth is to be preferred to a decayed one. All the disadvantages of the hollow tree are detailed in the Chapter 10, WOUND REPAIR.

** According to my interpretation, *all* trees are exogens, or, to put it another way, only exogens are trees. This definition does not exclude non-tree plants from being exogens but it does exclude non-exogens from being trees.

Trunk of a Spanish Oak tree.

In Mexico City, some of the fastest-moving items in curio shops are brightly decorated strips of various sizes of cork-like material that may be used as table mats or as wall hangings; these are sections of living bark stripped from the *amate* tree, a tropical species of fig. Some of our first writing tablets were made of bark; indeed, some etymologists have sought to connect the word *book* (of German *Buch,* plural *Bücher*) with the word *beech* for this very reason. It seems likely that the intertwined fibers of bark, or perhaps the criss-crossing, exposed fibers at the base of palm leaves, first suggested the idea of weaving.

Good-quality rope is made from the bark fibers of some tree species; that made from the linden is considered among the best, as the tree's alternate name reminds us (*basswood*, a corruption of *bastwood, bast* being inner bark). The very thick bark of the redwood, formerly treated as a nuisance because it interfered with sawing operations, is now utilized in the manufacture of various kinds of wood products. Special conducting cells found in the inner bark of some species transport such useful substances as latex and oleoresins from which we derive rubber, turpentine, incense, and various other products. The phloem sap of one kind of Brazilian tree resembles milk in color and consistency and is actually drunk as such, being sweet and nutritious.

Cambium

The cambium (from Latin "Exchange") is a layer of actively dividing cells theoretically only one cell thick arranged as a continuous cylinder near the outside of the trunk between the phloem (inner bark) and the xylem (the wood proper). This is the part of the stem responsible for all secondary diameter expansion; this ingenious location between phloem and xylem enables the trunk of exogens to increase continuously and indefinitely in girth. During the growth season, cells in the cambium layer divide and multiply continuously. Of the new cells formed, those on the outside become new phloem tissue and those on the inside new xylem tissue. Thus the cambium layer itself remains always of the same thickness while being steadily pushed outward, together with the phloem, by the new tissues of sapwood forming on the inside. In a young tree, one inch in diameter, the cambium layer lies just under the inner bark, one-half inch from the center of the stem. In an old tree, eight feet in diameter, the cambium layer still lies just under the inner bark, but both it and the bark now find themselves four feet from the trunk's center.

If phloem and xylem are formed in equal parts, why is there always more wood in the trunk than bark? Because, as pointed out above, the wood in a sound tree accumulates steadily in the center of the trunk, protected by the accident of its position from all external vicissitudes, while the bark, softer by nature and facing outward by the accident of *its* position, is steadily worn away by weathering and other attrition. If a tree grew flatly, like a board, with the cambium in the center, we could expect the layers of phloem on one side to equal in thickness the layers of xylem on the other; indeed, if both were exposed on their outer face, as the bark is on trees as they now exist, it is quite possible that the xylem would weather and decay faster than the phloem.*

Growth in diameter, then, is accomplished by the laying down of successive and concentric cylinders of sapwood (which appear as rings in cross-section), each one larger than the preceding one because forming around that one's rim, while at the same time and as a direct consequence of this inevitable radial expansion the embryonic cambium and the elastic phloem travel ever outwards. (Not elastic in the sense of a rubber band that stretches without increasing its substance, but elastic like the bony structure of a child's head that increases in size by intussusceptive growth while maintaining its proportions.) Every layer of sapwood was once cambium. Growth starts in the center of the stem and spreads out radially, just as a pebble dropped in a pond

---

* Examination of hollow trees where decay has had a free hand shows that such is indeed the case. Only a very thin shell of sapwood is to be found, sometimes hardly more than the layer formed in the current year, while the bark, both inner and outer, occurs in its customary dimensions.

produces ripples in all directions. The imagined solidification of these ripples furnishes a good analogy of what occurs in the tree. Each ripple represents a new layer of sapwood, and each layer, like each ripple, has its crest and its trough (spring growth and summer growth, together making up an annual ring); the ripples continue in ever-widening circles until the force of the original impulse is dissipated or until they encounter the margin of the pond. The energy contained in the fall of the pebble represents the original growth impulse, while the margin of the pond represents the limitations imposed by environment.

The healing of pruning cuts, bark wounds, and cavities is made possible by the cambium layer, which initiates the formation of callus tissue over the exposed region, growing from all sides towards the center. Callus tissue that forms over a concrete filling, for example, although different from undamaged stem tissue, comes with the passage of time to resemble undamaged tissue more and more, complete with xylem and phloem and embryonic cambium between the two; with every passing year new layers of bark and sapwood are added to the callus, so that, if the tree lives long enough, the concrete may be covered by 4, 5, 6, or more inches of good, sound wood. Since the endogens, as explained above, have their xylem and phloem located in fibrovascular bundles scattered throughout the stem instead of being concentrically arranged according to the ingenious plan of the exogens, they cannot expand continuously in girth nor can they heal over their wounds. A palm "tree" never forms callus tissue; wounds on its trunk remain open throughout its life. They may be filled with concrete plugs or treated with antifungal and waterproof paints, but they will never callus over. Although most organisms, both plant and animal, have the power of healing their wounds, so stately and beautiful a thing as a palm has no regenerative tissue in its trunk; once damaged, it's as powerless as a post to repair itself.*

Sapwood

The xylem, or wood proper, is of course the most familiar part of the tree, having entered into our daily lives in ways innumerable. Wood is basic: the first step in the vast industrial complex in which we live immersed. Probably there is not a single person alive today—and possibly none has ever lived during the whole history of mankind—who is not familiar with wood in one or other of the multiple forms in which it is fashioned; even those Eskimos and desert-dwellers who have never seen a tree are acquainted with wood and use it in some way in their daily life.

---

* Palms also suffer from the disadvantage that all their *vertical* growth is accomplished by the activity of one large terminal bud; when that bud is destroyed, growth ends and the plant dies. Decapitated palm trunks may be seen from time to time without a single sprig of new growth in evidence anywhere along the stem; so they will stand until they rot away or are cut down. Contrast this with the regenerative vitality of the true trees, the exogens, which however badly damaged persistently and undauntedly send up multitudes of new shoots from trunk, branches, and roots.

The xylem may be divided into two parts: sapwood and heartwood. These are not two different substances, as sometimes erroneously believed, but merely two different phases of the same substance. Heartwood is simply sapwood that has ceased to function; we cannot come to a proper understanding of wood until we thoroughly grasp that simple fact. Comprehending it, we see at once the fallacy in the following loosely entertained notions:

1. The sapwood grows faster than the heartwood. Correction: *neither* sapwood nor heartwood grows, in the strict sense of the word. As explained in the previous section, division and multiplication of cells in the cambium layer produces (annually in Temperate Zone trees, irregularly in tropical species) new cylinders; by this mechanism the stem expands in girth. But any cylinder of sapwood, once laid down, never moves from that position and never thereafter increases or decreases in size*. Thus, although more sapwood exists in a large tree than in a small one, its increase in size is due to accretion rather than to true growth (intussusception).** The same thing is true of the heartwood: not moving itself and certainly not growing (since growth implies life), it increases in size by successive increments from the older layers of sapwood that cease functioning and fill up with various metabolic by-products.

2. Sapwood rings are larger than heartwood rings. Correction: rings may be large or small in either sapwood or heartwood, the size of any given ring depending on whether conditions for cambial growth were favorable or unfavorable during the time it was laid down. Actually, since growth in older trees is generally slower than in younger trees, the first-formed rings tend to be the largest and the most recently formed rings the smallest. The first-formed rings, being the oldest, will necessarily be found in the heartwood, while the most recently formed rings, which in an old tree— but only in an old tree —tend to be the smallest, will be found of course in the sapwood.

3. There is always more heartwood in a tree than sapwood. (Or the opposite error, there is always more sapwood than heartwood.) Correction: The proportions of the two vary during the life of the tree. Young stems have no heartwood, the center usually being composed of pith and all the surrounding xylem layers of actively functioning sapwood. As the stem ages, the pith disappears, either being absorbed, desiccated, or crushed, and the older, inner layers of xylem stop functioning and change color by the filling and plug-

---

* Except for small daily fluctuations associated with the filling and partial emptying of its cells with water.

** Mineralogists will perhaps argue the point. Although crystals increase in size only by accretion, they lovingly think and speak of them as "growing".

ging of their cells; it is this non-functioning xylem that we call heartwood. Thus the very young stem has no heartwood, the somewhat older stem may have a small area of it and the older and thicker stem an ever larger proportion of it. The ratio between sapwood and heartwood will thus depend on the age of any given tree at the time it is examined; also on the species, some kinds beginning to show heartwood at a much earlier age than others.

The three functions of the sapwood are:

1. To convey water and dissolved minerals from the soil up to the leaves, where they are used in the manufacture of food,
2. To store food,
3. To provide rigidity.

As a supporting tissue, wood in the plant body corresponds to bone in the animal body, and just as it seems impossible that an animal of any size could exist without bones, so it seems impossible that a plant of any size could exist without xylem elements. Strictly speaking, even the veins of a leaf, composed as they are of fibro-vascular bundles, each with its xylem and phloem elements, partake of the nature of wood. Even the cacti, in spite of their thick, waxy covering and the extreme turgor of the moisture-repleted cells of their interior, are forced to construct xylem strands, continuous or discontinuous, in order to achieve larger dimensions. There are many interesting correspondences between bone and wood—but this could be a subject for a volume in itself. Enough here to say that in their weight-strength ratio they resemble each other strikingly (the degree of approximation depending, of course, on which wood and which bone is selected).

Microscopic examination of the sapwood shows it to be composed, in large part, of relatively long tubular cells arranged vertically end to end, the precise length of the cells varying according to species, something like a water pipe composed of one-, two-, or three-foot sections. The thickened cell walls help give the tissues their woody strength, while the large unobstructed interiors with the open ends make possible the rapid passage of water through the system.* In addition to these vessels, which make up its most prominent and most characteristic feature, the sapwood is further composed of (1) fiber-tracheids, which are additional supporting elements, (2) parenchyma strands made up of unspecialized cells serving for the storage of food and, to a limited extent, for the regeneration of lost parts, and (3) radially oriented ray cells which help transport water and dissolved materials back and forth from the stem's center to its circumference.

---

* Sap ascent through the wood is slowest in conifers (which have tracheids instead of open-ended vessels), faster in broad-leaved trees, (with considerable variation from species to species), and fastest of all in vines with their very large, completely open vessels. Under favorable circumstances sap may ascend through the sapwood at the velocity of three feet per minute.

The sapwood is at all times more or less replete with liquid—largely water drawn up from the soil with a greater or lesser admixture of sugars and starches that may have diffused into it from the adjacent phloem tissues. The sapwood of many trees is as moist, or moister, during winter as in spring or summer, as anyone who has ever sunk an axe into it knows. (Some trees, however, such as many species of ash, are curiously dry regardless of the season.) When a tree dies, it is evaporation of water from its tissues that makes the sapwood turn hard and dry; this also explains the loss of weight that dry wood shows over green wood. Those species whose pores (sapwood vessels seen in cross-section) are very large, such as the chinaberry, the tree-of-heaven, and the willow, lose much more weight in drying than those species whose pores are small, such as white oak, mesquite, Texas ebony, and ironwood. In other words, trees which are largely water to start with become almost substanceless when dry*, while slow-growing species with fine, close pores lose comparatively little weight when dried and, consequently, in general warp little. (The mesquite, for example, warps and shrinks negligibly in drying, being for this reason excellent material for levels, gun stocks, and other special uses.)

Among the oaks, two great groups—the red oaks and the white oaks—are distinguished by lumbermen according to the size of their pores, the former having large open pores and the latter fine closed ones. Through a two-inch block of red oak sapwood smoke may be blown, while through the tight, closed pores of the white oak neither liquids nor gases can make their way; hence the popularity of this wood for making whisky barrels. The pores of some woods are large enough to be distinguished by the naked eye; in some the point of a pin may be inserted.

In the Temperate Zones where decidious trees grow only, and evergreen trees mostly, during spring and summer, the sapwood is formed according to a definite pattern. Spring growth, which is most rapid, produces the largest cells, while the slower summer growth produces smaller and smaller cells as the months wear on. The contrast between the very small cells formed in late summer with the large ones formed in early spring constitutes a pattern easily recognizable: it is called a ring and represents, in the Temperate Zones, one year's growth. Counting the rings tells the age of the tree—one ring for each year. Counting them from the center outward reveals the history of the tree at any given age, for as the tree grows it leaves a permanent record of its experiences—a kind of frozen wake. Counting the rings from the circumference inwards is like traveling backward through time; we may read with surprising accuracy, once we learn the language, about events that happened in the distant past when no eye was present to see and

---

* The Argentinian *ombu,* made famous in the stories of W. H. Hudson, is the most remarkable case in point. When dry, a large branch, five or six feet long and six inches thick, can be picked up by a child of three.

no hand to record. Counting the rings of a branch tells the age of that branch but not of the tree proper. for even the oldest branch is necessarily at least a few years younger than the main stem (trunk) and often many years younger. In cases where the whole trunk has been destroyed by fire, wind, or some other cause, and a new stem has grown up to take its place, the rings of that new stem will not, or course, represent the true age of the tree, whose oldest parts will now be the first-formed roots.

Theoretically, rings near the center of trunk or branch should be the largest, since trees when uninhibited, grow faster when young, while as the rings get farther and farther from the center they should get progressively smaller, indicating the slowing down of growth that accompanies advancing age. But this correlation is by no means perfect, and in any given case dozens of factors may intervene to upset it. In a forest, for example, the young trees that grow in the deep shade cast by their fellows often grow very slowly, their first 25, 30, 50 years or more being marked by barely distinguishable rings. Should a large tree fall, any young tree in the immediate vicinity that had been marking time all those years will suddenly shoot upward in a veritable explosion of growth, and the rings formed during that frantic expansion period will of course be very much wider.

Other factors, such as drought, insect defoliation, and fire also affect the tree's growth rate, and all are faithfully reflected in its rings. Thus the theoretical picture of the rings being largest at and near the trunk's center and decreasing progressively in size outwards from the center is met with only under exceptional conditions. When examining any trunk section we may expect to find, not the symmetrical regularity of a draughtsman's drawing but the highly irregular, sometimes chaotic, and always unpredictable reflection of life itself: large and small rings alternating in no discoverable pattern, adversity yielding to prosperity or prosperity to adversity, or one or the other of these states unduly prolonged, or a jumbled pattern of regualr and irregular.

Two things the rings make unequivocally manifest: the tree's built-in tendency to grow and its sensitive reactivity to all external vicissitudes. This turns out to be a very convenient arrangement, for if we are vitalistically inclined, we may read into it an indomitable *élan vital* overcoming all obstacles, while if we are mechanistically disposed, we may see the tree as a stimulus-response mechanism, complex and endlessly interesting but still a mechanism, doing neither more nor less than that which the environment exacts of it.

Rings vary in thickness from a barely perceptible line in trees that have had a bad year or in those that are slow-growing by nature to an inch or more in fast-growing species under favorable conditions. The oldest of living things, the bristle-cone pine, growing in one of the world's harshest environments (rooted in the thin and rocky soil at the top of the White Mountains, buffeted incessantly by strong winds, frozen by night and burned by day by the sun hanging in a cloudless sky) grows so slowly that its rings are virtually indistinguishable without a hand lens. In contrast, such species as tree-of-heaven, red mulberry, cottonwood, willlow, and others may, when growing in well-watered locations, produce rings 1/2", 3/4", or even 1" thick. It must be remembered, of course, that the size of a ring represents only half of that year's trunk growth, for a ring that is 1/2" thick on the north side is (usually) also 1/2" on the south side. Thus the size of any given ring must be multiplied by two to give the true increase in trunk diameter. Sometimes, however, the geometrical center of the trunk and the location of the center ring do not correspond; moreover any given ring may not be of uniform thickness throughout. This condition indicates that something—perhaps a building, perhaps another tree—was forcing the tree to grow at an angle or in some way differentially affecting it, so that more sapwood was formed on one side than on the other. In such cases the ring is curiously shaped: almost flat during part of its arc and flaring out suddenly along another segment, forming an ellipse or irregular curve rather than a circle. In a forest of straight-trunked pines, on the other hand, where environmental pressure is even on all sides, the rings are of a nearly uniform width all the way around and describe a nearly perfect circle.

Since trees grow more in wet years than in dry years, other things being equal, the widest rings correspond to the wettest years and the narrowest rings to the driest years. This simple fact is the basis of a new and fruitful discipline—dendrochronology: the science of studying weather and climate in relation to the growth of trees. If you cut down a tree in Oregon in 1975 and, counting backward (from the outside towards the center) 25 years or so, suddenly come upon a series of six or seven unusually narrow rings beginning at that point, you may infer that from 1943 to 1950 Oregon received abnormally low precipitation. If you cut down numerous other specimens in different parts of the state and find them telling the same story, you may be sure of it. If to continue the investigation, you cut down trees in Washington, California, Nevada, Wyoming, and Montana and find the same evidence there, you will know that the drought was general over the Northwest.*

Applications of this technique on a grand scale are obvious. Wood specimens from trees, living and dead, all over the world can be compared to give continous climatological readings running back 3000 years and more.** For this purpose the longest-lived trees—the redwoods, firs, cypresses, pines—are of greatest value, although short-lived species may be used to help fill in the gaps. Even

---

* This is a hypothetical case. I do not know the actual weather pattern during the years indicated.

** It is no longer necessary to cut down a tree in order to count its rings. Sapwood and heartwood specimens may be extracted from a living tree by a special drill (increment borer) that pulls out an intact cylinder in which the rings are visible.

beams from ruins in Mexico, Guatemala, India, Egypt, and other countries have been pressed into service, and petrified logs from our Southwest as well. By a careful study of all these sources and a dovetailing of the pattern of one tree into that of another, a surprisingly accurate record of past events can be built up.

Tree rings thus constitute a great natural calendar, providing data of the highest value that may be correlated with data furnished by other natural phenomena, such as the deposition of silt in lake bottoms, the accumulation of pollen grains, the formation of new lakes and the drying up of old ones, the rate of wind and water erosion over given regions, etc., to help reconstruct the world's past climate. When the record furnished by tree rings and the sophisticated Carbon-14 dating technique fail to agree, as sometimes happens, it is interesting to note that the discrepancy is usually attributable to technical or interpretative errors connected with the latter method rather than to any "mistake" on the trees' part.

Very recent investigations have disclosed that not only the width of the rings is significant but also their chemical content, which furnishes an important clue to past sunspot activity.

In the tropics where seasons are wet and dry rather than hot and cold, tree rings do not have the same correlative value, for one ring does not necessarily mean one year. In some regions and with some species, growth is virtually continuous, no rings forming at all; in other regions several rings may form in one year, depending on the frequency of the rainy spells. In Florida, the lemon tree may lay down two or three rings of sapwood in a single calendar year.

The sapwood has a number of enemies, possibly the commonest being the borers that riddle it with their labyrinthine tunnels, eating the wood as they go along. Borers in cut mesquite are so numerous that a few feet away from a pile of logs their chewing may be heard like rain on the roof. Cases are on record of borers emerging out of wood (mesquite, cherry, walnut) ten or fifteen years after it has been made into furniture.

Although the heartwood of most trees is considered more valuable for lumber and furniture, the sapwood is also commonly used, either alone or in combination with the heartwood. Pine boards are commonly part sapwood. When a piece of lumber is so cut that it is part sapwood and part heartwood, it is harder to dry, since the sapwood contains much more water. Such differential drying is often responsible for warping, shrinking, and cracking.

Heartwood

Heartwood is that part of the stem xylem that no longer functions either in the conveyance of fluids or in the storage of food or in any other way, except passively as a hard, strong core constantly enlarging by accretion from the older sapwood layers, as explained in the preceding section.

Every heartwood ring was once a sapwood ring; and since this conversion process is always unidirectional—from sapwood to heartwood and never the other way around—it is obvious that the amount of heartwood becomes steadily larger as the tree ages. Young stems—whether twigs and small branches on a large tree or the main trunk itself of a small tree—have no heartwood, all the xylem being composed of functioning sapwood. As the tree continues to grow and its stems get older and larger, the sapwood rings nearest the center cease functioning; they dry out, harden, and fill up with various gums, resins, and other materials the tree no longer needs. A certain proportion between sapwood and heartwood comes to exist, the proportion being different for each kind of tree; moreover, this is a ratio that changes with age, the heartwood steadily gaining until in old trees of many species the greater part of the trunk and of the major limbs, both by weight and by volume, is heartwood.

Some species, such as certain hackberries, never form heartwood, even though their older sapwood rings cease functioning. At the other extreme is the black locust, which forms heartwood very early and so persistently that its trunk and larger limbs contain a greater proportion of heartwood than any other known tree, the sapwood being reduced to the thinnest of shells. Other species form heartwood slowly, like the persimmon, which needs 100 years to begin producing it.

Heartwood is harder than sapwood, drier, tougher, and of a different color, generally darker. While the sapwood is almost always white, creamish, or light brown, the heartwood is usually dark brown, bronze, or yellow; it may also be rose-colored, red, black, or any combination of these. The juxtaposition of heartwood and sapwood in a piece of lumber produces a very pleasing effect—the original two-tone. The heartwood of some species is extraordinarily beautiful and valuable: the satiny heart of mahogany, for example, or the rich warm heart of walnut, the glistening black heart of ebony, the deep rich redness of mesquite heart, the rose-colored huisache heart. Some heartwoods are amazingly hard, that of black locust having long since passed into legend and that of the Mexican ebony (*Pithecellobium,* or *Ebenopsis, flexicaule*) as resistant to nails as an iron post.

Although the heartwood has no physiological function, it is useful to the tree for support. While it is true, as explained in the preceding section, that a hollow tree, by virtue of inherent engineering principles, may support its heavy superstructure, it is obvious that a sound tree, strengthened by its core of heartwood, can do so much better. When limbs or trunks break off in high winds, the cause is usually decay of the heartwood.

Tough and strong as the heartwood is, it is susceptible to attack by a number of wood-rotting fungi. The very strong heartwood of oak that breaks teeth out of saws and mocks at the axe and wedge is quickly reduced to a pulpy, soggy mass by the strengthless filaments of the bracket fungi. Heart rot in forests causes the annual loss of millions of dollars' worth of timber, the pines, the balsam fir, the Douglas fir, and many other conifers figuring prominently among the victims. Fire damage and wind damage provide entrance points for the decay-producing fungi; so does poor pruning. Cabling, which helps prevent breakage; correct pruning, which helps prevent cavity formation; and skillful treatment of existing cavities are the indicated counter-measures for the prevention and control of heartwood rot.*

What is called grain in wood is the heartwood and sapwood rings and the vascular rays seen in different perspectives according to the way a log is sawed. When a log is cross-cut—sawed perpendicularly to its length—the rings are seen in their entirety: a series of concentric circles. When a log is cut lengthwise, the rings and rays appear in various interesting patterns, varying according to the distance of the board from the center, only a small arc of each ring, but the whole length of the rays, being visible. When a log is quarter-sawed, only those boards are cut that run out radially from the center of the log to its circumference, like the spokes of a wheel. Since this method shows up the beauty of the grain to greatest advantage, it is often practiced for special purposes with some of the finer woods; however, since fewer pieces can be cut from a given log, the method is wasteful and the product consequently more expensive.

Vascular Rays

The vascular rays (formerly called *medullary rays*) show up in cross-section as tiny lines running perpendicularly to the rings. These are channels by which food and water are transported radially throughout stems; they also serve for the storage of surplus food, and have, furthermore, interesting properties associated with their embryonic nature. Ray cells sometimes remain alive, even in the heartwood, long after all the longitudinally oriented cells that surround them have died. It is the exposed ends of the rays that, in some species, particularly tropical ones, are responsible for the regeneration of a new bark surface when the old one has been destroyed. When wood is split, it opens along its vascular rays.

The importance of the rays as radial conduction channels may be highlighted by an experiment performed a few years ago. Transverse saw cuts were made into the trunk of a tree all along its length at intervals of two feet or so in alternating order, that is, first from the left, then from the right, then from the left again, each cut passing about two-thirds

of the way through the trunk in such a manner that the vertical conducting system was severed in many different places. Yet in spite of these multiple cuts and the destruction of all vertical continuity, the upward conduction of sap proceeded in much the usual manner, with only a slightly impaired velocity. That the sap was able to rise by taking a zigzag path rather than a straight one illustrated dramatically the rays' conductive efficiency.*

Lenticels

Lenticels are small, slightly raised areas of loose cells scattered over the surface of roots, trunk, branches, and twigs. On trunks and major boughs they are generally invisible, hidden away among the furrows and scales of the coarse outer bark. On some species, however, they are clearly visible, even prominent, on all stems including the trunk itself; on the Chinese elm (*Ulmus parvifolia*), for example, they appear as tiny, raised, rust-colored islands occurring in such numbers as to give the stems their characteristic reddish look. They are also conspicuous on the tree-of-heaven. They are, it is presumed, avenues for the entrance of air into stems, analogous to the stomata which admit air to the leaves. Whenever a trunk or branch becomes too heavily covered with lichen, moss, or vine, the function of its lenticels may be interfered with.

In company with roots and twigs, the trunk and branches also serve for the storage of food. The rush of spring activity, including the unfolding and enlargement of leaves, the growth of twigs, and in some cases the formation of flowers and even seeds, before the leaves have begun to make food in any significant quantities, could not occur if it were not for the large amounts of food stored in the various stem tissues. All of which is by way of showing that the trunk is much more than a mere post connecting roots and crown and that the branches are much more than struts and griders: they are living organs with multiple functions and as such they must be supplied with air.

Part of this they get by way of the leaves through an internal air-conduction system, while another part they get by direct entry through the lenticels.

Many tree workers, either through ignorance or intent, persuade homeowners that lenticels are insects busily engaged in undermining the tree's vitality.

Indeed, without foreknowledge and the aid of a hand lens they do look convincingly like some obscure scale insect or like the fruiting bodies of a malignant fungus bursting its way through the bark to scatter its spores far and wide. Many thousands of persons are victimized annually by this close natural resemblance and by the plausibility of the proposed remedy, which is, of course, spraying. The unscrupulous practitioner starts up his spraying ma-

---

*In a living tree the heartwood, where exposed, decays more rapidly than sapwood. But in a dead tree it is usually the sapwood that decays first; this can be observed in fence posts, which rot away around the outside while their core remains sound. Some trees, however, like the California Valley Oak, are exceptional in that even in the living tree the sapwood—at least its oldest layers—may decay while the heartwood remains firm and untouched.

---

* What happened to this much-sawed tree was not disclosed in the experiment report. Obviously, if not braced in some way, it must have broken apart in the first wind of any consequence.

chine, douses the trees with unnumbered gallons of colored water, collects his fee, and moves on. *Caveat emptor!*

Superstructure

Many trees, such as the pines, have a single main stem, called trunk or bole, which gradually diminishes in diameter from bottom to top, forming a greatly elongated, more or less regular cone.* From the trunk the branches appear, from the branches the twigs, and from the twigs the leaves. Often, however, the pattern is not so neat at this: twigs— and sometimes even leaves—may spring directly from any part of the trunk, as indeed they do of necessity from its growing tip. Where the trunk ends and the branches begin

* Some few species depart grotesquely from this norm, like the Australian battle-tree or the African baobab. Many palms, too have trunks that, instead of being conical, swell and bulge in irregular curves.

is a point not always easy to determine, for sometimes branches appear along nearly the whole length of the trunk, while this, mast-like, continues straight upward; sometimes the trunk yields a tuft of branches at its very top; and sometimes it divides and subdivides in such a manner that its existence gradually merges with that of its limbs. Each species has it characteristic manner of branching; however, individual trees may depart from the species standard, in accordance with environmental peculiarities.

Based on their manner of branching, trees may be classified into two main forms: *deliquescent* and *excurrent*. (A third term, *decurrent*, is used by some botanists as a synonym for *deliquescent*, while others use it to designate a milder form of deliquescence.) The deliquescent form is that in which the trunk divides and subdivides repeatedly, losing its identity in that of the branches. This form of branching produces a gradual transition from trunk to twig and results generally in a broad, rounded crown, such as

Like a church spire, the Italian Cypress towers upward in faultless symmetry, forming a dense, immobile evergreen mass. Despite its narrowness and extreme elongation, it possesses an amazingly large photosynthetic surface.

that of oaks, elms, walnut, birch, willow, and most of our other familiar dooryard trees. The excurrent form is that in which the trunk grows, like a mast, throwing out branches more or less evenly on all sides but clearly preserving its identity from base to tip. This type is represented by pines, firs, spruces, deodars, redwoods, and most of the other conifers, which, because of their straight growth and little taper, people the ocean with masts and the land with telephone poles, in addition to providing the bulk of the world's lumber. In contrast to the broad, rounded head of the oaks and elms, most excurrent trees produce a conical, Christmas-tree-like shape; the fir is, in fact, the *Tannenbaum* so celebrated in carols, and the firs continue year after year, whether as small trees taken in their entirety or as the tops cut out of large trees, to supply us with the bulk of our Yuletide trees. Some species, such as young Sequoias (*gigantea*) with their lowest, longest branches resting on the ground, create in outline a cone almost as perfect as that formed by a paper cup placed base downward. Other conifers, however, habitually possess other shapes, some of the pines producing obdeltoid or irregular crowns. Others gradually change their shape with age; *S. gigantea* itself is perhaps the most conspicuous example of this modification, the perfect conical shape of its youth gradually giving way to a massive oval crown at maturity.

Some species represent a sort of compromise between the two main types, being sometimes deliquescent, sometimes excurrent, other times being, or trying to be, both at once; the sycamore and the cottonwood are instances. Although the sycamore may be considered predominantly excurrent, it is often found with divided bole, each part of which grows excurrently as if it were a single tree. The cottonwood exists in so many species and varieties that it is hard to generalize about. Often excurrent, it is as frequently deliquescent, being perhaps the most noticable borderline case of all.

Papayas and palms (which, it will be remembered, are not true trees according to my definition) and other tree-like tropical or semi-tropical forms have no branches at all, putting out instead from the meristematic tip a series of huge leaves on greatly thickened and elongated petioles. Some of the fan palms have leaves as large as an old-fashioned table top, while some of the feather palms produce leaves an unbelievable 40 or 45 feet long (including the saw-edged petiole which itself may measure 10, 12, or 15 feet). These, although simulating branches, do not function as such; they die back to the trunk and fall off just as oak and elm leaves fall from the twig. Because of this habit, growth continues only in an upward sense, never outward, and the crown of a palm 100 years old may extend no farther sideways than the crown of a palm 20 years old.

Tree stem and buds of a Post Oak.

Pussy Willow buds.

Square twigs—an oddity in nature. (Carolina Poplar, *Populus canadensis*)

The silhouette formed by each kind of tree according to the structure and arrangement of its branches is characteristic for the species, serving to identify the tree at a distance, both when in leaf and when bare, as surely as the shape of the leaves identifies it at close hand. And just as the different leaf shapes have special names, so the different silhouettes have each its name. Thus a tree may be conical like an incense cedar; cylindrical like a Texas elm or black acacia; globose like the southern live oak or the orange; spreading like the walnut; obdeltoid (vase-like) like the American elm; pointed (fastigiate) like the Lombardy poplar; or the Italian cypress; drooping like the weeping willow or the California pepper-tree; irregular like the hackberry, and so on. The tree in winter, stripped of leaves, flowers, and fruit, shows clearly and dramatically the scaffolding which the greenery of summer partially or totally conceals; study of both winter and summer forms in an exercise in esthetics. Although pruning will change its shape temporarily, the pruned tree will always tend to revert to its natural form. Even when the whole crown is destroyed, the new growth coming up from the stump tends to reshape the tree along the original lines.

Branch is a general term signifying any offshoot from the main stem; thus in the strict sense every secondary stem, from the largest to the smallest, can be called a branch. However, such a difference in size exists among these secondary stems that popular usage distinguishes among them, calling the largest ones *limbs* or *boughs*, the ones intermediate in size *branches,* the smaller ones *branchlets*, and the smallest of all *twigs.* Thus when the main stem or trunk divides into two parts, we say that it branches, but we avoid calling each part a branch, preferring the term "limb" or even referring to it as "a division of the trunk."

Every stem, whether bough, branch, twig, or the trunk itself, begins as a small, slender shoot, which then goes on to elongate and thicken so long as its life endures. The first shoot, rising vertically, becomes the trunk; shoots from it become the main lateral elements (limbs or boughs); shoots from these become branches; and shoots from branches become twigs. Boughs, branches, and twigs taken conjointly form the crown. In deliquescent types the passage from trunk to twig is usually a very gradual one, larger elements giving way to smaller elements by repeated bifurcation in orderly sequence. With continued growth each part, acquiring a kind of seniority, undergoes a transformation of roles: the twig becomes the branchlet, the branchlet the branch, the branch a bigger branch. Only the trunk itself and the major boughs do not ascend in this structural hierarchy, simply growing bigger and stronger in order to accommodate the increasing weight of their derivative members. In the excurrent type of tree with its single central

Buds on a Silver leafed Poplar.

Buds on a Sycamore.

mast this phenomenon of role-succession does not occur, or occurs to a much lesser degree. Branches tend to be more nearly uniform in size, particularly on small and medium-size trees, so that it is difficult to find any which we could call bough or major limb.(On the older conifers, however, some branches may become very much larger than others. On the large Sequoias, for example, some of the lower branches attain a diameter of 6, 7, or 8 feet while others, especially those near the top, remain small.)

Once a tree has grown large and its main outlines have been established, we too often make the mistake of believing its growth finished. Misled by analogy with animals, we believe that only young trees grow and that old ones merely maintain their status quo. Yet such is not the case; although true for animals and for small, non-woody plants, it is not true for trees. A tree continues to grow as long as it lives. It may grow at different rates, sometimes fast, sometimes slow, but it cannot stop growing, even though by continued growth it sometimes works its own destruction. Trees sometimes become so top-heavy that they split apart, particularly when whipped by the wind or weighted by ice. Great limbs sometimes break off under their own weight, even on perfectly still days. The California Valley Oak is notorious for this habit: on a day when no breath of wind is stirring, a sound limb may suddenly break off with a resounding crack and come hurtling to the ground. Apart from the danger to persons or objects underneath, such breakage nearly always leaves unhealing stubs that open avenues of infection to the heart of the tree, eventually causing or hastening its demise.

This phenomenon of continuing growth is of cardinal importance if we wish to understand our subject. As explained above, all exogens (which means all true trees, excluding such unbranched forms as the palms, yuccas, papayas, and others) have expandable stems whose nature not only permits them to keep on increasing in diameter but obliges them to do so. Any stem that possesses a continuous cambium cylinder positioned between its xylem and phloem must perforce increase in girth as long as it lives. While the cambium cells live, they will divide and multiply, and this division and multiplication inevitably results in stem enlargement. This is a case where life and growth are synonymous; to stop growing is to stop living. Regarded in one light, the presence of this perennially dividing cambium layer is a promise of immortality; regarded in another light is seems alarmingly cancer-like, in spite of the regularity and orderliness of its division pattern, for even though the tree would in many cases benefit from reaching a fixed size and remaining there, it cannot do so.

This built-in growth program presents the tree with its greatest problem: how to support a constantly larger and heavier superstructure from a central axis—increasing weight which even the strongest and toughest woods cannot withstand indefinitely. Only one kind of tree has found a solution to this seemingly insoluble problem: the banyan-tree of India and other of the tropical figs. (See the discussion in the section on roots.)

Leaves

Perhaps the most interesting and wonderful parts of the tree are its leaves. If the wood of the tree is its bones and the living bark is flesh, the leaves are its raiment, clothing it, giving it form, color, movement, life. As we modify our dress from season to season, so the tree changes the color of its leaves from the tender light green of spring through the darker green of summer to the yellows, browns, and crimsons of fall; and as we discard old garments in favor of new ones so the tree sheds each year's leaves in the fall and dresses itself anew each spring.

The green leaf—the world's most important factor. (Mulberry, *Movus rubva*).

Leaves perform a multitude of functions. They shelter and protect birds, shade and conceal animals, embellish the countryside. They interpose a barrier of green coolness between the sun and the ground, making possible human and animal existence in places otherwise uninhabitable.

They transpire great quantities of water into the air, humidifying and freshening it. By lowering the temperature of the ground underneath, they create minor ascending and descending air currents; at the same time they moderate the force of winds. They interrupt the fall of raindrops and so prevent impaction of the soil. When they die and fall to the ground, their bodies decompose, enriching and mulching the soil.

Leaves of a green elastic tree.

More than all this, leaves produce food for the tree and hence for all other forms of life dependent directly or indirectly on it. Indeed, this is their primary function; all other uses are secondary and incidental. Every leaf is a busy factory, the most marvelous factory in the world, whose motive power is the sun's rays and whose end-product is food. The green leaf—that of trees and other plants—is the *only* source of food on our planet. It is the bridge between the organic and the inorganic worlds. Only the green leaf is capable of manufacturing organic food out of inorganic elements. *No other power, natural or artificial, can accomplish this feat.* There are other ways by which food may be stored, transported, transformed, but only the green leaf can *manufacture* it. Hence all other life, animal and human, is dependent on the green leaf. Man, animals, insects, and plants without chlorophyll are all parasites in the sense that

Leaves of a Spanish Oak tree.

they cannot make their own food. We derive food from plants or animals or both. Carnivores derive theirs from herbivores which derive theirs from plants. If green plants disappeared from our planet tomorrow, all other forms of life—saprophyte, parasite, vertebrate, invertebrate, fish, fowl, insect, quadruped, man himself—would disappear shortly thereafter.* We cannot exist without green plants; on the other hand, they, with the exception of a few highly specialized forms dependent on our activities for pollination and propagation can exist very well without us.

Not only all our food but much of the energy we use to do the world's work comes from the green leaf. For it is by the activity of the leaf that the tissues of the tree are built, and it is the body of the tree burned as wood and coal that powers many of our machines. (It now seems that oil too is of vegetable origin, and consequently green-leaf-derived, although this point is not yet fully settled.) The energy of the sun's rays, transformed by the leaf into a form utilizable, storable, and controllable, is thus the ultimate source of the energy we need both for the construction and maintenance of our bodies and for our multifarious industrial uses. Only by exploiting atomic energy or by learning to use solar energy directly can we by-pass the green leaf.

The process by which the leaf manufactures organic food out of inorganic elements is called *photosynthesis*—Greek for "production-by-light." The raw materials used are carbon dioxide and water—the first taken in from the air by the leaves, the second absorbed from the soil by the roots

*Except certain bacteria.

and sent up through the sapwood to the leaves. When these two substances are brought together in the green leaf and when this is exposed to light, the substances are broken down and their elements are recombined: carbon dioxide and water are transformed into oxygen and sugar (dextrose). Chemically, the reaction is written thus:

$$6CO_2 + 6H_2O \xrightarrow{\text{sunlight}} 6O_2 + C_6H_{12}O_6$$

This is assuredly the most important chemical formula that exists on our planet, for both of its end-products are indispensable for the sustenance of animal life—not only the sugar (which is later changed to starch and other food products) but the oxygen as well. By constantly consuming oxygen and exhaling carbon dioxide during their respiratory cycle, animals would eventually vitiate the air to the point where they could no longer exist. Green plants, by reversing this process, that is, by using up carbon dioxide and emitting free oxygen, maintain the percentage of both substances at an approximately uniform level.* Each biotic kingdom consumes the other's waste products—a most

*Plants also respire as animals do, using up oxygen and giving off carbon dioxide. However, the effect of their respiration in comparison with the effect of photosynthesis, the reverse process, is almost negligible. They produce far more oxygen than they consume.

Leaves of the Box Elder tree.

convenient arrangement that has evolved over many millions of years. But this reciprocity, while obligatory for animals, is not so for plants.

The mechanism by which photosynthesis is accomplished is the object of intense study, not only because of its great theoretical interest but because of the practical possibilities inherent in our learning to use solar energy as a power source. Can we, imitating the leaf, learn to convert the radiant energy of light into the energy of the chemical bond? Can we use it to power our machinery? To divert rivers from their course? To produce rains at will? To modify global climate? At a time when the whole world is faced with its gravest energy crisis, the study of photosynthesis takes on a whole new dimension of importance. While we are struggling to manufacture a few hundred efficient and affordable solar batteries, a single tree produces them with cavalier prodigality—hundreds of thousands if we consider each leaf a battery; uncountable millions and quadrillions if, more properly, we equate the chloroplast with the battery—and then casts them off indifferently each fall to be trodden underfoot as the merest dust.

In spite of their great diversity of size and shape, all leaves consist of essentially the same parts: a petiole or stalk (sometimes absent) and a blade—a thin, flat sheet* extended in such a manner as to receive as much sunlight as possible. The blade in turn consists of:

1. A waxy covering or *cuticle*.
2. A single layer of cells called *epidermis* (cuticle and epidermis are on both top and bottom).
3. A layer of large upright cells called the *palisade layer*, each cell of which contains tiny bodies called *chloroplasts* inside which is found the vital chlorophyll.
4. A layer of irregularly shaped, loosely arranged cells forming the *spongy mesophyll*, also containing chloroplasts.
5. The veins or *fibrovascular bundles* that form the communication system, carrying liquids and nutrients to and from.

The large vein running down the leaf's center is called the midrib; the others are called lateral or secondary veins. In dicotyledonous leaves the two main patterns of veining are pinnate and palmate, each with its modifications. Pinnate venation reproduces the design of a feather; such leaves are usually narrowly oval like those of the elm. Palmate venation is characteristic of broad, spread-out leaves, like those of maple and sycamore; in each case the vein-pattern obviously follows the overall shape of the leaf. In addition to the midrib and the lateral veins there exist, in both types, a large number of criss-crossing smaller veins running in all directions between the large veins; hence, the dicotyledon-

*In Temperate Zone trees the blade is seldom more than a millimeter in thickness and usually less, but in some tropical species it may attain double or triple that thickness.

ous leaf is often referred to as having *netted venation.* In contrast, the monocotyledonous leaf, which is usually long, narrow, and sword-shaped like the leaves of lily and iris, has an entirely different pattern of venation characterized by a series of approximately parallel veins of uniform size running the length of the blade. Since there are few if any monocotyledonous trees, this type of leaf need not concern us here.

On the lower surface of the blade there are many thousands (10,000 to 20,000 per square centimeter) of tiny openings called *stomata,* each surrounded by two special *guard cells* that partially or completely close together at night and open during the day to allow gases from the atmosphere to enter and gases from the interior to escape. They also allow water to evaporate and by so doing make possible the entrance of more at the bottom of the hydrostatic system. On a hot day when the sun is beaming down and all the stomata are open, a tree transpires great quantities of water, drawing it in through the roots and evaporating it through the leaves—a living fountain driven by the sun.

It is through the stomata that many kinds of fungi gain entrance to the leaf's interior, deforming or killing it by absorbing its substance. Once inside the leaf, certain kinds of disease-producing organisms have the power to travel through the veins into the twigs and hence into all other parts of the tree. Working as they do from the inside, these vascular diseases are the most difficult of all to control. Although it is often impossible to eradicate them once they are established, they may sometimes be prevented by periodic spraying (see Chapter 7, SPRAYING), the purpose of which is to coat leaves with a protective layer of copper or some other substance through which the pathogenic fungi cannot pass.

In structure, leaves are simple or compound. A simple leaf is one undivided blade with or without petiole. Although its margin may be smooth, saw-toothed, or deeply lobed, the blade must be a single, continuous outgrowth at the end of its petiole or, if no petiole is present, seated directly on the parent twig; examples are leaves of oak, elm, maple, sycamore, fig, mulberry. A compound leaf is a series of discrete blades (leaflets), all growing directly or indirectly from a common petiole and hence forming one unit; when such leaves are shed, petiole and leaflets fall together. Leaves may be compound palmately, like those of the horse-chestnut wherein several leaflets spring radially from a common center, or compound pinnately like those of the locust or the tree-of-heaven, wherein from a central stalk (like the quill of a feather) paired leaflets grow out laterally. The compound leaf is usually larger than the simple leaf, although not necessarily so. The leaf of the banana is simple, while the leaf of the sweet acacia or huisache *(Acacia farnesiana)*, is compound, but the total leaf area of an average huisache tree, each leaflet of which is barely 1/8″ long, would not equal the area of a single ten-foot banana leaf.

Temperate-Zone leaves are usually medium-sized, like those of elms and oaks, ranging roughly from 1-1/2″ to 4″ in width and 3″ to 6″ in length, whereas tropical leaves tend to be either very small or very large. The leaflets of mesquite, huisache, and retama, small as they are in Texas, get progressively smaller as one goes south into drier, hotter Mexico. On the other hand, such plants as papayas, bananas, palms, and elephant-ears produce their immense leaves also under tropical skies.

In shape, leaves are so diverse that botanists have drawn on the resources of a dozen languages in an effort to describe them. They may be round, oblong, lance-shaped, sword-shaped, spindle-shaped, cross-shaped, egg-shaped, fan-shaped, and every other shape. No figure is too extravagant or too fantastic to be reproduced in a leaf form. Yet among all the many thousands of different kinds of trees no two have like leaves; although there may exist strong similarities, there are no duplications. Indeed, among the uncounted billions and trillions of leaves that exist or have existed or will exist there are no two identical, not even among those of the same kind, not even those of the same tree. We could not positively identify any given tree by its leaf-prints, nor even any given branch, for unlike a man who wears an unchanging set of finger-prints throughout his life, the tree discards its leaves (and with them its prints) annually and forms new ones that although almost identical are never quite so. Plant detectives, if any such existed, would be hard put to make their testimony stand up in court.

In color, leaves are of course predominantly green, although on many ornamental plants they show streaks of yellow, white, pink, and red. The foliage on young trees is frequently all red, as is the new growth on many old trees. New leaves on the mango-tree, for example, are always red, becoming green only several weeks after they have attained full size. The petiole and even midrib (sometimes also the lateral veins) on many well-known trees are reddish. The beautiful madrone is more red than green. Leaves of young eucalyptus trees and new shoots on older ones are definitely bluish; mature leaves are bluish-green. Leaves of many species are whitish underneath; the silver-leafed poplar is named for this peculiarity. Leaves of the shrub Texas silverleaf *(Leucophyllum texanum)* are gray on both surfaces.

Leaves on many coniferous trees, such as juniper and cypress, are formed on a different pattern: tiny scales wrapped closely around an axis, arranged overlappingly like shingles on a roof. Because of this arrangement and their small size, the leaves are not visible individually unless examined very closely; on a large tree their numbers are enormous. Other conifers, such as the pines, have leaves in the form of ''needles''—long, thin, flat, tough structures, built to resist desiccation by cold, heat, and wind and injury by snow. Different kinds of pines have different numbers of needles to a bundle, each bundle being enclosed by a slender sheath for a little distance along its base; some pines have two needles to a bundle, some three, some five. The structure of the conifer leaf is interesting in the extreme, being found on the oldest, the largest, and the most widely distributed trees on earth (cypress, redwood, fir, pine, spruce, juniper, cedar, etc.)

Some kinds of trees are evergreen, never seeming to lose their leaves.* The evergreen impression is accomplished by the more or less constant appearance of new leaves so that with the death of old ones the tree is at no time bare. Not all conifers are evergreen nor are all broad-leaved trees deciduous, although such is generally the case. Larches and bald cypress are as deciduous as elm or maple, while a number of oaks such as the southern live oak and the California live oak, are evergreen, retaining their thick, leathery leaves throughout the winter and shedding them only in March, at the time when the year's new leaves are already forming.

When leaves begin to turn color and fall off in the autumn, they do not do so of their own accord, there being no mechanism built into the leaf leading it to self-destruction. What happens is that the stem tissues form an abscission layer at the juncture of petiole with twig, a layer of impermeable tissue that functions like the closing of a valve so that no more movement of materials into or out of the leaf is possible, and it dies. Why do the stems form this layer? Because only in this way can the tree defend itself at a time when growing conditions are unfavorable: when the ground is frozen and no more water can be drawn up through the roots; also, at the other extreme and for the same reason, during prolonged droughts. Sensing in some way the water deficiency that develops under these conditions, the tree acts at once to reduce further evaporation; it sheds its leaves. So we amputate a limb to save a life; so a lizard sheds its tail to escape a pursuer.

If the tree did not observe this spartan discipline, if it retained its leaves, all busily evaporating water at a time when no more was being taken in by the roots, stem and root tissues would gradually be sucked dry of all their moisture reserves, and the whole tree would die. Thus the tree in its instinctive wisdom, or, if you prefer, by simple automatism, does what so many of us prove unable to do: it refuses to expend more than it can take in, and at the first sign of an overdraft it acts promptly, drastically, and mercilessly.*

On Temperate Zone trees leaves almost always appear at or near twig tips, these being the regions that contain the most embryonic tissue. On some tropical trees, however, such as the mango, leaves may grow directly from large branches or from the trunk itself without the intermediation of twig; the first sight of this growth habit is always startling. On most broad-leaved, Temperate Zone trees leaves form only during the springtime,** no more new leaves appearing during the season in normal circumstances. (However, if defoliated by insects or by mechanical means, a tree may produce new leaves from adventitous buds. Three times the tree may be defoliated during the course of a summer and each time respond with new foliage, drawing on its reserves, but with the fourth defoliation it dies.)*** In contrast to this pattern, many tropical trees, such as the yellow mombin *(Spondias),* and our better known mulberries and eucalypti produce new leaves continuously throughout spring and summer from the continuously growing stem tips. Defoliation of such a tree could hardly occur, since, hydra-like, it forms new parts as rapidly as the old ones are destroyed.

Many leaves have bristles at their tips and along their margins, usually at the termination of the veins. In some species, such as prickly ash, prickles occur on the leaf petiole and even along the midrib; in other species they may also be scattered along the blade. The lower surface of many leaves is covered with *tomentum*; a dense mass of very fine hair-like processes which must constitute a veritable jungle for the tiny insect that attempts to make its way through them. In most cases the tomentum is soft and woolly and may be rolled up in little balls between the fingers. In some cases, however, the leaf surfaces are roughened rather than softened; the leaf of the anaqua *(Ehretia anacua)* is so rough it will draw blood when rubbed sharply across the face or the back of the hand.

*Somehow the forming of the abscission layer has become incorporated into the genetic mechanism so that the tree need not wait for the actual onset of cold weather but may anticipate it by weeks or even months; probably it is the changing day-night ratio that triggers abscission. But for trees that shed their leaves during prolonged droughts (which occur irregularly) the day-night ratio would be of no help, and the response must be a direct one. Trees that retain their leaves for more than one year (see Footnote—leaf longevity) shed them for a different reason, probably because of a loss of photosynthetic efficiency.

**Actually, leaves are formed (in miniature) during the preceding spring and summer and wrapped up snugly within the protective leaf buds. They remain on the tree in this condition through fall and winter, dormant like a chrysalis in its cocoon; in the spring they swell, burst open the bud scales, and within a few days develop into full-sized leaves. At the same time *next season's* leaves and twigs are forming in miniature in their axils; and so the cycle goes on.

***Unless exceptionally well supplied with reserves. Some tropical species have unbelievable stores hidden away within their stem and root tissues and may continue to sprout even after five or six successive defoliations. In contrast, spruces, and other evergreen conifers are killed by a single defoliation.

*The longevity of some leaves is surprising. The following list is from Molisch (Fulling) in *The Longevity of Plants*:

Pinus pinsapo	11-15 years
Taxus baccata	8-10 years
Abies nordmanniana	3-5 years
Araucaria bidwilli	15 years
Laurus nobilis	4 years
Pittosporum tobira	3-5 years
Ilex aquifolium	2-4 years
Aucuba japonica	2-3 years
Osmanthus aquifolium	5 years

Certain leaves possess gland-like structures of unknown function. The leaf of the tree-of-heaven (Ailanthus) has two gland-like, circular swellings at its base. That of the eucalyptus has a curious circumferential vein that communicates with all its lateral veins. Some pinnately compound leaves sprout wings from their exposed midrib *(rachis)*.

Perhaps the most curious structures of all are the *pulvini*—enlargements at the base of the petiole by which movement is effected when a leaf is burnt, pinched, or sometimes only touched. The pulvini are small chambers or reservoirs which may be quickly emptied in response to stimuli: the resulting decrease in turgidity causes the leaf to droop, folding downward like a board on a hinge. Some doubly compound leaves have pulvini at the base of each leaflet and at the base of each pinna as well as the base of the primary petiole itself. When such a leaf is pinched, the leaflets (pinnules) fold together, the pinnae hang downward, and the whole leaf droops from the twig. If the stimulus is very slight, the reaction will affect only a part of the leaf; as the stimulus becomes progressively stronger the reaction becomes proportionally greater. Pulvini-equipped plants are fascinating to watch: the movement takes place with surprising quickness; you feel as if you were watching an animal. A number of tropical trees and smaller plants are endowed with those odd structures. Perhaps the best-known example is the sensitive plant (*Mimosa pudica*), immortalized in Shelley's poem of the same name; this occurs as a perennial in warmer parts of the globe, and is cultivated as an annual in colder climes.

The legend of man-eating trees and vines in the jungles of Brazil or Borneo or somewhere along the Congo that have the power of seizing animals and men in their movable "tentacles" is legend only. Quite another thing, however, is the fact that certain trees (and other plants) can produce skin lesions, blindness, and even death by caustic substances found in their tissues, usually in their leaves. Common examples are poison ivy, poison oak, and poison sumac. Many tropical trees contain juices much more virulent than these.

Organs of Reproduction

The reproductive parts of a tree are its flowers, fruits, and seeds. All trees except conifers (Gymnosperms) produce flowers, although these are often so small and so inconspicuously colored as to escape notice. Some trees, however, for a variety of reasons, do not produce fruits. Where fruit is present, it usually, but not always, contains seeds; sometimes the seeds abort. Here we have a true paradox: the tissues that enclose seeds, either partially or totally, are fruits by definition, yet while seeds cannot come into existence without an enveloping fruit, fruits can grow perfectly well even though they contain no seeds, Can a container exist without the presence of a contained object?

Physically it can, of course, but we know it to be a container only because we have seen it function as such in some other situation. Containment is a functional concept which we can transfer from the filled container to the empty one by virtue of our ability to manipulate symbols; we know that seedless grapes are fruits because we have eaten other grapes with seeds inside them. A more practical definition might read something like this: "Fruit: a more or less juicy and more or less tasty swollen bit of tissue found along plant stems closely following the appearance of the flowers." A gourmet definition would be stronger: "Fruit: a heaven-sent boon to the jaded palate; celestial ambrosia; drink in the desert; a foretaste of immortality; God's way of communicating to men the glad tidings that, although driven out of Paradise, not all is lost."

For the botanist the fruit is "The mature ovary, together with its adnate structures, containing developed or aborted seeds." This definition, which is both sharper and broader, is necessary for the inclusion of the thousands and thousands of non-edible fruits which greatly exceed in number the comparatively few edible ones. The apples, pears, and oranges are rare by the side of the vast numbers of elms, ashes, oaks, eucalypti, and others whose fruits are not the fruits of commerce.

Some kinds of trees reproduce themselves vegetatively, that is, without the formation of seed. Some kinds habitually reproduce in this way; others do so optionally; others only under extraordinary circumstances; others are unable to do so. A tree may reproduce vegetatively by:

1. Sending up shoots from the roots,
2. Growing a new individual from cut-off or broken-off twigs,
3. Growing a new individual from cut-off or broken-off branches,
4. Being grafted onto another stock;
5. By air-layering.

Examples of the first method are the southern live oak, the silver-leafed poplar, the jujube, and the hackberry, all of which sucker prolifically. Examples of the second and third methods are the willows, the gumbo-limbo *(Bursera simaruba),* and the wild plum *(Spondias lutea),* which, even though set into the ground as posts or sawed into firewood, grow new trees from each piece. (One of the reasons rivers are almost invariably lined with willows is that broken-off twigs and branches are carried downstream, lodge on sandbars, and grow into new trees.) Examples of the fourth kind are the grafts made on pecans, walnuts, apples, and other valued fruit trees. (Grafts are possible only among species genetically closely related: pecans may be grafted on hickories and apples on pears, but oaks may not be grafted on elms nor sycamores on pines.)

Vegetative reproduction is exact re-production, whereas sexual "reproduction" is not re-production at all but rather a constant experimenting with new forms. The vegetatively

A giant Arborvitae tree.

inflorescences of the elms to the showy, large-petaled flowers of the magnolia and the brilliant, dramatic color display of the Royal poinciana *(Delonix regia)*. Flowers are different size, in color, in structure, and in number of parts. Sepals and petals, although usually the most conspicuous parts, are not the essential parts; they may range in number from one to six or in cultivated varieties to many more, or they may be absent altogether. The essential elements are the stamens and the carpels; of the former some flowers possess fifty or more while others may have only two, three, four, or five. The pistil (organ formed by the union of carpels) is an enormously complex and variable structure and in itself the object of a life time of study.

The essential processes in the formation of seed are pollination and fertilization. Pollination is the transfer of pollen grains from stamen to pistil, and fertilization is the union of genetic material carried in the pollen grain with the genetic material residing in the ovule. If either of these processes is incomplete, no viable seed can be formed. Pollination is sometimes interfered with by heavy rains, snow, high winds, or other adverse weather conditions; it

Natural graft formed at a point about eight feet above the ground. Two originally separate trunks crossed each other or touched in some way and finally grafted together. (Live Oak, *Quercus virginiana)*

reproduced tree is genetically identical with its "parent"— is, in fact, merely a transplanted sections of its "parent"—or, more properly, of itself. Phrased another way, any tree may be extended indefinitely through space and time by subdivision of its parts, provided, of course, that these can be made to sprout. Such cloning, as this process is called, is invaluable when applied to an unusually desirable specimen; when we find the right tree, we can mass-produce it to our heart's content. (Biologists are already discussing the possibility of extending the cloning technique to animal and even human material; at some future date we may mass-produce our Einsteins and Darwins as we now do our avocados and prize roses.)

By contrast, in the genetic reshuffling that characterizes sexual "reproduction" there is no guarantee that the offspring, whether plant or animal, will resemble the parents: it may be similar or dissimilar, superior or inferior; it will never be identical.

As observed above, all trees (except conifers) produce flowers, varying in size from the inconspicuous, colorless may be prevented by certain kinds of sprays. Some plants produce pollen before the pistils are mature, and contrariwise some pistils mature before the pollen grains are ripe. Sometimes, in insect-pollinated trees, the needed insect fails to appear at the proper time. In all such cases, pollination and consequently fertilization cannot take place, and no seed is formed, even though stamens and pistils may be structurally and physiologically flawless.

A flower is said to be perfect when it contains both stamens and carpels. (A single carpel produces a simple pistil; several carpels united produce a compound pistil.) It is imperfect when it contains only stamens or only pistil. Flowers containing stamens only are said to be staminate or male, since the production of pollen is considered analogous to the production of spermatozoa in the animal body. Flowers that contain a pistil but no stamens are said to be pistillate or female, since it is in the ovary of the pistil that the embryo develops, as it is in the body of the female that the animal embryo develops. With few exceptions, perfect flowers may be either cross-pollinated or self-pollinated; while their organization seems to favor cross-pollination, they may fall back on self-pollination if the former is not forthcoming. Imperfect flowers are useless by themselves: if both staminate and pistillate flowers are too far apart or if they are not synchronized physiologically, pollination and resultant fertilization cannot occur.

On some kinds of trees all flowers are perfect. On other kinds—and these are in the majority—flowers are imperfect. The situation is complicated by the fact that the arrangement of the parts of imperfect flowers varies from species to species. Sometimes male and female flowers occur irregularly distributed on the same tree, sometimes on the same branch, sometimes in the same cluster. In some cases male flowers occur exclusively on one tree and female flowers exclusively on another; when this occurs, the species is said to be *dioecious* (which is the Greek way of saying that husband and wife live in separate houses). Where both male and female flowers occur on the same tree, the species is called *monoecious* (Greek for "living in the same house.") Willows, poplars, mulberries, Osage orange are dioecious. A tree of this kind must be either male or female; it cannot be both at the same time. Oaks, elms, and hackberries are monoecious. They can pollinate and fertilize themselves, so that one oak tree, for example, may produce acorns year after year even though all other oak trees in the world are destroyed.

The Bunya-Bunya *(Araucaria bidwillii)* makes an outstanding specimen tree in a park or large yard where it has plenty of room. Sixty years old, this specimen already overtops the large Sycamores and Maples around it.

For sculptured form few trees can equal the Coral tree *(Erythrina coralloides)*. Everything about this tree is unusual: the shape, the bank, the leaves, the flowers, and the regenerative vitality inherent in every broken-off branch.

Knowledge of a tree's sex has important practical applications. While monoecious trees and trees with perfect flowers present no problems, dioecious trees must be kept separate or planted together according to the goal sought. Where fruit is not desired because of messiness, bad odor, or non-edibility, the female should not be planted or should be planted only where there is no possibility of its being pollinated; the female ginkgo is an example of a disappointment that could have been avoided had the planter determined the sex in advance. Where fruit *is* desired, at least one male tree should always be interplanted with a group of female trees. As in animal husbandry one bull can serve a herd of cows, so one staminate tree will pollinate a large number of pistillate ones. Similarly, as animal breeders select the most vigorous bulls and cows for the production of a more vigorous race, so plant-breeders select the best trees for cross-pollination. Ancient pictographs represent the Egyptians of 3000 years ago hand-pollinating their date palms.

While the females of ginkgo, Osage orange, and mulberry are usually avoided, some dioecious trees are considered objectionable in both male and female form: the cottonwood, for example, whose staminate flowers form in long, sticky catkins that litter the streets and sidewalks and whose pistillate flowers produce the cottony tufts that float through the air for days.

Monoecious trees that are ordinarily self-pollinating may be cross-pollinated artificially by early removal of the stamens and subsequent transfer of pollen from another tree.

After pollination and fertilization have taken place, the part of the plant that becomes the edible portion is sometimes the seed itself, as in the various kinds of nuts; sometimes the enlarged and ripened ovary, as in the banana; sometimes the enlarged receptacle (end of the flower stem or pedicel to which are attached the floral parts), as in the apple. When we eat a pecan, we eat the seed proper and discard everything else. When we eat a banana, we eat the ovary and throw away the receptacle—in this case the skin. (The aborted seeds are visible as tiny black specks embedded in the fleshy ovary.) When we eat an apple, we eat the receptacle and throw away the ovary (the hard core with its seeds).

Trees are divided into two great groups, the Gymnosperms and the Angiosperms, according to their manner of producing seeds. The Gymnosperms ("naked seeds") are so called because their seeds lie exposed to view inside the structure bearing them. All the conifers—the pines, firs, spruces, cedars, cypresses, redwoods, and others—are Gymnosperms; in the pine, for example, the seeds are plainly visible at the base of each scale of the cone.

The Angiosperms ("covered seeds") receive their name from the fact that their seeds are entirely concealed within the enveloping fruit.* In the apple, the pear, the orange, the plum, the cherry, and virtually all our familiar fruits the seeds are concealed and well protected in the center. In popular terminology it is preferable to reserve the term "fruit" for the Angiosperms since its definition can hardly be broadened to include the cones or other seed-bearing structures of the Gymnosperms, although technically these too are fruits. All our familiar shade and ornamental broad-leaved trees are Angiosperms.

Tree fruits exhibit as much diversity in size, shape, and structure as do the leaves themselves. The difference between the pine cone and the apple are not more striking than the difference between a locust pod and a cherry, or between the winged samara of the maple and the dancing ball of the sycamore. Botanists have given special names to the many diverse kinds. The first and most obvious distinction among them is whether they are fleshy or dry; the second is whether they split open at maturity or remain intact. (Those that split open are called *dehiscent;* those that do not are *indehiscent).*

Fruits like those of the locust and mesquite and most others of the great Legume Family (including beans and peas) are *pods* and at maturity split open along two sutures. (The peanut, although a legume, is an exception: it does not dehisce.) Fruits like those of the milkweed are called *follicles,* dehiscing along one suture only. Fruits such as those of the lily that open along as many lines as there are carpels are called *capsules.* Fruits like the cherry, peach, and plum (stone fruits) are *drupes.* Dry winged fruits like those of ash, maple, and elm are *samaras.* Hard, dry, indehiscent fruits without wings are *achenes.* Fleshy fruits with the seeds distributed in a hard core, like apple, pear, and quince, are *pomes.* Structures like the strawberry, raspberry, and magnolia (developed from the partly fused ovaries of several flowers) are *multiple* or *collective fruits.*

Fruits serve not only as protective containers for the seeds within but also as distributing and propagating agencies. Since it is to the tree's advantage to send its offspring as far away from itself as possible so that they will not compete with it or with each other for *Lebensraum,* many ingenious mechanisms have been evolved for the furtherance of that end. Certain of the dehiscent pods open violently with a twisting motion that propels the seeds 20, 30, or 40 feet in all directions. The double samaras of the maple and the box elder are provided with wings that carry them away from the parent tree, even without wind, as they glide or twirl downward; so the single-winged samara of the ash.

---

*Anomalies exist, however. The cashew *(Anacardium occidentale)* bears its nut *outside* its fruit, pendent from its distal end. The Japanese Varnish-tree *(Firmiana simplex)* bears a dry pod which splits open along one suture to expose its pea-like seeds. The magnolia, the famous borderline case in more ways than one, bears its bright-red seeds, exposed, in a pine-like cone. In the strict meaning of the word these are Gymnosperms but for other reasons they are considered Angiosperms. All anomalous and intermediate forms are healthy reminders, forcing us to recognize, however reluctantly, that our classificatory schemes are at best arbitrary and artificial and that nature knows them not.

Ribbed and contorted trunk of Olive. As they age, Olive trees develop this characteristic pattern; the very old trees on the Spanish island of Mallorca show perhaps the most fantastically twisted and gnarled shapes of any trees.

On the fruit-balls of the sycamore each seed is outfitted with a tiny parachute that takes it far away with the aid of the slightest breeze. The coconut, with its thick, buoyant, air-filled husk on which salt water has no effect, is adapted for floating, sometimes circumnavigating the globe. Many fruits are furnished with hook-like appendages that stick to any passing animal; thus they hitchhike their way across the nation. Others, particularly small drupes, like those of

anaqua, hackberry, and mistletoe, are attractive to birds, which while eating them unavoidably carry away the seeds, either within their body or stuck to their feet or feathers.

Many fruits are eaten by animals; the seeds of these, having a hard coat that resists digestion, pass through the animal's alimentary canal unharmed and are deposited with the droppings, thereby being not only transported but fertilized. Birds transport many seeds in this way, from island to island, continent to continent. Some seeds have become so exquisitely adapted to alimentary canal dissemination that they will not germinate when deprived of their passage through that chemical processing plant. Moreover, some have become animal-specific, responding only to certain combinations of time, temperature, and ferments: the seed that will respond to a cow's interior may remain unaffected by a horse's, and the seed ingested and expelled by the Baltimore oriole may find during that short journey exactly the stimulus it needs and which no other bird could supply. Nor are birds and mammals the only distributors: ants, beetles, snails, bats, and even fish are known carriers of fruits and seeds. From the fruits that we ourselves eat seeds are transported in two ways: (1) accidentally, as when we spit out a grape seed or persimmon seed, and (2) intentionally, as when we seek out the best seeds and plant them.

In sum, plants' mechanisms for dissemination, although passive for the most part, are so varied, so ingenious, and so effective as to assure, with a very wide margin of safety, that their offspring will find their way into every viable niche on this globe and, once we begin space travel, on every other habitable planet. From one point of view their very passivity is an advantage, for while animals must spend great quantities of energy in moving about from one place to another,* plants as adults stand quietly in one place and as seeds are wafted, floated, and carried and thus enabled to channel all their energies into growth.

*Not only in maintenance but in reproduction as well. Merely to find a mate requires movement and energy-expenditure; courtship demands energy and time; and the act of mating itself consumes enormous quantities of energy, so much so that some animals die after one mating. The sperm must swim their way to the ovum, which, once fertilized, although not moving itself, imposes an unremitting burden on the mother, forcing her to forage incessantly for food.

14

Questions and Answers

Q. Why are some trees said to be male and others female?
A. Sexual differentiation is observable among the lowliest of plant and animal organisms; even the humble paramecium conjugate. Hence it is not surprising to find that trees, too, exhibit the familiar bipartite pattern of male and female; it would be surprising to find that they did not.

In certain species, such as the willows and cottonwoods, staminate flowers are borne by some individuals, while pistillate flowers are borne by others. These trees, then, and others like them, may legitimately be called male and female, although when neither flower nor fruit is present, it is impossible to tell one form from the other, there being no secondary sexual characteristics. Doubtless it would make recognition easier if male trees grew taller and sturdier and female trees smaller, slighter, with slenderer and more graceful limbs—but such is simply not the case. Such a species in which the two kinds of flowers occur on separate plants is called *dioecious.* (A word of Greek origin meaning "two houses.") A dioecious species will not set fruit and seed unless a male and female tree are fairly close together, so that pollen may be carried from male to female by wind or insects.

In other groups of trees such as the oaks, separate male and female flowers are borne on the same tree but in different places. Such a tree is said to be *monoecious.* (Greek for "one house.") Even when standing alone it is capable of setting fruit and seed.

Other species, especially those with showy blooms, may have both male and female parts combined in each individual flower. These are known as *perfect flowers.* A still different situation exists in the maples, in which there may be separate staminate and pistillate flowers as well as perfect ones all on the same tree. Then there is the avocado flower which may be male in the morning and female in the afternoon, or vice versa. And when we come to something like the papaya, still stranger things begin to happen. In addition to the familiar division into male and female flowers, with the latter producing the large luscious fruit, familiar to all Hawaiian visitors, we find male flowers that, at the end of a long, weak, and hollow stalk, obviously unsuited for the task, also bear fruits—smaller than the "authentic" ones but fruits nevertheless!

There is much more to the story of plant sexuality—so much more that whole encyclopedias can be written on this one topic alone. There are intermediate forms, intergrading forms, apomictic or skipped forms, hidden forms, and then, of course, there is the endlessly interesting subject of alternation of generations. Some day I will sit down and write a book with a title something like this: *Bizarre Sex Practices Among the East Indian Dipterocarps*—confident that it will become a best seller.

Q. Why do some trees have flowers while others have none?
A. All trees (except Gymnosperms) have flowers, for without flowers they cannot develop seeds, and without seeds they cannot reproduce. (Except for those versatile species able to reproduce vegetatively as well as sexually.) Although we are all familiar with the large, handsome flowers of the magnolia and the tulip tree, we are misled into believing that most trees do not flower because some species flower irregularly and others only in certain years (the extreme examples being the tree-like Oriental bamboos which flower only once every thirty years) and because the majority of our common shade trees bear very small, inconspicuous flowers that come and go before we are aware of them. Those of the American elm, for example, are seldom noticed, yet this tree (where unmolested by the Dutch Elm disease) unfailingly flowers and forms seed each year—often while snow is still on the ground, while it has not yet put out a single leaf and weeks before other trees awaken from their winter nap.

Tree flowers vary in size from the very large blossoms of the magnolia, measuring when fully open up to 10″ or more across, to the diminutive flowers of the fig, so tiny that they remain hidden *inside* the fleshy fruit (enlarged receptacle) and are never seen unless we cut open a green fruit and scrutinize its interior with a hand lens.

Anyone ever privileged to see a flame-tree *(Delonix regia)* with its incredible profusion of flamboyantly red, orchid-like blooms can never again doubt that trees can flower as magnificently as any plant of lesser stature.

A thorough coverage of Temperate-Zone tree flowers, with concise, lucid text and clear, striking photographs is *Tree Flowers of Forest, Park, and Street,* by Walter E. Rogers (Dover Publications).
Q. Do plants have emotions?
A. Many recent books allege that they do. Some of these have been highly successful, making handsome profits for

their authors. Similarly successful are books on flying saucers and treatises on astrology. In former generations it was sea serpents, the Cardiff Giant, and ectoplasmic materializations that stood the world on its ear.

Q. But what about the lie detector tests that prove that plants telepathically sense the approach of danger?

A. Such tests are extremely interesting and prove beyond the shadow of a doubt that lie detector testers have learned how to lie. Recent investigations by serious researchers at Cornell University (reported in the July-August, 1975, issue of *Science*) explode that substanceless and pernicious falsehood for all time.

Q. How many years can a seed lie around without being planted and still retain its capacity for germination?

A. A seed, like an egg, contains a living embryo and a large reservoir of food to nourish that embryo. Since it is a living thing, we expect it to breathe, albeit very slowly, and to undergo certain metabolic changes requisite for its development. It should, presumably, have an appointed time limit set for that development, and if such does not occur, we naturally expect the seed to die, its reserves used up or its enzymatic machinery in some way disrupted. Knowing that a shellacked or varnished egg will not hatch, its breathing pores being stopped up, we expect a similar response from the seed.

In general, this analogy holds good, with two significant differences: while some seeds are very short-lived, retaining their viability hardly longer than an egg, others are very long-lived—incredibly long-lived; moreover, their respiration, if it occurs at all is so slight as to be imperceptible. In fact, the coats of some seeds are so hard and so thick that they are impermeable to the passage of gases, whether in or out, so that varnishing or shellacking is a matter of the completest indifference.

Light, moist seeds with thin coats, such as those of elm, maple, willow, and poplar, live, under open air conditions, only a few weeks, sometimes only a few days. (Kept in sealed containers at low temperature their viability can be much extended.) Other seeds, such as those of certain pines, may survive 4 to 15 years or more, according to species and also depending on a number of variable factors, such as whether they have fallen to the ground or are retained within the cones. Seeds of legumes are generally extremely long-lived, possibly because of their extra-hard seed coats, those of *Cassia multijuga* having germinated after more than 150 years in storage. The all-time record, however, goes to the seeds of the water lily, *Nelumbo nucifera,* which germinated after having lain in a bog in Manchuria for more than 1000 years. (Age determined by radiocarbon dating.) The often-repeated stories about wheat seeds taken from Egyptian tombs after 2000 or 3000 years of interment and then obligingly germinating are believed to be fictional.

Anyway you look at it, the seed is an astonishing structure, a marvel of miniaturization, superficially simple yet stupendously complex. To polish a seed and mount it on a ring and then proudly to wear that ring could be taken as a mark of rusticity, the caprice of an eccentric, or the expression of an ever-deepening comprehension of things.

Q. If, then, the interior of a seed is enclosed in a coat so thick and so hard that it can resist the ravages of time for a hundred years or so, how does the embryo inside ever manage to emerge?

A. The question is an apt one, for although the thick, hard seed coat protects the embryo very efficiently against the slings and arrows of outraged fortune, it also imprisons it. The line between protection and restraint is not always easy to draw (as we repeatedly discover to our surprise in the social, political, and psychological realms as well as in the physical one); what seems to be a cozy and protective garment often turns out to be a strait-jacket. The embryo within the hard seed coat finds itself in the position of the genie in the bottle; however much it may want to get out, it must wait for some chance fisherman to pull the stopper. While the chick pecks its way out of the egg, and the baby alligator does the same by means of a tiny horn grown temporarily on the top of its snout for that purpose, how can the minuscule, tender, strengthless embryo, enclosed within a coat so hard that it cannot be cracked with a hammer, break through to freedom?

The various devices that nature has hit upon in the solution of this problem are sometimes direct, sometimes unbelievably roundabout, always ingenious. Some seeds will not germinate until eaten by animals, the digestive juices of stomach and intestines being the magic ingredients that soften and dissolve the seed coat; moreover, while for some democratically inclined seeds all alimentary canals are equally acceptable, others are highly selective: only one species of animal will do the trick. This must have a canal of specified length and specified chemical composition and the seed must be retained inside for a specified time; the journey through any other alimentary canal is simply an unfruitful detour.

Some seeds require an irreducible number of hours of weathering; they need the stinging lash of frost, the burning kiss of the sun, the revivfying touch of rain; hard as the coat is, it will soften and yield after prolonged exposure.

Some require the activity of micro-organisms acting on their coat to gradually break it down. Even the microscopic orchid seeds need the services of a fungus partner in order to germinate. (Not for the dissolving of the coat, which is fragile in the extreme, but for the supplying of absent nutrients.)

Some seeds require certain combinations of light, rainfall, and temperature, many as yet imperfectly understood—conditions which may occur only once in the space of many years.

Still other seeds will not liberate the imprisoned embryo until they are scarified or abraded mechanically. Horticulturists often perform this service with file and saw. How does nature manage it? In one very interesting case by the mechanism of flash floods! Certain desert seeds will not germinate until bumped and scraped along the rocky bottom and sides of stream beds. Only when the force of the water is sufficient to transport them the required distance and provide them with the requisite number of collisions will they germinate; by an exquisite coincidence this sudden spate of water moistens the soil sufficiently so that germination will not take place in vain; the seed sprouts when the conditions for survival of the seedling are most favorable.

Q. How is it possible for a seed to sprout—that is, to begin growing—when it has no root to draw water from the soil and no leaves to manufacture food?

A. This is a good question. Since nothing comes from nothing, how indeed does the unconnected seed put itself in motion and manage to send a shoot up and a root down? It is as if an electric motor began to rotate spontaneously, generating enough electricity to plug itself into a wall socket. It is easy enough to understand how the motor works *after* it is plugged in, but where does it get the energy to make that first connection?

Obviously, any such hypothetical motor would have to obtain its initial input of energy from built-in batteries. (There are now in existence experimental electro-mechanical robots equipped with sophisticated sensing devices which actually can locate wall sockets and plug themselves in.) And batteries, of course, are a form of stored energy, derived from some other source and placed in a state of potentiality for use at the owner's convenience.

Exactly the same mechanism is found in the seed. The "batteries" that make possible its germination are the cotyledons—one in the palms and yuccas, two in the broad-leaved trees, three or more in most conifers. These cotyledons—also called "seed-leaves"—make up the overwhelming bulk of most of our common seeds. The two halves of the peanut, for example, which fill the whole shell, are cotyledons, the embryo plant being a tiny knob-like thing barely visible at the cotyledon's base. The same is true of beans and related seeds. With the avocado seed, the cotyledons become truly enormous, and the embryo too is much larger and more easily examined, often sprouting while the seed is still within the fruit.

The cotyledons are vast storehouses of energy—capital accumulated in the bank, to change the metaphor—upon which the embryo plant can draw until it establishes itself in life. As the tiny plant begins to grow, sending its radicle downward and its diminutive stem upwards, it begins to use up those stored reserves. Little by little the cotyledons shrink, translocating into the growing plant their stores of water, fats, proteins, starches, sugars, minerals, and vitamins. Only after the plantlet has begun to manufacture its own food with its own minuscule leaflets and to imbibe its own moisture from the soil through its rapidly ramifying rootlets do the cotyledons cease to function. Often they are entirely used up, sometimes only partially so, but with the plantlet's independence, their role in the life cycle comes to an end, and their withered remains are soon sloughed off.

Some cotyledons, like those of the bean, are carried two inches or so into the air by the growing stem and function as leaves as well as food reservoirs. Others, like those of the avocado, remain at ground level. Still others, like those of the acorn (assuming the seed to have been planted underground), never emerge to the surface and consequently often go unperceived.

The reserves packed into the cotyledons are put there by the parent plant as part of the process of seed formation. The parent manufactures these highly concentrated materials, as it manufactures all the materials needed for its own growth, by the marvelous photosynthetic machinery contained in its leaves. And these machines are themselves essentially transforming stations converting the radiant energy of sunlight into the energy of the chemical bond. So that by a step-by-step process the energy that makes possible the germination of a seed is the energy emanating from the sun. The ancients were right: *nihil ex nihil,* and of all primitive religions the sun-worshippers came closest to the mark.

Q. How many seeds out of a tree's annual crop grow into new trees?

A. Of all the hundreds of thousands of seeds that your tree will produce this year the probabilities overwhelmingly indicate that very few will grow into an adult tree.

How can that be so? Is there something wrong with the seeds? Why should this year's crop be different from any other year's? And if so, what about next year's crop?

No, this year's crop is no different from any other year's, and the totally unbelievable fact is that few trees grew from last year's crop and a very few will grow from next year's crop. There is nothing wrong with the seeds. Each one is perfect. Each acorn, if it is an oak, each samara, if an ash, elm, or maple, is as exquisitely fashioned as those of any other year or any other tree; each is perfect and each contains all the potentialities needed to grow into a perfect tree. Why, then, do they not grow?

For a very simple reason: because there is no room for them. If this seems incredible, with a planet as big as ours and with so much empty space lying around waiting to be used, reflect a moment on the following facts:

First, the population explosion that is taking place now among our own ranks and that everybody is so concerned about already took place among the ranks of trees—myriads of years ago. (Where we produce one to fifteen children during our lifetime, a tree produces millions.)

Second, such being the case, trees very soon colonized all land propitious for their growth and have ever since maintained that maximum density figure. Although many are destroyed by the rising and lowering of the sea level, by the subsidence of the land, by the overflowing or drying up of lakes and rivers, by the advance of glaciers, and by other geological and geographical accidents, their progeny very rapidly regain all the lost territory, where possible, so that in a generation or two the environment again is exploited as its absolute maximum—tree-saturated.

Third, the deserts of the world, such as the Sahara, the Gobi, parts of our own Southwest, and large parts of India, although once covered with forests, will not now support any form of plant life except a few especially adapted species, and even these but sparsely. In those areas natural catastrophes were aided and abetted by unforesightful man, and if trees are ever to grow there again, man, in atonement, will have to intervene on a massive scale. As matters now stand, trees, unassisted, cannot recolonize those regions, regardless of how many seeds they may produce.

Fourth, in the Great Plains region of our Midwest and in the savannahs of Argentina and Brazil and in other comparable parts of the world trees do not grow for some strange reason that ecologists cannot agree on. Although many conditions seem favorable for them, somehow they do not take hold, and another great plant family—the grasses—claims these regions for its own. The plains, the savannahs, the pampas, are the world's grasslands, formerly the home of huge herds of buffalo, antelopes, deer, wild horses, now the great cattle ranges. By a kind of natural balance, the grasses and the trees divide the world between them, and the upsetting of that balance, even if it could be done, would be highly ill-advised.

Fifth, in most of the areas where we have established our sprawling urban complexes and in all their supplying hinterlands, trees could probably be made to grow again. The whole eastern part of our country, for example, from the Atlantic seaboard to the Missouri-Mississippi was virtually one solid block of forest which a squirrel, as it is said hyperbolically, could have traversed without once descending to the ground. Doubtless, much or all of this area could be replanted with forest, but since two objects cannot occupy the same place at the same time, what then would become of us?

Sixth, if all available land is already being used, what chance is there for new trees to grow? If there are 500 seats in a theater and all are occupied, how can we get more people in? Pack them in the aisles and let them stand through the performance? That was done long ago with trees—such is the meaning of the phrase *tree-saturated.* In the tropical rain-forest trees are crowded as close together as is physically possible, and as if that were not enough, trees (the epiphytic figs and others) grow on top of other trees, and all of them support thousands of forms of lesser plant life, both epiphytic and parasitic, while these, in turn, support other forms, still smaller. In short, every available

ecological niche is exploited. It is just as if in the theater not only were the seats taken and the aisles packed but people were standing on each other's shoulders, some were hanging from balconies, and others were twined together acrobatically to form human chains that criss-crossed the upper spaces in every direction, while perched on all these and hanging from them depended on protruded dwarfs, midgets, and many hundreds of alien forms.

Seventh, is it not obvious then that if every tree in the world produced in any given year two seeds that were destined to grow into adult trees, there would, within a generation, be three times as many trees in the world as there are now? Or if in any given generation, every tree in the world managed to produce just one more like itself, would there not be twice as many trees as there are now? And how could they possibly be fitted in, with all available land already maximally exploited?

Eighth, are we not led then to the mind-boggling conclusion that of all the seeds engendered by the giant Sequoia, living 3000 years or more and producing each year half a million seeds or so, each perfect, each capable of growing into a replica of its parent, yielding the stupendous total of a billion and a half seeds, give or take a million or so, perhaps not a single one will ever grow to maturity!

Ninth, it is obvious that *some* seeds must make it to adulthood, otherwise all species would die out, we see now that, on the average, *it is only one,* one single seed out of all those millions and billions, that can do so, and that seed is not necessarily superior in any respect to all its fellows that fell by the wayside but simply more fortunate: it just happens to be in the right place at the right time in the right stage of growth when its parent (or some other parent) dies, and it can therefore, occupy that momentarily vacated place.

Tenth, we seen then the race is not always to the swift nor the victory to the strong, and we are led to a kind of modified Darwinism. The existence of any tree anywhere (or of any animal or any person) implies, by pre-emption, the non-existence of billions, perhaps trillions, of others, all equally capable of occupying the same ecological niche. At their beginning all seeds have an equal chance for survival, albeit a very slim one: one in a hundred thousand or one in a million or a billion or whatever, depending on the longevity and fecundity of the parent tree. Whichever tree that makes it to adulthood is a living instance of the realization of astronomical odds. It is the drawing of a royal flush seven nights in succession when the pot is full; it is the red repeating itself twenty-nine times running in Monte Carlo. Its existence is totally incredible—and yet it occurs. And were any other tree to exist, instead of this particular one, exactly the same reasoning against the improbability of its appearance would also apply. So that in the grim struggle for existence it is not necessarily the fittest that survive: it is just as often, perhaps oftener, the luckiest.

Q. Why do bananas not have seeds?

A. Some bananas do. In the common supermarket banana the tiny black specks scattered through the center of the fruit are aborted seeds, seeds that failed to develop. But in many wild species of bananas and in the closely related plantain, those tiny specks grow to large, square or irregularly shaped seeds so hard that you have to break them with a hammer. The seedless variety sold in stores has been artificially selected and bred to enhance saleability, just as seedless grapes have.

(Incidentally, the banana is not a tree, although called by that name and growing almost tall enough to justify the appellation. It possesses no true wood and no true trunk. What seems to be the trunk is only a series of overlapping leaf bases, and when these are stripped off one by one, nothing is left.)

Q. Are woodpeckers harmful to trees?

A. Only the sapsucker. Most birds are, of course, beneficial to trees (and other plants) because of the large number of insects they eat. High on the list of beneficial birds are the woodpeckers, with their barbed extensible tongues especially designed for the capture of borers in their labyrinthine tunnels.

The sapsucker, however, is the black sheep of the woodpecker family. It makes a series of small holes along the bark of trunk and/or limbs in horizontal rows and comes back day after day to reopen them, consuming the sap and eating the insects that collect around the wounds. The numerous holes close together that are not permitted to heal over seriously interfere with the sap flow through the inner bark, weakening and in extreme cases killing the tree. The sapsucker is, moreover, a bird of catholic taste, attacking more than a hundred different tree species.

Q. Do squirrels harm trees?

A. Very little. Although squirrels live in tree cavities, they do not make the cavities but take possession of those that already exist. By constantly entering and leaving their homes, however, they prevent the mouth of the cavity from growing together. Also their scampering up and down trunks sometimes tears away bark, particularly on young trees or very smooth-barked ones. In the winter when food is scarce, they sometimes chew off twigs. Where nuts are available, they consume large quantities of these. On the other hand, by burying large numbers in different locations and neglecting to dig them up, they do the tree a favor by distributing and planting its seeds. On the whole, their damage is very small and is more then often offset by the interest and animation they lend to the tree in which they choose to live.

Q. If a tree is planted close to a house, will its roots crack the foundation?

A. The answer depends on the kind of tree and the kind of foundation. It is true that some tree species send out shallow and far-ranging roots that invade flower beds, penetrate sewer lines, heave sidewalks, and, in some cases, crack or even topple poorly built brick or stone structures. Since sidewalks are generally laid in sections and seldom exceed 7 or 8 inches in thickness, they are rather easily heaved by exploring roots; indeed, a strong man with a long iron bar can do as much. Similarly, any type of construction with pre-existing holes or cracks is an open invitation to those same wide-ranging roots. Remember that a root does not snake its way through the ground but *grows* its way along, a millimeter at a time. Each root begins as the slenderest of filaments, so slender that it may enter a tiny, almost invisible crack with the same ease with which we walk through our front door. Once inside the crack it begins to expand little by little, while its tip, always slender, continues to elongate. That inexorable expansion builds up enormous pressures, shattering rocks and concrete foundations with equal ease.

The proper protective measures are obvious: a well-built foundation made of firm concrete presenting no cracks along its face and adequately reinforced with iron rods. Where the roots cannot get a foothold, there is no danger of cracking; and as for heaving over the whole house, well, not even trees can do that.*

In the Temperate Zones, the worst offending roots for heaving and cracking are those of elms, hackberries, cottonwoods, and some species of ash. Worst for penetration of sewer lines are willows, cottonwoods, poplars, and elms.

Q. When is the best time to work on trees?

A. That depends in part on the work to be done, in part on the immediacy of the need. In general, *pruning* may be done at any time, although pruning wounds made early in the spring heal over most rapidly (by taking advantage of the subsequent growing season). Contrary to popular belief, most trees should be pruned when in full leaf, so that the pruner can better distinguish live from dead wood and can shape the tree artistically, seeing it in full dress. Profuse bleeders such as walnuts, birches, yellowwood, and hard maple, should be pruned *only* when in full leaf. (This is so because when sap is requisitioned by the leaves, less of it is available to bleed out of pruning wounds.)

The widespread idea that pruning should be done only in the dormant season is a carry-over from the days in which pruning was synonymous with dehorning. Such dehorning, or radical topping, should indeed be done only when the tree is dormant; but pruning, properly practiced, is a very different thing, and the removal of dead branches and the selective removal of a minor number of live ones may be done at any time.

Cavity repair may be done at any season and should be begun as soon as the cavity is discovered. However, since

---

*Not in one generation, that is. But given time enough and where the watchful eyes of the inhabitants are not around to detect their first encroachments, trees can overturn anything, not excepting the Empire State Building. Witness the ruins of Angkor Vat, where the prying roots of the gigantic tropical figs have heaved and toppled the huge stone building blocks weighing many tons.

growth occurs most rapidly in the spring, cavity fillings set in at that time will be most quickly sealed over at their edges by the healing callus. Concrete fillings should not be inserted during extremely cold weather because of the danger of freezing and cracking.

Cabling and *bracing* may also be done at any time and should be done as soon as the need is discovered. Cables installed when the tree is in full leaf may sometimes become slack when the leaves fall off, although slight slackness is not objectionable. Cabling is most often practiced in the spring to repair the damage done by ice storms; logically, of course, it would be better done before the storms.

Spraying is almost always done through the spring and summer as insects appear and plagues develop. However, some valuable preventive spraying can be done during the dormant season, in late winter or just before the buds break. *Removals* can, or course, be done at any time. But it should be taken into account that trees that have shed their leaves are smaller, easier to cut up, and easier to haul away.

Planting is usually done in fall or spring. In regions of severe cold it is best deferred until spring. In the South it may be done any time after the leaves fall; one month of the

Q. Does it make any difference whether a branch is cut off at one place or another?

A. It makes all the difference between good and bad pruning. A branch should be cut off at a joint, flush with the trunk if it stems from the trunk, or flush with the lines of whatever limb it does stem from. When not cut at a joint but four or five inches distant from it, as is common in amateurish endeavors, a stub is left and one of two undesirable consequences ensues: (1) if the tree is vigorous, the stub may produce a multitude of new shoots, forming a spot of dense and tangled growth out of harmony with the clean and open lines which characterize, or should characterize, the rest of the tree; (2) if the tree is not a vigorous sprouter, the stub will lie there and decay, the living tissues of the trunk or parent limb in most cases being unable to grow around it; such an unhealing stub provides an open door for the easy entrance of insects and disease organisms into the heart of the tree. Even if the stub is a very short one, some trees are curiously unable to grow around it; indeed, it may not be a complete stub but only a lip caused by attempted flush-cutting with imperfect alignment of the saw, and it may still prevent healing.** Thus flush-cutting becomes the single most important measure for the prevention of decay.

Twig tips, on the other hand, may be clipped off indifferently at any point along their length. (Ideally, they should be cut to a bud, but on a tall tree this is impractical.) Since they contain much embryonic tissue, they can regenerate from any point.

**Some trees, such as the California Valley Oak, have extraordinary powers of healing and manage to form new bark surfaces over stubs up to 10 or 12 inches long. Such exceptional trees present a very curious appearance, their healed-over stubs sticking out like amputated human limbs.

winter is as good as another. In California, planting is a year-around activity, although peaking in the spring. Moist, cloudy days are best for transplanting.

In the colder parts of the country, spring planting should be undertaken before the buds begin to swell, since the roots will have become active several weeks earlier. Bare-rooted trees are better not moved after leafing out, although careful digging and stripping of the leaves sometimes makes the move possible. Since evergreens are always moved with a ball of earth and often are sprayed with a wax solution to retard evapotranspiration, one time is about as good as another. Theoretically, any tree, evergreen or deciduous, can be moved at any time if a large enough ball of soil is moved with it. In practice, however, the cost of moving a ball of earth large enough to accommodate a deciduous tree in full leaf makes it wiser to wait until the leaves have been shed. Possibly the worst time to move any tree is in the late summer, when the spring growth impulse has been exhausted and before dormancy has set in.

Fertilizing is best done in early spring so that its effect may be felt immediately. It is less effective in midsummer and autumn and not effective at all, of course, in the winter, although not lost, since the materials remain in the soil ready to enter the roots in early spring. Heavy fertilizing right before the advent of freezing weather should be avoided because it forces new growth and keeps older tissues succulent at a time when they may be harmed by the cold. However, most authorities agree that a sick tree should be fed and watered whenever its sickness is discovered, regardless of the season.

Q. How can a stump be kept from resprouting?

A. Although salt and kerosene were formerly the two materials most commonly used against stumps, they are not as effective against stubborn species as some of the newer chemicals. Ammonium sulfamate continues to be the most popular for this purpose. It may be applied as a liquid, painted across the cut stump surface, or as crystals, poured into downward-slanting holes or into cuts made along exposed roots. The chemical gradually makes its way through all parts of the stump, causing its death. Some species, however, are very resistant and may require repeated treatments. Among the hardest to kill are beech, hickory, sweet gum, hackberry, and mesquite. 2,4-D and 2,4,5-T are also effective stump-killers; they are sometimes mixed with fuel oil and applied as a drench to the basal area from which new shoots might be expected to arise. Penetration is facilitated by first scraping off the outer bark.

Q. Can a tree be killed by driving a copper nail into it?

A. No. This is a popular fallacy. Copper in low concentrations or even pure copper in small quantities is not harmful to trees. If it were, it would not be so widely used as the chief ingredient in so many fungi-inhibiting compounds. Sprayed directly on the tree, it kills the molds and rusts but leaves the tree unharmed. Similarly, copper nails, although embedded firmly in tree roots, trunk, or branches, produce no observable ill effect. They are, in fact, in standard use for the installation of lightning rods.

Q. Will driving iron nails into its trunk help a fruit tree to bear?

A. In certain cases it may indeed do so. Everything depends on the kind of tree and whether or not is is suffering from a nutritional deficiency. The trace elements (so called because they are needed in very small quantities only) that sometimes hinder the full development of a plant are iron, zinc, copper, boron, sulfur, manganese, molybdenum, and aluminum. An apple, pear, or quince tree with a zinc deficiency sometimes shows a dramatic improvement when zinc nails are driven into its trunk, and with the improvement of its general health a non-bearing tree will often begin to bear.

Generally, however, if your tree is suffering from iron deficiency, you will correct the condition more effectively by boring downward-slanting holes, 2″ deep and 1/2″ or 3/4″ wide, at intervals around the trunk and inserting capsules of ferric phosphate, which will quickly dissolve in the sap stream. But perhaps iron deficiency is not the reason for the inability to bear. Try first punch-bar feeding in the soil, using a 5-10-5 mixture or some similar ratio and augmenting it with small amounts of iron sulfate.

Q. Can a fruit tree be made to bear by girdling its trunk?

A. Oddly enough, it can, although the practice is potentially dangerous. When a tree is girdled—that is, when a continuous horizontal band of inner bark is stripped away—it is stimulated to bear a heavy crop of fruit, often the heaviest in its history. The peasants of medieval Europe flogged their non-bearing trees, with gratifying results—the heavier the beating the more abundant the following season's crop. (In Russia, where bits of metal were often worked into the knout, the correlation was most striking.) Doubtless, using a psychological analogy, they believed the trees frightened into obedience. Our former explanation, although a bit more sophisticated, was no less anthropomorphic. We endowed the girdled tree with prescience: foreknowing its death, it reproduced as prolifically as possible, sending out into the world hundreds of thousands of fruits and seeds so that its name might not perish from the earth.*

The correct explanation is simplicity itself. As we have seen, food is manufactured in the leaves (sunlight driving the wheels) and sent down through the inner bark to nourish all parts of the plant body. When a continuous horizontal strip of that bark is removed, the needed food cannot pass the gap, no more than a convoy of trucks can pass over a destroyed bridge. The interrupted food supplies re-ascend

*This analogy is used by John Steinbeck in *Tortilla Flat,* in which he compares the sexual excesses of a man foreseeing his own death with the reproductive prodigality of a girdled tree.

the tree and gradually accumulate above the gap to such an extent that the upper parts of the tree find themselves with a food surplus and so form fruits and carry them to maturity. (The curious practice of flogging, while not totally girdling the trees, destroyed large areas of bark, interrupting or greatly reducing the phloem stream and eventuating in the same result. On larger trees with thicker outer bark the flogging would, of course, be totally useless.)

Girdling really works. Year after year the largest tree of my avocado grove, although flowering and producing thousands of tiny fruits, aborted all but the merest handful. Although I never got around to flogging it, I very seriously considered cutting it down, putting off that operation only because of the perennial hope that next year it would do better. Finally, as a last resort, I girdled it, just as it came into full flower. Sure enough, the fruits did not fall off but grew to full size for the first time in the tree's history. I took care, of course, that the girdle was a narrow one, not exceeding half an inch, and I watched the trunk carefully for signs of regeneration. Everything proceeded on schedule. New callus began to form almost immediately, and by the end of the season the severed portions had completely rejoined.

These, then, are the two precautions to observe if you decide to girdle a non-bearing fruit tree: first, make the girdle in the early spring, and second, keep it narrow enough so that the separated parts will be able to reunite.

If you wish to kill the tree, do the direct opposite and make the girdle as wide as possible. Sometimes broadly girdled trees are seen standing in a field for years on end, later to be cut down when thoroughly dry. You may wonder why, if somebody wished to kill a tree, he would go about it so deviously instead of cutting it down in a single operation. There's a method in the madness, however, because a girdled tree allowed to stand will die roots and all (in fact, the roots, unable to receive food from the leaves, die first, having in the meantime exhausted all their reserves by continuing to supply the top with the customary nutrients), whereas when a tree is cut off at or near ground level, the root system remains both physically intact and physiologically capable (in some species) of sending up new shoots in profusion.

Since there are exceptions to all rules, we find some trees that send up new shoots below the girdle, regardless of its width, and (provided these are not cut off), so save themselves. We also find others, such as most of the conifers (the redwoods being notable exceptions), that when cut off never sprout.

Q. Is it true that the underground parts of a tree repeat the pattern of the above-ground parts—a root for every branch and a tap root going down as far as the trunk goes up?

A. For both structural and physiological reasons it seems fitting that the tree should have half its bulk above ground and half below, and indeed certain species in certain environments very closely approximate this ideal, insofar as it has been possible to weigh and measure them. Excessive fondness for this idea, however, leads us straight to the theory of archetypes and ideal forms, and we run the danger of being tempted, Procrustes like, to force all trees into this formal and arbitrary pattern. Moreover, and most interestingly, there lingers in the notion that there is a root for every branch, a faint flavor of the medieval "doctrine of correspondences."

As a matter of fact, trees vary greatly in their above-ground/below-ground ratios, according to species and environment. The pecan has a very long tap-root, going down, down, down—nobody is really sure exactly how far. Other species have no vertical roots at all—nothing but a mass of far-extending side roots. The tallest of all, the redwood, is very shallowly rooted although sending lateral roots hundreds of feet in all directions—a giant poised on a disk. The mesquite, when growing in good soil and receiving abundant water, becomes a 30 or 35 foot tree with massive curving limbs and a reasonable proportion between crown and root system; but when growing in the desert it goes underground with a vengeance, descending 75 feet or so in its search for water and exposing to the searing heat above only a score or so of slender, thorny switches.

The palm with its massive, nearly untapered trunk 100 feet or more tall crowned by broad, heavy leaves mounted on long, strong stalks resists the fury of the fiercest winds without the help of a single vertical root, being anchored only by a multitude of pencil-like rootlets of uniform width running laterally in all directions.

That the roots and branches correspond point for point is certainly not true; however, since both tend to spread in all directions from a common starting point, they usually end up with a design roughly similar. Moreover, since the roots, unlike the branches, grow through a medium that supports them, they extend much farther than these, sometimes two, three, four times farther or even more. That the tap root goes down as far as the top goes up is true only in a few special cases.

Q. Must a transplanted tree be set in the same relation to the points of the compass as it grew before being moved?
A. No. If this were necessary, all trees and plants growing in nurseries would need to have their stems marked *north, south, east,* and *west* so that, when moved, they could be planted in exactly the same orientation. Thus a plant could not be turned with its most presentable face forward unless that side happened to face the same way as in the original location. Actually, of course, when setting out a tree you turn it this way and that until you line up the branch pattern to your satisfaction. Much more important than attempting to preserve the original orientation is to set the transplant at the same depth at which it formerly grew.

One concession. While all this applies to nursery-grown trees which are often moved from one field to another several times during their life and hence are habituated to no fixed orientation, trees taken directly from the woods may suffer a a certain amount of shock at any modification of their position. This may be especially evident in high latitudes where the difference between southern and northern exposure is extreme. Transplants which are turned so that their north side that had never felt the heat of the sun is now directly exposed to it may experience severe sunburn or bark and cambium. Other, less measurable damage, possible due to altered geomagnetic fields, may also exist.

Q. Does an evergreen tree keep the same leaves throughout its life?
A. No, like a deciduous tree, the evergreen sheds its old leaves and forms new ones, but unlike the deciduous tree it does not shed them all at the same time. New ones are formed before the old ones fall off, hence the evergreen impression. The process may be, with some species, more or less continuous, or it may occur in bursts, with production alternating with abscission, but the plant is never entirely bare. Some leaves, such as those on an evergreen oak, last only one year, falling off in March as the new ones come on with a rush. Others have surprising longevity, those of the yew *(Taxus baccata)* lasting 8 to 10 years and those of the bunya-bunya *(Araucaria bidwilli)* hanging on a full 15 years before giving up the ghost.

We could, if we like, compare the evergreen tree and its leaves with a city and its inhabitants. We know that at whatever time we enter a city, day or night, winter or summer, spring or fall, we will find people there. Although the older inhabitants are continually dying off, new ones are continually being born; the tree is never entirely bare.*

Q. When are the leaves of a deciduous (non-evergreen) tree formed?
A. Generally at least a year before they make their debut. The buds containing *this* year's leaves were formed in *last* year's spring. While you watch *this* year's leaves pushing out from the bud and unfolding, *next* year's leaves are already forming, in miniature, in the angle between the base of the tiny leaf stalk and the stem it is attached to. (The bud scales obscure the sight, but if you pull them away and apply a hand lens, you will be able to see for yourself.) These *avante-garde* leaves remain snugly curled up as axillary buds all through summer, fall, and winter, ready to come out next year when calendar and weather give the signal. Thus is the process repeated endlessly, the leaves being always ready a year beforehand.

It is this preformation that is responsible for the very rapid spring growth that perenially astonishes us. One day the ground is covered with snow, and the next day the whole landscape begins turning green. We drive down a broad street with the trees respectfully distant and the

*Extending the metaphor, we could call each city a twig, each state a branch, each nation a tree. According to our inclinations we could then make humanity a forest composed of separate trees belonging to distinct species, or we could make it one mighty tree with each nation a massive bough.

branches bare and come back a few days later to find the street transformed into a narrow lane, invaded by leafy shoots from both sides. Leaves may unfold and shoots grow 6 to 8 inches in a week or less. Without performation the tree would have to build its foliage from scratch each year and would lose precious time doing it, missing the growing opportunity provided by melting snow and early spring rains.

Q. If I drive a nail into a young tree at a certain distance above the ground, will it remain at the same level or will it be carried upward as the tree grows?

A. It is natural to believe, by analogy with animals, that a tree grows more or less equidistantly along its entire length, and that just as a baby's knee gets farther and farther from the ground as he grows into a man, so any given point on a tree trunk ought to get farther and farther from the ground as the tree grows taller. But analogies are often wrong, and in this case the error is not partial but total. Although some plants, like the reeds, do grow equidistantly along their stems, and others, like the grasses, grow basally, trees and woody shrubs can grow in length only by elongation of their non-woody twig tips. Woodiness is by its very nature a kind of prison: woody tissues, once laid down, never move again. Only the succulent tender tips, not yet lignified, are capable of elongation; and after their first burst of growth, they too become lignified and thenceforth forever immobile. From their embryonic tip comes the next flush of growth, and so on as long as the tree lives. To use another analogy, and a more nearly correct one, we may say that stem growth proceeds like the building of a smokestack: once the bricks are in place and the mortar becomes set, no brick ever moves again; the stack grows by continual superimposition of newer bricks on top of the older ones. Such being the case, a nail driven into the tree at any level and at any stage of its life will always remain at precisely that same level, regardless of how tall the tree becomes.

If this were *not* the case, if any driven-in nail or screwed-in hook were carried upward as the tree grew, we could not attach swings or clotheslines and could not nail boards to tree trunks with any assurance of their staying put; and we would have to keep on hand a pair of stilts—adjustable—to continue getting into our hammock year after year. We would, with Heraclitus, conclude mournfully that no man could sleep in the same hammock twice. Jungle dwellers, empirical to the core, often lay their roof's centerpiece from tree crotch to tree crotch. What if *that* were to be carried skyward as the tree impishly insisted on pushing up from the ground!

What we often overlook—and here the smokestack analogy breaks down—is that the trunk of the tree like all its other stems—boughs, branches, and twigs—although not growing in length grows continually in diameter. Each stem continues to thicken as long as it lives.* The twig thickens

*Most monocots excepted.

into a branchlet, the branchlet into a branch, the branch into a major bough, and all the time the trunk continues its steady expansion until, if it should happen to be a Sequoia, it becomes so massive that fifty couples could dance on its cut-over stump and have room to spare.

A nail driven into a tree will neither move upward nor outward; it will remain fixed in its original position as long as the tree stands. Such a nail would serve admirably as a reference point if it would be located by X-rays or in some other way, for, not moving itself, it would soon be engulfed by the outward-expanding trunk and would thus remain hidden within the constantly enlarging woody core. On the contrary, any mark made on the *bark*—the familiar heart with inscribed initials, for example—will both remain visible and move outward as the tree continues to grow, only gradually becoming distorted and indistinct, like a figure drawn on a toy balloon that is then inflated.

Q. At what age does a tree stop growing?

A. A tree never stops growing. Unlike most animals, ourselves included, that cease their growth at a certain age, which we call adulthood, trees continue to grow as long as they live. Since old trees, however, grow more slowly than young ones, many people mistakenly believe their growth pattern analogous to our own. This error can have serious practical consequences. Believing that large trees have ceased all growth, and, like us, are simply maintaining the status quo, people erect buildings so close beside them that wall and trunk may touch, or they build their house around a tree, putting the living trunk within the study or the kitchen or the bedroom, according to the caprice of the moment. Such arrangements are, of course, impractical in the extreme, eventuating in damage to both building and tree.

Some trees, such as the palms and the yuccas (endogens and by some criteria not true trees), after reaching a certain size grow only, or chiefly, at the tip, getting taller but not thicker. All our commonest species, however, such as oak, elm, ash, pine, hickory, cottonwood, eucalyptus, etc.(exogens), continue to get both taller and thicker every year of their life. The trunk and branches increase annually in girth, and the twigs grow annually in length.

Very old trees, like very old people, may recede from their maximum height values—but for very different reasons. Where we become stooped with age and our tissues shrink, old trees may decrease in height by the simple process of breakage. If the top of an old tree breaks off, the replacement shoots are unlikely to grow as tall. Unless the tree is totally dead, however, some shoots will grow from it, and these will increase in length with every passing year, and the trunk, broken, scarred, and decayed though it may be, will increase inexorably in girth by the annual laying down of new woody rings.

Q. Is there any way to tell the age of a tree other than by counting its rings?

A. Counting the rings of the trunk is the only accurate way.

Estimates based on size are only approximations, since growing conditions may change greatly during the life of a tree and since trees planted at the same time in different locations may grow at widely differing rates. Fortunately, however, it is no longer necessary to cut down a tree to examine its rings. You may use an increment borer, a hand-operated device which drills a small hole into the trunk and brings out a core section. The rings are clearly visible in this section, as is also of course the tree's inner condition: whether sound, rotten, checked, stained, etc. The hole (usually less than half an inch in diameter) is readily stopped up with asphalt, putty, or cement, and the tree remains unharmed.

The correlation one ring/one year is, however, limited to the Temperate Zone where the seasons follow one another in definite sequence. Rings are created by the juxtaposition of rapidly growing spring wood with more slowly growing summer wood, no growth at all taking place in autumn and winter. In the tropics where the spring-summer-fall-winter sequence does not occur, there is no fixed correlation between rings and years. Growth is dependent chiefly on rainfall, which may be highly irregular. Thus it is possible that in one calendar year three or more rings may be formed, while another year may produce only one ring, or possibly none. Even in subtropical Florida the lemon tree may show three rings per year.

Severe insect defoliations (in whichever Zone) may also affect the production of rings, resulting either in a very narrow ring or in none at all. Other environmental abnormalities show up clearly in the rings, making it possible to reconstruct the climate of past centuries with surprising accuracy.

Q. Why does a tree die?

A. This is a very interesting question and one on which there are conflicting opinions. Some authorities maintain that each species has its appointed span and that when its time has come, nothing can save it. How else explain the striking differences in longevity among such trees as the peach, living only 15-20 years, the apple living 50-75, the oaks living 100-400 according to species, the olive 500-600, some species of pine 700-900, the coast redwood 2000-3000, the interior redwood 3000-4000, and the bristle-cone pine 5000 years and over?

Other authorities allege that a tree (not specifying which kind) dies only because of neglect, accident, or disease, that it has no inborn mechanism limiting its days, that if properly cared for it could live indefinitely. Perhaps both viewpoints are partly right. It is undeniable, as we established in a preceding section, that intelligent care can prolong any tree's life, but precisely how long that prolongation can be made to last is the unsettled question. In our present state of knowledge it seems impossible that a peach tree could ever be made to equal or outlast a bristlecone pine. But with new discoveries continually being made, perhaps some day potential immortality for every tree may become a reality.

One of the reasons trees die is the mechanical difficulty of continuing to increase in size. Growth is a built-in feature of all exogens (meaning all our common trees except palms, yuccas, and similar monocots); they cannot stop growing so long as they live. Where *we* reach our maximum vertical growth sometime in our twenties and then stop (although often continuing to expand in girth for another twenty or thirty years), trees continue to grow both in height and in circumference. Imagine what would happen to adults if every year we grew a few inches taller. Giantism is by no means the advantage we sometimes fondly imagine it to be. Getting enough to eat would become even more of a problem than it already is, and just moving about would be burdensome in the extreme. There are indeed a few unfortunate individuals (acromegalics) who do keep on growing at their extremities, somewhat like a tree; most of them end up as circus freaks, and all of them die young.*

These are precisely the problems that face the continually growing tree. In order to get enough to eat and drink—mostly drink—its roots must range ever farther afield. And although it does not move about, it is confronted with a not unsimilar spatial problem: how to support an increasingly heavy mass from a single central axis. As its branches extend farther and farther, they reach a point when they can no longer stand the strain; they break off under their own weight, and this breakage, by admitting the agents of decay, usually marks the beginning of the end. The redwoods, the largest and also the longest-lived of trees (always excepting the bristlecone pine, squat and grotesque but not to be argued away), have partially solved that problem by limiting their branch growth to a scant 20 or 30 feet in any direction; and by building a single, massive, slightly tapering trunk of the lightest possible weight consistent with the demands for strength, they have almost solved the height problem. Four hundred years ago Galileo set 360 feet as the maximum height to which a tree could grow, proving mathematically that any tree exceeding that height would be not only compressed but bent by its own weight. Some of the coast redwoods have managed to exceed that figure by 10 or 20 feet, but that seems to be the absolute limit. And after reaching that limit, sooner or later they either break under their own weight or are broken by the wind or blasted by lightning.

The tropical figs have taken an alternative approach to the spatial problem. Rather than attempting to grow tall, they grow laterally, and they solve the problem of how to support their ever-lengthening branches by dropping down, at needed intervals, slender filaments that contact the ground, take root, thicken, and form posts. Such a tree has, theoretically, no limit set to its growth; it can cover acres, and many of them do.

*Robert Wadlow of Alton, Illinois, one of these unfortunates, was paraded about the country in the 1930's as a walking advertisement by one of the shoe manufacturers. At his death at around 28 or 29 he had reached approximately nine feet in height, and his shoe size was something on the order of two feet.

Men have intervened to solve the spatial problem by simply cutting the tree off every time it reaches a certain size and then allowing it to regenerate. This may be done either by cutting it at ground level and forcing it to build a whole new top, or by topping it at any arbitrary level. In Europe and in South America, pollarded willows and cottonwoods are common sights, their height always remaining the same while their trunks get thicker and thicker with every passing year. While no statistics are available, it seems undeniable that these trees live much longer than they normally would. Forced regeneration may be the most certain means to rejuvenation.

An interesting question that arises is this: if a tree is cut off at ground level and comes up anew, is it the same tree or is it a different one? It is different in that it occupies a different position in time and a different position in space, (for its shape, although similar, can never be identical, absolute identity of form under such conditions being an impossibility.) It is the same in the sense that it is constructed according to the genetic specifications contained in the original seed. This is true because a cut-off tree must be considered not killed but only pruned; a full half of it—the root system—is left untouched and under the right conditions will rebuild the destroyed top.* Every cell in the new top is thus genetically identical with every cell in the old top (excluding the possibility of somatic mutations). Thus by one criterion the regenerated top is a different tree, while by another criterion it is the same tree. Most arguments result from failure to define and agree on terms, and in this question of what constitutes an individual the semantic pitfalls are everywhere. The important thing, however, from the standpoint of the present discussion, is that it is a *rejuvenated* tree.

Similar rejuvenation is experienced in cloning—and a similar semantic difficulty. Cloning is the vegetative reproduction of a plant as distinguished from its sexual reproduction. That is to say, when by clipping off from any plant a twig or a piece of root or in some cases only a leaf or a bud, you stick these in the ground and a new plant grows up, you may expect it to be genetically identical with the original. Cloning is thus *re-production* in its purest form. "Sexual reproduction" is really a misnamed process: involving as it does a continual reshuffling of genetic material, it is not so much reproduction as a perpetual experimentation with new forms in which the identity of the parents is always altered, sometimes almost beyond recognition.

In the early days of avocado growing, every avocado tree in California was a first, second, or third generation offshoot from a single tree in Atlixco, Mexico (in the state of Puebla). Only the scions of this tree were found hardy enough to resist the California winters. All these trees collectively formed a clone—a pure line undiluted by any type of sexual cross. What happened to individuality here?

*Some species, however, never regenerate from roots.

Should each plant be considered a separate tree, or do all together make a single tree? This again admits of several interpretations while at the same time demanding the sharpest possible definition of terms. (For those interested in the philosophic implications of the problem, I recommend Schelling's *Essay on Individuation*.)

This much is certain: cloning, like radical pruning, results in rejuvenation. Although the original avocado tree is now long dead, its cloned offspring, all genetically identical, continue to flourish.*

Q. Does a tree feed itself by means of its roots?

A. This question, so seemingly simple, has more to it than meets the eye. One's first inclination is to answer "yes"; otherwise why do we speak of feeding a tree when we apply fertilizer to the soil? Primitive peoples hold it as dogma that the soil not only feeds the plant but actually engenders it; they speak of the "strength" of the soil and believe without question that every form of plant life, from the most diminutive herb to the tallest tree, is a direct outgrowth from it, as our hair is an outgrowth from our skin. (Actually, of course, plants do not grow out of the soil—they invade it.) In *Paradise Lost* Milton, following the Biblical version, depicts not only plants but animals emerging, fully formed, directly from the soil, as a butterfly struggles to free itself from the split cocoon. Joyce Kilmer added his bit to the confusion when in his oft-quoted "Trees" he speaks of the tree "whose hungry mouth is pressed to earth's sweet-flowing breast."

We know that everything that lives must eat, and we speak of all animals and plants as being connected in a vast and complex food chain (or food web, to be more precise), in which all exist by virtue of destroying each other. While partly true, this is not altogether the case, of course, and can never be the case, for we would then have a zero-sum game which very quickly would come to an end. Green plants are the vital exception. They are the primary producers without whose activities the supporting strand of the food web would be broken and the whole structure be destroyed. Every animal and every nongreen plant is thus, in the exact sense of the word, a parasite depending for its sustenance directly or indirectly on the green plant. (We too, of course, are included in that ethically uncomfortable category, although we prefer to call our means of feeding "heterotrophic" rather than using the blunter word "parasitic".)

Green plants have a unique talent: by means of the chlorophyll in their leaves and stems *they can convert the radiant energy of sunlight into the chemical bond*. This is their tremendous—and as of now—incommunicable secret. Utilizing the motive power of sunlight they effect a chemical combination between carbon dioxide and water—the

*Apparently this process cannot be continued indefinitely, however. Studies on Lombardy poplars show that long-continued clones show a decline in vigor. Comparable studies on animals asexually propagated also show that an occasional sexual cross is necessary to restore vigor to the stock.

first taken into the leaves directly from the air, the second absorbed from the soil by the roots and transported to the leaves. Combining these substances to form sugars and starches and then incorporating other substances drawn in by the roots to form complex proteins they thus construct the building blocks necessary for the erection of their own bodies, while at the same time—inadvertently, of course and not intentionally as we used so complacently to believe—providing the food necessary to sustain the whole mass of animal life with which the planet teems.

Which, then, are the tree's true mouths—the millions of tiny stomata (even the word *stoma* means *mouth* in Greek) opening on the leaf's surface or the roots that incessantly explore the soil for the absorption of water and dissolved minerals? This is somewhat like asking which is more important, men or women. Both are necessary, and the tree as we know it could not exist without either organ. Taking a broader view of the plant kingdom, however, we see that the leaf, with its attendant stomata, takes precedence over the root. Many plants exist without roots of any description, absorbing moisture and even minerals through their leaves and stems. In light of these facts, we are forced to conclude that the root, however wonderful, is essentially an accessory organ, specialized for the extraction of water from the soil (where most of it is to be found) and later put to all sorts of secondary uses, such as becoming a storehouse of manufactured food, supplying a supporting network that makes possible the erection of a towering superstructure, and functioning as a launching platform from which a new top can quickly be sent skyward, once the old one has been destroyed.

The one entity (for we can hardly call it an organ) which cannot be dispensed with and for which no substitute has ever been devised, either by nature or by human artifice, is the chloroplast, whether in leaf or stem; it is this minuscule organelle which, to repeat, performs the stupendous feat of converting the radiant energy of sunlight into the energy of the chemical bond and so makes possible the existence of all life on earth.

Q. When a tree's top is cut off or broken off, how is it possible for the trunk and main branches to produce shoots where none grew before? How can a tender new shoot, easily crushed by the slightest pressure of the fingers, force its way through the hard, compact wood of old stems?

A. Such new shoots may come from either *dormant buds* or *adventitious buds.* Dormant buds are those that are formed fairly early in the tree's life, usually in a leaf's axil. For one reason or another they do not develop but remain quiescent or dormant, the tip growing just enough to keep outside each year's newly formed woody cylinder, while remaining hidden beneath the bark. Thus each bud becomes in effect an embedded, miniature branch endowed with the potential for sprouting once the forces that inhibit it are removed. The destruction of the tree's top is precisely such an inhibition-

removal mechanism. When that happens, the dormant buds scattered up and down the length of trunk and main branches are now suddenly exposed to full sunlight and, more important, are freed from the chemical inhibitions formerly sent downward through the bark by the growing stem tips. Their hour of glory strikes. The activated bud tip pushes its way, partly by mechanical pressure and partly by the dissolving action of the enzymes that it secretes, through the soft bark which is all that stands between it and freedom. (Not through the hard wood of the central cylinder, for it has avoided being caught in that trap). Once into the open air, the bud expands, sends forth leafy shoots, and goes on to grow from shoot to twig, twig to branchlet, branchlet to branch, branch to major bough.

Adventitious buds, by contrast, develop from scratch, not from deeply buried and long suppressed branch traces. They may arise from the cambium layer (which is outside the woody cylinder, of course) or from callus tissue around wounds. They are formed on the spur of the moment— created out of the void, as it were—in response to the same factors that activate the dormant buds.

It is easy to tell whether a shoot comes from a dormant or an adventitious bud. Deeply embedded within the wood of the tree, the shoots formed from dormant buds are tough and strong and cannot be pulled out. Shoots from adventitious buds, on the contrary, being formed *de novo* between bark and wood and having no roots, so to speak, can very easily be pulled out or broken off; in fact, with so weak a base, they often break off under their own weight. Only after many years, when its base can gradually be absorbed by the expanding wood cylinder of the parent stem, does the adventitious shoot become firm enough to be of any permanent value. However, its service to the tree as an emergency leaf-bearing shoot, functioning in co-operation with the shoots from dormant buds, should not be underestimated.

Most species of broad-leaf trees form both kinds of buds and consequently, when these are activated, both kinds of shoots. Conifers, on the other hand, form few adventitious buds, and some species form few dormant buds. It is for this reason that so many fail to form a new top when their original one is destroyed.

Q. When a tree's leaves are eaten by insects or destroyed by fire or frost or any other cause, how does it manage to produce new ones? And how many times can it do so?

A. This question is similar to the preceding one. When a tree is defoliated, its resting buds are immediately activated and soon begin sending forth new leaves and shoots. A resting bud lies in the axil of a leaf, containing within it, largely preformed, future leaves and shoots in miniature; it is like an auxiliary soldier, partially equipped and placed in a state of suspended animation, ready to be awakened and rushed into battle when his comrade falls. (Since it is entirely in the open, a resting axillary bud is not the same as a dormant stem bud. If not activated, however, it may become a dormant bud grown over and concealed by the bark of the ever-expanding stem, growing each year just enough to keep its tip outside the enlarging woody cylinder, like a swimmer just managing to keep his head above water.)

Defoliation is the stimulus that awakens the resting buds, or, to speak more precisely, it is the event that removes the subsisting inhibitions that have hitherto kept them in the resting state. Those inhibitions removed, they go on to develop in the normal way.

Such development is made possible by the same mechanism that enables new leaves to appear every spring: by the temporary exploitation of prudently accumulated reserves. During its growing season, the tree, unenlightened by Keynesian economics, not only manufactures food enough for its own growth and maintenance but also manufactures a surplus which it foresightedly puts aside for a rainy day. (Actually for an un-rainy day, drouth being one of the many emergencies that a tree must be prepared for.) Just as an animal stores surplus food in the form of fat distributed at various points throughout its body, so the tree stores its reserves in the form of fats and starches and other substances in various parts of its body—principally in roots and stem. Without these reserves, which must be easily translocatable and readily metabolized, the tree would go under at the first adverse blow of fortune.

Tree species vary greatly in the quantity of reserves they manage to accumulate. Most broad-leaved trees have stores enough to enable them to resist three successive defoliations; conifers, on the other hand, sometimes die after the second defoliation and some species even after the first. Broad-leaved tropical species excel all other kinds in their regenerative capacity, hence presumably also in the amount of food reserves they build up and in the amount of embryonic tissue scattered about throughout all parts of their body. I have cut down unwanted avocado trees and then watched in amazement as from the cut-over stump they continued to sprout for the next four or five years, sending up new leafy shoots with undiscouraged persistence as fast as I could cut them off. If the avocado is cut high, five or six feet of the trunk being left, the sprouting is even more vigorous and continues for even a longer period. Other tropical trees, such as the wild plum (Spondias lutea) are considered immortal by the Guiana natives because of their prodigious sprouting ability, the cut-up wood never rotting, each piece growing into a new tree.

Q. How fast does sap rise in a tree?

A. This depends on the kind of tree, the spread between the slowest and the fastest velocity being surprisingly large. In conifers water has been found to ascend through the xylem at a rate averaging about 15 inches per hour. This relative slowness is attributable to the nature of conifer wood: the sap must rise through long, narrow cells (tracheids) arranged end-to-end whose walls, although perforated, necessarily oppose resistance to the passage of liquid, just as a pipe would do if it were composed of a multitude of small sections each having at each end a plate pierced by a number of small holes. In the broadleaved trees, by contrast, sap rises through a series of long, slender open tubes (vessels) that may vary in length from a few inches to several feet in diffuse-porous species (maple, birch, beech, poplar, alder, and others) to much greater lengths in ring-porous species (red oak, American elm, white ash, and others), sometimes equaling the height of the whole tree so that the vessels are uninterrupted from ground level—or even possibly from root-tip—to topmost twig.

In the diffuse-porous species measurements indicate that the sap rises at mid-day at velocities ranging from 3 to 18 feet per hour, while the same measuring technique applied to ring-porous species yields a velocity ranging from 75 to 180 feet per hour. Translated, the maximum velocity figure comes out at 3 feet per minute—a rather remarkable speed for the vegetable world in which we expect processes to take days, weeks, months, and even years. If we could dye the sap and make it visible by putting it in a glass tube, like mercury in a thermometer, even the most impatient of us would have no difficulty observing its upward movement. Three feet per minute is a velocity not to be sneezed at even in our own hectic domain. In traffic jams such steady advance is often a consummation devoutly to be wished. At three feet per minute we could stroll leisurely along the whole length of the Great Wall of China in a mere five years, enjoying the scenery as we progressed. At the same gentlemanly rate we could make it from the earth to the moon in 820 years or so. In short, three feet per minute is no inconsiderable speed: if our thoughts moved at half that rate, most of us would notice the change.

Q. If tree care is so important, how is it that trees managed to exist in those dark ages B.T.S. (Before the Tree Surgeon) and how is it that trees in the woods survive and flourish even today although receiving no attention?

A. It is true that there are and always have been thousands, millions, hundreds of millions of trees scattered about the world that receive no attention and yet live on. But it is not true that all of these are flourishing. Although many are in excellent health, many others, less fortunate, are flying a clear distress signal. Virtually every tree that exists, even the healthiest, could be helped by intelligent care, even if this might be no more that the removal of a single dead branch. The key word in this statement is "intelligent". If the tree surgeon's intervention is to be anything less than intelligent, the tree had better be left to its own resources. The first obligation of the tree expert, like that of the medical doctor, is *Primum non nocere*—"First do no harm." There are, alas, unscrupulous and unknowledgeable practitioners in every art, craft, and science, including doctors, lawyers, accountants, bankers, mechanics, barbers, masseurs, pretzel-manufacturers, and even—even—arborists. Just as Leonardo da Vinci, when he felt illness coming on, would lock himself up in his room and hide the key so no doctor could get at him, so many a tree, if it could feel, think, and act, would sink into the ground and scoop earth and leaves over its crown at the sight of a tree butcher advancing ruthlessly upon it.

But where intelligent and conscientious care is practiced, the tree is benefited, make no mistakes about that. If trees are always with us, this is merely a proof of their recuperative capacity and their reproductive fecundity, not a proof of exemption from the need of care. Just as our own lives can be prolonged by intelligent and affectionate care, so that of trees can be prolonged. Where the average life expectancy at the time of Cro-Magnon men was perhaps 27 and at the time of Shakespeare hardly better (35), it has now risen to around 70, with future limits optimistically set at 140. Exactly the same situation applies to trees: the average life expectancy of every species can be raised beyond its present limits.*

Go out and examine any tree in the forest. The chances are a hundred to one that it is weighted down with dead branches or parasitized by mistletoe or invaded by fungi or riddled by borers or honeycombed by termites or disfigured by gaping cavities. Even the untrained eye can find something wrong with it, while to the critical, practiced eye it is too often a museum of horrors. Consider cavities alone. In a report recently published by an American dental survey 800,000,000 cavities in need of attention are estimated to lie there rotting away in the mouths of we 200,000,000 taxpayers—four to every citizen! How many cavities, gaping and otherwise, do you then suppose there are in the uncounted millions of trees within our national borders? Enough to make every tree surgeon in the business as rich as Croesus. How then can it be said that trees in the woods need no care?

Q. Is it better to have tree work done on a contract basis or a cost-plus basis?

A. It is better on a cost-plus basis. While laying bricks or building automobiles may be calculated at an invariable price per unit, tree work cannot be so calculated; it cannot be mass-produced. Each tree is different: a different size, a different kind, and in a different condition. No man that lives can name to the hour the time it will take to prune or repair a given tree. The homeowner, not realizing this, often demands that tree work, like other forms of labor more easily calculable, be contracted for on a flat-rate basis. By so doing, he exposes himself to two dangers: (1) the danger of being overcharged, as when the arborist, forced to name a flat figure, protects himself by charging more than he actually expects the bill to come to; and (2) the danger of getting a poor job, as when the arborist, anchored to a figure

from which he cannot pull loose, skimps on the work when it turns out to be more than he had bargained for.

You should make up your mind in advance that good work cannot be secured at bargain prices and should put behind you for all time the seductive illusion of the lowest bid. When purchasing an article of merchandise, the buyer may haggle days or weeks or months and has nothing to lose except the time since he has already presumably inspected the goods and knows exactly what he is getting. Even in building a house, it is common practice to accept the lowest bid, since the architect is on hand to see that the contractor meets all the specifications. But tree work is different. Here you, as homeowner, have no architect and no inspector to protect your interests. You must rely entirely on the integrity of the arborist, and the arborist, however well meaning, cannot be expected to put forth his best efforts when he finds himself coming out financially on the little end.

Q. How can I tell a reputable tree man from an unreliable one?

A. This question naturally arises out of the preceding one. Reputable arborists fortunately seem to be on the increase, in part because of the efforts of the National Shade Tree Conference and of the recently formed American Society of Consulting Arborists, which strive constantly to raise the standards among tree workers and which serve as nerve centers for the dissemination of information.

This increase in reputable practitioners is, however, merely an increase in total numbers—a natural result of the increase in national population. It is not necessarily, nor even probably, a *relative* increase. Percentagewise, the number of reputable workers as compared with the questionable ones is still highly unsatisfactory. Quacks abound, and in wealthy communities they multiply like rabbits in clover. If you value your trees—and your money—be on guard against the itinerants without telephone or address, men who drift in and out, having no roots in the community and no interest in building a reputation. Beware of doorknockers, unlettered trucks, phony references, and glib talkers who know all the answers.

Much can be inferred from the worker's equipment. Adequate equipment in good condition indicates a prosperous past usually (but not always) synonymous with a long record of satisfied customers. Sometimes, however, the most brazen quacks will have the best-looking equipment: bright and shiny new trucks, garnishly lettered and washed daily, spotless uniforms, supernumerary chain saws, and impressive-looking spraying rigs. Too often, alas, these items are designed for show rather than use—mere false fronts like Hollywood building facades with nothing behind them.

Many times information about a man can be supplied by the local Chamber of Commerce, the Better Business Bureau, or the County Agriculture Agent. A good (but not infallible) indication of reliability is membership in one of

---

*Just as there have always been Methuselahs among men, so there have always been redwoods among trees. But far from squashing the argument, this confirms it, as establishing realistic targets to shoot at.

the organizations mentioned above, not forgetting, however, that with these; as with the American Medical Association, a certain inevitable percentage of those who join are status seekers only while many good men choose to remain unaffiliated.

Little by little, well educated men are getting into tree care. Some are graduates of forestry schools, some are spin-offs from the larger companies; Men who have in some way received special training are obviously better prepared than those whose experience is limited to two or three months of running a chain saw in a logging camp.

Q. How can I tell whether my tree is properly repaired or not?

A. It is hoped that reading this book will make you better able to tell. Few people have more than the vaguest knowledge about the way a tree is built and the way it grows, consequently competent judges of the work are as scarce as competent workers. One of the curious features of tree work is that a man may do it badly and never be detected—for who is there to expose him? If a plumber repairs your hot water heater or a mechanic your car motor, you know at once or within a few days whether the work was properly done or not; the results speak for themselves. But if an unscrupulous tree quack gives you third qualtiy work, you may never discover the fact. Trees have such great regenerative power that they often survive all the injuries that ignorance and malice can heap on them, just as a tough human patient may struggle on for years in the hands of a charlatan doctor. Unfortunately, tree care is crowded with charlatans—men without training or conscience who get into it because they see a chance to make easy money, capitalizing on the public's lack of knowledge.

If you are really interested in the fate of your trees, you should, first, make an effort to learn the basic principles of tree care yourself, and, second, get the best man you can find to work on them. Landscape architects are usually in touch with competent arborists and, with few exceptions, are reliable advisers.

Q. Is damage done to trees and shrubs deductible from my income tax?

A. Yes. According to Section 23 (e) 3 of the Federal Revenue Act of 1938, trees and shrubs are considered an integral part of the entire estate, and not a separate entity. For this reason damage done by storms, lightning, hail, etc., may be deducted from the income tax, the amount of the deduction being the difference in appraised value of the estate before and after the casualty. Incidentally, many insurance policies, particularly the more liberal of the fire-protection policies, cover damage to trees and shrubs by natural agencies or by errant automobiles or other similar freakish possibilities.

Q. Who has control over trees along the highways?

A. Along state highways the State Highway Department has full jurisdiction over such trees. Although sometimes the departments get the help of private tree organizations, they more often use their own crews for planting, repairing, and removing. Along country roads the procedures vary from state to state and locality to locality.

Q. Do the utility companies have a right to trim my trees so that their wires may pass through them?

A. They often act as if they have such a right, carving a passageway through your favorite trees with the presumptive assurance of a medieval lord exercising the *droit du seigneur*. While they do indeed have a right-of-way in the name of the public domain along certain designated strips at the edge of streets and or the edge of alley-ways and can legally cut away branches that interfere with their poles or overhead wires, they cannot cross your property line without your permission nor can they touch any parts of your trees that lie exclusively within your property limits. On the other hand, from the moment you request telephone or electrical service, you expressly or tacitly give the right of entry to the linemen and guarantee access to the line. In practice the linemen will attempt to make the shortest possible connection between their pole and your house and if a tree stands in the way will cavalierly thread the line through it, cutting off interfering branches as they go. But if you object strongly enough, the linemen will seek another access route, even though by so doing they will be forced to use more wire and spend more time.

You can win your point by being firm or even nasty. The simplest way, however, is to be nonchalant, light a Murrad, and gently point out the obvious: to wit, that as the tree continues to grow, its branches will rub on the wire and push it up or down or to one side, so that sooner or later it will have to be replaced or relocated. Since enforced propinquity entails the rubbing away of your tree's bark and their wire's insulation, both your interest and the company's interest are patently and essentially the same in spite of any ephemeral and superficial conflict of interest; such being the case, why not do the sensible thing and by-pass the tree at the very beginning and so avoid all subsequent two- to three-month nuisance calls, etc., etc.,

Q. Do I have a right to cut off branches from my neighbor's tree when they are overhanging my property?

A. Yes. According to law, you do have a right to cut such branches back to the point where they intersect your property line. You also have a right to cut any encroaching roots. Moreover, you may do so without notifying the owner of the tree or asking his consent. However, the parts cut off belong to the owner and must be given to him if he so requests.

In the case of fruit trees, the fruit legally belongs to the owner of the tree, and (if the branches have not been cut off) he has a right to reach over on the adjoining property and pick the fruit. (Hoffman v. Armstrong, 46 Barb. (N.Y.) 337.) **NOTE:** It is always advisable to check local ordinances and neighbors before any action on your part.

Q. Does my neighbor have a right to mutilate or cut down a tree on the boundary line between our properties?

A. No. Nor do you. Such a line tree belongs to both parties and, according to a ruling of a New York court, may not be mutilated or destroyed by either party without consent of the other. If either party acts contrary to this ruling, the other may sue for treble damages.

Q. Am I liable if my tree falls over on my neighbor's property?

A. If you can be proved negligent in any respect, you are liable for damage. If the tree is decayed or weakened or split or damaged at its roots and you have been apprised of its condition, or if you are presumed to have been aware of its condition, then you are considered negligent. On the other hand, if the tree was apparently sound and no negligence on your part can be proved, then the fall is considered an act of God, and you are not liable.

In many cases the testimony of the tree expert is needed to help decide whether the owner could have been reasonably supposed to know about the tree's impaired condition. Where considerable damage is involved, this point can be a delicate one.

Q. Do I have a right to prune, repair, or remove trees in the parkway in front of my property?

A. Parkway trees (those between the sidewalk and street) are in many communities considered city property and hence should not be touched except by explicit permission of the city authorities. In municipalities that retain a city forester the parkway trees cannot be removed or worked on without permission from the forester's office, and the men who are to do the work must be licensed by that office. In other communities the city has its own crew charged with planting, maintenance, and removal of parkway trees.

In smaller communities that do not have a city forester, the parkway trees, although technically owned by the city, are often planted, cared for, and removed by the property owner at his discretion.

Q. If the parkway trees in front of my property are injured, can I recover damages?

A. Yes. Although the trees may belong to the city, you have a special interest in them and may recover damages to the extent that accidental injury or willful abuse practiced on them lessens the value of your property. (Murtaugh v. Chicago Motor Coach Co. 269 Ill. App. 290, 1933.)

Q. Does a tree have legal rights in and of itself?

A. The notion that a tree—and other natural objects—may have legal standing and may actually secure representation in the courts is now being seriously considered by some of our avant-garde thinkers, however absurd the proposition may seen at first blush. In the famous law suit Sierra Club v. Walt Disney Corporation revolving around the opening up of California'a Mineral King Valley to sophisticated resort use, the minority view (opposing such use), expressed by

Justices Douglas, Brennan, and Blackmun, came out strongly for the rights of natural objects against trespass, encroachment, and abuse. Expanding the Justices' arguments, Christopher Stone has written a brilliant essay, now published in book form, entitled *Should Trees Have Standing?* in which he argues for the affirmative, adducing a multitude of philosophical, ethical, and legal precedents, analogies, and supportive arguments. According to this viewpoint, trees and all other forms of plant life, all forms of animal life, as well as waterfalls, lakes, rivers, mountains, and other natural objects, should have the right to sue, through some pre-designated human agency, any person, persons, corporation, or agency affecting their "natural and inalienable" right to existence.

The idea is a very interesting one and, if it gains force and is properly implemented, may come to the rescue, in the very nick of time, of this Polluted Planet.

If we wish to quibble, we can, of course, find countless absurdities in the notion. Could, for example, the tree sue the insects that defoliate it? Or could it sue the Forest Service for not spraying it opportunely and so protecting it against insect invasion? Or could the insects (those that survive) sue the Forest Service *for* spraying and so destroying them? Could a waterfall sue an earthquake for producing irreversible and prejudicial alterations in the rivers that give it being? Could a mountain sue the clouds for the discharge of an unwanted quantity of water in any given year, effecting an unreasonable, inconsiderate, and disproportionate amount of erosion of its unprotected slopes? So could the absurdities be multiplied. But to detect the greatest absurdity of all we would have to reread that fable of Aesop in which he presents two mice quarreling over the division of a piece of cheese. Unable to agree, they refer the quarrel to an arbitrator—by ill choice a cat. This arbitrary cat cuts the cheese in half, weighs each piece in his paws, decides that one is heavier, takes a bite out of it to equalize the weight, then decides that the other is heavier, takes a bite out of it, finds *it* heavier, takes another bite, and so on until the cheese is entirely gone and the quarrel is at an end.

This, then, is the danger: if we endow natural objects with legal rights, it is the lawyers who are likely to be the real beneficiaries in all ensuing actions. (If not convinced by Aesop, we need only recall the current medical malpractice scandals.) All we can do is to balance this danger against the possibility of reduced pollution and destruction of the environment. The *threat* of a lawsuit is always an effective deterrent, and if lawyers did not exist, we would be forced to invent them. We may presume that if the mice found a second piece of cheese, they would try to settle their differences amicably rather than to seek the lip service of an arbitrator.